The Genius of Jane Austen

ALSO BY PAULA BYRNE

Perdita: The Life of Mary Robinson
Mad World: Evelyn Waugh and the Secrets of Brideshead
The Real Jane Austen: A Life in Small Things
Belle: The Slave Daughter and the Lord Chief Justice
Kick: The True Story of JFK's Sister
and the Heir to Chatsworth

AS CO-EDITOR

Stressed Unstressed: Classic Poems to Ease the Mind

The Genius of Jane Austen

Her Love of Theatre and Why She Works in Hollywood

Paula Byrne

HARPER PERENNIAL

NEW YORK • LONDON • TORONTO • SYDNEY • NEW DELHI • AUCKLAND

For Jonathan

HarperCollins books may be purchased for educational, business, or sales promotional use. For information, please email the Special Markets Department at SPsales@harpercollins.com.

Originally published in Great Britain as *Jane Austen and the Theatre* in 2002 by Hambledon and London.

Updated edition first published in Great Britain by Williams Collins in 2017.

FIRST US HARPER PERENNIAL EDITION PUBLISHED 2017.

Library of Congress Cataloging-in-Publication Data has been applied for.

ISBN 978-0-06-267449-4

17 18 19 20 21 LSC 10 9 8 7 6 5 4 3 2 1

Contents

Illustrations

Unless otherwise stated, all pictures are from the author's private collection, © Paula Byrne.

Professional versus Private Theatricals: *Blowing up the Pic Nics* by James Gillray. Sheridan, manager of Drury Lane, leads a protest against the amateur aristocratic Pic Nic Society. The amateurs are performing *Tom Thumb*, while the professionals march under the banner of Shakespeare and Kotzebue (author of the German original of *Lovers' Vows*).

Dora Jordan as the Comic Muse. John Hoppner, *Mrs Jordan as the Comic Muse*: The Royal Collection © Her Majesty Queen Elizabeth II

The Comic Muse unveils herself and inspires the pen of Hannah Cowley: Jane Austen had particular admiration for comic plays written by women.

The Pantheon in Oxford Street where Austen's brother Henry owned a box.

Early nineteenth-century theatre-going: pit, boxes and stage, showing the experience that Jane Austen loved.

The 'illegitimate' Astley's, visited by Jane Austen and the location of the rekindling of the love affair between Harriet Smith and Robert Martin in *Emma*.

Jane Austen's favourite comic actor: her 'best Elliston'.

Eliza O'Neill as Juliet: Jane Austen called her 'an elegant creature' who 'hugs Mr Younge [her co-star] delightfully' – but did not live up to the example of the great Mrs Siddons. George Dawe, *Study for Miss O'Neill as Juliet*: Folger Shakespeare Library, Washington DC, licensed under a Creative Commons Attribution-ShareAlike 4.0 International License (CC BY-SA 4.0)

Sarah Siddons as Constance in Shakespeare's *King John*: 'I should particularly have liked seeing her in Constance, and could swear at her for disappointing me,' wrote Austen in 1811.

Frontispiece to the published text of *Lovers' Vows*, revealing its risqué content.

Mrs Inchbald's version of *Lovers' Vows* was immensely popular. Staged at the Theatre Royal, Bath, when Austen lived there, in 1799 it travelled as far as Philadelphia. Playbill for *Lovers' Vows*, New Theatre, Philadelphia. Pennsylvania, 25 May 1799: Library of Congress, Rare Book and Special Collections Division.

Emma Woodhouse, alias Alicia Silverstone as Cher, *Clueless* in Beverly Hills. Alicia Silverstone as Cher Horowitz in *Clueless*, directed by Amy Heckerling, © Paramount Pictures, 19 July 1995/Alamy Stock Photos

Fanny Price and Mary Crawford in Patricia Rozema's controversial *Mansfield Park*. Frances O'Connor and Embeth Davidtz in *Mansfield Park* (1999), directed by Patricia Rozema, © Moviestore Collection Ltd/Alamy Stock Photos

Mansfield Park made *Metropolitan* in upper-crust Manhattan. Isabel Gillies and Taylor Nichols as Cynthia Mclean and Charlie Black in *Metropolitan*, directed by Whit Stillman, © New Line Cinema, 23 March 1990/Alamy Stock Photos

Lady Susan: Whit Stillman's *Love & Friendship* takes Austen back to her comic origins. Chloë Sevigny and Kate Beckinsale in *Love and Friendship* (2016), directed by Whit Stillman, © Roadside Attractions/Amazon Studios/Atlaspix/Alamy Stock Photos

Foreword to the New Edition

Fifteen years ago, I published *Jane Austen and the Theatre*, a book whose central argument was that Austen's comic genius was shaped by her love of theatre. *Mansfield Park* was the first Austen novel I read, and, like many readers, I was intrigued by the spectacle of the amateur theatricals at the heart of the plot. Stuck in the country and bored to death, the young people decide to stage a play. But, as with Hamlet's 'play-within-the-play', the production is riddled with double meanings, intrigue and alarming consequences.

It seemed to me then, and does so now, that Austen's play-within-a-novel operates as a wonderful vehicle for exploring illicit flirtations between the young people, especially in the absence of a reliable chaperone. The play *Lovers' Vows* works as a meta-text for exploring important relationships between the characters. Edmund Bertram, the pious, shy clergyman, who is in love with a gorgeous, witty *femme fatale*, Mary Crawford, undertakes to play the part of a pious, shy clergyman who is seduced by a gorgeous, witty *femme fatale*, played by Mary Crawford. So many plot parallels, intrigues, allusions, moments of drama are contained in the amateur theatricals episode, which dominates the first quarter of the novel.

The play comes to a sticky end, and gives the reader one of the funniest moments in Austen's canon (and, incidentally, the only moment in Austen without a woman present), when the master of the household, Sir Thomas Bertram, returns from his slave plantations in Antigua to find himself on a stage next to a ranting young actor, who is a complete stranger to him. It's a beautifully orchestrated, highly comic scene, which humiliates Sir Thomas, giving him grave grounds for concern about the conduct of his children. His revenge is to burn all the unbound copies of the play. But the flirting doesn't stop.

Nevertheless, I was puzzled by the critical consensus, which, following the influential critic Lionel Trilling, took the view that the *Lovers' Vows* debacle meant that Jane Austen morally disapproved of theatre. Because Sir Thomas and the heroine, Fanny Price, disapprove of the play, then this must mean that Austen did too. This made no sense to me in the light of her letters and her other novels, which contain copious allusions to the theatre and to playwrights, from Shakespeare to Sheridan. Jane Austen wrote plays as a child and acted in amateur theatricals at home. She herself was said to be a fine actor, and played the part of Mrs Candour in Sheridan's *The School for Scandal* with great aplomb.

Furthermore, it seemed to me that a writer with such comic gifts (often overlooked in the pursuit of the romantic courtship and marriage plot) owed a debt to the plays she watched and read. This book is my attempt to redress that misconception and to examine the roots of Austen's comic genius. Her love for Shakespeare is well known (she pays tribute to him in *Mansfield Park*), but she also loved farce and comedies, especially those of now largely forgotten female dramatists, such as Hannah Cowley and Elizabeth Inchbald.

Some years ago, the book went out of print, partly the consequence of being with a small publishing house that no longer exists. Many of my readers have, over the years, expressed interest in the book, which was so generously reviewed. The bicentenary of the death of Jane Austen (2017) seemed to William Collins, the loyal publisher of my five subsequent books, a very good moment to reissue the book, with a new title and new material, as a companion to my full-scale biography *The Real Jane Austen: A Life in Small Things*.

The extra chapter takes a distinctive look at Austen in Hollywood, exploring a number of stage and film adaptations, from A. A. Milne (creator of *Winnie-the-Pooh*) to Whit Stillman, who recently adapted the juvenilia for the silver screen. The vogue for stage adaptations of the novels began in the early 1930s, but the explosion of interest in recent years has seen her novels refashioned, reworked and updated on stage, on screen and in the ever-expanding world of the Internet.

Fascination with Jane Austen does not wane. The bicentenary witnesses the appearance of her image on the ten-pound banknote. There are exhibitions about her life and work in Hampshire, where she was born and where she died. But the popular image of her is too often that of a novelist interested only in romance and marriage. Of course marriage is the traditional endpoint of comedy, but what really interested Austen were the misunderstandings and incongruous encounters along the way, not the happy ending. This book is an attempt to place Jane Austen where she properly belongs: alongside Shakespeare as one of the world's greatest comic writers. It was conceived as a love letter to the comic theatre of the late eighteenth and early nineteenth centuries, which I began to explore twenty years ago during a magical year in the incomparable setting of the Huntington Library in Los Angeles. While I was there, I regularly crossed town to Pasadena, Burbank, Hollywood and Westwood, in order to watch the latest movie releases. Among them were Emma Thompson's sparkling *Sense and Sensibility* and Roger Michell's tender, sombre *Persuasion*. Then there came a day when my partner said that he was going to take me to a teen movie called *Clueless* that was set in Beverly Hills. He was a Shakespeare scholar, also research-ing in the Huntington, so this seemed a very peculiar choice – until five minutes into the film, when I realised what was going on. I leant over and whispered, 'She's Emma, isn't she?' Since the film did not explicitly acknowledge at any point that it was a reworking of *Emma*, I think he was rather impressed that I worked it out so quickly. Perhaps that was why, soon after, he asked me to marry him.

As Jane Austen said herself, 'Let other pens dwell on guilt and misery. I quit such odious subjects as soon as I can.'

Acknowledgements

I am grateful to the Centre for Kentish Studies, Maidstone, for permission to quote from Fanny Knight's unpublished journals, and the Hampshire Record Office, Winchester, for permission to quote from Eliza de Feuillide's unpublished letters and James Austen's prologues and epilogues to the Austen family theatricals.

Abbreviations

Sense and Sensibility	(1811)	*SS*
Pride and Prejudice	(1813)	*PP*
Mansfield Park	(1814)	*MP*
Emma	(1816)*	*E*
Northanger Abbey	(1818)	*NA*
Persuasion	(1818)	*P*

All quotations of the above are from *The Novels of Jane Austen*, ed. R. W. Chapman, 5 vols (3rd edn, Oxford: Oxford University Press, 1932–34).

Minor Works	*MW*

Quotations are from *The Works of Jane Austen*, vi, *Minor Works*, ed. R. W. Chapman, rev. B. C. Southam (London: Oxford University Press, 1975).

Jane Austen's Letters, ed. Deirdre Le Faye (3rd edn, Oxford: Oxford University Press, 1995) is cited throughout as *Letters*.

Lovers' Vows	*LV*

Quotations are from *Lovers' Vows: A Play, in Five Acts. Performing at the Theatre Royal, Covent-Garden. From the German of Kotzebue. By Mrs Inchbald.* (fifth edn, London, 1798), reprinted in Chapman's edition of *MP*.

---

* Published December 1815.

Introduction

In 1821, four years after the death of Jane Austen, a critic in the *Quarterly Review* compared her art to Shakespeare's. 'Saying as little as possible in her own person and giving a dramatic air to the narrative by introducing frequent conversations', she created her fictional world 'with a regard to character hardly exceeded even by Shakespeare himself.'[1]

In the Victorian era, Austen was dubbed 'the Prose Shakespeare'.[2] George Eliot's common-law husband, George Henry Lewes, developed the comparison in an influential *Blackwood's Magazine* article on 'The Novels of Jane Austen':

> But instead of *description*, the common and easy resource of novelists, she has the rare and difficult art of *dramatic presentation*: instead of telling us what her characters are, and what they feel, she presents the people, and they reveal themselves. In this she has never perhaps been surpassed, not even by Shakespeare himself.[3]

Yet another nineteenth-century writer, the novelist Thomas Lister, ascribed her genius to revelation of character through dramatic dialogue: 'She possessed the rare and difficult art of making her readers intimately acquainted with the character of all whom she describes ... She scarcely does more than make them act and talk, and we know them directly.'[4] Austen herself had a strong sense of the importance of dramatic dialogue in the novel. She and her family, like many others of their class, loved to read aloud together. The Austen women ranked novels according to how well they stood up to repeated group readings. Thus Charlotte Lennox's *The Female Quixote* remained a firm favourite (*Letters*, p. 116), whereas Sarah Burney's *Clarentine* failed the test: 'We are reading

Clarentine, & are surprised to find how foolish it is. I remember liking it much less on a 2nd reading than at the 1st & it does not bear a 3rd at all' (*Letters*, p. 120).

Jane Austen also had strict notions about how characters in her own novels should be rendered dramatically. To her chagrin, her mother botched the dialogue badly when *Pride and Prejudice* was read aloud to some friends: 'Our 2nd evening's reading to Miss Benn had not pleased me so well, but I beleive [*sic*] something must be attributed to my Mother's too rapid way of getting on – & tho' she perfectly understands the Characters herself, she cannot speak as they ought' (*Letters*, p. 203).

Perhaps Austen's frustration stemmed from her own aptitude for dramatic renditions. Her brother Henry noted her skill in the biographical notice written soon after her death: 'She read aloud with very great taste and effect. Her own works, probably, were never heard to so much advantage as from her own mouth; for she partook largely in all the best gifts of the comic muse.'[5] Her niece Caroline Austen recorded in her *Memoir*. 'She was considered to read aloud remarkably well. I did not often hear her but *once* I knew her take up a volume of *Evelina* and read a few pages of Mr Smith and the Brangtons and I thought it was like a play.'[6]

In *Mansfield Park*, it is typically tongue-in-cheek that Austen endows her villain Henry Crawford with her own gift for reading aloud. Edmund's commendation of Henry's reading of Shakespeare, 'To read him well aloud, is no every-day talent' (*MP*, p. 338), is seconded by Lady Bertram's approving comment, which curiously prefigures Caroline Austen's: 'It was really like being at a play' (*MP*, p. 338).

Austen's nineteenth-century critics defined her genius in terms of her dramatic powers. Her great achievement was in character study. As in Shakespeare, the fools are as distinctive and perfectly discriminated as are the heroines, and all the characters reveal themselves, unhampered by an obtrusive authorial presence, through dramatic presentation and conversations – by a kind of 'dramatic ventriloquism'.[7] Yet in the twentieth century there was a common perception that Jane Austen had a deep distrust of the dramatic arts. This was principally due to the notorious amateur theatricals in *Mansfield Park*: the disruption caused to the household by the performance of *Lovers' Vows* during Sir Thomas

Bertram's absence from home was taken as proof of the author's own distaste for theatre.[8]

There are, however, a range of judgements upon 'home representation' in *Mansfield Park*, not all of them hostile. It is an error to assume that Fanny Price's astringent judgement on the theatricals is Austen's own; after all, Fanny is by no means a disinterested commentator. Unlike her demure creation, who has never seen the inside of a theatre and is manifestly afraid of 'exposing herself' on stage, Austen herself was fascinated by professional theatre, visited it frequently, and, far from condemning private theatricals, participated in them herself, both when she was a child and when she was a woman in her thirties. Strikingly, only two years before writing *Mansfield Park*, she took part in a private performance of perhaps the most popular contemporary play of the Georgian period, Richard Brinsley Sheridan's *The School for Scandal*.

Jane Austen's letters reveal that she was steeped in theatre. As a young woman, she wrote short plays. She copied her brothers in the writing of burlesques in the style of Sheridan and Henry Fielding. She even turned her favourite novel, Samuel Richardson's *Sir Charles Grandison*, into a five-act comedy. Her interest in the theatre, both amateur and professional, and her lifelong preoccupation with the drama undoubtedly influenced her mature writing. She lived through a golden age of English stage comedy. Yet critics of Austen have barely touched upon this rich source, save in occasional nods to her extraordinary gift for theatrical dialogue and the creation of sustained comic characterisation.

This book offers the first comprehensive account of Jane Austen's interest in the theatre, but, more than this, it also suggests that her play-going and her reading of plays were a formative influence on her comic art. Part One of the book reveals her interest in the world of theatre and drama, while Part Two suggests that there is something intrinsically dramatic about her vision of the world in many of her major novels – not only *Mansfield Park*, but also *Sense and Sensibility*, *Pride and Prejudice* and *Emma*.

I make a number of passing references to *Northanger Abbey*, in which the heroine, Catherine Morland, resembles the naive 'country girl' of the comic tradition in the theatre, but of course the main thrust of this book's comedy is its parody of the Gothic novel. My argument about the importance of the theatre for Jane Austen is in no respect intended to diminish the importance of her engagement with the traditions of the novel. I draw attention to many neglected theatrical allusions in her work, but there are also many – frequently documented – allusions to eighteenth-century fiction. Indeed, it is an important part of my argument that from Fielding and Richardson through to Austen and her peers, especially Fanny Burney and Elizabeth Inchbald, there was vigorous two-way traffic between the new form of the novel and the ancient art of the drama. It must, however, be acknowledged that, unlike Inchbald and Burney, Austen never expressed the desire actually to write for the public stage.

Although Austen's final works are less obviously theatrical than her earliest ones – I do not offer a detailed account of *Persuasion*[9] – she participated in private theatricals well into her adult life, as may be seen from some fascinating and little-known passages in the unpublished journals of her niece Fanny Knight. She also took Fanny to the theatre whenever she got the chance. Her periods of residence in London, Bath and Southampton provided ample opportunities for theatre-going with her brood of nieces and nephews. In her letters she recorded her relish for the performances of the renowned tragedian Edmund Kean and the celebrated comic actress Dora Jordan, as well as her particular fondness for Robert Elliston, the star of the Bath Theatre Royal, whose fortunes she followed when he moved to the London stage. Even when in the country, when she was far away from the theatres, she maintained her interest by reading plays, both old and new. She also picked up theatre gossip from the newspapers and would have been able to keep up with reviews of new performances, for this was the age when professional theatre-reviewing grew to maturity.

Twentieth-century criticism was fixated on the assumption that Jane Austen was immovably attached to village life and deeply suspicious of urban pleasures – the theatre foremost among these.[10] This book presents quite another picture: an Austen who enjoyed urban life, who attended the theatre whenever she could, and who took enormous pleasure in the theatrical scene. A recovery of the theatrical Austen makes it difficult to persist in regarding her as a supremely parochial novelist, much less as an isolated, defensive, class-bound or reactionary one.

The first part of the book establishes Jane Austen's knowledge of the world of the theatre. The second part explores how that knowledge shaped her own art. It demonstrates how she makes allusions that assume considerable theatrical knowledge – of a kind now lost to us – on the part of her first readers. And it examines the ways in which the novels adapt a wide range of techniques from the stage tradition, including dramatic entrances and exits, comic misunderstandings, ironic reversals and tableaux.

A particularly important device is what I call the 'set-piece': chapters or episodes framed as set-pieces are often analogous in shape and length to a scene in a play. It is helpful here to cite a comment of Henry James, another nineteenth-century novelist much interested in scenic construction – and indeed in the writing of plays. His novel *The Awkward Age* was organised entirely on scenic principles. In his author's preface, James pictured each of his episodes as a lamp:

> Each of my 'lamps' would be the light of a single 'social occasion' in the history and intercourse of the characters concerned, and would bring out to the full the latent colour of the scene in question and cause it to illustrate, to the last drop, its bearing on my theme. I revelled in this notion of the occasion as a thing by itself, really and completely a scenic thing.[11]

The building bricks of Austen's novels were also dramatic scenes. This is one reason why they adapt so well to film representation.

We naturally think of Jane Austen as a pioneer of the nineteenth-century realist novel. But she also lived through a great age of English stage comedy. The aim of this book is to restore her to the company of such admired contemporaries as Richard Brinsley Sheridan and Hannah Cowley, while also setting her in the great tradition of English drama that stems from Shakespeare.

PART ONE

The Novelist and the Theatre

A love of the theatre is so general ...

Mansfield Park

1

Private Theatricals

The fashion for private theatricals that obsessed genteel British society from the 1770s until the first part of the nineteenth century is immortalised in *Mansfield Park*. The itch to act was widespread, ranging from fashionable aristocratic circles to the professional middle classes and minor gentry, from children's and apprentices' theatricals to military and naval amateur dramatics.[1]

Makeshift theatres mushroomed all over England, from drawing rooms to domestic outbuildings. At the more extreme end of the theatrical craze, members of the gentrified classes and the aristocracy built their own scaled-down imitations of the London playhouses. The most famous was that erected in the late 1770s at Wargrave in Berkshire by the spendthrift Earl of Barrymore, at a reputed cost of £60,000. Barrymore's elaborate private theatre was modelled on Vanbrugh's King's Theatre in the Haymarket. It supposedly seated seven hundred.[2]

Private theatricals performed by the fashionable elite drew much public interest, and had profound implications for the public theatres.[3] On one occasion in 1787 a motion in the House of Commons was deferred because too many parliamentarians were in attendance at a private performance of Arthur Murphy's *The Way to Keep Him* at Richmond House.[4] Such private performances often drew more attention in the newspapers than the theatres licensed for public performance.

From an early age Jane Austen showed her own mocking awareness of what the newspapers dubbed 'the Theatrical Ton'. In a sketch called 'The Three Sisters', dating from around 1792, she portrayed a greedy, self-seeking young woman who demands a purpose-built private theatre as part of her marriage settlement (*MW*, p. 65). In *Mansfield Park*, the public interest in aristocratic private theatricals is regarded ironically: 'To be so near happiness, so near fame, so near the long paragraph in praise of the private theatricals at Ecclesford, the seat of the Right Hon. Lord Ravenshaw, in Cornwall, which would of course have immortalised the whole party for at least a twelve-month!' (*MP*, p. 121). Austen carefully distinguishes between the fashionable elitist theatricals of the aristocracy, of the kind that were mercilessly lampooned by the newspapers, and those of the squirearchy.[5] While Mr Yates boasts that Lord Ravenshaw's private theatre has been built on a grand and lavish scale, in keeping with aristocratic pretensions, Edmund Bertram shows his contempt for what he considers to be the latest fad of the nobility:

'Let us do nothing by halves. If we are to act, let it be in a theatre completely fitted up with pit, box and gallery, and let us have a play entire from beginning to end; so as it be a German play, no matter what, with a good tricking, shifting after-piece, and a figure dance, and a horn-pipe, and a song between the acts. If we do not out do Ecclesford, we do nothing.' (*MP*, p. 124)

Edmund's mocking comments are directed to his elder brother. But despite Tom Bertram's efforts to professionalise his theatre, the Mansfield theatricals eventually fall back on the measure of converting a large room of the family home into a temporary theatre for their production of *Lovers' Vows*. In reality, this was far more typical of the arrangements made by the professional classes and the minor gentry who had also adopted the craze for private theatricals. The private theatricals of Fanny Burney's uncle at Barbone Lodge near Worcester, for example, took place in a room seating about twenty people. At one end of the room was a curtained off stage for the actors, while the musicians played in an outside passage.[6]

In 1782, when the craze for private theatricals first reached Steventon rectory, Jane Austen was seven. The dining parlour was probably used as a makeshift theatre for the early productions.[7] The first play known to have been acted by the Austen family was *Matilda*, a tragedy in five acts by Dr Thomas Francklin, a friend of Dr Samuel Johnson and a fashionable London preacher. The part of the tragic heroine Matilda was later popularised by Mrs Siddons on the London stage. At Steventon the tragedy was acted some time during 1782, and James Austen wrote a prologue and an epilogue for the performance.[8] Edward Austen spoke the prologue and Tom Fowle, one of Mr Austen's Steventon pupils who later became engaged to Cassandra Austen, the epilogue.[9]

Francklin's dreary play, set at the time of the Norman Conquest, dramatises a feud between two brothers. Morcar, Earl of Mercia, and his brother Edwin are both in love with Matilda, the daughter of a Norman lord. Matilda has chosen Edwin. Morcar separates the lovers, sets up plans to murder his brother, and tries (unsuccessfully) to win over and marry Matilda. The tragedy takes an unexpected twist with Morcar's unlikely reformation: he is persuaded to repent of his crimes, reunite the lovers and become reconciled to his brother.

Matilda was a surprising choice for the satirically-minded Austen family. Its long, rambling speeches and dramatic clichés of language and situation made it precisely the kind of historical tragedy that Sheridan burlesqued in *The Critic*. The tragedy had only six speaking parts, however, and was perhaps manageable in the dining room.[10] Jane Austen was surely only a spectator at this very first Steventon performance, but it is probable that she disliked the play, given the disparaging comment she makes in her juvenilia about another historical drama, *The Tragedy of Jane Shore*, 'a tragedy and therefore not worth reading' (*MW*, p. 140). Perhaps the manager/actor James felt the same, for after *Matilda* no more tragedies were performed at Steventon.

Matilda was followed two years later by a far more ambitious project. In 1784, when Jane was nine, Sheridan's *The Rivals* was acted at Steventon. Once again James Austen wrote the prologue and an epilogue for the play performed in July 'by some young Ladies & Gentlemen at Steventon'.[11] Henry spoke the prologue and the actor playing Bob Acres (possibly James himself) the epilogue. James's prologue suggests that there was an audience for this production.[12] The play has a cast of twelve, and it seems that the Austens had no qualms about inviting neighbours and friends to take part in their theatricals. The Cooper cousins and the Digweed family probably made up the numbers.[13] Biographers speculate that Jane Austen may have taken the minor role of Lydia Languish's pert maid, Lucy, but perhaps it is more likely that she was a keen spectator.[14]

James's prologue is unequivocal in its praise of satirical comedy, rather than sentimental tragedy:

> The Loftier members of the tragic Lyre;
> Court the soft pleasures that from pity flow;
> Seek joy in tears and luxury in woe.
> 'Tis our's, less noble, but more pleasing task,
> To draw from Folly's features fashion's mask;
> To paint the scene where wit and sense unite
> To yield at once instruction and delight.[15]

Jane Austen was undoubtedly influenced by her Thespian brothers, and it is therefore unsurprising that one of their favourite comic writers was to have a major impact on her own writing. While Sheridan's influence is discernible in Austen's earliest works, his presence can be felt most strongly in her mature works, which, unlike the juvenilia, also set out to instruct and to delight, and sought to combine 'wit and sense'. In particular, the influence of *The Rivals* can be most keenly felt in Austen's own satire on sentimentalism: her first published novel, *Sense and Sensibility*. It is all the more bewildering that this aspect of her comic genius has been so sorely neglected.

It was shortly after the performance of *The Rivals* that Cassandra and Jane were sent off to boarding school in Reading. The eccentric headmistress of the school was a Mrs La Tournelle, née Sarah Hackitt, who (much to the amusement of her pupils) could not speak a word of French. She was notorious for having a cork leg, for dressing in exactly the same clothes every day, and for her obsession with every aspect of the theatre. She enthralled her young charges with lively accounts of plays and play-acting, greenroom anecdotes, and gossip about the private lives of leading actors. Plays were performed as an integral part of the girls' education. The Austen sisters' interest in the drama was fostered at this school. Jane later recalled their time here with memories of fun and laughter, reminding her sister of a schoolgirl expression: 'I could die of laughter … as they used to say at school' (*Letters*, p. 5).

When the girls returned home from school for good in 1786, they were delighted to be in the company of a real French-speaking person, their exotic cousin, Eliza de Feuillide, a French countess. Eliza had taken part in theatrical activities since she was a child and had also acted in private theatricals staged by her aristocratic French friends. In a letter to Philadelphia Walter (also a cousin of Jane Austen), Eliza regaled her cousin with tales of private theatricals: 'I have promised to spend the Carnival, which in France is the gayest Season of the year, in a very agreeable Society who have erected an elegant theatre for the purposes of acting Plays amongst ourselves, and who intend having Balls at least twice a week.'[16]

Family tradition records that the Steventon barn was used on occasions as a temporary theatre, but probably not until the Christmas theatricals of 1787 when Eliza was a guest at the rectory.[17] In a letter written in September of that year, Philadelphia Walter wrote: 'My uncle's barn is fitting up quite like a theatre and all the young folks are to take their part.'[18]

During September 1787 Eliza had asked her cousin to join her for the Tunbridge Wells summer season, and had requested that the comedies *Which is the Man?*, by Hannah Cowley, and *Bon Ton: or High Life Above Stairs*, by Garrick, be presented at the local theatre. Much to her delight, the house was full on both occasions.[19] These two modern comedies were clearly great favourites with Eliza. *Bon Ton* was an amusing satire on fashionable French manners, while *Which is the Man?* depicted a fascinating young widow, Lady Bell Bloomer, on the brink of remarriage. Eliza clearly longed for an opportunity to perform these plays at Steventon. Later, Philadelphia Walter informed her brother in a letter that these plays were to be given at Steventon that Christmas: 'They go at Xmas to Steventon and mean to act a play *Which is the Man?* and *Bon Ton*.'[20]

Eliza had already made plans with the Austen family for the Christmas festivities. James was home from his foreign travels and keen to begin organising theatricals on a grander scale than before, egged on by Eliza. Both she and the Austen family wished Philadelphia to be part of the theatrical ensemble, but, like Fanny Price, the meek and timid Phila resolutely declined the offer: 'I should like to be a spectator, but am sure

I should not have courage to act a part, nor do I wish to attain it.'[21] Eliza urged Phila, on behalf of the Austens, to take one of the 'two unengaged parts' that were waiting to be filled:

> You know we have long projected acting this Christmas at Hampshire and this scheme would go on a vast deal better would you lend your assistance … and on finding there were two unengaged parts I immediately thought of you, and am particularly commissioned by My Aunt Austen and her whole family to make the earliest application possible, and assure you how very happy you will make them as well as myself if you could be prevailed on to undertake these parts and give us all your company.[22]

In the same letter, Eliza assured her cousin that the acting parts set aside for her were 'neither long nor difficult', and reminded her that the acting party were well-equipped: 'Do not let your dress neither disturb you, as I think I can manage it so that the *Green Room* should provide you with what is necessary for acting.' At the close of the letter she tried another means to persuade her shy cousin: 'You cannot possibly resist so many pleasures, especially when I tell you your old friend James is returned from France and is to be of the acting party.'[23]

Eliza was clearly used to getting her own way. But Philadelphia's firm resolve not to act surprised both Eliza and the Austen family:

> I received your letter yesterday my dear friend and need not tell you how much I am concerned at your not being able to comply with a request which in all probability I shall never have it in my power to make again … I will only allow myself to take notice of the strong reluctance you express to what you call *appearing in Publick*. I assure you our performance is to be by no means a publick one, since only a selected party of friends will be present.[24]

According to Eliza, Philadelphia's visit to Steventon was dependent on her compliance with joining the acting party: 'You wish to know the exact time which we should be *satisfied with*, and therefore I proceed to acquaint you that a fortnight from New Years Day *would do*, provided however you could bring yourself to act, for my Aunt Austen declares "she has not room for any *idle young* people".[25]

Despite Eliza's repeated assurances that the parts were very short, Philadelphia resisted her cousin's efforts and stayed away. Eliza appears to have attributed this to Mrs Walter's interference: 'Shall I be candid and tell you the thought which has struck me on this occasion? – The insuperable objection to my proposal is, some scruples of your mother's about your acting. If this is the case I can only say it is [a] pity so groundless a prejudice should be harboured in so enlightened [and so] enlarged a mind.'[26] The Austens showed no such prejudice against private theatricals and *Bon Ton* was performed some time during this period. There is a surviving epilogue written by James.[27]

The first play that was presented at Steventon in 1787 was not, however, Garrick's farce, but Susanna Centlivre's lively comedy, *The Wonder: A Woman Keeps a Secret* (1714). As usual James wrote a prologue and an epilogue. *The Wonder* was an excellent choice for Eliza: she played the part of the spirited heroine, Donna Violante, who risks her own marriage and reputation by choosing to protect her friend, Donna Isabella, from an arranged marriage to a man she despises. The play engages in the battle-of-the-sexes debate that Eliza particularly enjoyed. Women are 'inslaved' to 'the Tyrant Man'; and whether they be fathers, husbands or brothers, they 'usurp authority, and expect a blind obedience from us, so that maids, wives, or widows, we are little better than slaves'.[28]

The play's most striking feature is a saucy proposal of marriage from Isabella, though made on her behalf by Violante in disguise, to a man she barely knows. Twenty-seven years later, Jane Austen would incorporate private theatricals into her new novel, and the play, *Lovers' Vows*, would contain a daring proposal of marriage from a vivacious young woman.[29]

The Austen family clearly had no objection whatsoever to the depiction in Centlivre's comedy of strong, powerful women who claim their rights to choose their own husbands, and show themselves capable of loyalty and firm friendship. James's epilogue 'spoken by a lady in the character of Violante' leaves us in no doubt of the Austens' awareness of the play's theme of female emancipation:

In Barbarous times, e'er learning's sacred light
Rose to disperse the shades of Gothic night
And bade fair science wide her beams display,
Creation's fairest part neglected lay.
In vain the form where grace and ease combined.
In vain the bright eye spoke th' enlightened mind,
Vain the sweet smiles which secret love reveal,
Vain every charm, for there were none to feel.
From tender childhood trained to rough alarms,
Choosing no music but the clang of arms;
Enthusiasts only in the listed field,
Our youth there knew to fight, but not to yield.
Nor higher deemed of beauty's utmost power,
Than the light play thing of their idle hour.
Such was poor woman's lot – whilst tyrant men
At once possessors of the sword and pen
All female claim with stern pedantic pride
To prudence, truth and secrecy denied,
Covered their tyranny with specious words
And called themselves creation's mighty lords –
But thank our happier Stars, those times are o'er;
And woman holds a second place no more.
Now forced to quit their long held usurpation,
Men all wise, these 'Lords of the Creation'!
To our superior sway themselves submit,
Slaves to our charms, and vassals to our wit;
We can with ease their ev'ry sense beguile,
And melt their Resolutions with a smile.[30]

Jane Austen's most expressive battle-of-the-sexes debate, that between Anne Elliot and Captain Harville in *Persuasion*, curiously echoes James Austen's epilogue. Denied the 'exertion' of the battlefield and a 'profession', women have been forced to live quietly. James's remonstrance that 'Tyrant men [are] at once possessors of the sword and pen' is more gently reiterated in Anne Elliot's claim that 'Men have had every advantage of us in telling their story … the pen has been in their hands' (*P*, p. 234).

There were two performances of *The Wonder* after Christmas. The evident success of the play was followed up in the new year by a production of Garrick's adaptation of *The Chances* (1754), for which James, once again, wrote a prologue. This play was to be Eliza's final performance for some time.

Once again James and Henry chose a racy comedy: originally written by Beaumont and Fletcher, the play had been altered by the Duke of Buckingham and in 1754 'new-dressed' by Garrick. Although Garrick had made a concerted effort to tone it down, the play was still considered to contain strong dialogue. So thought Mrs Inchbald in her *Remarks*, which prefaced her edition of the play: 'That Garrick, to the delicacy of improved taste, was compelled to sacrifice much of their libertine dialogue, may well be suspected, by the remainder which he spared.'[31]

The Austen family did not share such compunction. Like *The Wonder*, Garrick's play depicts jealous lovers, secret marriages and confused identities. The two heroines, both confusingly called Constantia, are mistaken for one another. The first Constantia is mistaken for a prostitute, although she is in fact secretly married to the Duke of Naples. It is likely that the feisty Eliza played the role of the low-born 'second Constantia', a favourite of the great comic actress Mrs Jordan.

Eliza had played her last role, as the return of Mr Austen's pupils in the new year signified her imminent removal from Steventon. Both James and Henry Austen were 'fascinated' by the flirtatious Eliza, according to James's son, who wrote the first memoir of Jane Austen. Most critics and biographers accept that a flirtation between Henry and Eliza was begun around this time and resulted eventually in their marriage ten years later. Some critics have conjectured that the flirtation which the young Jane Austen witnessed between Henry and Eliza during rehearsals may have given her the idea for the flirtation between Henry Crawford and Maria Bertram in *Mansfield Park*.[32] That the young girl was acutely aware of the flirtation seems clear from one of her short tales, 'Henry and Eliza', where there are a series of elopements including one by Henry and Eliza, who run off together leaving only a curt note: 'Madam, we are married and gone' (*MW*, p. 36).

By all accounts, Jane Austen was an intelligent observer of the intrigues, emotions and excitement of private theatricals; of rehearsals, the reading over of scripts, and the casting of parts. James Edward Austen's *Memoir* claims that his aunt Jane 'was an early observer, and it may be reasonably supposed that some of the incidents and feelings which are so vividly painted in the *Mansfield Park* theatricals are due to her recollection of these entertainments'.[33]

In *Mansfield Park*, Jane Austen devoted her creative energies to the rehearsal process rather than the performance. Furthermore the singular strength of the theatrical sequence lies in its depiction through the eyes of an envious observer. It has been suggested that in writing the *Lovers' Vows* sequence Austen distilled some of her own experience as an outsider, a partially excluded younger sister.[34] There is, however, no evidence to suggest that Jane was excluded from the family theatricals. Even if her youth prevented her from taking part in the actual performances, she began, at this time, to write her own short playlets. These were probably performed as afterpieces to the main play.

Henry Fielding's outrageous burlesque *The Tragedy of Tom Thumb* was 'acted to a small circle of select friends' on 22 March 1788 at Steventon, and this was followed some time later by 'a private Theatrical Exhibition'. Regrettably, James's prologue to the latter gives no indication of the play performed, though it imitates Jacques's 'seven ages of man' speech. The prologue also satirises the hypocrisy of the sentimental age where 'to talk affecting, when we do not feel' is described as a form of 'acting'.[35] The family perhaps wrote the entertainment themselves. It was probably at this time that Jane wrote and participated in her own burlesque playlet, 'The Mystery'.[36]

The last plays performed at Steventon in 1788–89 were *The Sultan: or A Peep into the Seraglio*, a farce by Isaac Bickerstaffe, and another farce by James Townley, *High Life Below Stairs*. Bickerstaffe's farce was first performed in London in 1775, but had only been recently published, in 1784. It was yet another comedy that depicted a bold, spirited heroine, posing a challenge to male prerogative and authority. Roxalana is an Englishwoman who has been captured for the Sultan's seraglio. She displaces the favourite concubine, Elmira, by winning the honourable affections of the Sultan. Moreover, she condemns his harem and demands the freedom of all his wives: 'You are the great Sultan; I am your slave, but I am also a free-born woman, prouder of that than all the pomp and splendour eastern monarchs can bestow.'[37] James's epilogue was yet another provocative declaration of female superiority over men, opening with the words,

> Lord help us! what strange foolish things are these men,
> One good clever woman is fairly worth ten.[38]

Two of the most popular contemporary choices for private representation were Fielding's *Tom Thumb* and Townley's *High Life Below Stairs*. The Burneys acted *Tom Thumb* in Worcestershire in 1777, ten years before the Austens chose it for performance. The part of the diminutive hero Tom Thumb was often played by a child, whose high-pitched voice would add to the comic incongruity.[39]

James Townley's satire on plebeian manners, *High Life Below Stairs* (1759), depicts a household of lazy servants who behave as badly as their masters. They ape their masters' manners, assume their titles, drink their expensive wine, gamble and visit the theatre. Like Gay's *Beggar's Opera* and Foote's *Mayor of Garett*, Townley's farce was a comedy that used low life to criticise high society. It was also an extremely popular choice for amateur theatricals. In part, this was because it was more prudent to poke fun at the lower orders in the safety of one's own home than in the professional theatre house. In 1793 a performance of *High Life Below Stairs* in an Edinburgh public theatre incited a row between a group of highly offended footmen and their masters.

George Colman the Younger's comedy about social transformations, *The Heir at Law*, was also a popular choice for the gentry to indulge themselves in stereotypical 'low' roles. Austen was to explore this contentious issue in *Mansfield Park* when the heir of Mansfield insists on staging *The Heir at Law* so that he can play the stage Irishman, Duberley.

Jane's playlet, 'The Visit', dedicated to James, contains a quotation from *High Life Below Stairs*, which suggests that she composed it around the same time as the family performance of Townley's farce, perhaps as a burlesque afterpiece. Austen repeats Townley's phrase, 'The more free, the more welcome', in her play. The allusion seems to be a nod to the main play performed that day at Steventon. Austen's habit of repeating phrases from the plays performed, or even merely contemplated for performance, at Steventon remained with her for a long time. Though Hannah Cowley's play *Which is the Man?* was considered for performance, it was finally rejected. Yet Austen quoted a phrase from it in a letter dated 1810, some twenty-nine years later.[40]

Which is the Man? is alluded to in Austen's 'The Three Sisters', written around 1788–90 (*MW*, p. 65). In this story, a spoilt young woman demands to play the part of Lady Bell Bloomer, just as Eliza had wished to in the 1787–88 Christmas theatricals. Again, a quotation from Cowley's popular comedy *The Belle's Stratagem* appears in a letter of 1801: 'Mr Doricourt has travelled; he knows best' (*Letters*, p. 73).

Though Eliza was now in Paris and unable to partake in the Steventon theatricals, the Cooper cousins came to Steventon for Christmas 1788–89 and Jane Cooper filled the gap left by Eliza. In a letter to Philadelphia, Eliza had hastily, though wistfully, scribbled a last message: 'I suppose you have had pressing accounts from Steventon, and that they have informed you of their theatrical performances, The Sultan & High Life below Stairs, Miss Cooper performed the part of Roxelana [*sic*] and Henry the Sultan, I hear that Henry is taller than ever.'[41] No prologue or epilogue by James has survived for *High Life Below Stairs*, but the prologue he provided for Bickerstaffe's comedy is (confusingly) dated 1790 and states it was 'spoken by Miss Cooper as Roxalana'.[42]

The Sultan and *High Life Below Stairs* ended the theatricals at Steventon, although there is a family tradition which claims that they were resumed in the late 1790s. The main reason why actor-manager James abandoned private theatricals seems to be that he was turning his mind to other literary interests, namely the production of a weekly magazine, *The Loiterer*. This periodical, like the theatricals at Steventon, was also to prove an important influence on Jane Austen's early writings.

Henry Austen tells us in his 'Biographical Notice', published in the first edition of *Northanger Abbey* and *Persuasion*, that his sister Jane was acquainted with all the best authors at a very early age (*NA*, p. 7). The literary tastes of Catherine Morland have often been read as a parody of the author's own literary preferences.[43] Catherine likes to read 'poetry and plays, and things of that sort', and while 'in training for a heroine', she reads 'all such works as heroines must read to supply their memories with those quotations which are so serviceable and so soothing in the vicissitudes of their eventful lives' (*NA*, p. 15): dramatic works, those of Shakespeare especially, are prominent among these. *Twelfth Night*, *Othello* and *Measure for Measure* are singled out. Catherine duly reads Shakespeare, alongside Pope, Gray and Thompson, not so much for pleasure and entertainment, as for gaining 'a great store of information' (*NA*, p. 16).

In *Sense and Sensibility*, Willoughby and the Dashwoods are to be found reading *Hamlet* aloud together. In *Mansfield Park*, the consummate actor Henry Crawford gives a rendering of *Henry VIII* that is described by Fanny Price, a lover of Shakespeare, as 'truly dramatic' (*MP*, p. 337). Henry memorably remarks that Shakespeare is 'part of an Englishman's constitution. His thoughts and beauties are so spread abroad that one touches them every where'. This sentiment is reiterated by Edmund when he notes that 'we all talk Shakespeare, use his similes, and describe with his descriptions' (*MP*, p. 338). Though Emma Woodhouse is not a great reader, she is found quoting passages on romantic love from *Romeo and Juliet* and *A Midsummer Night's Dream*.

Henry and Edmund agree on very little. It is therefore a fair assumption that, when they do concur, they are voicing the opinion of their author. Their consciousness of how Shakespeare is assimilated into our very fibre, so that 'one is intimate with him by instinct', reaches to the essence of Jane Austen's own relationship with him. She would have read the plays when a young woman, but she would also have absorbed famous lines and characters by osmosis, such was Shakespeare's pervasiveness in the culture of the age. She quotes Shakespeare from memory, as can be judged by the way that she often misquotes him. Her surviving letters refer far more frequently to contemporary plays than Shakespearean ones, but Shakespeare's influence on the drama of the late eighteenth and early nineteenth century was so thoroughgoing – for instance through the tradition of the 'witty couple', reaching back to *Love's Labour's Lost* and *Much Ado About Nothing* – that her indirect debt to his vision can be taken for granted.

In her earliest works, however, Jane Austen showed a certain irreverence for the national dramatist. Shakespeare's history plays are used to great satirical effect in *The History of England*, a lampoon of Oliver Goldsmith's abridged *History of England*. Austen mercilessly parodied Goldsmith's arbitrary and indiscriminate merging of fact and fiction, in particular his reliance on Shakespeare's history plays for supposedly authentic historical fact. Austen, by contrast, is being satirical when she makes a point of referring her readers to Shakespeare's English history plays for 'factual' information about the lives of its monarchs.[44] Just as solemnly, she refers her readers to other popular historical plays, such as Nicholas Rowe's *Jane Shore* and Sheridan's *The Critic* (*MW*, pp. 140, 147). The tongue-in-cheek reference to Sheridan compounds the irony, as *The Critic* is itself a burlesque of historical tragedy that firmly eschews any intention of authenticity.

From such allusions in the juvenilia it is clear that Jane Austen was familiar with a wide range of plays, although these are probably only a fraction of the numerous plays that would have been read over as possible choices for the private theatricals, read aloud for family entertainment, or read for private enjoyment. While it is impossible to calculate the number of plays that she read as a young girl, since there is no extant record of Mr Austen's ample library, the range of her explicit literary allusions gives us some idea of her extensive reading – references to over forty plays have been noted.[45]

Jane Austen owned a set of William Hayley's *Poems and Plays*. Volumes one to five are inscribed 'Jane Austen 1791'; volume six has a fuller inscription 'Jane Austen, Steventon Sunday April the 3*d*. 1791'.[46] Hayley was well known as the 'friend and biographer' of William Cowper, Austen's favourite poet, though he fancied himself as a successful playwright. The most well-thumbed volume in Austen's collection of Hayley was the one containing his plays. It contained five dramas in all: two tragedies, *Marcella* and *Lord Russel*, and three comedies in verse, *The Happy Prescription: or the Lady Relieved from her Lovers*; *The Two Connoisseurs*; and *The Mausoleum*.[47]

Like the Sheridan plays which the Austens adored, Hayley's comedies depict the folly of vanity and affectation in polite society. By far the best of them is *The Mausoleum*, which dramatises excessive sensibility and 'false refinement' in the characters of a beautiful young widow, Sophia Sentiment, and a pompous versifier, Mr Rumble, a caricature of Dr

Johnson. Lady Sophia Sentiment erects a mausoleum to house her husband's ashes and employs versifiers to compose tributes for the inscription on the monument. The comedy explores the self-destructive effects of sensibility on the mind of a lovely young widow, who refuses to overcome her grief because of a distorted conception of refined sentiment. The tell-tale sign of misplaced sensibility is Lady Sophia's obsession with black:

> If cards should be call'd for to-night,
> Place the new japann'd tables alone in my sight;
> For the pool of Quadrille set the black-bugle dish,
> And remember you bring us the ebony fish.[48]

But this sentiment is amusingly undercut by its correlation to hypocrisy and false delicacy:

> Her crisis is coming, without much delay;
> There might have been doubts had she fix'd upon grey:
> But a vow to wear black all the rest of her life
> Is a strong inclination she'll soon be a wife.[49]

This comedy is of particular interest as the main character has the name that was adopted in a satirical letter to James Austen in his capacity as editor of *The Loiterer*. The letter complains of the periodical's lack of feminine interest:

> Sir, I write this to inform you that you are very much out of my good graces, and that, if you do not mend your manners, I shall soon drop your acquaintance. You must know, Sir, that I am a great reader, and not to mention some hundred volumes of Novels and Plays, have in the two last summers, actually got through all the entertaining papers of our most celebrated periodical writers.[50]

The correspondent goes on to complain of the journal's lack of sentimental interest and offers recommendations to improve its style:

Let the lover be killed in a duel, or lost at sea, or you make him shoot himself, just as you please; and as for his mistress, she will of course go mad; or if you will, you may kill the lady, and let the lover run mad; only remember, whatever you do, that your hero and heroine must possess a great deal of feeling, and have very pretty names.[51]

The letter ends by stating that if the author's wishes are not complied with 'may your work be condemned to the pastry-cooke's shop, and may you always continue a bachelor, and be plagued with a maiden sister to keep house for you'. It is signed Sophia Sentiment.

It is highly probable that Jane Austen wrote this burlesque letter to her brother. It is very close in spirit to her juvenilia of the same period. *Love and Freindship* also has a sentimental heroine named Sophia. It seems plausible that *The Mausoleum* was among the comedies considered for performance by the Austens when they were looking at material for home theatricals in 1788. This may have been the time that Jane first became acquainted with the name Sophia Sentiment. If Austen was indeed Sophia Sentiment, by her own admission, she was a great reader of some hundred volumes of novels and plays.

Austen also owned a copy of Arnaud Berquin's *L'ami des enfans* (1782–83) and the companion series *L'ami de l'adolescence* (1784–85). Berquin's little stories, dialogues and dramas were much used in English schools for young ladies towards the end of the eighteenth century, being read in the original for the language or in translation for the moral. Berquin states in his preface to *L'ami des enfans* that his 'little dramas' are designed to bring children of the opposite sex together 'in order to produce that union and intimacy which we are so pleased to see subsist between brothers and sisters'.[52] The whole of the family is encouraged to partake in the plays to promote family values:

Each volume of this work will contain little dramas, in which children are the principal characters, in order that they may learn to acquire a free unembarrassed countenance, a gracefulness of attitude and deport-ment, and an easy manner of delivering themselves before company. Besides, the performance of these dramas will be a domestic recreation and amusement.

Berquin's short plays and dramatic dialogues were intended to instruct parents and children on manners and morals, on how to conduct themselves in domestic life, how to behave to one another, to the servants, and to the poor, and how to cope with everyday problems in the home. Some were directed towards young women, warning against finery and vanity. *Fashionable Education*, as its name suggests, depicts a young woman (Leonora) who has been given a fashionable town education, 'those charming sciences called drawing, music, dancing', but has also learned to be selfish, vain and affected.[53] The blind affection of Leonora's aunt has compounded her ruin. The moral of this play is that accomplishments should embellish a useful education and knowledge, not act as a substitute for them. A similar play, *Vanity Punished*, teaches the evils of coquetry, vanity, selfishness and spoilt behaviour.

Intriguingly, one of the playlets in the collection carries the same plot-line as Austen's *Emma*. In *Cecilia and Marian*, a young, wealthy girl befriends a poor labourer's daughter and 'tastes the happiness of doing good' when she feeds her new playmate plum cake and currant jelly:

> Cecilia had now tasted the happiness of doing good. She walked a little longer in the garden, thinking how happy she had made Marian, how grateful Marian had shewed herself, and how her little sister would be pleased to taste currant jelly. What will it be, said she, when I give her some ribbands and a necklace! Mama gave me some the other day that were pretty enough; but I am tired of them now. Then I'll look in my drawers for some old things to give her. We are just of a size, and my slips would fit her charmingly. Oh! how I long to see her well drest.[54]

Cecilia continues to enjoy her patronage until she is roundly scolded by her mother for her harmful and irresponsible conduct. By indulging and spoiling her favourite, Cecilia has made her friend dissatisfied with her previous life:

> MOTHER: But how comes it, then, that you cannot eat dry bread, nor walk barefoot as she does?
> CECILIA: The thing is, perhaps, that I am not used to it.

MOTHER: Why, then, if she uses herself, like you, to eat sweet things, and to wear shoes and stockings, and afterwards if the brown bread should go against her, and she should not be able to walk barefoot, do you think that you would have done her any service?[55]

Cecilia is an enemy to her own happiness and that of her 'low' friend Marian. She is only saved by the intervention and guidance of her judicious mother. In *L'ami des enfans*, mothers are often shown instructing, advising and educating their daughters: the plays were aimed at parents as well as children. In *Emma*, the variant on Berquin's plot-line is a similarly meddlesome, though well-meaning, young woman who painfully lacks a mother figure.

Like Berquin, Austen wrote her own short plays and stories for domestic entertainment.[56] But, rather than teaching morals and manners, Austen's playlets parody the moral didacticism of Berquin's thinly disguised conduct books. There are three attempts at playwriting in Austen's juvenilia. The first two, 'The Visit' and 'The Mystery' in *Volume the First*, were written between 1787 and 1790.[57] The third, 'The First Act of a Comedy', is one of the 'Scraps' in *Volume the Second* and dates from around 1793.

As mentioned earlier, 'The Visit' was probably written in 1789, the same time as the Steventon performance of Townley's *High Life Below Stairs*. The play depicts a dinner engagement at Lord Fitzgerald's house with a party of young people. Dining room etiquette is satirised in this piece, as the characters pompously make formal introductions to one another, then promptly discover that there are not sufficient chairs for them all to be seated:

MISS FITZGERALD: Bless me! there ought to be 8 Chairs & there are but 6. However, if your Ladyship will but take Sir Arthur in your Lap, & Sophy my Brother in hers, I beleive we shall do pretty well.
SOPHY: I beg you will make no apologies. Your Brother is very light.
(*MW*, p. 52)

The conversation between the guests is almost wholly preoccupied with the main fare of 'fried Cowheel and Onion', 'Tripe' and 'Liver and Crow'. The vulgarity of the food on offer is contrasted with the polite formality of the guests:

> CLOE: I shall trouble Mr Stanley for a Little of the fried Cowheel & Onion.
> STANLEY: Oh Madam, there is a secret pleasure in helping so amiable a Lady –.
> LADY HAMPTON: I assure you my Lord, Sir Arthur never touches wine; but Sophy will toss off a bumper I am sure to oblige your Lordship. (*MW*, p. 53)

Banal remarks about food and wine lead irrationally to unexpected marriage proposals for the three young women at the table, who eagerly accept without a second's hesitation.

On the surface, Austen's parody of a dull social visit derives its comic impact from the farcical touches and the juxtapositions of polite formalities with vulgar expressions. The young heroine, Sophy, like so many of Austen's early creations, is portrayed as a drunk who can 'toss off a bumper' at will. Above all, there is an irrepressible delight in the sheer absurdity of table manners. The Austens performing this play would, of course, be expected to maintain their composure when solemnly requesting 'fried Cowheel & Onion' and 'Liver & Crow' (*MW*, p. 53).

Austen's playlet, deriding the absurdity and pomposity of table etiquette, provides a mocking contrast to the morally earnest tone of Berquin's instructive playlets. His *Little Fiddler* also dramatises a social visit, where the exceptionally rude behaviour of a young man to his sister (Sophia) and to her visitors, the Misses Richmonds, leads to expulsion from the family circle. Charles, the ill-mannered brother and deceitful, greedy son, is eventually turned out of his father's house for his treachery and lies, and for his cruel treatment of a poor fiddler. In Berquin's play, the virtues of polite conduct are piously upheld:

> SOPHIA: Ah! how do you do, my dear friends! [*They salute each other, and curtsy to Godfrey, who bows to them.*]

CHARLOTTE: It seems an age since I saw you last.

AMELIA: Indeed it is a long time.

SOPHIA: I believe it is more than three weeks. [*Godfrey draws out the table, and gives them chairs.*]

CHARLOTTE: Do not give yourself so much trouble, Master Godfrey.

GODFREY: Indeed, I think it no trouble.

SOPHIA: Oh, I am very sure Godfrey does it with pleasure, [*gives him her hand.*] I wish my brother had a little of his complaisance.

The stilted artificiality of such social visits is precisely the target of Jane Austen's satire in 'The Visit'. She seemed to have little time for plays which dictated appropriate formal conduct, preferring comedies which satirised social behaviour. Jane Austen mocks Berquin and simultaneously begins to explore the incongruities and absurdities of restrictive social mores.[58]

As noted, a more direct source for 'The Visit' was Townley's *High Life Below Stairs*. Austen's quotation 'The more free, the more welcome' (*MW*, p. 50) nods to Townley's farce, where fashionably bad table manners are cultivated by the servants in an attempt to ape their masters. Berquin wrote didactic plays instructing the correct ways to treat servants, both honest and dishonest. Townley's hilarious farce of social disruption dramatises a lord who disguises himself as a servant to spy on his lazy servants, so that he can punish them appropriately for taking over his house.[59]

Austen dedicated 'The Visit' to her brother James. Intriguingly, in her dedication, she recalled two other Steventon plays. These 'celebrated comedies' were probably written by James, since Jane describes her own 'drama' as 'inferior' to his:

Sir, The Following Drama, which I humbly recommend to your Protection & Patronage, tho' inferior to those celebrated comedies called 'The School for Jealousy' & 'The travelled Man', will I hope afford some amusement to so respectable a *Curate* as yourself; which was the end in veiw [*sic*] when it was first composed by your Humble Servant the Author. (*MW*, p. 49)

James had recently returned from his travels abroad, so 'the travelled Man' may have been based on his adventures. The two play-titles echo the form of several favourites in the eighteenth-century dramatic repertoire: Goldsmith's *The Good-Natur'd Man* (1768), Arthur Murphy's *The School For Guardians* (1769), and Richard Cumberland's *The Choleric Man* (1774), Sheridan's *The School for Scandal* (1777), and Hannah Cowley's *School for Elegance* (1780).

'The Mystery' was probably performed as an afterpiece to the Steventon 1788 'Private Theatrical Exhibition'.[60] Austen dedicated it to her father, and it may well have been a mocking tribute to one of his favourite plays. It has been suggested that the whispering scenes in this playlet were based on a similar scene in Sheridan's *The Critic*.[61] Jane Austen's parody is, however, closer to Buckingham's burlesque, *The Rehearsal*, which Sheridan was self-consciously reworking in *The Critic*.[62] It is most likely that Austen was parodying the whispering scene in *The Rehearsal*, where Bayes insists that his play is entirely new: 'Now, Sir, because I'll do nothing here that ever was done before, instead of beginning with a Scene that discovers something of the Plot I begin this play with a whisper':

PHYSICIAN: But yet some rumours great are stirring; and if Lorenzo
     should prove false (which none but the great Gods can tell) you
     then perhaps would find that – [*Whispers.*]
BAYES: Now he whispers.
USHER: Alone, do you say?
PHYSICIAN: No; attended with the noble – [*Whispers.*]
BAYES: Again.
USHER: Who, he in gray?
PHYSICIAN: Yes; and at the head of – [*Whispers.*]
BAYES: Pray, mark.
USHER: Then, Sir, most certain, 'twill in time appear. These are the
     reasons that have mov'd him to't; First, he – [*Whispers.*]
BAYES: Now the other whispers.
USHER: Secondly, they – [*Whispers.*]
BAYES: At it still.
USHER: Thirdly, and lastly, both he, and they – [*Whispers.*]
BAYES: Now they both whisper. [*Exeunt Whispering.*][63]

'The Mystery' is closely modelled on this whispering scene. Austen's playlet is comprised of a series of interruptions and non-communications. It opens with a mock mysterious line, 'But hush! I am interrupted!', and continues in a similarly absurd and nonsensical manner:

DAPHNE: My dear Mrs Humbug how dy'e do? Oh! Fanny, t'is all over.
FANNY: Is it indeed!
MRS HUMBUG: I'm very sorry to hear it.
FANNY: Then t'was to no purpose that I ...
DAPHNE: None upon Earth.
MRS HUMBUG: And what is to become of? ...
DAPHNE: Oh! thats all settled. [*whispers Mrs Humbug*]
FANNY: And how is it determined?
DAPHNE: I'll tell you. [*whispers Fanny*]
MRS HUMBUG: And is he to? ...
DAPHNE: I'll tell you all I know of the matter. [*whispers Mrs Humbug and Fanny*]
FANNY: Well! now I know everything about it, I'll go away.
MRS HUMBUG & DAPHNE: And so will I. [*Exeunt*]
(*MW*, p. 56)

The play ends with a further whispering scene, where the secret is finally whispered in the ear of the sleeping Sir Edward: 'Shall I tell him the secret? ... No, he'll certainly blab it ... But he is asleep and won't hear me ... So I'll e'en venture' (*MW*, p. 57). In 'The Mystery', we are never told any information about the conversations between the characters, and it becomes as incongruous as Bayes's own 'new' play, which he proudly insists has no plot.

Austen's third playlet, 'The First Act of a Comedy', parodies musical comedy, an extremely popular mode of dramatic entertainment in the latter part of the eighteenth century.[64] A satirical passage from George Colman's *New Brooms* (1776) targets the vogue for comic opera:

Operas are the only real entertainment. The plain unornamented drama is too flat, Sir. Common dialogue is a dry imitation of nature, as insipid as real conversation; but in an opera the dialogue is refreshed by an air every instant. – Two gentlemen meet in the Park, for example, admire the place and the weather; and after a speech or two the orchestra take their cue, the musick strikes up, one of the characters takes a genteel turn or two on the stage, during the symphony, and then breaks out –

When the breezes
Fan the trees-es,
Fragrant gales
The breath inhales,
Warm the heart that sorrow freezes.[65]

Austen, like Colman, satirises the artificiality of the comic opera, its spontaneous outbursts of songs, and distinctive lack of plot.[66] Austen's playlet concerns the adventures of a family *en route* to London, and is set in a roadside inn, a familiar trope of the picaresque form popularised in Fielding's novels *Joseph Andrews* and *Tom Jones*.[67] Austen's play also nods towards Shakespeare's comic scenes set in 'The Boar's Head' in *Henry IV, Parts One and Two*. Three of the female characters are called 'Pistoletta', 'Maria' and 'Hostess'.

Chloe, who is to be married to the same man as Pistoletta, enters with a 'chorus of ploughboys', reads over a bill of fare and discovers that the only food available is '2 ducks, a leg of beef, a stinking partridge, & a tart'. Chloe's propensity for bursting into song at any given moment echoes Colman's burlesque of the inanities of comic opera: 'And now I will sing another song.'

SONG
I am going to have my dinner,
After which I shan't be thinner,
I wish I had here Strephon
For he would carve the partridge
If it should be a tough one.

CHORUS
Tough one, tough one, tough one,
For he would carve the partridge if it should be a tough one.
(*MW*, p. 174)[68]

As will be seen in the next two chapters, Austen clearly enjoyed musical comedy, even if, like Colman, she was conscious of its deficiencies as an 'imitation of nature'.

The three playlets in the juvenilia are parodic and satirical, and a strong sense prevails that Austen was writing to amuse her sophisticated, theatre-loving brothers. Whether she was composing a mocking counterpart to Berquin's instructive dramatic dialogues, or writing burlesques in the style of plays like *The Rehearsal* and *The Critic*, she endeavoured to impress her siblings with her knowledge of the drama. Two of her playlets, 'The Mystery' and 'The First Act of a Comedy', allude specifically to what was popular on the London stage, and mock it by drawing attention to its limitations and artificiality. 'The Visit' nods to the popular comedy *High Life Below Stairs*, so often dramatised for the private theatre, and begins to explore the incongruities and absurdities of genteel social behaviour.

In contrast with Berquin and William Hayley, who self-consciously used their plays to instruct, Austen entertains. Furthermore, even as she abandoned plays and turned to fiction, she began an apprenticeship in the art of dramatic dialogue and quasi-theatrical techniques that was to distinguish her mature writing. Austen's juvenilia reveals a deep familiarity with the most popular plays of the period: the works of Garrick, Fielding, Sheridan and Cowley.[69]

The Steventon theatricals took place between 1782 and 1790, coinciding with the period in which Jane Austen's juvenile literary works were written. Given the abundance of dramatic entertainment that she was exposed to at this time, it is not at all surprising that there were attempts at playwriting among her youthful literary efforts. Contrary to popular belief, however, it was not only in her childhood at Steventon that Austen developed her interest in the drama. In the period between the composition of the early versions of *Northanger Abbey*, *Pride and Prejudice* and *Sense and Sensibility* and the completion of the mature novels, Austen was taking part in private theatricals, writing dramatic dialogues and turning her favourite novel into a five-act comedy.

Jane Austen took part in private theatricals in 1805 when she was thirty. The death of her father early in the same year had a profound effect on the lives of the three dependent women whom he left behind, who were not to find a permanent home until they settled at Chawton in 1809. Some time after her father's death Austen may have redrafted and put the finishing touches to a short epistolary novel, *Lady Susan*. In June, the Austen sisters left Gay Street in Bath, collecting their niece Anna on the way, and set out for her brother Edward (Austen) Knight's Godmersham home. During her time at Kent, Jane spent many hours amusing her favourite nieces, Fanny and Anna, with play-acting. It was here that Anne Sharp, the children's governess, formed a friendship with Jane Austen that was to last for the rest of the latter's life. In the Godmersham private theatricals, Miss Sharp played the male roles and was clearly a great success.

The unpublished diaries of one of those nieces, Fanny Knight, reveal that aunt Jane had no scruples about play-acting. Fanny records a game of 'school' in which her aunts, grandmother and governess dressed up and took part:

Wednesday 26 June. We had a whole holiday. Aunts and Grandmama played at school with us. Aunt C was Mrs Teachum the Governess Aunt Jane, Miss Popham the teacher Aunt Harriet, Sally the Housemaid, Miss Sharpe the Dancing Master the Apothecary and the Serjeant, Grandmama Betty Jones the pie woman and Mama the bathing woman. They dressed in Character and we had a most delightful day. – After dessert we acted a play called *Virtue Rewarded*. Anna was the Duchess St Albans, I was the Fairy Serena and Fanny Cage a shepherdess 'Mona'. We had a bowl of Syllabub in the evening.[70]

Although improvisational play was part of the fun, the small company of women also included their own plays in their repertoire. *Virtue Rewarded* may well have been composed by Anne Sharp, with roles written specifically for the children.[71]

The theatricals continued throughout June and July. Then on 30 July Fanny recorded two more amateur performances, including a play possibly written by Anne Sharp called *Pride Punished: or Innocence Rewarded*:[72] 'Aunt C and J, Anna, Edward, George, Henry, William and myself acted *The Spoilt Child* and *Innocence Rewarded*, afterwards we danced and had a most delightful evening.'[73] Bickerstaffe's *The Spoilt Child* was a great favourite on the London stage, popularised by Mrs Jordan who played the cross-dressed role of 'Little Pickle', the naughty child of the title. If Fanny played the part of Little Pickle and Anne Sharp his father, it is plausible that Jane Austen took the role of the spinster aunt, Miss Pickle. The most popular scene in the play is when the naughty child catches his aunt and her lover in the garden reciting love poetry and planning their elopement, and sews their clothes together.

It was during the 1805 Kent visit that Jane Austen read Thomas Gisborne's dour *Enquiry into the Duties of the Female Sex*. She would have been amused to discover Gisborne's assertion that play-acting was injurious to the female sex through encouraging vanity and destroying diffidence 'by the unrestrained familiarity with persons of the other sex, which inevitably results from being joined with them in the drama'.[74] Jane wrote to Cassandra, 'I am glad that you recommended Gisborne for having begun, I am pleased with it, and I had quite determined not to read it' (*Letters*, p. 112). This remark suggests a softening of her prior scepticism towards Gisborne, yet she clearly had no intention of putting his prescriptions into practice and giving up her involvement with private theatricals.[75] Jane Austen not only acted in plays at the same time that she was reading Gisborne, she also committed the grave offence of luring children into this dangerous activity, a practice that Gisborne particularly abhorred:

> Most of these remarks fully apply to the practice of causing children to act plays, or parts of plays; a practice of which parents, while labouring to vindicate it, sometimes pronounce an emphatical condemnation, by avowing a future purpose of abandoning it so soon as their children shall be far advanced in youth.[76]

Gisborne's prejudice directly opposes Arnaud Berquin's championing of the moral efficacy of family theatricals. Austen appears to have been more sympathetic to Berquin's view, judging by her enthusiasm for private theatricals among Edward Knight's young family at Kent. Perhaps she was rekindling memories of happier days at Steventon in her present uncertain state of home (she was to live at yet another brother's home in Southampton before eventually settling at Chawton).

In the meantime she continued not only to act with the children, but also returned to drama writing. It may well have been at this time that, with the help of her niece Anna, she put the finishing touches to her five-act play, *Sir Charles Grandison: or The Happy Man*, a burlesque dramatisation of her favourite novel, Richardson's *The History of Sir Charles Grandison*.[77]

There are two more notable occurrences that reflect Austen's interest in the drama. There still exists in the Austen-Leigh family collection a short unidentified document, untitled and consisting of two dramatic dialogues on the business of child-rearing in the early nineteenth century. From 1806 to 1809 Mrs Austen, her two daughters and Martha Lloyd were living in Southampton, for part of the time with Frank Austen and his newly pregnant wife Mary Gibson. As was the convention, the women read novels and plays aloud. This provided Jane Austen with another opportunity for the composition of amusing playlets on the subject of baby-care and motherhood.[78]

In these dramatic dialogues, a first-time mother, Mrs Denbigh, is seen neglecting her child, and spending almost all of her time in the garden looking at her auriculas. She pleads ignorance in child-rearing as 'I was just come from school when I was married, where you know we learnt nothing in the way of medicine or nursing'. The incompetence of Mrs Denbigh (and her Irish nanny) is contrasted with the sensible advice and practical skills of her friend Mrs Enfield:

MRS ENFIELD: [*Endeavours to look at the back*] Ah Nurse his shirt
    sticks! Do bring me some warm water & a rag.
MRS DENBIGH: [*rising*] I shall faint if I stay.
MRS ENFIELD: I beg you will stay till we can see what can be done.

MRS DENBIGH: [*takes out her smelling bottle*] I will try – how unfeeling [*aside*].

MRS ENFIELD: [*applies a mild plaister*] Now nurse you must change the plaister night & morning, spread it very thin, & keep a few folds of soft linen over it – Will you bring me a clean shirt.

NURSE: [*going out*] Yes Ma'am, if I can find one – I wish she and her plaister were far enough [*aside*].[79]

The dialogues are didactic, as they are meant to be, but the selfish Mrs Denbigh is comically drawn. Her rattling conversations perhaps foreshadow the monologues of Miss Bates and Mrs Elton in *Emma*.[80]

The other significant event in these later years took place in 1809. It was then, only two years before starting work on *Mansfield Park*, that Austen acted the part of Mrs Candour in Sheridan's *School for Scandal*. In writing of Sir William Heathcote of Hursley Park, Hampshire, in 1898, the novelist Charlotte M. Yonge recalled: 'His mother was Elizabeth, daughter of Lovelace Bigg-Wither of Manydown Park in the same country … She lived chiefly in Winchester, and it may be interesting that her son remembered being at a Twelfth day party where Jane Austen drew the character of Mrs Candour, and assumed the part with great spirit.'[81]

There is no reason to doubt this evidence. Jane Austen's friendship with the Manydown family lasted all her life. Both she and Cassandra often used to spend the night at Manydown when they attended the Basingstoke balls as girls. Jane informed Cassandra of a twelfth day party at Manydown in her letter to Cassandra of 27 December 1808:

> I was happy to hear, cheifly [*sic*] for Anna's sake, that a Ball at Manydown was once more in agitation; it is called a Child's Ball, & given by Mrs Heathcote to Wm – such was its' beginning at least – but it will probably swell into something more … it is to take place between this & twelfth-day. (*Letters*, p. 160)

The postscript to her next letter (10 January 1809) suggests that she attended the festivities: 'The Manydown Ball was a smaller thing than I expected, but it seems to have made Anna very happy. At *her* age it would not have done for *me*' (*Letters*, p. 165). If this was the same party that Sir

William recollected, then Jane Austen was acting in a Sheridan play only two years before she began writing *Mansfield Park*. This would seem to be still stronger evidence against the notion that the novel offers an unequivocal condemnation of amateur theatricals.

Jane Austen's artistic development was clearly influenced by the vogue for private theatricals that swept Britain in the late eighteenth and early nineteenth century. Contrary to popular belief, it was not merely as a passive spectator that she was exposed to private theatricals as a young girl. Her plays show that she was actively engaged in the amateur dramatics at Steventon, and her involvement in private theatricals in Kent, Southampton and Winchester confirm an interest that was to be crystallised in the writing of *Mansfield Park*.

2

The Professional Theatre

In 1790 Jane Austen wrote *Love and Freindship*, a parody of the popular heroine-centred, sentimental novel. The cast of characters includes two strolling actors, Philander and Gustavus, who eventually become stars of the London stage. As a final joke, these two fictional characters are transformed into real figures: 'Philander and Gustavus, after having raised their reputation by their performance in the theatrical line in Edinburgh, removed to Covent Garden, where they still exhibit under the assumed names of *Lewis & Quick*' (*MW*, p. 109).

William Thomas ('Gentleman') Lewis (1748–1811) and John Quick (1748–1831) were well-known comic actors of the Covent Garden Company. The roles of Faulkland and Bob Acres in Sheridan's *The Rivals* were created for them, and Quick was also the original Tony Lumpkin in Goldsmith's *She Stoops to Conquer*. 'Gentleman' Lewis earned his appellation for his rendering of refined roles. A fellow actor, G. F. Cooke, called him 'the unrivalled favorite of the comic muse in all that was frolic, gay, humorous, whimsical, and at the same time elegant'.[1] Leigh Hunt considered that 'vulgarity seems impossible to an actor of his manners',[2] and Hazlitt's testimony ranked him high above the comedians of his day: 'gay, fluttering, hare-brained Lewis ... all life and fashion, and volubility, and whim; the greatest comic *mannerist* that perhaps ever lived.'[3]

Quick, conversely, was a fine 'low' actor, 'the prince of low comedians'.[4] He was a diminutive man who breathed life into the roles of clowns, rustics and servants before he became famous with his performance of Tony Lumpkin. Unsurpassed in playing old men, he was George III's favourite actor.[5] Hazlitt records that he 'made an excellent self-important, busy, strutting, money-getting citizen; or a crusty old guardian, in a brown suit and a bob-wig'.[6]

By the 1790s Lewis and Quick were among the highest-paid actors in the Covent Garden Company.[7] Austen's reference to this comic duo reveals her knowledge of the contemporary stars of the London stage, and suggests the young girl's eagerness to be included in the theatre-loving clan of her brothers and her cousin Eliza de Feuillide, to whom *Love and Freindship* was dedicated (*MW*, p. 76). The joke is more than merely a glancing and amusing allusion to an immensely popular pair of eighteenth-century comedians: it also reveals a striking and specific interest in the nuanced world of high and low comedy in the late Georgian theatre. This interest was to have a strong influence on Austen's comic vision. As will be demonstrated, her sense of the interplay between genteel characters and low ones was an important part of her awareness of how comedy works.

The first reference to the professional theatre in Austen's letters is a mention of Astley's Theatre in London, in August 1796: 'We are to be at Astley's tonight, which I am glad of' (*Letters*, p. 5). The history of this theatre, and its importance in the growth of the illegitimate stage, has been overlooked by Austen scholars.

Astley's Amphitheatre was an equestrian theatre built on the south side of the river in Lambeth by Philip Astley in 1770.[8] When first opened it was merely an open-air circus ring with covered seats. By 1780 Astley had roofed over the whole of his ring, which was now called the Amphitheatre Riding House. It was renamed the Royal Grove in 1784, when Astley obtained a royal patent, and in 1787, he added 'burletta' to his amphitheatre licence.[9] It was popular not only for equestrian events, but for acrobatics, swordsmanship, musical interludes, songs and dancing. In 1794 the amphitheatre was burnt to the ground. It was rebuilt in the following year with the new name, the Amphitheatre of Arts.[10] In 1796, when the Austens visited Astley's, the entertainment was more elaborate than ever before. Thirty-five new acts were advertised, and, as a special attraction, two Catawba Indian chiefs performed dances and tomahawk exercises.[11] Astley's Amphitheatre survived two fires and lasted until 1841.

As with many of the minor, unpatented London theatres, Astley's circumvented the licensing laws by exploiting the ambiguity of the term 'burletta' and slipping in straight plays among the main entertainments.[12]

The Licensing Act of 1737 confined legitimate theatrical performances to two patent playhouses in London, Drury Lane and Covent Garden. The Act prohibited the performances of plays elsewhere for 'hire, gain or reward' and gave the Lord Chamberlain statutory powers to examine all plays.[13] The monopoly of the patents was broken in 1740, however, by Henry Giffard who re-established his theatre in Goodman's Fields and avoided the 'hire, gain or reward' clause by claiming to charge only for the music and giving the play free. The authorities tolerated Giffard's theatre until David Garrick joined the company in 1741. The unprecedented success of Giffard's new actor ensured that both he and Garrick were offered engagements at Drury Lane, and Goodman's Fields was closed once more.

Giffard had demonstrated that the law could be circumvented. Other theatre managers followed suit and found ways of evading the £50 fine and the threat of the loss of their licence. Samuel Foote sold tickets inviting the public to 'drink a dish of chocolate with him' at noon, and provided entertainments free of charge, thereby inventing the matinee. This led to his obtaining a summer patent for his Little Theatre in the Haymarket in 1766.[14]

Foote's patent was followed by a number of patents for provincial theatres. In London, by the early nineteenth century, the proliferation of illegitimate theatres posed a formidable challenge to the patents. By 1800 there were seven minor theatres offering regular entertainment: Sadler's Wells, Astley's, the Royal Circus, the Royalty in east London, Dibdin's Sans Souci, the King's, Pantheon and the first Lyceum.[15] In 1826 Edward Brayley included eleven minor theatres in his *Historic and Descriptive Accounts of the Theatres of London*, and F. G. Tomlins, in *A Brief View of the English Stage* (1832), listed thirteen minor theatres operating in London.[16]

Astley's was not only visited by Jane Austen. It was also chosen by her as the location for a major turning point in *Emma*.[17] It is Astley's Theatre where Robert Martin meets Harriet and rekindles the love affair between them, thus clearing the way for Emma and Mr Knightley to be united. Scholars have assumed that Austen was referring to the equestrian amphitheatre by Westminster Bridge in Lambeth. But following the success of his amphitheatre, which only operated on a summer licence, Astley opened a new theatre on Wych Street in the Strand in 1806.[18] He called his new theatre the Olympic Pavilion, but it was also known as Astley's Pavilion, the Pavilion Theatre, the Olympic Saloon, and sometimes simply Astley's.[19] The theatre specialised in equestrian events, but Astley also obtained a licence, through the influence of Queen Charlotte, for music and dancing.[20]

According to the testimony of one nineteenth-century theatre historian, though Astley conducted several other establishments, the new Olympic theatre was '*par excellence*, "Astley's" – a name which has become historic'.[21] It was an especially popular place to take children. Astley had built his new theatre from the remains of some old naval prizes that he had bought. The deck of the ship was used for the stage and the floors.[22] The new theatre was built like a playhouse, with a stage, orchestra, side-boxes, galleries and a pit surrounding the ring. It was the largest of London's minor theatres and accommodated three thousand people.[23] In writing about Astley's in his *A Brief View of the English Stage*, Tomlins notes that it was 'a name at which the youthful heart bounds, and the olden one revives. Jeremy Bentham pronounced it to be the genuine English theatre, where John Bull, whatever superior tastes he might ape, was most sincerely at home'.[24]

Jane Austen was not absolutely precise about dates in *Emma*: the theatre visit takes place some time in late summer and Harriet marries Martin shortly afterwards, in late September. This opens up the possibility of the Astley's reference being to either the summer amphitheatre in Lambeth or the winter Olympic house off Drury Lane. Strictly speaking, the summer season commenced on Easter Monday and closed about the end of September or the beginning of October.[25] Given that the Austens patronised the Lambeth Amphitheatre, Jane may well have intended the same theatre. On the other hand, the genteel John Knightleys visit Astley's as a treat for their young boys, and Harriet, on quitting their box, is made uneasy by the size of the crowds. This suggests the superior Olympic Pavilion.[26] The Lambeth Amphitheatre also had its own separate entrance for the boxes and the pit, with the gallery entrance fifty yards down the road, so it would be more likely that Harriet encountered large crowds at the Olympic.[27]

Nevertheless, whichever of Astley's playhouses Austen intended when she was writing *Emma* in 1813, the allusion is of considerable interest, as the long-standing battle between the minor theatres and the patents had once again flared up that year, with the name 'Astley's' at the centre of controversy. When Elliston opened up Astley's in 1813 with the provocative name 'Little Drury Lane Theatre', he was almost immediately forced to close. He was able to reopen the theatre by reverting to its old name. In 1812 Astley had sold his theatre and licence to Robert Elliston for £2800.[28] Almost as soon as the management passed into Elliston's hands, he remodelled the playhouse in the hope of attracting a superior type of audience. He introduced a mixed programme of farce, pantomime and melodrama, all of course concealed under the term 'burletta'. Though many of the minor theatres circumvented the law by similar methods, none had dared to do so in the direct vicinity of the patents. Perhaps Austen was sympathetic to Elliston's crusade to compete against the patents, for he was one of her favourite actors, and, as we will see, she followed his fortunes throughout his career.

Astley's was known for its socially diverse audience. It was 'a popular place of amusement for all classes'.[29] A friendly and unpretentious theatre, its tickets were priced well below those of the patents.[30] The spectacle that it offered clearly appealed to families, and to people of all classes, much as the West End musical attracts thousands of people today. Austen had no compunction about visiting the minor theatres when she stayed in London, and her reference to Astley's in *Emma* may indeed have been a gesture in support of them in their long battle to break the monopoly of the patents.

Given Jane Austen's scrupulous sense of class and realism, and the particular concern in *Emma* with fine discriminations within social hierarchies, it is by no means fanciful to attach considerable weight to her choice of Astley's for the reconciliation between Harriet and Robert Martin. Precisely because of its status as a minor, illegitimate theatre, it was a place where a yeoman farmer and a girl who is without rank (carrying the 'stain of illegitimacy', we are reminded in the same chapter) could mingle freely with the gentry.

Austen does mention the patented theatres in her other novels. In *Sense and Sensibility*, Willoughby 'ran against Sir John Middleton' in the lobby of Drury Lane Theatre, where he hears that Marianne Dashwood is seriously ill at Cleveland. In *Pride and Prejudice* Lydia Bennet, in complete disregard to the disgrace that she has brought on the family by her elopement, can only prattle: 'To be sure London was rather thin, but however the Little Theatre was open' (*PP*, p. 319). Lydia's elopement takes place in August, and, as Austen was aware, the 'Little Theatre' in the Haymarket was the only house licensed to produce regular drama during the summer season. This is a fine example of Austen's scrupulous sense of realism working in conjunction with her knowledge of the London theatre world. It is also worth noting that her favourite niece, Fanny Knight, with whom she often went to the theatre, was particularly fond of the 'little' theatre in the Haymarket, as opposed to the vast auditoriums at Covent Garden and Drury Lane. In her unpublished diaries Fanny complained that 'Drury Lane is too immense' and that she preferred 'the dear enchanting Haymarket.'[31]

There is only one other mention of playgoing in *Pride and Prejudice*, a vague reference to an 'evening at one of the theatres' in which Elizabeth Bennet and Mrs Gardiner talked over intimate family matters in what was presumably a theatre box, while the rest of the party watched the action on the stage (*PP*, pp. 152–54). In *Persuasion*, Austen includes only a few vague references to the Theatre Royal on Orchard Street in Bath.[32] However, she uses the same theatre in *Northanger Abbey* to structure an important plot link between John Thorpe and General Tilney. It is at the theatre that Thorpe, 'who was never in the same part of the house for ten minutes together' (*NA*, p. 95), falsely boasts to General Tilney that Catherine is the heiress to the Allen fortune, thus encouraging the General's plan to invite her to Northanger Abbey.

In *Sense and Sensibility*, *Northanger Abbey* and *Emma* Jane Austen uses the forum of the public theatre to implement crucial plot developments. In this, she was influenced by Fanny Burney, whose novels about the London *ton* used the playhouses as important meeting grounds for the advancement of plot lines. For example, in *Evelina* the heroine first attends Drury Lane to see Garrick in *The Suspicious Husband* and is later reunited with Lord Orville at a performance of Congreve's *Love for Love*. Here she is subjected to impertinent remarks by the fop Lovel, who compares her to the character of Miss Prue, an ignorant rustic young hoyden, a role made famous by the comic actress Frances Abington.[33] As

Burney and Austen demonstrate in their novels, the public theatres provided an arena for the exchange of news and gossip.

In *Northanger Abbey* there is a special irony at play, for Austen's novel about an ingenue's entrance into Bath society self-consciously mirrors Burney's *Evelina: or The History of a Young Lady's Entrance into the World.* In one of the more subtle allusions to *Evelina*, Catherine quotes from Congreve's *Love for Love* when she tells John Thorpe that she hates the idea of 'one great fortune looking out for another' (*NA*, p. 124). Like Evelina, Catherine delights in going to the play, though she has been told that the Theatre Royal Bath is 'quite horrid' compared to the London stage (*NA*, p. 92).

Northanger Abbey's status as a burlesque Gothic novel has unwittingly deflected attention away from Austen's parody of the heroine-centred sentimental novel popularised by female writers like Burney and Edgeworth. Instead of London's *beau monde*, unfamiliar terrain to Austen, the resort city of Bath becomes her microcosm of fashionable high society. *Northanger Abbey* was written in 1798–99. As Jane Austen and her mother were at Bath during the later part of 1797 visiting the Leigh-Perrots, her account could well have been based on actual experience.

In 1799 Jane Austen revisited Bath, staying at Queen Square with her brother Edward Knight. This visit included a trip to the Theatre Royal: 'The Play on Saturday is I *hope* to conclude our gaieties here, for nothing but a lengthened stay will make it otherwise' (*Letters*, p. 47). She does not name the play, but the account in the *Bath Herald and Reporter* for 29 June 1799 reveals that she saw Kotzebue's drama *The Birth-Day* and 'The pleasing spectacle of Blue-Beard' on that occasion. In the eyes of the Bath newspapers, the new Kotzebue comedy was considered to be a vast improvement on his previous works, which were notable for their immorality:

> If the German Author has justly drawn down censure for the immorality of his productions for the stage, this may be considered as expiatory – this may be accepted as his *amende honoyrable* [sic]; it is certainly throughout unexceptionable, calculated to promote the best interest of

virtue, and the purest principles of benevolence: and though written in the style of Sterne, it possesses humour without a single broad Shandyism.[34]

James Boaden, a professed admirer of Kotzebue, described the play as 'the *naval* pendant to the *military* Toby and Trim', and thought it contained 'one of the best delineations of human nature coloured by profession'.[35]

The Birth-Day, a comedy in three acts, was translated from Kotzebue's play *Reconciliation*, and adapted for the English stage by Thomas Dibdin (1771–1841).[36] The plot is centred on a feud in a Bertram family. Twin brothers, estranged over a law suit, are finally reconciled on their sixty-third birthday by the efforts of their children, cousins who are in love with each other. The heroine, Emma Bertram, is devoted to her father and has vowed never to marry until she is finally persuaded by her cousin: 'But if a man could be found, who would bestow on your father a quiet old age, free from every sorrow; who, far from robbing the father of a good daughter, would weave the garland of love round three hearts, who would live under his roof, and multiply your joys, by reconciling your father and your uncle'.[37]

Two of the best comic characters in *The Birth-Day* are a boatswain, Jack Junk, and a meddling housekeeper, Mrs Moral, who has taken over Captain Bertram's household and has contributed to the family estrangement for her own devious means.[38] *Mansfield Park*, in which a different Kotzebue adaptation is staged, shares with this other Kotzebue play not only the family name Bertram but also similar comic stereotypes in the persons of the bullying, interfering Mrs Norris and the rum-drinking, oath-swearing Mr Price.[39]

In May 1801 Jane Austen moved more permanently to Bath to live with her parents. She stayed until July 1806. Owing to the absence of letters during this time, very little is known of her theatrical activities there.[40] Her residence in Bath coincided, however, with one of the most prosperous and exciting times in the history of the local stage. The period from 1790 to the opening of the new theatre in Beaufort Square in 1805 marked an unprecedented time of 'prosperity, of brilliancy and of progress'.[41]

Bath was a fashionable resort town and was able to support a theatre of considerable standing for the society people who flocked there to take the waters. The theatre was run in tandem with the Bristol playhouse and was regarded as one of the best in the country. Provincial theatres in the Georgian era were not merely seasonal or summer playhouses, playing in the London off-season, but year-round operations. Their importance to the life and culture of their cities is suggested in the increasing numbers of royal patents granted by 1800.[42] The Bath theatre had been patented in 1768, becoming the first Theatre Royal of the English provinces.[43]

Outside London, Bath was one of the most important theatres, maintaining a regular company which was supplemented by London stars.[44] Many of the London stars had indeed cut their teeth in the Orchard Street playhouse. It was described variously as 'a dramatic nursery for the London stage' and a 'probationary school of the drama to the London stage'.[45] Mrs Siddons had begun her career there in 1778, and retained such an affection and loyalty to the theatre that she often returned during the summer seasons.[46]

One of the theatre's main assets was Robert William Elliston (1774–1831). Intended for the church, the young Elliston ran away to Bath and made his first appearance in Orchard Street in 1793.[47] Remarkably, he stayed until 1804, although 'by permission of the Bath manager' he was loaned to the London theatres, where he played once a fortnight, reinforcing the already strong links between the London and Bath playhouses. One of the reasons why Elliston refused to leave Bath, despite lucrative offers from both Drury Lane and Covent Garden, was his marriage. In 1796 he eloped with and married Elizabeth Rundall, a dance teacher, who, despite her husband's success, continued her occupation.[48]

Despite Sheridan's efforts to hire him, Elliston refused a permanent engagement at Drury Lane. His new wife had recently gone into partnership running a dance and deportment academy, and Elliston enjoyed his position as Bath's star attraction. Even when he was finally lured to Drury Lane in 1804, Mrs Elliston remained in Bath. Jane Austen was aware of the unusual arrangements of Elliston's private life. In February 1807, she shared with Cassandra some Bath gossip gleaned from her Aunt

Leigh-Perrot: 'Elliston, she tells us has just succeeded to a considerable fortune on the death of an Uncle. I would not have it enough to take *him* from the Stage; *she* should quit her business, & live with him in London' (*Letters*, p. 122). This remark, which has not hitherto drawn comment from Austen scholars, demonstrates her loyalty to Elliston, both in his professional and his private life. Even though Elliston was now based in London, Austen continued to take an interest in him, and she clearly disapproved of his wife's determination to remain with her academy in Bath.

Elliston's last engagement on the Bath stage, before leaving for London, was as Rolla in Sheridan's adaptation of Kotzebue's *Pizarro*.[49] Rolla was not a surprising choice for Elliston. His performance of the noble, virtuous warrior was one of his most acclaimed tragic roles. It was also the role that he played for his Drury Lane debut, later that year, when he took over from Kemble.[50]

Another Kotzebue adaptation, *Lovers' Vows*, was performed at least seventeen times in Bath from 1801 to 1806.[51] This suggests that Austen was familiar with the play long before she used it in *Mansfield Park*. Elliston played the part of Frederick. Kotzebue adaptations such as *The Birth-Day*, *Pizarro*, *The Stranger* and *Lovers' Vows* continued to flourish at Bath, despite objections by the *Anti-Jacobin Review* to 'the filthy effusions of this German dunce'.[52] In September 1801 Siddons played Elvira in *Pizarro* alongside Elliston at the Orchard Street Theatre.[53] Elvira, in particular, incited vicious attacks by the *Anti-Jacobin Review* which, with typically excessive rhetoric, described her as one of the most reprehensible characters that had ever been suffered to disgrace the stage. Such charges cut no ice with playgoers, who flocked to the Bath theatre to see Siddons as Pizarro's dignified paramour.

Another comment suggesting that the Austens were theatregoers while living in Bath is to be found in a letter written by Jane's mother to her daughter-in-law Mary Austen: 'Cooke, I dare say will have as full houses tonight and Saturday, as he had on Tuesday.'[54] George Frederick Cooke (1756–1811) was the name of the Covent Garden actor whose brilliance as a tragic actor was overshadowed by his notorious drinking problem. He was one of the great actors of the English stage, the hero of Edmund Kean. After Cooke's death brought on by hardened drinking,

Kean arranged for his remains to be removed to a better location, and kept the bone of the forefinger of his right hand as a sacred relic.[55] Cooke's reputation as a drunkard has obscured his acting abilities. His performances of Richard III and Iago were legendary, but he was considered to be an unreliable and erratic actor. One of his critics, to Cooke's great mortification, described him in the following terms: 'No two men, however different they may be, can be more at variance than George Cooke sober and George Cooke in a state of inebriety.'[56] At Covent Garden in 1803, while playing Sir Archy MacSarcasm in *Love à la Mode*, Cooke was so drunk that he was hissed off stage and the curtain dropped.

Like Kean and Siddons, Cooke started his career as a provincial actor before he became famous on the London stage.[57] In December 1801 Cooke returned to Bath where he played Richard III, Shylock and Sir Archy MacSarcasm. In that season, the same time that Mrs Austen was writing of him, he also played Iago to Elliston's Othello. Cooke wrote in his journal: 'I received the greatest applause and approbation from the audiences.'[58]

The last five seasons at the Orchard Street Theatre before the opening of the new playhouse in 1805 saw the introduction of several London actors onto the Bath stage. The appearance of such London stars gave prominence to the playhouse, and, coupled with the allure of Elliston, ensured its reputation as a theatre of the highest standing. Austen was fortunate in residing in Bath at a time when the theatre was in 'the zenith of its glory',[59] and where she could see her favourite actor performing all the major roles. Elliston's most famous roles in comedy were Charles Surface, Doricourt, Ranger, Benedick, Marlow, Lord Ogleby, Captain Absolute, Lord Townley and Dr Pangloss. In tragedy, Hamlet, Macbeth, Othello, Douglas, the Stranger, Orestes and Rolla were just a few of the characters that her 'best Elliston' made his own.[60]

Elliston was unusual in being a player of tragic and comic parts. Leigh Hunt declared Elliston 'the only genius that has approached that great actor [Garrick] in universality of imitation'. Though Hunt preferred him in comedy, he described him as 'the best lover on the stage both in tragedy and comedy'.[61] Others praised his diversity. Byron said that he could conceive nothing better than Elliston in gentlemanly comedy and in some parts of tragedy.[62] His obituary stated that 'Elliston was undoubtedly the most versatile actor of his day'.[63] Even William Oxberry's disparaging memoir conceded that 'Mr Elliston is the best versatile actor we have ever seen'.[64] Charles Lamb honoured him with high praise in his 'Ellistonia': 'wherever Elliston walked, sate, or stood still, there was the theatre'.[65]

Elliston finally moved on to the London stage, where Austen saw him perform. She complained, however, of the falling standards of Elliston's acting when she saw him in London. Austen's observations on his demise reveal her familiarity with his work from the Bath years. With the majority of Austen's letters from this time missing, destroyed after her death, much has been lost, for, as her London letters reveal, she was a discerning and perceptive critic of the drama.

When Austen left Bath in 1806 to live with Frank Austen and his wife, Mary, in Southampton, she was forced to make do with the French Street Theatre, a far cry from Bath's Theatre Royal. It was also during the first few months at Southampton that Austen wrote her two little playlets on baby-care. Frank Austen's young wife was pregnant with their first child, and writing the plays proved a welcome diversion during the winter evenings. Austen also attended the public theatre in Southampton. In her list of expenses for 1807 she noted that she had spent 17s. 9d. for water parties and plays during that year.[66]

The French Street Theatre in Southampton was served mainly by provincial companies, but stars from the London stage made occasional visits. Sarah Siddons and Dora Jordan made visits of a few days in 1802 and 1803.[67] The less talented Kemble brother, Charles Kemble, and his wife played there for a few nights in August 1808.[68] John Bannister (1760–1836), one of the most popular comedians of the London stage, was also well known to the provinces. His *Memoirs* record that he played the provinces during the summer months from 1797 to 1812. In the course of his career he took on the roles of some 425 characters.[69]

Although there is no record by Jane Austen of the plays that she saw at the French Street theatre, her niece recorded one of the performances that she attended with her two aunts. In September 1807 Edward Knight and his family visited his mother and sisters in Southampton. Austen's attachment to her niece Fanny Knight is revealed in her description of her as 'almost another sister' (*Letters*, p. 144). Austen had amused her niece with private theatricals in 1805, and when Fanny came to stay they visited the playhouse. Fanny recorded in her journal that on 14 September 1807 the party saw John Bannister in *The Way to Keep Him* and the musical adaptation of Kotzebue's *Of Age Tomorrow* for his benefit.[70]

Bannister's role in Arthur Murphy's comedy *The Way to Keep Him* was Sir Bashful Constant, a man of fashion in possession of the shameful secret that he is in love with his own wife, his '*Cara Sposa*'.[71] Jane Austen employed this fashionable Italianism to brilliant effect in *Emma*. For Emma, there is no clearer mark of Mrs Elton's vulgarity than her references to her husband as 'Mr E.' and 'my *caro sposo*': 'A little upstart, vulgar being, with her Mr E., and her *caro sposo*, and her resources, and all her airs of pert pretension and under-bred finery' (*E*, p. 279). Scholars have debated the source of Austen's use of the phrase, but no one has noticed its presence in Murphy's comedy, where, spoken by the coxcomb Sir Brilliant Fashion, it surely got a laugh in the theatre.

Bannister was best known for his low roles. Leigh Hunt claimed that 'no actor equals him in the character of a sailor'.[72] The sailor, Jack Junk, in Thomas Dibdin's adaptation of Kotzebue's *The Birth-Day* was one of his best-loved roles. Bannister was also praised for his ability to transform himself into many different roles: 'The greatest comedians have thought themselves happy in understanding one or two characters, but what shall we say of Bannister, who in one night personates six, and with such felicity that by the greatest part of the audience he is sometimes taken for some unknown actor?'[73] Leigh Hunt was thinking, in particular, of *A Bold Stroke for a Wife*, where Bannister transmigrated into five different characters. However the comic after-piece, *Of Age Tomorrow*, that Austen saw in Southampton was also used as a vehicle for Bannister's versatility.

Thomas Dibdin adapted *Of Age Tomorrow* from Kotzebue's *Der Wildfang*. Dibdin had already adapted Kotzebue's *The Birth-Day* and *The Horse and Widow*.[74] Michael Kelly, in his *Reminiscences*, records that Bannister persuaded Kelly and Dibdin to adapt *Der Wildfang* for Drury Lane.[75] Kelly describes *Of Age Tomorrow* as a great favourite. The ballad 'No, my love, no', according to Kelly, was 'the most popular song of the day ... not only to be found on every piano-forte, but also to be heard in every street'.[76]

Dibdin's musical farce showed Bannister adopting three different disguises in his endeavours to woo his lover, Sophia, who is guarded by a dowager aunt, Lady Brumback, who stands to lose half her fortune if her niece marries. Bannister's disguise as Fritz the *frizeur* was extremely popular, especially for his comic rendering of a story of his master breaking his leg over a bannister, to which Lady Brumback remarks, 'Poor fellow! I wish there were no Bannisters in the world'.[77] Kelly wrote: 'Bannister's personification of the Hair Dresser, was excellent; had he served a seven years' apprenticeship to the trade, he could not have been more *au fait* in it, nor have handled the comb, curling irons and powder puff, more skillfully.'[78] Bannister's transformations into a Swiss soldier and a (cross-dressed) abandoned mother of a foundling child showed his powers of imitation at their very best.[79]

The appearance of London stars at the French Street theatre may be attributed to the rising popularity of Southampton as a spa town. Charles Dibdin, the Southampton-born dramatist,[80] partly ascribed this transformation to the increasing number of 'genteel families who have made it their residence', and also to the tourists who came to Southampton for the sea-bathing.[81] Though the theatre had acquired a poor reputation by the end of the eighteenth century, a new playhouse was opened in July 1803 by one John Collins.[82]

The French Street theatre also housed amateur theatricals from the local grammar school. The school's headmaster, George Whittaker, was passionate about the theatre and encouraged his pupils to stage amateur theatricals for charitable purposes. In 1807 Home's famous tragedy *Douglas* was acted for the benefit of British prisoners of war in France, to 'an uncommonly crowded house'.[83] In *Mansfield Park*, Tom Bertram's comic remarks about the efficacy of schoolboys reciting the part of young Norval in *Douglas* may have been an echo to such performances lingering in Jane Austen's memory of amateur theatricals.

Her comments a year later, in 1808, about the playhouse suggest that she had taken a dislike to its shabbiness: '*Our* Brother [James] we may perhaps see in the course of a few days – & we mean to take the opportunity of his help, to go one night to the play. Martha ought to see the inside of the Theatre once while she lives in Southampton, & I think she will hardly wish to take a second veiw [sic]' (*Letters*, p. 155).

Another family descendant, Richard Arthur Leigh, observed that while Jane Austen was living in Southampton she became friendly with a Mr Valentine Fitzhugh, whose sister-in-law was an ardent admirer of Mrs Siddons who would assist her in dressing and make-up for her shows.[84] There is, however, no record of any conversation that Austen might have had with Fitzhugh about the theatre, which is hardly surprising given that he was so deaf 'he could not hear a Canon, were it fired close to him' (*Letters*, p. 160).

During the Bath and Southampton years Austen's writing was put on hold. She had produced three full-length novels before leaving Steventon in 1801, and began working on them again in 1809. Biographers and critics have been puzzled by Austen's eight-year silence, attributing it to her evident unhappiness and displacement. But perhaps Bath and Southampton simply had more to offer in the way of public diversions and amusements than Hampshire and Kent. At Chawton Austen turned her mind once more to her novels and, with the help and encouragement of her brother Henry, began to think about publication. When Jane spent time in London with Henry, negotiating with publishers, she rarely missed a chance to visit the London theatres.

Had the majority of Jane Austen's letters not been destroyed after her death in 1817, we would have had a much more detailed sense of her passion for the theatre. But there is enough evidence in the few surviving letters to suggest that she was utterly familiar with contemporary actors and the range and repertoire of the theatres. Her taste was eclectic; she enjoyed farces, musical comedy and pantomime, considered to be 'low' drama, as much as she enjoyed Shakespeare, Colman and Garrick.

3

Plays and Actors

The year 1808 was a particularly busy one for Jane Austen. She spent most of the time travelling between her various brothers and family friends. After playing Mrs Candour in *The School for Scandal* at the Manydown Twelfth Night party, she visited the Fowles at Kintbury and in May she visited Henry and Eliza Austen at 16 Michael Place in Brompton. The latter two, whose love of the theatre went back to the home theatricals at Steventon, were delighted to live in close proximity to several famous London stars. The actress and singer Jane Pope lived next door to them at No. 17. She had been the original Mrs Candour in *The School for Scandal*, playing the part until she was in her sixties. By this time, she was the only member of the original cast left on the stage.[1] Having herself played the part of Mrs Candour earlier that year, Jane Austen must have been amused to be living next door to the actress who had inspired the original role.

At No. 15 Michael Place was Elizabeth Billington, the celebrated soprano singer. John Liston the comedian lived at No. 21.[2] Jane Austen stayed until July, enjoying the rounds of dinner-parties, theatre trips and concerts arranged by Henry and Eliza. Henry Austen owned his own box at one of the illegitimate theatres, the Pantheon in Oxford Street.[3] The Pantheon had originally opened in 1772 as a place of assembly for masquerades and concerts, which were all the rage in the 1770s.[4] Boswell and Dr Johnson visited and admired the magnificent building in 1772, and Fanny Burney distilled her own experience of the new Pantheon into *Evelina*; her heroine is 'extremely struck with the beauty of the building' when she is taken to a concert there.[5]

The Pantheon was converted into an opera house in 1791 but was destroyed by fire a year later, losing its hope of a royal patent to the King's

Theatre in the Haymarket. Thereafter the Pantheon was rebuilt and resumed its original function as a place of concerts and masquerades until 1812, when it reopened as the Pantheon Theatre, staging the usual mixed bill of burlettas and ballet to circumvent the licensing law.

Henry Austen's patronage of minor playhouses such as the Pantheon and the Lyceum, as well as the legitimate patent houses, suggests his unflagging interest in the theatre. Like his sister, he had no compunction about supporting the minor theatres. Unlike his brother James, who lost interest in the theatre after he was ordained, Henry's passion for the theatre carried on into maturity; and, whenever Jane and Cassandra were in town, he was to be found arranging seats at the various London theatres. Although there are few surviving letters to fill in the details of Jane's activities at this time (the letters stop altogether from 26 July 1809 until 18 April 1811), she surely took advantage of Henry's and Eliza's hospitality as she did in the following years. Starting at the latter date, there is a sufficient amount of information to provide a fair estimate of her theatrical activities up to 28 November 1814, the last time she is known to have attended a theatre.

In order to be available for the proof-reading of *Sense and Sensibility*, she went to London in April 1811, staying with Henry and Eliza at their new home in Sloane Street. Shortly after her arrival she expressed a desire to see Shakespeare's *King John* at Covent Garden. In the meantime, she sacrificed a trip to the Lyceum, nursing a cold at home, in the hope of recovering for the Saturday excursion to Covent Garden:

> To night I might have been at the Play, Henry had kindly planned our going together to the Lyceum, but I have a cold which I should not like to make worse before Saturday ... [Later on Saturday] Our first object to day was Henrietta St to consult with Henry, in consequence of a very unlucky change of the Play for this very night – Hamlet instead of King John – & we are to go on Monday to Macbeth, instead, but it is a disappointment to us both. (*Letters*, pp. 180–81)

Her preference for *King John* over *Hamlet* may seem curious by modern standards, but can be explained by one of the intrinsic features of Georgian theatre: the orientation of the play towards the star actor in the lead role. Her disappointment in the 'unlucky change' of programme from 'Hamlet instead of King John' is accounted for in her next letter to Cassandra:

> I have no chance of seeing Mrs Siddons. – She *did* act on Monday, but as Henry was told by the Boxkeeper that he did not think she would, the places, & all thought of it, were given up. I should particularly have liked seeing her in Constance, & could swear at her with little effort for disappointing me. (*Letters*, p. 184)

It was not so much *King John* that Austen wanted to see as Siddons in one of her most celebrated roles: Queen Constance, the quintessential portrait of a tragic mother. In the words of her biographer and friend, Thomas Campbell, Siddons was 'the imbodied image of maternal love and intrepidity; of wronged and righteous feeling; of proud grief and majestic desolation'.[6] Siddons's own remarks on this 'life-exhausting' role, and the 'mental and physical' difficulties arising from the requirements of playing Constance provide a striking testimony to her all-consuming passion and commitment to the part. Siddons records:

> Whenever I was called upon to personate the character of *Constance*, I never, from the beginning of the play to the end of my part in it, once suffered my dressing-room door to be closed, in order that my attention might be constantly fixed on those distressing events which, by this means, I could plainly hear going on upon the stage, the terrible effects of which progress were to be represented by me.[7]

Though her part was brief – she appeared in just two acts – Siddons's impassioned interpretation was acclaimed. Constance's famously eloquent speeches and frenzied lamentations for her dead boy were newly rendered by Siddons, for she didn't 'rant' and produce the effects of noisy grief but was stunningly understated, showing grief 'tempered and broken', as Leigh Hunt put it.[8] While admitting that *King John* was 'not written with the utmost power of Shakespeare', Hunt nevertheless viewed the play as a brilliant vehicle for Siddons's consummate tragic powers.[9] Her biographer, Thomas Campbell, also claimed that Siddons's single-handedly resuscitated the play, winning over the public to 'feel the tragedy worth seeing for the sake of *Constance* alone'.[10]

Jane Austen certainly felt that 'Constance' was worth the price of a ticket. Though Henry Austen was misinformed by the box-keeper and Siddons had indeed appeared in *Macbeth* on Monday (22 April), Jane was less sorry to have missed her in Lady Macbeth than in Constance, which may imply that she had previously seen her in *Macbeth*. Sarah Siddons acted Lady Macbeth eight times and Constance five times that 1811–12 season, before retiring from the London stage, so perhaps Jane finally got her wish.[11]

On Saturday (20 April) the party went instead to the Lyceum Theatre in the Strand, where the Drury Lane company had taken their patent after the fire in 1809.[12] They saw a revival of Isaac Bickerstaffe's *The Hypocrite*.

> We *did* go to the play after all on Saturday, we went to the Lyceum, & saw the Hypocrite, an old play taken from Moliere's *Tartuffe*, & were well entertained. Dowton & Mathews were the good actors. Mrs Edwin was the Heroine – & her performance is just what it used to be. (*Letters*, p. 184)

In *The Hypocrite*, the roles of Maw-Worm, an ignorant zealot, and the religious and moral hypocrite Dr Cantwell were acted by the renowned comic actors Charles Mathews (1776–1835), and William Dowton (1764–1851), singled out by Jane Austen for praise. Dowton was famous for his roles as Dr Cantwell, Sir Oliver Premium and Sir Anthony Absolute.[13] Leigh Hunt described his performance in the *Hypocrite* as 'one of the few perfect pieces of acting on the stage'.[14]

The great comic actor Charles Mathews was also a favourite of Hunt's: 'an actor of whom it is difficult to say whether his characters belong most to him or he to his characters'.[15] Mathews was so tall and thin that he was nicknamed 'Stick'; when his manager Tate Wilkinson first saw him he called him a 'Maypole', told him he was too tall for low comedy and quipped that 'one hiss would blow him off the stage'.[16]

Mathews himself described the success of *The Hypocrite* at the Lyceum, and recorded his experiment in adding an extra fanatical speech for Maw-Worm, thus breaking the rule of his 'immortal instructor, who says "Let your clowns say no more than is set down for them". His experiment worked, and the reviews were favourable: 'It was an admirable representation of "Praise God Barebones", an exact portraiture of one of those ignorant enthusiasts who lose sight of all good while they are vainly hunting after an ideal perfectibility.'[17] Jane Austen dearly loved a fool – in *Pride and Prejudice* she portrayed her own obsequious hypocrite and ignorant enthusiast, in Mr Collins and Mary Bennet.

Elizabeth Edwin (1771–1854), the wife of the actor John Edwin, performed the part of Charlotte, the archetypal witty heroine, for which she was famous.[18] The Austen sisters were clearly familiar with Mrs Edwin's acting style. She had played at Bath for many years, including the time that the Austens lived there, and she was also a favourite of the Southampton theatre, where the sisters may have seen her perform.[19]

Elizabeth Edwin was one of many actors from the provinces who had begun her career as a child actor in a company of strolling players. She was the leading actress at Wargrave at the Earl of Barrymore's private theatricals.[20] She was often (unfairly) compared to the great Dora Jordan, whose equal she never was, though they played the same comic roles. Jane Austen's ambiguous comment about Edwin suggests that she did not rate her as highly as Dowton and Mathews, whom she regarded as the 'good actors' in *The Hypocrite*. Oxberry's 1826 memoir observed that although Edwin was 'an accomplished artist … she has little, if any, genius – and is a decided mannerist'.[21] She was an 'artificial' actress who betrayed the fact that she was performing:

> Though we admired what she did, she never carried us with her. We knew that we were at a display of art, and never felt for a moment the illusion of its being a natural scene.[22]

The preoccupation with the play as a vehicle for the star actor, popularly called 'the possession of parts', went hand-in-hand with the theatre's proclivity towards an established repertory.[23] It was common to see the same actor in a favourite role year in, year out. Dora Jordan's Rosalind and Little Pickle, both of them 'breeches' roles, were performed successfully throughout her long career. Siddons's Lady Macbeth and Constance were staples of her repertory throughout her career, and, even after her retirement, they were the subject of comparison with other performances. The tradition of an actor's interpretation of a classic role, which still survives today, was an integral part of an individual play's appeal. Critics and the public would revel in the particularities of individual performances, and they would eagerly anticipate a new performance of a favourite role, though innovations by actors were by no means a guarantee of audience approbation.

In the early autumn of 1813, Jane Austen set out for Godmersham, stopping on the way in London, where she stayed with her brother Henry in his quarters over his bank at Henrietta Street, Covent Garden. On the night of 14 September, the party went by coach to the Lyceum Theatre, where they had a private box on the stage. As soon as the rebuilt Drury Lane had opened its doors to the public, the Lyceum had no choice but to revert to musical drama. The Austens saw three musical pieces. The first was *The Boarding House: or Five Hours at Brighton*; the second, a musical farce called *The Beehive*; and the last *Don Juan: or The Libertine Destroyed*, a pantomime based on Thomas Shadwell's *The Libertine*. Once again, Jane Austen's reflections on the plays were shared with Cassandra:

> I talked to Henry at the Play last night. We were in a private Box – Mr Spencer's – Which made it much more pleasant. The Box is directly on the Stage. One is infinitely less fatigued than in the common way … Fanny & the two little girls are gone to take Places for tonight at Covent Garden; Clandestine Marriage & *Midas*. The latter will be a fine show for L. & M. – They revelled last night in 'Don Juan', whom we left in Hell at half-past eleven … We had Scaremouch & a Ghost – and were delighted; I speak of *them*; *my* delight was very tranquil, & the rest of us were sober-minded. Don Juan was the last of 3 musical things; – Five hours at Brighton, in 3 acts – of which one was over before we arrived, none the worse – & The Beehive, rather less flat & trumpery. (*Letters*, pp. 218–19)

The Beehive was an adaptation of Kotzebue's comedy *Das Posthaus in Treuenbrietzen*. Two lovers who have never met, but who are betrothed to one another, fall in love under assumed names. The young man discovers the ruse first and introduces his friend as himself; meanwhile the heroine, Miss Fairfax, in retaliation pretends to fall in love with the best friend. In the light of *Emma*, the conjunction of name and plot-twist is striking.

Austen clearly preferred the Kotzebue comedy to *Five Hours at Brighton*, a low comedy set in a seaside boarding house. Her 'delight' in *Don Juan* is properly amended to 'tranquil delight' for the sake of the upright Cassandra. Byron had also seen the pantomime, in which the famous Grimaldi played Scaramouch, to which he alludes in his first stanza of *Don Juan*:

> We all have seen him, in the pantomime,
> Sent to the devil somewhat ere his time.[24]

Scaramouch was one of Grimaldi's oldest and most frequently revived parts.

In her letter to Cassandra, Jane gives her usual precise details of the theatre visit, even down to the private box, 'directly on the stage'. Again, the Austens showed their support for the minor theatres, and Henry is arranging trips to the Lyceum. Perhaps he had an arrangement with his friend Mr Spencer to share each other's boxes at the minor theatres. Being seated in a box certainly meant that Jane could indulge in intimate discussion with Henry – as Elizabeth Bennet does with Mrs Gardiner in *Pride and Prejudice*.[25]

As planned, the very next night the party went to Covent Garden Theatre, where they had 'very good places in the Box next the stage box – front and second row; the three old ones behind of course'.[26] They sat in Covent Garden's new theatre boxes, presumably in full consciousness that, at the opening of the new theatre, riots had been occasioned by the extra number of private and dress boxes.[27] The parson and poet George Crabbe and his wife were in London and Jane Austen joked about seeing the versifying vicar at the playhouse, particularly as the 'boxes were fitted up with crimson velvet' (*Letters*, pp. 220–21). The remark skilfully combines an allusion to Crabbe's *Gentleman Farmer*, 'In full festoons the crimson curtains fell',[28] with detailed observation of the lavish fittings of the new Covent Garden Theatre, recently reopened after the fire of 1809.

Edward Brayley's account of the grand new playhouse also singled out the 'crimson-covered seats',[29] and described the grand staircase leading to the boxes, and the ante-room with its yellow-marble statue of Shakespeare.

The Austens saw *The Clandestine Marriage* by David Garrick and George Colman the Elder, and *Midas: an English Burletta* by Kane O'Hara, a parody of the Italian comic opera.[30] One of the attractions was to see Mr Terry, who had recently taken over the role of Lord Ogleby in *The Clandestine Marriage*.

> The new Mr Terry was Ld Ogleby, & Henry thinks he may do; but there was no acting more than moderate; & I was as much amused by the remembrances connected with Midas as with any part of it. The girls were very much delighted but still prefer Don Juan – & I must say I have seen nobody on the stage who has been a more interesting Character than that compound of Cruelty & Lust. (*Letters*, p. 221)

Daniel Terry (1780–1829) had made his debut at Covent Garden on 8 September, just a few days before Jane Austen saw him.[31] Sir Walter Scott was a great friend and admirer of Terry (who adapted several of the Waverley novels for the stage),[32] and claimed that he was an excellent actor who could act everything except lovers, fine gentlemen and operatic heroes. Scott observed that 'his old men in comedy particularly are the finest I ever saw'.[33] Henry Austen showed a little more tolerance than his sister in allowing Mr Terry teething troubles in the role of one of the most celebrated old men of eighteenth century comedy.

Henry Austen's faith in Terry's capacity to grow into a beloved role reflects the performer-oriented tendency of the age. But Jane's powerful and striking description of *Don Juan* is a far less typical response. Here a more discerning and discriminating voice prevails. Rather than the performer being the main focus of interest, she is responding to the perverse appeal of the character beneath the actor. The famous blackguard was still obviously on her mind, belying her earlier insistence upon 'tranquil delight' and 'sober-mindedness'.

Jane Austen's reference to *Midas* confirms that she had seen this entertainment at an earlier date. Garrick and Colman's brilliant comedy *The Clandestine Marriage* had also been known to her for a long time. The title appears as a phrase in one of her early works, *Love and Freindship*, and, as will be seen, the play was a source for a key scene in *Mansfield Park*.

Austen was disappointed with her latest theatrical ventures, though had she stayed longer in London she might have been disposed to see Elliston in a new play, *First Impressions*, later that month.[34] When she wrote to her brother Frank, she complained of the falling standards of the theatres:

> Of our three evenings in Town one was spent at the Lyceum & another at Covent Garden; – the Clandestine Marriage was the most respectable of the performances, the rest were Sing-song & trumpery, but did very well for Lizzy & Marianne, who were indeed delighted; but *I* wanted better acting. – There was no Actor worth naming. – I beleive the Theatres are thought at a low ebb at present. (*Letters*, p. 230)

Austen's heart-felt wish for 'better acting', or, in Edmund Bertram's words, 'real hardened acting', was soon to be realised.

Drury Lane had indeed reached its lowest ebb for some years when it was rescued by the success of a new actor, Edmund Kean (1787–1833), who made his electrifying debut as Shylock in January 1814. The story of his stage debut has become one of the most enduring tales of the theatre. The reconstructed Drury Lane Theatre, rebuilt after it was destroyed by fire in 1809, was facing financial ruin, greatly exacerbated by the ruinous management of R. B. Sheridan, when a strolling player from the provinces, Edmund Kean, was asked to play Shylock.[35] Kean, in his innovative black wig, duly appeared before a meagre audience, mesmerising them by his stage entrance. At the end of the famous speech in the third act, the audience roared its applause. 'How the devil so few of them kicked up such a row', said Oxberry, 'was something marvelous.'[36] Kean's mesmerising appearance on the stage was given the seal of approval when Hazlitt, who after seeing him on the first night, raved: 'For voice, eye, action, and expression, no actor has come out for many years at all equal to him.'[37]

The news of Kean's conquest of the stage reached Jane Austen, and in early March 1814, while she was staying with Henry during the negotiations for the publication of *Mansfield Park*, she made plans to see the latest acting sensation:

> Places are secured at Drury Lane for Saturday, but so great is the rage for seeing Keen [*sic*] that only a third & fourth row could be got. As it is in a front box however, I hope we shall do pretty well. – Shylock. – A good play for Fanny. She cannot be much affected I think. (*Letters*, p. 256)

The relatively short part of Shylock is thus considered to be a suitably gentle introduction to Kean's powerful acting for the young girl. But Austen's own excitement is barely contained in her description of the theatre party: 'We hear that Mr Keen [*sic*] is more admired than ever. The two vacant places of our two rows, are likely to be filled by Mr Tilson & his brother Gen. Chownes.' Then, almost as if she has betrayed too much pleasure in the absence of her sister, she writes: 'There are no good places to be got in Drury Lane for the next fortnight, but Henry means to secure some for Saturday fortnight when You are reckoned upon' (*Letters*, p. 256).

Another visit to see Kean was intended, and Henry's acquaintance with the theatre world again emphasised. The party went to Drury Lane on the evening of 5 March, attending the eighth performance of *The Merchant of Venice*. Austen's initial response to the latest acting phenomenon was calm and rational: 'We were quite satisfied with Kean. I cannot imagine better acting, but the part was too short, & excepting him & Miss Smith, & *she* did not quite answer my expectations, the parts were ill filled & the Play heavy' (*Letters*, p. 257). Hazlitt, too, frequently complained that one of the problems of the star system was filling up the smaller parts. In his review of *The Merchant of Venice*, he was only grudgingly respectful of the minor roles.

Kean was still very much on Austen's mind, for in the same letter, in the midst of a sentence about Henry Crawford and *Mansfield Park*, she unexpectedly reverted to the subject of him with greater enthusiasm: 'I shall like to see Kean again excessively, & to see him with You too; – it appeared to me as if there was no fault in him anywhere; & in his scene with Tubal there was exquisite acting' (*Letters*, p. 258).

Jane Austen was conscious of the dramatic demands of Shylock's scene, which required the actor to scale, alternately, between grief and savage glee. Her singling out of this particular scene was no doubt influenced by the reports of the opening night, where the audience had been powerless to restrain their applause. Kean's biographer noted the subtle intricacies of the scene in the third act ending with the dialogue between Shylock and Tubal:

> Shylock's anguish at his daughter's flight, his wrath at the two Christians who had made sport of his suffering, his hatred of Christianity generally, and of Antonio in particular, and his alternations of rage, grief and ecstasy as Tubal enumerated the losses incurred in the search of Jessica – her extravagances, and then the ill-luck that had fallen on Antonio; in all this there was such originality, such terrible force, such assurance of a new and mighty master, that the house burst forth into a very whirlwind of approbation.[38]

For many critics, the greatest quality of Kean's as Shylock was his ability to change emotional gear at high speed, to scale the highest points and the lowest. Thus Hazlitt:

> In giving effect to the conflict of passions arising out of the contrasts of situation, in varied vehemence of declamation, in keenness of sarcasm, in the rapidity of his transitions from one tone and feeling to another, in propriety and novelty of action, presenting a succession of striking pictures, and giving perpetually fresh shocks of delight and surprise, it would be difficult to single out a competitor.[39]

Kean's acting style was hereafter characterised as impulsive, electric and fracturing. 'To see him act', Coleridge observed famously in his *Table Talk*, 'is like reading Shakespeare by flashes of lightning.'[40]

In contrast to her reaction to Kean, Jane Austen was disappointed with the performance of her old favourite Elliston. The programme that night included him in an oriental 'melodramatic spectacle' called *Illusion; or The Trances of Nourjahad*. The Austen party left before the end:

> We were too much tired to stay for the whole of Illusion (Nourjahad)
> which has 3 acts; – there is a great deal of finery & dancing in it, but I
> think little merit. Elliston was Nourjahad, but it is a solemn sort of part,
> not at all calculated for his powers. There was nothing of the *best Elliston*
> about him. I might not have known him, but for his voice. (*Letters*, pp.
> 257–58)

Henry Crabb Robinson also saw Elliston as Nourjahad and wrote in his
diary that 'his untragic face can express no strong emotions'. Robinson
admired Elliston as a 'fine bustling comedian', but thought that he was a
'wretched Tragedian'.[41] Austen's observation that Elliston's brilliance lay
especially in his comic powers was a view shared by his critics and
admirers. Charles Lamb thought so too, but was afraid to say so when
Elliston recounted how Drury Lane was abusing him. Lamb recorded:
'He complained of this: "Have you heard ... how they treat me? they put
me in *comedy*." Thought I – "where could they have put you better?"
Then, after a pause – "Where I formerly played Romeo, I now play
Mercutio."'[42]

Austen's 'best Elliston' was altered from his glory days at Bath and his
early promise at Drury Lane as a result of physical deterioration brought
on by hard drinking. His acting powers had steadily declined. From
managing various minor and provincial theatres, he finally became the
lessee and manager of Drury Lane from 1819 until 1826, when he retired,
bankrupt through addiction to drinking and gambling.

Elliston's acting talent suffered when he threw his energies into his
multifarious business ventures. The *London Magazine and Theatrical
Inquisitor* observed that in later years he had fallen into 'a coarse buffoonery of manner' and Leigh Hunt oberved that he had 'degraded an
unequivocal and powerful talent for comedy into coarseness and vulgar
confidence'.[43]

Three days after seeing Kean and Elliston at Drury Lane, Jane Austen
went to the rival house Covent Garden to see Charles Coffey's farce, *The
Devil to Pay*. 'I expect to be very much amused', she wrote in anticipation
(*Letters*, p. 260). Dora Jordan played Nell, one of her most famous comic
roles. The party were to see Thomas Arne's opera *Artaxerxes* with
Catherine Stephens (1794–1882), the celebrated British soprano who

later became Countess of Essex. She was, however, less excited by the opera than the farce: 'Excepting Miss Stephens, I dare say Artaxerxes will be very tiresome' (*Letters*, p. 260). Catherine Stephens acted Mandane in *Artaxerxes*, a role in which Hazlitt thought she was superb, claiming that he could hear her sing 'forever': 'There was a new sound in the air, like the voice of Spring; it was as if Music had become young again, and was resolved to try the power of her softest, simplest, sweetest notes.'[44] Austen's response was just as she expected: 'I was very tired of Artaxerxes, highly amused with the Farce, & in an inferior way with the Pantomime that followed' (*Letters*, p. 260). However, she was unimpressed with Catherine Stephens and grumbled at the plan for a second excursion to see her the following night: 'I have had enough for the present' (*Letters*, p. 260).

Nevertheless, in spite of a cold, she joined the party to see Stephens as Mrs Cornflower in Charles Dibdin's *The Farmer's Wife*, a role created for her musical ability and her talent in low comedy:

Well, we went to the Play again last night … The Farmer's Wife is a musical thing in 3 acts, & as Edward was steady in not staying for anything more, we were at home before 10 – Fanny and Mr J. P. are delighted with Miss S. & her merit in singing is I dare say very great; that she gave *me* no pleasure is no reflection upon her, nor I hope upon myself being what Nature made me on that article. All that I am sensible of in Miss S. is, a pleasing person & no skill in acting. We had Mathews, Liston and Emery: of course some amusement. (*Letters*, p. 261)

Though disappointed with Stephens, she enjoyed the performances of Mathews, Liston and Emery, who were three of the great comedians of the day. Tall and skinny, Charles Mathews was noted for his brilliance as 'officious valets and humorous old men'.[45] His long-time friend and fellow-actor, the inimitable John Liston, often appeared alongside him.[46]

Liston (1776–1846) was the highest paid comedian of his time.[47] Hazlitt described him as 'the greatest comic genius who has appeared in our time'.[48] He was noted for his bumpkin roles and humorous old men. Leigh Hunt observed that his 'happiest performances are ignorant rustics … he passes from the simplest rustic to the most conceited pretender with undiminished easiness of attainment'.[49] Liston's grave and serious face added to the effect of his comedy, Lamb wrote: 'There is one face of Farley, one of Knight, one (but what a one it is!) of Liston'.[50] For Hazlitt, Liston had 'more comic humour oozing out of his features and person than any other actor'.[51] He was a particularly fine Baron Wildenhaim in *Lovers' Vows*.

John Emery (1777–1822) also played in the same line of old gentle-men and rustics, and was compared to Liston: 'If our two stage-rustics, Emery and Liston, are compared, it will be found that the former is more skilled in the habits and cunning of rusticity, and the latter in its simplic-ity and ignorance.' But Hunt later claimed of Emery that, in playing the countrymen, the field was 'exclusively and entirely his'.[52] Hazlitt also observed that 'in his line of rustic characters he is a perfect actor'.[53]

The Farmer's Wife was a vehicle for the singing arts of Stephens and the comic talents of Mathews, Liston and Emery. It tells a rather tired tale of an innocent (Emma Cornflower) abducted by a debauched aristocrat (Sir Charles). Mathews plays a village apothecary, Dr Pother. Liston played a cunning London manservant to Sir Charles. This served as a comic contrast to Emery's ignorant but good-hearted Yorkshireman, servant to Farmer Cornflower.[54] The play's comic juxtapositions of high and low characters drew on a convention long associated with the stage: the contrast between town and country, a theme that Austen had been working on in *Mansfield Park*.

Jane Austen's blunt assertion that Stephens had 'no skill in acting' is refreshing and to the point, in an age distinguished by its over-elaborate encomiums of actors and their roles. Furthermore her remark reveals a strong and discerning voice, one that knows what 'good hardened acting' is, and isn't, and is confident in its own critical judgement without being unduly influenced by the current favourite of the stage. After revealing the details of the previous night's theatre to Cassandra, she wrote of plans for yet another excursion to Covent Garden to see Kean's rival, Charles Mayne Young (1777–1856), acting in *Richard III*: 'Prepare for a Play the very first evening. I rather think Covent Garden, to see Young in Richard' (*Letters*, p. 261).

Young had been the leading tragedian of the London stage before Kean challenged his supremacy in 1814. Young was in the Kemble school of acting, and was noted for his heroic, dignified acting style, though he was often compared unfavourably with his predecessor Kemble: 'His most striking fault, as a tragic actor, is a perpetual imitation of Mr Kemble.'[55] He was often criticised for his lack of passion: 'Mr Young never gives himself up to his feelings, but always relies upon his judgement – he never acts from the heart, but the head.'[56] Leigh Hunt was lukewarm about his abilities, describing him as an actor of 'elegant mediocrity', and Hazlitt was even more disparaging, especially of Young's Hamlet: 'he declaims it very well, and rants it very well; but where is the expression of the feeling?'[57] Since Cassandra was coming to London, and presumably accompanied her sister to see Young's Richard, there is no letter describing Jane's reaction to his rendering of the part. But the critical consensus was that the performance was not a success.

The opposition between the Kemble/Young and the Cooke/Kean school of acting was often couched as a conflict between reason and feeling, judgement and passion. It is striking that Austen, who is so often associated with 'sense' rather than 'sensibility', clearly admired Kean's acting but seems to have had little enthusiasm for the Kemble school. Though she names most of the major stars of the London stage in her surviving letters, there is not a single mention of John Philip Kemble himself.

Jane Austen did see Young again, this time with the new acting sensation, Eliza O'Neill, who had made her triumphant debut a month earlier as Juliet and was heralded as the only tragedian worthy to take over the mantle of Sarah Siddons. Just as Drury Lane had been saved from the brink of financial ruin by the advent of Kean, so Covent Garden was desperate to bring forward its own star in reply.[58] Byron refused to see O'Neill out of his loyalty to Kean and Drury Lane, and for fear that he would like her too much: 'No I'm resolved to be un-"Oneiled".'[59] As with Kean's debut earlier that year, audiences acclaimed O'Neill as a genius from the provinces; it was claimed that some spectators fainted under her spell.[60]

Jane Austen's last known visit to the professional theatre took place late in 1814. She was as keen to see Covent Garden's new star as she had been to see Kean, and on the night of 28 November Henry and Edward arranged for her to see *Isabella*, a tragedy adapted by Garrick from

Thomas Southerne's *The Fatal Marriage: or The Innocent Adultery*, in which O'Neill played the leading female role. Jane, writing to her niece Anna Lefroy, was disappointed with O'Neill's performance:

> We were all at the Play last night, to see Miss O'neal [*sic*] in Isabella. I do not think that she was quite equal to my expectation. I fancy I want something more than can be. Acting seldom satisfies me. I took two Pocket handkerchiefs, but had very little occasion for either. She is an elegant creature however & hugs Mr Younge [*sic*] delightfully. (*Letters*, p. 283)

She shows discernment in her rather cool response to O'Neill's performance. Even O'Neill's most ardent admirers admitted that she was less good in maternal parts, like *Isabella*, but was more suited to playing innocent young girls, such as the lovesick Juliet, and repentant fallen women, such as Jane Shore and Mrs Haller: 'She could not represent maternal affection; her love was all the love of fire, youth and passion.'[61]

Isabella, the tragedy of a devoted wife and mother who is persuaded to marry again only to find her beloved husband is alive, was considered to be one of Siddons's finest roles. She had established herself on the London stage with her performance in the part. O'Neill suffered from the inevitable comparisons drawn between the two women. Even Hazlitt, who admired O'Neill's Isabella, thought it lacked Siddons's grandeur and power: 'Nothing can be more natural or more affecting than her noble conception of the part. But there is not that terrible reaction of mental power on the scene, which forms the perfection of tragedy, whether in acting or writing.'[62] Oxberry's biography described her performance in *Isabella* as 'artificial' and suggested that it 'savoured strongly of adoption from the style of Kean'.[63]

Austen was clearly intimate enough with the theatre world to know about the nuances of O'Neill's acting style. Her joking reference to her two pocket handkerchiefs alludes to O'Neill's reputation as an actress of excessive sensibility whose magic was to 'raise the sigh' and who provoked tears rather than terror. O'Neill's biographer observed that her 'triumph, it has been justly said, is in tears'.[64] For Hazlitt, O'Neill's power lay in her extraordinary ability to draw sympathy from the audience. It was her 'reaction' to Romeo's death that characterised her unique acting style: 'In the silent expression of feeling, we have seldom witnessed anything finer.'[65]

The telling phrase '[she] hugs Mr Young delightfully' suggests that there was a kind of intimate theatrical code between Austen and her niece. As they were both aware, coupled with O'Neill's ability to elicit sympathy and tears was her reputation as a 'hugging actress'. This appellation appears to have been given by Thomas Amyot, according to the testimony of Crabb Robinson's diary: 'Saw Miss O'Neill in Isabella. She was as Aymot well said, "a hugging actress". Sensibility shown in grief and fondness was her forte, – her only talent.'[66]

The deleterious effects of excessive sensibility are a recurrent theme of Austen's fiction from her earliest jokes in *Love and Freindship* to *Sanditon*. Her joke about O'Neill's sensibility is shared not only with Anna but also with her other favoured niece Fanny Knight:

> I just saw Mr Hayter at the Play, & think his face would please me on acquaintance. I was sorry he did not dine here. – It seemed rather odd to me to be in the Theatre, with nobody to *watch* for. I was quite composed myself, at leisure for all the agitation Isabella could raise. (*Letters*, p. 285)

Austen's ironic remark, 'It seemed rather odd to me to be in the Theatre, with nobody to *watch* for', comically portrays herself in the role of the chaperone of her young nieces, guarding their exposure to excessive sensibility or 'agitation'. Earlier, we saw her worrying about Fanny's agitation on seeing Kean. As indicated, both Kean and O'Neill were reputed to have the power of making their audience faint under their spell. Towards the close of this letter, Austen makes a striking reference to the two most famous tragediennes of the age, and uses the ardent acting style of O'Neill to express the contrasting natures of her young nieces:

> That puss Cassy, did not shew more pleasure in seeing me than her Sisters, but I expected no better; – she does not shine in the tender feelings. She will never be a Miss O'neal; – more in the Mrs Siddons line. (*Letters*, p. 287)

This passage, perhaps more than any other single reference to the theatre, is revelatory of Jane Austen's intimacy with the late Georgian theatre. As she was clearly aware, one of the current debates in the theatre world was the contrasting acting styles of Mrs Siddons and Miss O'Neill. The latter's 'extreme natural sensibility' was played off against the former's classical nobility. For Hazlitt, Siddons was the embodiment of 'high tragedy', O'Neill of 'instinctive sympathy'.[67]

O'Neill's biographer, Charles Inigo Jones, complained of 'the rather too invidious comparisons constantly kept up betwixt her and Mrs Siddons', and yet proceeded to make his own comparisons, contrasting not only the acting styles of the two women but their physical attributes which, he believed, embodied their acting styles. Thus Siddons's 'grandeur and dignity are pictured in her appearance', and O'Neill's 'excess of sensibility is predominant ... and well pourtrayed in her countenance'.[68]

One of the best comparisons of the two tragedians is made in Oxberry's memoir of O'Neill:

> Miss O'Neill was a lovely ardent creature, with whose griefs we sympathized, and whose sorrows raised our pity. Mrs Siddons was a wonderful being, for whom we felt awe, veneration, and a more holy love ... Miss O'Neill twined most upon our affections, but Mrs Siddons made an impression on our minds, that time never eradicated.[69]

Austen's observations in the scanty correspondence that survives offer decisive, hitherto neglected, evidence of her deep familiarity with the theatre of Siddons and O'Neill. In addition, her manner of comparing social conduct to theatrical models such as her niece's Siddons-like dignified behaviour denoting a lack of sensibility ('the tender feelings') betrays a striking propensity to view life through the spectacles of theatre.

In January 1801, Cassandra Austen was compelled to abandon a trip to London, where she had intended to visit the Opera House to see the celebrated comic actress Dora Jordan (1761–1816). Jane wrote to her: 'You speak with such noble resignation of Mrs Jordan & the Opera House that it would be an insult to suppose consolation required' (*Letters*, p. 71).

The King's Theatre or Italian Opera House in the Haymarket had been built by Vanbrugh in 1705. The Opera House was destroyed by fire in 1789 and was rebuilt on a vast scale in 1791.[70] On the opening night, Michael Kelly sang in *The Haunted Tower* and Dora Jordan performed in Kemble's farce, *The Pannel*.[71] In 1799 the interior of the Opera House was partly remodelled by Marinari, the principal scene painter at Drury Lane.[72] Austen's sympathy for Cassandra's double disappointment was therefore equally distributed between seeing the new Opera House and seeing the great Mrs Jordan.

In 1801 Dora Jordan was at the height of her powers, and the star of Drury Lane. As Siddons was the Tragic Muse of the London stage, so Jordan was the Comic Muse.[73] Hoppner's portrait of Jordan as 'The Comic Muse' was a huge success at the Royal Academy in May 1786.[74] Not even Jordan's long-term liaison with the Duke of Clarence (to whom she bore ten children over a period of twenty years) could stem the tide of 'Jordan-Mania' that swept the country in the late eighteenth and early nineteenth centuries. Her image was everywhere: in the theatre, in theatrical engravings in print shop windows, and in the numerous caricatures by Gillray and Cruikshank. Sheet music of the songs that she sang at Drury Lane were sold on the streets.

Dora Jordan was unparalleled in comedy.[75] She appealed to both the critics and the theatre-going public who flocked to see her. Coleridge, Byron, Hazlitt and Lamb were among her admirers.[76] Hazlitt described her as 'the child of nature, whose voice was a cordial to the heart, because it came from it ... whose laugh was to drink nectar ... who "talked far above singing" and whose singing was like the twang of Cupid's bow'.[77] Leigh Hunt also singled out her memorable laugh and melodious voice: 'Mrs Jordan seems to speak with all her soul ... her laughter is the happiest and most natural on the stage.'[78]

Jordan's extensive range was unusual in an era during which actors tended to be restricted to specific kinds of role. She played genteel ladies, such as Lady Teazle and Widow Belmour, and romantic leads such as Lydia Languish and Kate Hardcastle. She was also famous for her 'low' roles, playing chambermaids, romps and hoydens to much acclaim. Miss

Prue, Miss Hoyden, and Nell in *The Devil to Pay* were among her favourites. She was also famous for her 'breeches roles', playing the cross-dressed Hippolita, Harry Wildair, Rosalind, Viola, and Little Pickle in the farce *The Spoilt Child*. The theatre chronicler John Genest claimed that she 'sported the best leg ever seen on the stage'.[79]

Jordan's performance as the innocent country girl in Garrick's adaptation of William Wycherley's highly risqué Restoration comedy *The Country Wife* combined the role of a hoyden with a 'breeches part'. She played the Country Girl for fifteen seasons at Drury Lane from 1785 to 1800. In one of the most memorable scenes, Peggy takes a walk in St James's Park, disguised as a young boy, as her jealous guardian is determined to protect her from other men. In a letter of 1799, Austen uses the notion of the 'Country Girl' to express doubts about the behaviour of an acquaintance, Earle Harwood, who had married a woman of obscure birth:

> I cannot help thinking from your account of Mrs E. H. [Earle Harwood] that Earle's vanity has tempted him to invent the account of her former way of Life, that his triumph in securing her might be greater; – I dare say she was nothing but an innocent Country Girl in fact. (*Letters*, p. 48)

Austen's instinctive and imaginative way of using stage characters as a point of reference in her letters, coupled with her habit of weaving in quotations from favourite plays, offers yet another striking example of the range and extent of her familiarity with the drama. She is viewing the world around her through the spectacles of theatre, and, simultanously, showing her awareness of the intricacies and nuances of the kinds of social stratification reflected in the drama. The invention of 'Country Girl' innocents out of low-born characters in order to reflect favourable light upon the inventor is precisely the kind of dubious behaviour that Austen fictionalises so adroitly in *Emma*.

The life of the low-born and illegitimate Dora Jordan echoed the theatre's predilection for plays depicting social metamorphosis. From her humble, obscure origins, she had risen to be the mistress of a prince and a royal estate.[80] Epilogues were written for Jordan with pointed reference to her private circumstances. In 1791, when the Duke was stepping up his courtship of Jordan, she played for her benefit an adaptation of Fletcher's *The Humorous Lieutenant* called *The Greek Slave: or The School for Cowards*.[81] Jordan played the part of a slave girl who is in love with a prince, and is eventually discovered to be of noble birth. The epilogue drew attention to her assumption of genteel roles, both on and off stage:

> How Strange! methinks I hear a Critic say,
> What, *She* the serious Heroine of the Play!
> The Manager his want of Sense evinces
> To pitch on *Hoydens* for the love of Princes!
> To trick out *Chambermaids* in awkward pomp –
> Horrid! to make a Princess of a *Romp*.[82]

The epilogue also drew attention to the fact that, while she was acclaimed for her 'low' parts, her roles in polite comedy were often condemned. It seems that Jordan, even among her admirers, was considered to be a 'natural' at low parts. Even her adoring biographer Boaden described her low parts as 'natural ... the genuine workings of nature within her'.[83] Leigh Hunt believed that Jordan was at her best in low comedy, and declared that she was 'all deficient in the *lady*' and unable to bring off genteel roles because of her lack of 'a certain graceful orderliness, an habitual subjection ... of impulse of manner', claiming, however, that 'If Mrs Jordan were what she ought to be in the lady, we more than doubt whether she could be what she is in the boarding school-girl or the buxom woman'.[84]

Hunt's remarks betray a consciousness about the ease with which actresses could play the lady on stage and cross social boundaries off stage. Perhaps this was because so many former actresses married into aristocratic circles. Famously, one of Mrs Jordan's co-stars, Elizabeth Farren, quit the stage to marry the Earl of Derby.[85] Catherine Stephens married the Earl of Essex and Miss O'Neill retired early to become Lady Wrixon Beecher. Jordan's rise from illegitimate child-actor to royal mistress, crossing almost every social barrier, added an extra comic dimension to her role as Nell in Charles Coffey's farce *The Devil to Pay*.

In 1814 Jane Austen saw Jordan in this play, in what was perhaps her most famous role, that of a timid cobbler's wife who is magically transformed into an aristocratic society mistress.[86] Jordan played the part of the downtrodden wife who makes a better wife to Sir John, and a kinder mistress to her servants, than the irascible Lady Loverule. Lady Loverule's metamorphosis into the cobbler's wife eventually brings about her moral transformation. The rough treatment she experiences at the hands of the cobbler is partially responsible for the change in her attitude towards her exalted position:

> There's nought but the devil
> And this good strap
> Could ever tame a scold.[87]

The comedy had long amused the public, who enjoyed seeing Jordan's metamorphosis from rags into riches, just as she herself had been transformed, seemingly, by her liaison with the Duke of Clarence. Jordan was dubbed 'Nell of Clarence' by Horace Walpole, who intended a reference to her famous predecessor as royal theatrical mistress, Nell Gwynne.

By the time that Jane Austen saw *The Devil to Pay* in 1814, however, Jordan was separated from the duke and had returned to the stage.[88] Austen declared herself 'highly amused' with the farce. She was in good company – Hazlitt described Jordan's Nell as 'heavenly':

> Her Nell … was right royal … Miss Kelly is a dexterous knowing cham-
> bermaid: Mrs Jordan had nothing dexterous or knowing about her. She
> was Cleopatra turned into an oyster-wench, without knowing that she
> was Cleopatra, or caring that she was an oyster-wench. An oyster-
> wench, such as she was, would have been equal to a Cleopatra; and an
> Antony would not have deserted her for the empire of the world![89]

The Devil to Pay, the play that was so closely associated with Dora Jordan, exemplifies the drama's obsession with the concept of social mobility, and its endless play on rank and manners. The metamorphosis of a timid country girl and a termagant wife and society mistress highlighted the same sort of class tensions initiated by the unprecedented success of Richardson's *Pamela*. Goldsmith's *She Stoops to Conquer* was another

favourite eighteenth-century comedy that examined uneasy social strat-
ifications by a series of ironic reversals.

It is striking, but perhaps not surprising, that Austen favoured comedies where social roles were turned topsy-turvy, such as Coffey's *The
Devil to Pay*, Townley's *High Life Below Stairs* and Colman's *The Heir at
Law*.[90] Such comedies were popular with a wide and varied audience.
Theatre historians have shown how the need for public theatres to
appeal to a socially diverse audience of box, pit and gallery led to a
mixed programme of entertainment.[91] The opposition between 'high'
and 'low' became a perennial theme in eighteenth-century comedy,
depicting the dramatic situations and comic scenes that arise when a
person crosses the boundaries from low life to high, or vice-versa. The
device of bringing together contrasting types, whereby different styles
of action and language are attached to different classes and ironically
juxtaposed, allowed the writer to exploit the comic potential of 'high'
and 'low' life in Georgian England, and please the upper galleries as well
as the pit.

Pleasing the upper galleries and the boxes was, however, only part of
the intention. Writers for the theatre also knew that fashionable comedy
was genteel, and that its audience was predominantly middle class; therefore farces that criticised aristocratic manners and poked fun at 'low'
characters were particularly successful. The increasingly frequent
appearance of wealthy merchants, sympathetically treated in the plays of
the 1790s, has been ascribed to the development of 'middle-class'
attitudes.[92]

Ever since the success of Gay's *Beggar's Opera*, writers for the stage had
used low life as a means of satirising high. In Cowley's *Which is the Man?*
one of the 'low' characters duly exclaims: 'He must be a Lord by his want
of ceremony.' In *The Devil to Pay*, Nell's gentle manners and innate
dignity reflect badly on Lady Loverule. In *Pride and Prejudice*, Austen
was also to depict the moral defeat of a high-ranking aristocrat (another
Lady Loverule?) by a young woman 'of inferior birth ... without family,
connections, or fortune' (*PP*, pp. 355–56). In *Mansfield Park* the rendi-
tion of Fanny's 'low' family in Portsmouth exploits the dramatic situations and comic scenes resulting from a woman's movement across the
boundaries between high life and low. Yet, in the end, it is the

lower-ranking Price children (William, Fanny and Susan) who turn out better than the high-bred Bertrams.[93]

It is evident throughout her work, distinguishable even from the early reference to Lewis and Quick, that Jane Austen was particularly attuned to the discrepancies between rank and manners within the tightly circumscribed social structure of her world. That understanding was shaped and informed by her interest in the drama. Her special interest in social metamorphosis, with its comic interplay between high and low types, was stimulated by the influence of eighteenth-century comedy.

The year 1814, in which *Mansfield Park* was published, saw the birth of a new age in the English theatre. Between the years of Kean's birth in the late 1780s and his death in 1833 the theatre underwent unprecedented change. The two patent houses had been closed by catastrophic fires in 1808–9 and had then been rebuilt on a more lavish and grander scale than had been seen before. Kemble's raised prices had incited sixty-seven nights of rioting in Covent Garden until he was forced to capitulate to the demands of the rioters. Edmund Kean and Eliza O'Neill had taken over the mantle of Kemble and Siddons, bringing to the stage a new style of intuitive acting characteristic of the 'Romantic' era. The rise of the illegitimate theatres and the impact of a 'theatrical revolution' in the advent of Kean (cemented by the praise of the cockney young literary radicals, Keats, Leigh Hunt and Hazlitt) marked a new age of vitality in the theatre.

This tumultuous period in the history of the theatre also happened to coincide with Jane Austen's own birth and death. She attended the first performances of Kean and O'Neill, witnessed the transformations taking place in the theatre, and remained in touch with its nuances and foibles. Austen's interest in the drama has been overlooked in the persistently mistaken notion that she was morally opposed to the theatre. Yet this assumption is in flagrant defiance of the evidence of the letters.

In the early part of 1814, in the middle of negotiations for the publication of *Mansfield Park*, and in the space of four days, Austen visited the professional theatre three times to see Kean, Jordan and Stephens. In the same short period she wrote of two more excursions to see Kean again and also his rival Young. It is a striking irony that the completion of

Mansfield Park, the novel that has been viewed almost universally as Austen's rejection of the theatre, coincided with a particularly busy theatre-going period for the author.[94]

Judging by Austen's earlier theatre-going periods, visits in such close proximity were not unusual. Her visit to Henry and Eliza in 1811 was planned with the Lyceum on Thursday, followed by two more visits to Covent Garden on Saturday and Monday. In 1813 she was found at the playhouse two nights in a row. This was by no means untypical and is an acute reminder of the frequency with which the Georgians visited the playhouse. On average, there were about 180 nights each season on which the patent houses offered the play-going public some kind of dramatic entertainment. The two winter patent houses alone could command a total of four hundred performances per season.[95] Whenever Jane made extended visits to town, she seems to have taken advantage of Henry's close connections with the theatre.

Theatre in the late Georgian period became an essential part of fashionable middle-class life.[96] One of the consequences of the system of stock companies was that the audience became familiar with the same actors, seeing them in a variety of different roles and plays of all types, coming to know not only their styles of acting, but the details of their private lives.[97] The proliferation of stage-related literature meant that readers were able to know the intimate details of actors' lives. In the words of one historian: 'The public's appetite for news, gossip and scandal about the stage was insatiable, its sense of intimate acquaintance with actors unique. A successful player could only have a public private life.'[98] To sate the audience appetite for theatre there were actors' diaries, journals, memoirs, biographies of playwrights and managers, histories and annals of the theatre, periodicals, and magazines. Between 1800 and 1830 some one hundred and sixty different periodicals devoted exclusively to the theatre came into existence in Britain.[99]

William Hazlitt, in the preface to his *A View of the English Stage*, describes the allure of the theatre in late Georgian England: 'the disputes on the merits or defects of the last new piece, or a favourite performer, are as common, as frequently renewed, and carried on with as much eagerness and skill, as those on almost any other subject'.[100] With Hazlitt's words in mind, one of the most striking features of Austen's letters is her discussion of the theatre as a part of everyday conversation, to be written about as she writes about other quotidian matters like shopping and gossip.

Austen's letters are a neglected historical source for her interest in and love of the theatre. The fundamental place the theatre occupied in her life is revealed in the manner in which it can be joked about, admired, even be taken for granted. Her mock-insult to Siddons, 'I could swear at her for disappointing me', reflects the way in which the sisters often consoled one another for missing particular performers. Her tantalising observation that Mrs Edwin's performance 'is just what it used to be' speaks a language of intimate theatrical knowledge that we can only begin to guess at.

There is something paradoxically casual and yet essential about the way that Austen 'converses' about the theatre. At times her letters reveal a striking language of precision and economy in respect to the drama; details of the seating arrangements are often as important as descriptions of the plays, sometimes a cursory remark such as 'no skill in acting' is enough for the sisters and nieces, who are in tune with one another; no further elaboration is necessary, but it still needs to be said, because the interest is there between them. That interest lasted throughout Jane Austen's life and, as I will demonstrate, had a profound effect on her fiction.

PART TWO

The Theatre and the Novels

She partook largely in all the best gifts of the comic muse

Henry Austen, 'Biographical Notice' of his sister

4

Early Works

The impact of private theatricals and the vitality of the professional theatre in the late Georgian period gave Jane Austen a comprehensive and
longstanding interest in the drama. From her earliest attempts at
play-writing to the systematic incorporation of quasi-theatrical techniques into her mature novels, the influence of the drama rarely left her.
Throughout the canon there is an abundance of resonances and allusions
to eighteenth-century plays, many of which the author expected her
readers to recognise. It is, however, in Austen's juvenilia, written to amuse
her family, and not intended for public consumption, where the marks
of her early exposure to the drama can most clearly be seen.

Jane Austen's chief literary tool in her early works was the art of
burlesque.[1] In this she was influenced by her brothers' Oxford literary
journal, *The Loiterer*, which ran for sixty numbers between 1789 and
1790, and made a duty of burlesquing 'novel slang' and the absurdities of
popular fiction. Henry Austen's burlesque of the literary conventions of
courtship, entitled 'Peculiar Dangers of *Rusticus* from the Attacks of a
Female Cousin', is particularly striking.[2] In this parody of a sentimental
novel, the unlucky hero is besieged by the attentions of his cousin. The
hero of Henry's sentimental tale is lured into seducing his fair cousin:
'She begged me for the loan of an arm. My arm she accordingly took, and
in the course of all her frights and false steps, pinched it so hard and so
often, that it is still quite black and blue, through sheer tenderness.'
Following his cousin's admission of loving 'cropt Greys to distraction', he
is a lost man:

There was no standing this … I thought she never looked so much like an angel. In short, I know not where my passion might have ended, had not the luckiest accident in the world at once roused me from this rapturous dream of fancied bliss, to all the phlegm of cool reflection and sober reality. A sudden puff of wind carried off two luxuriant tresses from her beautiful Chignon, and left her (unconscious to herself) in a situation truly ridiculous. The delicate thread of sentiment and affection was broken, never to be united.[3]

Henry Austen's burlesque technique of juxtaposing a serious and sentimental reflection with a quasi-farcical action is echoed throughout Jane Austen's *Volume the First*. Also typical is the taste for absurd detail and witty aphorism. Henry's tale ends with a description of the hero's unsuccessful attempts to be rid of his cousin; getting 'completely cut' and spilling lemonade over her dress prove fruitless: 'But she wouldn't be provoked, for when once a woman is determined to get a husband, I find trifling obstacles will not damp her hopes or sour her temper.'[4]

The Loiterer was not the only influence on Jane Austen. As has been shown, she was writing burlesque sketches at least two years before its publication, during the time of the Steventon private theatricals.[5] James and Henry's taste for satirical comedies ensured that she was exposed at a very early age to those masters of burlesque plays, Henry Fielding and Richard Brinsley Sheridan. Fielding's *Tom Thumb: or The Tragedy of Tragedies* (1730) and Sheridan's *The Critic* (1779) were two of the most successful examples of eighteenth-century theatrical burlesque. Jane Austen alludes to both plays in her juvenilia.

Fielding had been hailed as a master of political satire after the commercial success of his theatre burlesques, *The Author's Farce, Tom Thumb, Pasquin* and *The Historical Register*. His repeated attacks on the Whig government came to a head in *The Historical Register*, where he was more openly hostile to Sir Robert Walpole than he had been in his earlier burlesques. The success of this play finally provoked the government into passing the Theatre Licensing Act of 1737, whose long-term repercussions were to include the growth of closet drama and a transfer of creative energy from the theatre to the novel.[6] Fielding gave up writing and turned to the law, until the publication of Richardson's *Pamela*

(1740) provoked him into writing again. Once again he used burlesque to ridicule literary pretension and hypocrisy: *Shamela* and *Joseph Andrews* are different burlesques of the same book.

Fielding's theatre burlesques relied upon a subtle blending of theatrical and political satire. *Tom Thumb: or The Tragedy of Tragedies*, which the Austens acted at Steventon on 22 March 1788, was chiefly a parody of contemporary tragedy, although Walpole was implicitly satirised in the portrayal of Tom Thumb, 'the great man'. It was intended to be ludicrous and nonsensical. The original audience was delighted by the incongruity of a 'tragedy' designed to make them laugh. Fielding was satirising the way in which modern tragedy was unintentionally absurd.

Set in King Arthur's Court, Fielding's travesty ruthlessly caricatured conventional heroic tragedy. The play contains the full panoply of Neoclassical tragedy, but the superhuman giant-killing hero, Thumb – 'whose soul is as big as a mountain' – is a midget. The other 'noble' personages of the court are just as ridiculous. The royal couple are a quarrelsome pair. The noble King Arthur is bullied by his wife Dollalolla, a queen 'entirely faultless, saving that she is a little given to drink', and in love with the captive queen, Glumdalca, a giantess, who is in love with the dwarf, Thumb. The romantic sub-plot common in heroic tragedy is also parodied in the love triangle of the gluttonous Princess Huncamunca and her rivals, Lord Grizzle and Tom Thumb. The King's loyal courtiers, Noodle, Doodle and Foodle, are foolish and inept, and the play ends with a ludicrous massacre of all the characters.

Burlesque appealed to Austen, for her main concern in her early writings was to excite laughter. She approved of its uncomplicated aim to raise laughter by comic exaggeration and from the sheer absurdity of language and image. But, like Fielding, she was aware that parody acts as a form of criticism, a way of elucidating the absurdities and limitations of a particular art form.

Austen shared Fielding's irreverence for literary and artistic convention. Her characters are no more heroic than Fielding's, and often as physically odd or repulsive. In a deliberate echo of *Tom Thumb*, Austen set her stories in villages called Pammydiddle and Crankhumdunberry. Like Fielding, she took the clichéd situation and rendered it absurd. In 'Frederick and Elfrida' she parodied the novelistic convention of depicting two antithetical sisters, one beautiful and foolish, the other ugly and clever. In this topsy-turvy world it is the ugly Rebecca who charms the hero:

> Lovely & too charming Fair one, notwithstanding your forbidding Squint, your greazy tresses & your swelling Back, which are more frightful than imagination can paint or pen describe, I cannot refrain from expressing my raptures, at the engaging Qualities of your Mind, which so amply atone for the Horror, with which your first appearance must ever inspire the unwary visitor. (*MW*, p. 6)

In *Tom Thumb*, Princess Huncamunca is confounded by the ugliness of Glumdalca: 'O Heaven, thou art as ugly as the devil.' Queen Dollalolla, meanwhile, is permanently drunk:

> Oh, Dollalolla! do not blame my love;
> I hoped the fumes of last night's punch had laid
> Thy lovely eyelids fast.[7]

Just as Fielding's heroes are characterised by their unheroic qualities, such as physical ugliness, drunkeness and violence, Austen's earliest characters are also drunkards, murderers and adulterers. Jealous sisters poison each other, landowners beat their workers with a cudgel on a whim, and children bite off their mother's fingers. Austen's letters suggest that she long continued to find physical ugliness, illness and death amusing.[8]

Jane Austen does not raise a laugh merely through the employment of knockabout farce and violent imagery. Her grasp of verbal incongruities is equally impressive. Thus, in 'Frederic and Elfrida', the physically abhorrent Rebecca is finally sought in marriage by the aged Captain Rogers: 'Mrs Fitzroy did not approve of the match on account of the tender years of the young couple, Rebecca being but 36 & Captain Roger little more than 63. To remedy this objection, it was agreed that they should wait a little while till they were a good deal older' (*MW*, p. 7).

Absurdity of language is coupled with farcical action to achieve the maximum comic effect: 'From this period, the intimacy between the Families of Fitzroy, Drummond, and Falknor, daily increased till at length it grew to such a pitch, that they did not scruple to kick one another out of the window on the slightest provocation' (*MW*, p. 6). In this instance, Austen is parodying the formal rhetoric of the sentimental novel and elucidating its absurdities while simultaneously observing the quasi-farcical conventions of slapstick stage-comedy.

Similarly, in 'Jack and Alice', Austen moves swiftly from the educational motif of the 'improving' novel to a punch-line that is pure farce:

> Miss Dickens was an excellent Governess. She instructed me in the Paths of Virtue; under her tuition I daily became more amiable, & might perhaps by this time have nearly attained perfection, had not my worthy Preceptoress been torn from my arms, e'er I had attained my seventeeth year. I never shall forget her last words. 'My dear Kitty she said, Good night t'ye.' I never saw her afterwards', continued Lady Williams wiping her eyes, 'She eloped with the Butler the same night'. (*MW*, p. 17)

The technique of juxtaposing a mock-grandiose sentiment with a comic action is influenced by the burlesque methods of Henry and James Austen in *The Loiterer*. But, as this passage reveals, the rhythms and cadences of stage comedy also shape the narrative. The pompous diction of the second sentence culminates in the hackneyed sentimental expression 'torn from my arms', only to be comically deflated by the governess's brisk goodnight. The gesture of 'Lady Williams wiping her eyes' before continuing her story introduces a theatrical pause between the two clauses of the final sentence – and the governess eloping with the butler is a twist straight out of stage farce.[9]

The egocentricity of the heroine's blithe remark, 'I daily became more amiable, & might perhaps by this time have nearly gained perfection', is inserted almost incidentally into the narrative. Here the comic touch is more finely tuned. Jane Austen is already going beyond mere slapstick. Similarly, in the same story, the 'perfect' Charles Adams, a character based on Richardson's idealised hero Sir Charles Grandison, memorably remarks, 'I expect nothing more in my wife than my wife will find in me – Perfection' (*MW*, p. 26).

Austen's heroine in 'Jack and Alice' is an absurd figure whose only fault is, in the style of Fielding's Dollalolla, a propensity for liquor. Even

Lady Williams's benevolent nature is strained by her tippling companion: 'When you are more intimately acquainted with my Alice you will not be surprised, Lucy, to see the dear Creature drink a little too much; for such things happen every day. She has many rare & charming qualities, but Sobriety is not one of them. The whole Family are indeed a sad drunken set' (*MW*, p. 23).

As in the 'tragic' ending of *Tom Thumb*, 'Jack and Alice' becomes increasingly absurd and farcical. At the tender age of seventeen, Lucy is poisoned by the envious Sukey, who is promptly hauled off to the gallows for murder. The hero of the story (presumably 'Jack') is finally introduced only to be killed off instantly:

> It may now be proper to return to the Hero of this Novel, the brother of Alice, of whom I beleive I have scarcely ever had occasion to speak; which may perhaps be partly oweing to his unfortunate propensity to Liquor, which so compleatly deprived him of the use of those faculties Nature had endowed him with, that he never did anything worth mentioning. (*MW*, pp. 24–25)

The real hero and heroine of Austen's story are, of course, not the ludicrous drunkards Jack and Alice of Pammydiddle, but those more sinister figures, monsters of ego and self-interest, Lady Williams and Charles Adams, who are united in marriage having found their ideal of perfection in each other.

In *Volume the Second*, Austen continued to show her allegiance to burlesque. Where Henry Fielding had been an important influence in *Volume the First*, she now turned to Richard Brinsley Sheridan, his great successor in the art of literary parody. In *The History of England*, a burlesque of Oliver Goldsmith's 'partial, prejudiced and ignorant history', Austen mocks the way in which supposedly factual history is tempered by sensationalised fiction in order to popularise its appeal. To this end, she refers her readers to Sheridan's *The Critic*.

Sir Walter Raleigh flourished in this & the preceding reign, & is by many people held in great veneration & respect – But as he was an enemy of the noble Essex, I have nothing to say in praise of him, & must refer all those who may wish to be acquainted with the particulars of his life, to Mr Sheridan's play of the Critic, where they will find many interesting anecdotes as well of him as of his freind [sic] Sir Christopher Hatton. (*MW*, p. 147)

There are several further gestures towards *The Critic* in Austen's full-length burlesque of sentimentalism, *Love and Freindship*. This work was dedicated to Eliza de Feuillide, who had taken the part of Miss Titupp in the Steventon production of the Garrick's *Bon Ton*. As has been noted, the title of Jane's own burlesque had appeared as a phrase in Garrick's play: 'Love and Friendship are very fine names to be sure, but they are merely visiting acquaintance; we know their names indeed, talk of 'em sometimes, and let 'em knock at our doors, but we never let 'em in, you know.'[10]

Eighteenth-century 'sentimentalism' is a particularly slippery concept to define, not least because what was first an approbatory term increasingly became a pejorative label.[11] A quality of emotional excess – the indulgence or luxuriance in emotion for its own sake – was the particular target of Austen's satire in *Love and Freindship*.[12] This burlesque novella is a parody of the heroine-centred, epistolary novel of sensibility, exemplified by Charlotte's Smith's *Emmeline: or The Orphan of the Castle* and Fanny Burney's *Evelina*.[13] *Love and Freindship* duly contains all the clichés of romantic fiction: swooning heroines, unknown parentage and improbable chance meetings. But Austen's burlesque should not be viewed solely in the context of the sentimental novel. The deluded romantic heroine was also a theatrical type. So it was that *The Critic* gave Austen a precedent for her parody of the excesses of sentimentalism.

One of the traditions of sentimental drama was the 'discovery scene', in which some dramatic (and usually emotionally charged) revelation occurs. Sheridan parodied the device mercilessly. In the play-within-the-play, Puff's risible tragedy *The Spanish Armada*, there is the requisite improbable chance meeting with a stranger who is 'discovered' to be a long-lost relative:

JUSTICE:
What is thy name?

SON:
My name's Tom Jenkins – *alias*, have I none –
Tho' orphaned, and without a friend!

JUSTICE:
Thy parents?

SON:
My father dwelt in Rochester – and was,
As I have heard – a fishmonger – no more.

PUFF: What, Sir, do you leave out the account of your birth, parentage and education?
SON: They have settled it so, Sir, here.
PUFF: Oh! oh!

LADY:
How loudly nature whispers to my heart!
Had he no other name?

SON:
I've seen a bill
Of his, sign'd *Tomkins*, creditor.

JUSTICE:
This does indeed confirm each circumstance
The gypsey told! – Prepare!

SON:
I do.

JUSTICE:
No orphan, nor without a friend art thou –
I am thy father, *here's* thy mother, *there*
Thy uncle – this thy first cousin, and those
Are all your near relations!

MOTHER:
O ecstasy of bliss!

SON:
O most unlook'd for happiness!

JUSTICE:
O wonderful event!

[They faint alternately in each others' arms]

PUFF: There, you see relationship, like murder, will out.[14]

The specific object of Sheridan's parody is the famously sentimental discovery scene in John Home's immensely popular tragedy, *Douglas* (1756). In the second act, Lady Randolph 'discovers' a sheep-tender and is struck by the fact that, had her son lived,

He might have been like this young gallant stranger
And paired with him in features and in shape.

The stranger, who really is Lady Randolph's lost son, describes his life story in an eloquent, long-winded speech. In *The Critic*, the 'My name is Norval' speech is condensed into the two lines

My name's Tom Jenkins – *alias*, have I none –
Tho' orphaned, and without a friend!

In *Mansfield Park* Jane Austen alludes to the famous scene in *Douglas* when Tom Bertram recalls play-acting as a boy: 'How many times have we mourned over the dead body of Julius Caesar, and *to be'd* and *not to be'd*, in this very room for his amusement! And I am sure, *my name was Norval*, every evening of my life through one Christmas holidays' (*MP*, pp. 126–27). Long before this, in *Love and Freindship*, she had already parodied the obligatory discovery scene:

> Never did I see such an affecting Scene as was the meeting of Edward & Augustus.
>
> 'My life! my Soul!' (exclaimed the former) 'My adorable Angel!' (replied the latter) as they flew into each other's arms. It was too pathetic for the feelings of Sophia and myself – We fainted Alternately on a Sofa. (*MW*, p. 86)

The final line is a clear allusion to the parody of *Douglas* in *The Critic*, with its climactic stage direction, '*They faint alternately in each others' arms*'.

The allusion to Tom Jenkins's 'discovery scene' is sustained in the sentimental reunion of Austen's heroine, Laura. She also discovers, unexpectedly, the existence of a wealthy grandfather and benefactor: 'At his first Appearance my Sensibility was wonderfully affected & e'er I had gazed at him a 2*d*. time, an instinctive Sympathy whispered to my Heart, that he was my Grandfather' (*MW*, p. 91). Laura's friend and confidante, Sophia, discovers that the same venerable old man is a relative: '"Oh!" replied Sophia, "when I first beheld you the instinct of Nature whispered me that we were in some degree related – But whether Grandfathers, or Grandmothers, I could not pretend to determine"' (*MW*, p. 91).

Austen's heroines echo Sheridan's phrase, 'whispered to my heart'. This clichéd phrase indicates the trademark of sensibility: the heroine's grasp of the supremacy of instinctive intuition over the rational or intellectual. In *The Critic*, the implausible discovery scene is followed by a quick succession of equally implausible reunions:

I am thy father, *here's* thy mother, *there*
Thy uncle – this thy first cousin, and those
Are all your near relations!

Austen's own discovery scene is only completed when two more long-lost grandchildren, the strolling actors Philander and Augustus, enter the inn, much to the Grandfather's dismay:

'But tell me (continued he looking fearfully towards the Door) tell me, have I any other Grand-Children in the House'. 'None my Lord'. 'Then I will provide for you all without further delay – Here are 4 banknotes of 50£ each – Take them & remember I have done the Duty of a Grandfather –'. He instantly left the room & immediately afterwards the house … You may imagine how greatly surprised we were by the sudden departure of Lord St Clair. 'Ignoble Grand-sire!' exclaimed Sophia. 'Unworthy Grandfather!' said I, & instantly fainted in each other's arms. (*MW*, p. 92)

The swooning scene once again borrows the stage direction in *The Critic* that calls for mutual fainting. The last-minute discovery of a benevolent guardian appears in most of the sentimental plays of the period. Celebrated examples include Stockwell in Cumberland's *The West Indian* and Sir Oliver Surface in Sheridan's own *The School for Scandal*.[15]

As well as the conventional discovery scene, Puff's tragedy incorporates fainting fits and madness, the symptoms of extreme sensibility in both drama and fiction. Hence the stage direction, '*Enter Tilburina and Confidante mad, according to custom*'.

TILBURINA:
The wind whistles – the moon rises – see
They have kill'd my squirrel in his cage!
Is this a grasshopper! – Ha! no, it is my
Whiskerandos – you shall not keep him –
I know you have him in your pocket –
An oyster may be cross'd in love! – Who says
A whale's a bird? – Ha! did you call, my love?

– He's here! He's there! – He's everywhere!
Ah me! He's no where![16]

In *Love and Freindship*, madness and swoons are the prerequisites for the distressed heroines, who witness the death of their husbands from an upturned carriage: 'Two Gentlemen most elegantly attired but weltering in their own blood was what first struck our Eyes … Yes dearest Marianne they were our Husbands. Sophia shrieked & fainted on the Ground – I screamed and instantly ran mad.' Laura descends into madness: 'My Eyes assumed a vacant Stare, My face became as pale as Death, and my Senses were considerably impaired' (*MW*, pp. 99–100). Laura's mad speech echoes the incongrous jumble of images in Tilburina's:

'Talk not to me of Phaetons' (said I, raving in a frantic, incoherent manner) – 'Give me a violin – I'll play to him & sooth him in his melancholy Hours – Beware ye gentle Nymphs of Cupid's Thunderbolts, avoid the piercing Shafts of Jupiter – Look at that Grove of Firs – I see a Leg of Mutton – They told me Edward was not Dead; but they deceived me – they took him for a Cucumber'. (*MW*, p. 100)

In *Love and Freindship*, Austen's allusions to *The Critic* are deliberate and blatant. Her mockery of the conventions of sentimentalism is shaped by Sheridan's burlesque techniques and she acknowledges the debt in her close and deliberate echoes of the play. But the Sheridan play that has most resonance with Austen's satire on sensibility is *The Rivals*. *Love and Freindship* has been seen as an early burlesque version of *Sense and Sensibility*, and in both works Austen is indebted to *The Rivals*.

One of the conventions of sentimentalism that both Sheridan and Austen exploit is the conflicting attitudes of the young and their more prudent elders, particularly when it comes to marriage.[17] What leads to a tragic outcome in *Clarissa*, the most influential example of parental tyranny in eighteenth-century fiction, is for Sheridan in *The Rivals* a subject for burlesque. *Love and Freindship* follows Sheridan's inversion of the convention, whereby the benign impulses of parents are wilfully misunderstood by their children. The absurd hero, Edward, opposes his father, even though the opposition is contrary to his own wishes:

'My father, seduced by the false glare of Fortune and the Deluding
Pomp of Title, insisted on my giving my hand to Lady Dorothea. No
never exclaimed I. Lady Dorothea is lovely and Engaging; I prefer no
woman to her; but know Sir, that I scorn to marry her in compliance
with your wishes. No! Never shall it be said that I obliged my Father.'
(*MW*, p. 81)

The comic impact arises from the contrast between Edward's sentimental
outburst and his father's level-headed response, which is to rebuke his
quixotic son for using language that is inflated and melodramatic:

'Sir Edward was surprized; he had perhaps little expected to meet with
so spirited an opposition to his will. "Where Edward in the name of
wonder (said he) did you pick up this unmeaning Gibberish? You have
been studying Novels I suspect." I scorned to answer: it would have been
beneath my dignity.' (*MW*, p. 81)

The problem with Sir Edward's cretinous son is that he has read too
many novels. In *The Loiterer*, Henry and James Austen had satirised
women for reading trashy novels, but Austen retaliated in *Love and
Freindship* by making a young *man* the target of her satire. Sir Edward
accuses his son of gleaning absurdly romantic notions from the pages of
sentimental fiction, just as Laura and Sophia make partial judgements
based upon the sentimental novels they read:

We soon saw through his Character ... They said he was Sensible, well
informed, and Agreeable; we did not pretend to Judge of such trifles, but
as we were convinced he had no soul, that he had never read the Sorrows
of Werter, & that his Hair bore not the slightest resemblance to Auburn,
we were certain that Janetta could feel no affection for him, or at least
that she ought to feel none. (*MW*, p. 93)

In the late eighteenth century, the epitome of the misguided reader of
romantic novels was Lydia Languish in *The Rivals*. But Sheridan was not
the first playwright to burlesque the giddy female novel reader. Lydia
Languish follows on from a tradition of quixotic stage heroines such as

Richard Steele's Miss Biddy in *The Tender Husband* (1705) and George Colman the Elder's *Polly Honeycombe* (1760).

Sheridan, like Austen, had limited tolerance for financially imprudent marriages. Lydia embraces the idea of love in a cottage with Ensign Beverley – 'How charming will poverty be with him'. In *Love and Freindship*, Edward also prefers the romance of living in poverty, but the absurdity of his sentimental notions is made apparent by the cool scepticism of his clever sister, Augusta:

'Never, never Augusta will I so demean myself ... Support! What Support will Laura want which she can receive from him?'

'Only those very insignificant ones of Victuals and Drink' (answered she.)

'Victuals and Drink!' (replied my Husband in a most nobly contemptuous Manner) 'and dost thou then imagine that there is no other support for an exalted Mind (such as is my Laura's) than the mean and indelicate employment of Eating and Drinking?'

'None that I know of, so efficacious' (returned Augusta).

'And did you then never feel the pleasing Pangs of Love, Augusta?' (replied my Edward). 'Does it appear impossible to your vile and corrupted Palate, to exist on Love? Can you not conceive the Luxury of living in every Distress that Poverty can inflict, with the object of your tenderest Affection?'

'You are too ridiculous (said Augusta) to argue with.' (*MW*, pp. 83–84)

The device of contrasting a cool, level-headed character with a foolish one had also been deployed by Hugh Kelly in his play *False Delicacy* (1768), where Mrs Harley and Cecil provide a rational norm by which the excesses of absurd sensibility can be measured. The contrasts and conflicts arising from clashes between Romantic idealism and prudent conservatism provide the comic dynamic of both Austen's and Sheridan's satire, and – as will be shown later – Austen was to rework this comic device in *Sense and Sensibility*.

Even in her earliest works, the harmful effects of excessive emotion are satirised, although the chief emphasis in *Love and Freindship* is upon the hypocrisy of sentimentalism. The two anti-heroines, Laura and Sophia, justify selfish and malicious behaviour by their skewed vision of sentimental duty. In the name of sentimentalism, they persuade Janetta to elope with an unprincipled fortune hunter, and abandon the honourable man that she really loves:

> The very circumstance of his being her father's choice too, was so much in his disfavour, that had he been deserving her, in every other respect yet *that* of itself ought to have been a sufficient reason in the Eyes of Janetta for rejecting him ... we had no difficulty to convince her that it was impossible she could love Graham, or that it was her duty to disobey her Father. (*MW*, pp. 93–94)

What is worse, their destructive interference in a young girl's happiness is twisted into the appearance of a noble and generous act. Beneath the veneer of sensibility lie egotism and selfishness. Laura and Sophia steal, lie and cheat – all in the name of sensibility. It was, after all, a code of conduct that unashamedly placed the individual first. Thus, when Sophia is caught *in flagrante delicto* stealing money from her host, in her own words 'majestically removing the 5th bank-note' from her cousin's private drawer, she responds in the injured tones of a virtuous heroine whose personal integrity has been violated, a parody on Clarissa Harlowe in Richardson's novel:

> Sophia ... instantly put on a most forbidding look, & darting an angry frown on the undaunted culprit, demanded in a haughty tone of voice 'Wherefore her retirement was thus insolently broken in on?' The unblushing Macdonald, without even endeavouring to exculpate himself from the crime he was charged with, meanly endeavoured to reproach Sophia with ignobly defrauding him of his money ... The Dignity of Sophia was wounded; 'Wretch' (exclaimed she, hastily replacing the Bank-note in the drawer) 'how darest thou to accuse me of an Act, of which the bare idea makes me blush.' (*MW*, p. 96)

Clarissa of course has every right to object to her violation, whereas Sophia does not, for she is stealing. Just as Laura and Sophia steal unashamedly from their guests, Edward and Augustus 'scorned to reflect a moment on their pecuniary distresses and would have blushed at the idea of paying their debts' (*MW*, p. 86). This 'gentlemanly' attribute derives from Charles Surface in *The School for Scandal*, who is encouraged by his friend Careless to put off paying his huge debts with the money that he has borrowed from Premium:

> CARELESS: Don't let that old Blockhead persuade you – to squander
> any of that money on old Musty debts, or any such Nonsense for
> tradesmen – Charles, are the most Exorbitant Fellows.
> CHARLES: Very true, and paying them is only Encouraging them.[18]

In *The Rivals* Sheridan had satirised absurd sentimentalism, but in *The School for Scandal* he made explicit the connection between sensibility and hypocrisy. Comedies by playwrights such as Steele, Colman and Kelly had satirised foolish sentimentalism, but the darker *School for Scandal* showed how the cult of sensibility was abused when it became a front for prudery and hypocrisy.[19]

In *Love and Freindship* Austen also shows how sensibility is abused by unscrupulous characters. In an allusion to Sheridan's smooth hypocrite Joseph Surface, Laura's 'refined' feelings are disturbed by the sound of 'loud and repeated snores' in a carriage journey, inciting a misplaced outburst of emotion:

> What an illiterate villain must that Man be! (thought I to myself) What
> a total Want of delicate refinement must he have who can thus shock our
> senses by such a brutal Noise! He must I am certain be capable of every
> bad Action! There is no crime too black for such a Character. (*MW*, p.
> 103)

This speech is an imitation of Joseph's hypocritical protestations when he persuades Sir Peter Teazle that his brother Charles is Lady Teazle's lover, rather than himself:

Oh, 'tis not to be credited – There may be a man capable of such Baseness to be sure – but for my Part 'till you can give me positive Proofs – I can not but doubt it. However if this should be proved on him He is no longer a Brother of mine! I disclaim kindred with him – for the Man who can break thro' the laws of Hospitality – and attempt the wife – of his Friend deserves to be branded as the Pest of Society.[20]

The 'artful, selfish and malicious' man who 'studies sentiment' and is a member of Lady Sneerwell's circle of malicious slanderers disguises his perfidy beneath a veneer of sensibility and tells the audience that, instead of the 'silver ore of pure Charity', he prefers to use 'the sentimental French plate'. Jane Austen's mockery of the hypocritical cant of sensibility owes much to Sheridan's example. Though her characters in *Love and Freindship* are rarely permitted to stray beyond the boundaries of burlesque, in *Sense and Sensibility* the genuine sensibility of the Dashwood sisters is used to reflect upon the false sensibility of other characters. Even in this later work, however, she doesn't altogether abandon burlesque methods.

Austen's roots were in literary parody: she loved burlesque and never altogether abandoned it. From her earliest full-length satire of the sentimental and Gothic novel, *Northanger Abbey*, to her final uncompleted novel, she continued to use elements of it in her work. *Sanditon* is extremely close in spirit to the juvenilia, a dying return to Austen's natural medium of satire and her love of the ridiculous.[21]

The Critic and *Tom Thumb* were probably the two most popular burlesques of the eighteenth century. Austen's development as a comic writer and her affinity with literary parody can be attributed, in part, to the example set by these plays. Furthermore, the distinctive element of both plays was the degree of authorial control maintained by the authors. Fielding's satirical author's notes to the text of *Tom Thumb*, and Sheridan's rehearsal play, with its author-within-the-play, permitted the writers an unusual degree of authorial control of a kind that greatly appealed to Jane Austen.

In the move from the drama to the novel, Fielding pioneered the way of successfully integrating quasi-theatrical techniques with third-person narration. Jane Austen also experimented with both dramatic and epistolary form – both of which lack a narrator's voice – before turning to third-person narration.

5

From Play to Novel

Jane Austen's chief models in the art of burlesque were Sheridan and Fielding in the dramatic tradition, and Charlotte Lennox's *The Female Quixote* in the novel tradition. In her mature fiction Austen honed her use of the technique without ever abandoning it fully. But before she began refining her first novels for publication in the early part of the nineteenth century, she put the finishing touches to two important transitional works: a play that burlesques Richardson's novel *Sir Charles Grandison* and an epistolary novel, *Lady Susan.*

An analysis of these works reveals a crucial development in the trajectory of Austen's writing career: her final experimentation with, and eventual rejection of, dramatic and epistolary forms, both of which lack a controlling narratorial voice, in favour of third-person narration. In this respect, the novels of Henry Fielding and Elizabeth Inchbald – both playwrights who became novelists – were an important influence on Austen's style. They assisted her in the search for a medium of writing that incorporated quasi-theatrical techniques with third-person narration.

Jane Austen's little five-act comedy 'Sir Charles Grandison' depends upon a close knowledge of Samuel Richardson's novel of the same name.[1] She sub-titled her play 'The Happy Man', in allusion to the way that Richardson irritatingly overused this phrase throughout his novel. Austen had previously made Richardson's 'perfect hero' the butt of many jokes in her juvenilia. He was the 'happy man' in 'Jack and Alice': 'an amiable, accomplished & bewitching young Man; of so dazzling a Beauty that none but Eagles could look him in the Face' (*MW*, p. 13).

The most obvious joke in Austen's 'Sir Charles Grandison' is its very brevity. It reduces Richardson's seven-volume, million-word novel into a stage lampoon of five short acts, without any marked alteration to the plot. The heroine, Harriet Byron, is stolen away at a masquerade ball by a notorious blackguard, Sir Hargrave Pollexfen, before being rescued and married to the hero Sir Charles Grandison. In the novel the reader, like the heroine, has to wait for five volumes before the hero is free to marry the woman he loves.

Samuel Johnson famously said that a man who read Richardson for the story might as well go hang himself. The telescoping of the notoriously long narrative into a short play is in the tradition of Fielding's reduction of *Pamela* into the sixty-page lampoon *Shamela*. The success of burlesque partly depends on its brevity, as Fielding realised, and Austen showed a similar awareness of this necessity in her juvenilia, where she rarely permitted the joke to be laboured. In 'Grandison' she compounded the comic impact by showing that Richardson's thin plot and million-word novel could be transposed into a short play.

It seems to have been written over a number of years.[2] Austen was probably working on it from the 1780s, when the family was engaged in private theatricals. For example, Act One is very similar in style to her playlets of this period, whereas the manuscript of Act Two is watermarked 1799. The final version was probably completed around 1805. The dating is important because it was the completion of 'Grandison' that heralded the way ahead for Austen's adoption of third-person narration.

By turning her favourite novel into a burlesque play, Austen showed her implicit awareness of Richardson's dramatic inheritance. Richardson was keen on the public theatre, and was friendly with such dramatists as Colley Cibber, Aaron Hill and Edward Young. He was deeply influenced by the drama and gleaned a diversity of techniques and materials from his knowledge of plays.[3] Indeed, he perceived himself as a dramatic novelist. In the postscript to *Clarissa*, he describes that work as a 'Dramatic Narrative', and at the front of *Clarissa* and *Sir Charles Grandison* he places the 'Names of *the* Principal Persons' as a *dramatis personae*. In all of his novels Richardson has parenthetical insertions like stage directions such as '*Enter Dorcas in haste*', '[*rising*]' and '[*Rising again*]' and even directions for the characters, '[Lips drawn closer: eye raised]'.[4]

One of the most striking theatrical borrowings in *Clarissa* is the scene before Hampstead, where Lovelace writes:

> And here, supposing my narrative of the dramatic kind, ends Act the First. And now begins
>> ACT II. Scene, Hampstead Heath, continued
>> *Enter my Rascal.*[5]

Lovelace is a recognisable theatrical character (he is in many respects based on Nicholas Rowe's Lothario), and the fate of Clarissa may even have been based on the plot of a play called *Caelia* by Charles Johnson (1733), where a virtuous heroine is placed in a brothel.[6] Lovelace's relish for role-playing and for stage-managing the action of the novel reveal his open allegiance to the archetypal stage rake.[7]

A further development of Richardson's dramatic art in *Clarissa*, which he was to perfect in *Sir Charles Grandison*, was his implementation of dialogue in the style of a play-book. This can be seen in the comic description of Anna Howe's account of Uncle Anthony's courtship of Mrs Howe. The dialogue between mother and daughter is set out like a play:

> I *think* you shall have the *dialogue* …
>
> MOTHER: I have a very serious matter to talk with you upon, Nancy, when you are disposed to attend to matters *within* ourselves, and not let matters *without* ourselves wholly engross you …
>
> DAUGHTER: I am *now* disposed to attend to everything my mamma is *disposed* to say to me.
>
> MOTHER: Why then, child – why then, my dear – (and the good lady's face looked *so* plump! *so* smooth! and *so* shining!) – I see you are all attention, Nancy! – but don't be surprised! – don't be uneasy! – but I have – I have – where is it? – (And yet it lay next her heart, never another near it – so no difficulty to have found it) – I have a *letter*, my dear! – (and out from her bosom it came: but she still held it in her hand) – I have a *letter*, child – It is – it is – it is from – from a gentleman, I assure you! – lifting up her head, and smiling.[8]

Richardson knew that he was writing for a public used to reading play-books. Not for nothing had Pope quipped 'Our wives read Milton and our daughters plays'.[9] Though Richardson explicitly made use of play-book narration in *Clarissa*, he drew upon it even more extensively in *Sir Charles Grandison*. Though *Clarissa* (and *Pamela I*) were centred on a single plot situation that could be perceived as dramatic in origin, *Sir Charles Grandison* is more episodic. Richardson builds his script tech-nique into the novel, recounting long dramatic conversations in the narrative with increasingly rare authorial intervention.

Paradoxically, *Sir Charles Grandison* has little dramatic action and is more concerned with everyday social behaviour, aside from the Clementina sub-plot. Yet Lady Bradshaigh, among others, saw the dramatic potential of the novel as genteel comedy when she remarked that a play worthy of David Garrick might be formed out of it.[10] The dramatic method of narrative is actually described in the novel itself, when Harriet explains her epistolary style to Lucy:

> By the way, Lucy, you are fond of plays; and it has come into my head, that to avoid all *says-I's* and *says-she's*, I will henceforth, in all dialogues, write names in the margin: so fansy, my dear, that you are reading in one of your favourite volumes.[11]

Richardson's pioneering method of narration was a significant influ-ence on writers such as Fanny Burney and Jane Austen. Parts of Burney's early journals, for example, were written as conversations between different characters, following what she called 'the Grandison way of writing Dialogue'.[12] Later, she coined her own word to describe her method of writing: 'I think I shall occcasionally *Theatricalise* my Dialogues.'[13]

It is striking, but not surprising, that Jane Austen should have turned her very favourite novel into a burlesque, and in so doing have height-ened many of its weaknesses. The very act of transcribing the novel into a play was a sly hit at Richardson's claim to be a dramatic novelist. Thus Austen parodies Richardson's use of elaborate stage-directions: '*The Library at Colnebrook, a few minutes later. Curtain draws up and discovers* Miss Grandison *reading*.'[14] Austen's stage directions mockingly recall the way in which Richardson describes action, gesture and facial expression in his dramatic dialogues:

> SIR CHARLES: I have a letter of his to answer. He is very urgent with me for my interest with you. I am to answer it. Will you tell me, my sister (giving her the letter) what I shall say?
>
> MISS GRANDISON: [*after perusing it*] Why, ay, poor man! he is very much in love.[15]

Though she admired *Grandison*'s comedy of manners, Austen was irreverent about the exaggerated parts that she found comically absurd and highly artificial. One example is the incident when Harriet Byron's stomach is squeezed in a door by the villainous seducer Sir Hargrave Pollexfen. Austen dramatises the action and mocks Richardson's melodramatic dialogue, 'So so, you have killed me, I hope – Well, now I hope, now I hope you are satisfied.'[16] Austen also parodies Richardson's stagecraft in act one scene two of her play, where there are twelve hurried entrances and exits centred upon Harriet's abduction. In Richardson's novel, Pollexfen behaves in the manner of a stage villain, and in the space of one paragraph makes numerous entrances and exits. Here it was easy to turn drama into farce.[17] The parts of *Sir Charles Grandison* that Jane Austen least enjoyed were the excessive sentimental and melodramatic elements, such as the abduction of Harriet and the madness of Clementina. Austen was aware that Richardson's debt to the dramatic tradition was best expressed in his conversations and the 'battle of the sexes' combats in the drawing room and the cedar parlour.

Richardson's comic types are drawn from Restoration and eighteenth-century comedy. In particular, Charlotte Grandison (later to become the married Lady G.) derives from the witty, teasing heroines of stage comedy – Harriet in Etherege's *The Man of Mode*, Harriot in Steele's *The Funeral* and Lady Betty Modish in Cibber's *The Careless Husband*.[18] Above all, Charlotte resembles Congreve's Millamant in *The Way of the World*. Though her wit and raillery provoke censure from her brother, he confesses that he loves her '*With all your faults, my dear*, and I had almost said, *for* some of them'.[19] Sir Charles is surely alluding to Mirabell's description of Millamant: 'I like her with all her Faults; nay, like her for her Faults. Her Follies are so natural, so artful, that they become her; and those Affectations which in another Woman wou'd be odious, serve but to make her more agreeable.'[20] Mirabell's remarks are also echoed in Knightley's feelings about Emma, when he describes her as 'faultless, in spite of all her faults' (*E*, p. 433) and claims that he has always doted on her 'faults and all' (*E*, p. 462).[21]

Austen's burlesque of Harriet, who loses all her spirit and interest as soon as she falls in love, is thrown into relief by her evident admiration of Charlotte Grandison. Throughout Richardson's *Sir Charles Grandison*, few characters get the better of Charlotte, and she is usually the winner in the various wit combats which pervade the narrative. Charlotte dislikes the subordination of women in marriage and delights in her own independence. Even as she is led up to the altar she is overheard to say, very much in the manner of Millamant, 'You don't know what you are about, man. I expect to have all my way: Remember that's one of my articles before marriage.'[22] Unusually for the fiction of the time, Charlotte remains an unreformed coquette even after her marriage to her bashful and doting husband.

Austen demonstrates her awareness of Charlotte Grandison's stature as the real heroine of the novel, and simultaneously burlesques one of Richardson's duller characters, Mr Reeves, by reversing his character, and enabling her own Charlotte to confess that Mr Reeves 'disputes charmingly. I thought he would have got the better of me.' Later Austen has Miss Jervois satirically observe of Lord G., Charlotte's betrothed: 'he will certainly get the better of you at last. He did it once, you know.'[23] Austen's dramatisation of *Sir Charles Grandison*, and in particular her use of the burlesque tradition to highlight its artificial elements, was a way of exorcising the parts of the novel she liked least, of escaping from the excessive sentimentality and melodramatic elements of Richardson's narrative method. It liberated her to produce her own ironised version of the sentimental novel. But she discovered that the dramatic form was unable to give her the authorial control she required, and she was now to reject it. It is surely no coincidence that she was also doing something similar with the epistolary tradition, that quasi-dramatic form of narration of which Richardson had been the pioneer.

* * *

Around the same time as she put the finishing touches to her burlesque play of *Sir Charles Grandison*, Jane Austen was completing *Lady Susan*. This short epistolary novel was probably first drafted around 1794–95, but Austen seems to have carefully copied it out around 1805, when she also added an author's conclusion in the third person.

Lady Susan is Jane Austen's most ambitious early work. It is her only extant epistolary novel of substance, and it is here that she really began to explore the possibilities of the letter as a narrative form. *Lady Susan* reveals how Austen recast inherited conventions by means of ongoing experiments with narrative voice. It also shows how she was still strongly influenced by Richardson.

Lady Susan playfully reworks the structure of Richardson's great tragic novel, *Clarissa*. It reproduces the first part of Richardson's plot, where a daughter is imprisoned for her refusal to marry the man of her parents' choice. As Lovelace is the traditional rake (of both stage and page), so Lady Susan is the temptress, manipulating men by employing her personal charms; she is charming and witty, and morally corrupt. Lady Susan justifies her attempt to ensnare the young hero on two accounts: partly to amuse herself with the challenge of subduing an 'insolent spirit', and also to avenge herself on the Vernon family, whom she despises, 'to humble the Pride of these self-important Courcies still lower' (*MW*, p. 254). These are exactly the two reasons why Lovelace literally ensnares Clarissa: 'Then what a triumph would it be to the *Harlowe pride*, were I now to marry this lady?'; 'Why will she not *if once subdued* be *always subdued*.'[24]

Lady Susan was Austen's first novel to contrast the town and the country. Events that occur at the country house of the Vernons are set against those which occur in London. This device, which the novel absorbed from stage comedy, was used to fine effect in Richardson; Jane Austen used it again in *Sense and Sensibility* and *Mansfield Park*. Unlike Richardson, who is brilliant in the London scenes, Austen is at her finest when she is depicting events in the country. She recast inherited stage conventions by having the Londoners entering the country and causing trouble, rather than the ingenues entering London society, as was conventional both in stage comedy and the novels of Fanny Burney and Maria Edgeworth.

Lady Susan was an important transitional work. Unlike *Love and Freindship*, which merely parodied the novel-of-letters, this work is a serious trial of the epistolary form. In *Clarissa*, Richardson mastered and perfected the epistolary form. The same characters and events are seen and judged from a variety of viewpoints; different characters reveal how all actions are open to many layers of interpretation and potential distortion.

The double yet separate correspondence of *Lady Susan* echoes that of Clarissa and Anne Howe, Lovelace and Belford. The psychological richness of Lovelace's character is rendered by Richardson's complex interweaving of letters between the four correspondents, and his careful manipulation of point of view. Just as Richardson's letters permit us to enter into the mind of the villainous Lovelace, Austen allows us into the mind of the equally unscrupulous Lady Susan. Through the juxtaposition of Lady Susan's first two letters, the novelist establishes her heroine's villainous potential. The tone and content of Lady Susan's deferential opening letter is contrasted and highlighted by the sheer force of her stylishly defiant second epistle, with its insolent self-justification of her villainous conduct. Despite the fact that Austen damns her heroine, Lady Susan's rebelliousness and her lively epistolary style, reminiscent of Lovelace's, make her an appealing villain. But, unlike Richardson, Austen does not sufficiently develop counter-balancing epistolary voices.

Lady Susan reproduces the first part of the *Clarissa* plot, but considers it from a different perspective. Like Clarissa, Lady Susan's daughter Frederica is imprisoned. Though Frederica is not imprisoned in a brothel, nor drugged, raped and left alone to die, her fate is nevertheless a devious form of confinement orchestrated by her mother. Clarissa is defined by her letters and her freedom to write; even after her 'literal death' her posthumous letters confirm and sustain her existence in the life of the novel. By contrast Frederica is forced to suffer a diametrically opposed, but equally significant, form of confinement. Frederica's punishment for trying to escape from her mother is the ban on her freedom to speak. Frederica has no voice. Nor does Austen give her a pen, save for one brief letter. The young heroine is silenced. This causes a potential problem for Austen; since we have Clarissa's letters, we can judge Lovelace's villainy. Without Frederica's letters, and without the counter-balancing voice of a strong male character, there is a danger that Lady Susan will completely dominate the novel.

Austen tries to get round this problem by contrasting her heroine with another strong female character, the sagacious and perceptive Mrs Vernon. Letter 24 is crucial in this regard. Here Austen demonstrates her own 'command of language' (*MW*, p. 251) in a scene that anticipates the vigour and sophistication of her later dialogues. This is a brilliant set-piece. Like so many of her later set-pieces, it is an arresting confrontation between two women in conflict over a young man. This motif reappears in the confrontation between Elinor Dashwood and Lucy Steele in *Sense and Sensibility*, and Elizabeth Bennet and Lady Catherine De Bourgh in *Pride and Prejudice*.

The dispute is induced by Frederica's plea for help, the substance of her first and only letter. Austen establishes the tone of this dramatic confrontation by Lady Susan's exultant acknowledgement of her manipulative powers: 'Did not I tell you, said she with a smile, that your Brother would not leave us after all?' (*MW*, p. 287). Lady Susan is barely able to contain her derision at her daughter's guilelessness: 'had Frederica possessed the penetration, the abilities, which I could have wished in my daughter, or had I even known her to possess so much as she does, I should not have been anxious for the match' (*MW*, p. 288). Mrs Vernon's defence of Frederica is equally spirited: 'It is odd that you alone should be ignorant of your Daughter's sense' (*MW*, p. 288).

The dialogue is continued in this vein, with Lady Susan's tears, vindications and excuses contrasted with Mrs Vernon's brusque, impatient rejoinders. Austen's delivery of Lady Susan's animated utterances, with its affected tone of injured virtue, is beautifully controlled. Before Letter 24 we have heard much of Lady Susan's linguistic arts, but in this letter we see them fully in action:

> Can you possibly suppose that I was aware of her unhappiness? that it was my object to make my own child miserable, & that I had forbidden her speaking to you on the subject, from a fear of your interrupting the Diabolical scheme? Do you think me destitute of every honest, every natural feeling? Am I capable of consigning *her* to everlasting Misery, whose welfare it is my first Earthly Duty to promote? (*MW*, p. 289)

Through the dramatic force of this confrontation, Austen blurs the distinction between reported and immediate action. Following Richardson's model, Austen punctuates her speeches with added commentary, almost like stage directions: 'here she began to cry', 'with a smile', 'taking me by the hand'. Mrs Vernon's interjections are used to draw attention to Lady Susan's theatrical skills and they also reveal one of the strengths of the epistolary form. The letter simultaneously allows for the correspondent's retrospective viewpoint of the action, while providing immediate access to the character's writing 'of the moment'. Austen's device of switching between direct and reported speech also enables the flow of the heated exchange to gain full momentum. In response to Lady Susan's impassioned pleas and theatrical gestures, Mrs Vernon's reply is uncompromisingly brusque: 'The idea is horrible. What then was your intention when you insisted on her silence?' (*MW*, p. 289).

Mrs Vernon's resistance is, however, short-lived, and she is finally defeated by the sheer intellectual vigour of Lady Susan. That the day is the latter's is suggested in Lady Susan's closing barb: 'Excuse me, my dearest Sister, for thus trespassing on your time, but I owed it to my own Character; & after this explanation I trust I am in no danger of sinking in your opinion' (*MW*, p. 290).

Stunned by this final example of her opponent's effrontery, Mrs Vernon, like all Lady Susan's enemies (including her own daughter), is reduced to silence: 'It was the greatest stretch of Forbearance I could practise. I could not have stopped myself, had I begun' (*MW*, p. 291). Lady Susan's following letter rejoices over this major victory: 'I call on you my dear Alicia, for congratulations. I am again myself; gay and triumphant' (*MW*, p. 291).

Following the defeat of Mrs Vernon, the pace of the novel increases with a series of short letters, which serve to wind up the plot. Like Lovelace, Lady Susan wreaks revenge on all who have crossed her, and her favourite place to execute her plans is London. Richardson and Burney both made London the immoral centre of corrupt society. Lovelace's plot is chiefly dependent upon the lax morals of the prostitutes in the London brothel, and he insists that his intrigues can only work in a place that has the anonymity of the capital. Similarly, Lady Susan adores the bustle and intrigue of the town, 'for London will be always the fairest field of action' (*MW*, p. 294).

Austen devotes little space to the events in London, and swiftly moves to the denouement of plot, the exposition of Lady Susan's continuing affair with Manwaring, and its subsequent disclosure. The ensuing self-revelatory letters reveal the depths of Lady Susan's villainy. This is the weakest part of the novel; Austen seems impatient to wind up the plot. She abandons the letters and rounds off the ending with an author's summary, a cursory account of the fate of the main characters in a distinctive third-person narratorial voice that makes fun of the epistolary device that she has been used hitherto. Seemingly frustrated with a villain who has got out of hand, Jane Austen assumes a studied indifference to the fate of her essentially unsympathetic supporting cast. The novel ends rather predictably with the promise of Frederica's and Reginald's marriage, but by now the author doesn't really care: 'Frederica was therefore fixed in the family of her Uncle & Aunt, till such time as Reginald De Courcy could be talked, flattered & finessed into an affection for her … Three months might have done it in general, but Reginald's feelings were no less lasting than lively' (*MW*, p. 313).

Austen's conclusion also represents a light-hearted attack on the epistolary style: 'This Correspondence … could not, to the great detriment of the Post office Revenue, be continued longer' (*MW*, p. 311). The breakdown of the epistolary form is the price that Jane Austen has to pay for Lady Susan's domination of the narrative. In the absence of strong balancing forces, and with the silencing of Frederica and the defeat of Mrs Vernon in Letter 24, the epistolary form cannot provide Austen with a sufficiently powerful means of being both inside and outside her protagonist.

Far from guiding our moral responses, the brisk conclusion leaves readers to decide for themselves if the characters' fates are justified. Lady Susan marries the rich fop Sir James and we assume gets what she deserves: 'The world must judge from Probability. She had nothing against her, but her Husband, & her Conscience.' The author's own sympathy is devoted to one of her minor characters who loses her lover to Lady Susan: 'For myself, I confess that *I* can pity only Miss Manwaring, who coming to Town & putting herself to an expense in Cloathes, which impoverished her for two years, on purpose to secure him, was defrauded of her due by a Woman ten years older than herself' (*MW*, p. 313). And on that tantalising jibe, the novel ends, somewhat unsatisfactorily in its own terms, but leaving us eager to hear more of that ironically detached *I*.

Austen's rejection of Richardson, through her burlesque play 'Grandison' and through *Lady Susan*, was a casting aside of both epistolary and dramatic form. Neither of these were suitable mediums for her desire to be simultaneously inside and outside her characters, something which she eventually achieved by her use of irony and free indirect speech in third-person narration. Though *Lady Susan* was a serious experiment in epistolary narrative, Austen rejected it precisely because the epistolary technique is itself 'dramatic'; it formally banishes the authorial voice, though the 'author' or 'editor' is still implicit as the coordinator of juxtapositions, sequences, contrasting tones and parallelisms. Richardson's effacement of the authorial voice through the epistolary was clearly uncongenial to the mature Austen.

Austen also rejected the epistolary form's claim to be able to create the illusion of 'writing to the moment'. Lovelace's own phrase, 'I love to write to the moment',[25] suggests that the events are happening in the present tense, giving the reader a sense of the story's immediacy. The characters are always in the middle of their own experience, a feature which Fielding had been quick to satirise in *Shamela*: 'You see I write in the present Tense'.[26] Austen engaged in a similar parody in her juvenilia, notably in a story called 'Amelia Webster' (*MW*, pp. 47–49).

Anna Barbauld, in the introduction to her 1804 edition of Richardson's correspondence, described what she considered to be the differences between conventional methods of novelistic narration and the inherent drama of the epistolary method:

This method unites, in good measure, the advantages of the other two; [the 'narrative' or 'epic' found for example in Cervantes and Fielding, and the 'memoir' found in Smollett and Goldsmith] it gives the feelings of the moment. It allows a pleasing variety of stile, if the author has sufficient command of the pen to assume it. It makes the whole work dramatic, since all the characters speak in their own persons.[27]

While writing *Sir Charles Grandison*, Richardson described to his friend, Lady Bradshaigh, the paradoxes of his narrative method in which the author's presence is banished and yet can simultaneously be identified with any one of the characters:

> Here I sit down to form characters. One I intend to be all goodness; All goodness he is. Another I intend to be all gravity; All gravity he is. Another *Lady G* – ish; All *Lady G* – ish she is. I am all the while absorbed in the character. It is not fair to say – I, identically I, am anywhere, while I keep within the character.[28]

This dramatic projection allows him to enter into the points of view of all of his characters; there is no single reliable authorial voice.

In her mature works Jane Austen used free indirect speech to achieve an even more sophisticated effect: she writes from both within and without her characters. Free indirect speech is the device whereby a novelist writes from the point of view of an individual character, but retains the distance provided by third-person narrative. Austen uses this technique most fully in *Emma*: 'The hair was curled, and the maid sent away, and Emma sat down to think and be miserable. – It was a wretched business, indeed! – Such an overthrow of every thing she had been wishing for ... Such a blow for Harriet! – that was the worst of all' (*E*, p. 134). The first sentence appears to belong to the voice of the author, but as the passage continues, we seem to be given a verbalisation of the heroine's own thoughts.

It is for this reason that film and television adaptations – brilliantly as they may render the surface of Jane Austen's comic world – can never fully satisfy the serious reader of the novels themselves. Screenwriters find it almost impossible to render the ironic third-person authorial voice that is so important to Austen's narrative method.[29] Important as the drama was to the making of her fictional worlds, Austen was in the end a novelist.

Whereas dramatic dialogue and epistolary form render the *words* of the characters, free indirect discourse renders their *thoughts* – and, since it does so in the third person rather than the first, the author is able to be simultaneously inside and outside the consciousness of the character, to be both engaged and ironic. This technique is unique to the novel, but Austen only fully developed it after having experimented with dramatic and epistolary forms. In direct opposition to the Richardsonian imperative, she discovered that she favoured the authorial voice, the voice that we hear at the end of *Lady Susan*. By adding her author's conclusion to *Lady Susan*, Austen bid farewell to the epistolary form. It seems to have been after this that she reworked the epistolary 'Elinor and Marianne' into the third-person *Sense and Sensibility*.

Richardson remained, nevertheless, an important influence on Austen's narrative art. His pioneering use of dramatic-style dialogue was crucial to her development, and she assimilated both epistolary and quasi-theatrical techniques into her mature novels. Austen had parodied Richardson in her juvenilia and in 'Grandison', and in *Lady Susan* she had paid tribute to the epistolary tradition, before transcending her favourite writer. Paradoxically, the writer whose narrative style she now turned to was Richardson's great opponent, Henry Fielding, who pioneered the successful integration of quasi-theatrical techniques with third-person narration.

While she learned much from Richardson's mastery of revelation of character through dialogue, she also learned from Fielding. It is an irony that Richardson was singled out for his dramatic powers and imagination, while the playwright-turned-novelist Fielding was characterised by his obtrusive authorial presence, and his distrust of the epistolary form.

Fielding's metamorphosis into a novelist provided a powerful model for Austen. He began by burlesquing the epistolary tradition and highlighting its weaknesses and artificiality in *Shamela*, then developed a sophisticated third-person narratorial voice in *Joseph Andrews*. Austen not only shared his love of burlesque, but, like him, also successfully made the transition from burlesque to high comedy and from epistolary to third-person narration. Yet even as they rejected the drama, each of them retained a wealth of quasi-theatrical devices in their plotting, characterisation, dialogue, use of set-pieces and formal tableaux, coincidences, wit-combats and cross-purposes.[30] In direct opposition to Richardson's epistolary style, which they both parodied, Fielding and Austen favoured authorial mediation and a controlling intelligence. The stylisation wrought by theatrical techniques within the non-theatrical form of the novel highlighted the workings of that intelligence.

A comparable case is that of Elizabeth Inchbald, who, like Fielding, was a playwright turned novelist. Her highly acclaimed first novel, *A Simple Story*, was loosely based on Shakespeare's *Winter's Tale*. Austen knew Inchbald's adaptation of *Lovers' Vows*, which she used in *Mansfield Park*. She also perhaps alludes to Inchbald's controversial novel in *Emma*, where Mr Knightley describes the news of Harriet's engagement to Robert Martin as a 'simple story' (*E*, p. 471).

Inchbald's interpolation of dramatic detail into the novel, the product of her long experience as both a dramatist and an actress, was highly praised by her contemporaries. Like Fielding, she found new opportunities in her move from theatrical to narrative writing. An emphasis on direct speech and telling gesture was used to achieve dramatic revelation of character. The *Monthly Review* noted: 'The secret charm, that gives a grace to the whole is the art with which Mrs Inchbald has made her work dramatic. The business is, in a great degree, carried on in dialogue. In dialogue the characters unfold themselves. Their motions, their looks, their attitudes, discover the inward temper.'[31]

With the minimum of authorial intervention, Inchbald promised to let her heroine reveal herself: 'And now – leaving description – the reader must form a judgment of her by her actions; by all the round of great or trivial circumstances that shall be related.'[32] In her lively and irreverent dialogue, the heroine Miss Milner is indebted to the witty stage heroines of Restoration and eighteenth-century comedy. From her first exchange with the austere guardian/priest Dorriforth, she shows herself capable of forthright charm and candour: 'in some respects I am like you Roman Catholics; I don't believe from my own understanding, but from what other people tell me.'[33] In contrast, Dorriforth's repressed nature is conveyed in the stilted and wooden tones by which he endeavours to conceal his passion for his vivacious ward.

Inchbald's theatrical training is evident in the numerous reversals and parallels of incident and characterisation and the tightly-structured comedy of misunderstandings and misreadings between her intimate group of characters. Dorriforth ascribes Miss Milner's blushes to excessive modesty, but her embarrassment betrays something other than maidenly virtue:

> 'How can I doubt of a lady's virtue, when her countenance gives such evident proofs of them? Believe me, Miss Milner, that in the midst of your gayest follies; while you thus continue to blush, I shall reverence your internal sensations.'
>
> 'Oh! my lord, did you know some of them, I am afraid you would think them unpardonable.'[34]

The characters not only misunderstand each other, they also often dwell in ignorance of their own feelings. It is only Dorriforth's jealousy of a rival lover that forces him to acknowledge his illicit love for his ward.

Inchbald's art of dramatic presentation is further revealed in her deployment of comic parallels and contrasts to the main action. A comic device that she uses to great effect in *A Simple Story* is that of showing a series of reactions to the same incident. When Dorriforth's confessor, Sandford, tells the ladies that Dorriforth is to fight a duel over Miss Milner, they respond in a variety of ways:

> Mrs Horton exclaimed, 'If Mr Dorriforth dies, he dies a martyr'.
>
> Miss Woodley cried with fervour, 'Heaven forbid!'
>
> Miss Fenton cried, 'Dear me!'
>
> While Miss Milner, without uttering one word, sunk speechless on the floor.[35]

The dramatic detail that was absorbed into her novel elicited high praise from Maria Edgeworth: 'I am of the opinion that it is by leaving more than most other writers to the imagination, that you succeed so eminently in affecting it. By the force that is necessary to repress feeling, we judge of the intensity of the feeling; and you always contrive to give us by intelligible but simple signs the measure of this force.'[36] Edgeworth's remarks provide an important insight into Inchbald's technical innovation in narrative writing: the power of 'intelligible but simple signs'. Actions in *A Simple Story* often render dialogue or authorial elaboration unnecessary. The movement of a knife and fork in Miss Milner's hand, a mistake made while playing cards, or thrusting her head outside the window to cool her flushed face: all convey the strongest emotion beneath the exterior.[37]

Jane Austen's comparable interest in different reactions to the same incident, and the depiction of strong emotion beneath the surface of polite conduct, is evident in her first published novel, *Sense and Sensibility*. Signs or actions, as when a character rolls a paper or cuts with scissors, are used to suggest emotional turmoil within, very much in the manner of an actor's use of props and gestures on stage.

Fielding and Inchbald metamorphosed themselves from playwrights into novelists, and in so doing introduced theatrical effects into the novel. Austen correspondingly abandoned the dramatic and epistolary forms because they lacked a controlling narratorial voice. By adopting the best parts of Richardson's comedy of manners and the quasi-theatrical innovations of Fielding and Inchbald, she achieved a synthesis that enabled her to find her own unique novelistic voice.

6

Sense and Sensibility

Sense and Sensibility, Jane Austen's first published novel, is usually read in the context of the tradition of the sentimental novel, as *Northanger Abbey* is read in the context of the Gothic novel. But for Austen, the figure of the giddy female reader who falls into misadventures as a result of wishing to be like the sentimental heroines of fiction does not only derive from the novel form itself. There are other exemplars – and they offer further, hitherto neglected, evidence of the importance for her of the theatrical tradition.

In *Love and Freindship*, Austen had satirised sensibility and its harmful effect on the minds of young lovers who imbibe distorted romantic notions from the pages of sentimental novels. Like Henry Austen's burlesque heroine in *The Loiterer*, Austen's sentimental heroines, Laura and Sophia, are influenced by Goethe's *The Sorrows of Young Werther*. Literary parody associated with the harmful effects of reading on the young naive mind is to be found among the papers of the *Spectator* and in novels such as Charlotte Lennox's *The Female Quixote* (1752). Yet the key tradition in this respect was that of the theatre, where since 1705 there had been a comic paradigm of the giddy novel reader. Versions of this figure re-emerged in plays throughout the century. She was usually female, and she was often portrayed as mad or, at the very least, misguided and foolish.

In the late eighteenth century the epitome of the misguided reader of romantic novels was Lydia Languish in *The Rivals* (1775). Sheridan's brilliant portrayal of sentimental delusion made Lydia a household name, and helped to perpetuate the idea that novels were an inferior form of fiction, producing harmful effects on the minds of their undiscerning readers:

Here, my dear Lucy, hide these books. – Quick, quick. – Fling *Peregrine Pickle* under the toilet – throw *Roderick Random* into the closet – put *the Innocent Adultery* into *The Whole Duty of Man* – thrust *Lord Aimworth* under the sopha – cram *Ovid* behind the bolster – there – put *the Man of Feeling* into your pocket – so, so, now lay *Mrs Chapone* in sight, and leave *Fordyce's Sermons* open on the table.[1]

Sheridan's burlesque of the reader of the sentimental novel follows on from a tradition of quixotic stage heroines such as Richard Steele's Miss Biddy in *The Tender Husband* (1705) and George Colman the Elder's *Polly Honeycombe* (1760).[2]

Austen clearly knew *The Tender Husband*, as she alludes to Miss Biddy in *Love and Freindship*:

She was a Widow & had only one Daughter, who was then just Seventeen – One of the best of ages; but alas! she was very plain & her name was Bridget ... Nothing therefore could be expected from her – she could not be supposed to possess either exalted Ideas, Delicate Feelings or refined Sensibilities – She was nothing more than a mere good tempered, civil & obliging Young Woman; as such we could scarcely dislike her – she was only an Object of Contempt (*MW*, pp. 100–1).

Steele's Bridget objects to her own name: 'How often must I desire you, Madam, to lay aside that familiar name, Cousin *Biddy*? I never heard of it without Blushing – did you ever meet with an Heroine in those Idle romances as you call 'em, that was term'd *Biddy*?'[3]

The literary tradition of the female quixotic was popularised by Charlotte Lennox's novel, though her heroine Arabella was in fact based on Steele's Biddy Tipkin. When Polly Honeycombe condemns her loathed suitor she likens him to fictional characters from the novels she reads, 'you are as deceitful as Blifil, as rude as the Harlowes, and as ugly as Doctor Slop',[4] and is met with the same incredulous reaction as that of Lennox's lovely but absurd heroine, whose head has been turned by reading novels.[5] In *The Rivals*, Sir Anthony Absolute cries, 'the girl's mad! – her brain's turn'd by reading'.[6] If Lydia Languish and Polly Honeycombe should be viewed in the light of Lennox's heroine, attention should also be paid to Steele's earlier model from which it is more likely that they derive.

The final speech of Polly's exasperated father is a warning to fathers that 'a man might as well turn his Daughter loose in Covent garden, as trust the cultivation of her mind to a circulating library'. In *The Rivals*, Sir Anthony Absolute continues the tradition of fathers fulminating against the evils of the circulating library. Both Sir Anthony Absolute and Mr Honeycombe single out young girls as the targets for the circulating library, as did many other eighteenth-century critics.

Historically speaking, however, the flighty novel-reader was as likely to be male as female.[7] Certainly Jane Austen took this view from the beginning of her writing career to the end. In *Love and Freindship* it is Edward who is directly accused of gleaning absurd notions from reading novels, and in *Sanditon* Sir Edward Denham is a quixotic figure ludicrously enthralled by sensational novels and determined to be 'a dangerous man, quite in the line of the Lovelaces' (*MW*, p. 405). Willoughby loves 'all the same novels' as Marianne and has the same respectful, if detached, admiration for Pope, 'no more than what is proper'. Henry Tilney claims to have 'hundreds and hundreds' of novels and teasingly defends his rights as a male reader of novels, 'for they read nearly as many as women' (*NA*, p. 107).

Austen's fullest attempt at drawing her own giddy quixotic heroine, and avid reader of sensational fiction, Catherine Morland, paradoxically reveals a surprising doubleness, where the novel-reading heroine, contrary to expectation, *does* in fact learn about life from books.[8] Austen's defence of the novel in chapter 5 of *Northanger Abbey* is compounded by Catherine's epiphany at the end of the novel: 'Catherine, at any rate, heard enough to feel, that in suspecting General Tilney of either murdering or shutting up his wife, she had scarcely sinned against his character, or magnified his cruelty' (*NA*, p. 201).

Nor does Austen conform to the view that circulating libraries were the repositories of pap. She used circulating libraries and in 1798 commented on the opening of a subscription library which she intended to join: 'As an inducement to subscribe Mrs Martin tells us that her collection is not to consist only of Novels, but of every kind of Literature &c &c – She might have spared this pretension to *our* family, who are great Novel-readers & not ashamed of being so' (*Letters*, p. 26). One of Fanny Price's compensations for being exiled from Mansfield is the discovery of the joys of Portsmouth's circulating library.

The idea that giddy readers of fiction were not necessarily female is borne out by the practice of both the great comic dramatist and the great comic novelist of the period: as will be shown, both Richard Brinsley Sheridan and Jane Austen reveal that men as well as women are susceptible to absurd and self-destructive sentimentalism. Both writers burlesqued literary sentimentalism and its hackneyed features that arose in the genres of both fiction and drama, often interchangeably.[9] Austen and Sheridan's shared sense of literary parody has already been discussed. Here I want to suggest that the debate about the giddy female reader is but one aspect of a much more profound link between *The Rivals* and *Sense and Sensibility*. This connection is a paradigm for Austen's reworking of theatrical techniques from eighteenth-century dramatic models.

In *The Rivals*, Sheridan exploits the quasi-farcical device of mistaken identity in the character of Jack Absolute, who disguises himself as the penniless Ensign Beverley so that his lover can marry beneath her. *The Rivals* has two contrasting heroines: one sensible and level-headed (Julia Melville); the other excessively romantic and filled with quixotic notions (Lydia Languish). The amorous entanglement of Lydia and Jack is paralleled by that of Julia and Faulkland.

By this principle of pairings Sheridan is able to provide contrasts and comparisons between his two female characters, as well as the male. The sensible Julia acts as a foil to the captious sentimentalist, Faulkland, as Lydia's sensibility is mocked by Absolute. But Julia also acts as a foil to Lydia's romantic attitudes, as Jack censures Faulkland's self-destructive impulses. The contrasts and conflicts arising from clashes between romantic idealism and prudent conservatism provide the comic dynamic of Sheridan's satire.

Lydia's quixotic notions threaten her own happiness. She invents a quarrel with Jack Absolute by writing a letter to herself, defaming his character, and is grievously disappointed to be denied a Gretna Green elopement. The association of the name Lydia with elopement is, of course, echoed in *Pride and Prejudice*, where the foolish Lydia writes to

Mrs Forster of her hopes of eloping to Gretna Green.[10] Both Lydia Bennet and Lydia Languish are denied the full romance of illicit love:

> LYDIA: There had I projected one of the most sentimental elopements!
> – so becoming a disguise! – so amiable a ladder of Ropes! –
> Conscious Moon – four horses – Scotch parson – with such
> surprize to Mrs Malaprop – and such paragraphs in the
> Newspapers! – O, I shall die with disappointment.
> JULIA: I don't wonder at it! …
> LYDIA: How mortifying, to remember the dear delicious shifts I used
> to be put to, to gain half a minute's conversation with this fellow! –
> How often have I stole forth, in the coldest night in January, and
> found him in the garden, stuck like a dripping statue! – There
> would he kneel to me in the snow, and sneeze and cough so
> pathetically! he shivering with cold, and I with apprehension! and
> while the freezing blast numb'd our joints, how warmly would he
> press me to pity his flame, and glow with mutual ardour! – Ah,
> Julia! that was something like being in love.
> JULIA: If I were in spirits, Lydia, I should chide you only by laughing
> heartily at you.[11]

Julia's level-headed response to her friend's misplaced misery throws into relief the comic absurdity of Sheridan's sentimental heroine. Furthermore, Julia is paralleled with Jack, for both characters needlessly suffer at the hands of their incorrigible lovers. The sympathy between them is suggested by Julia's heartfelt rebuke of Lydia's affectation: 'I entreat you, not to let a man, who loves you with sincerity, suffer that unhappiness from *caprice*, which I know too well caprice can inflict.' Lydia's response confirms the parallelism of character: 'What does Julia tax me with caprice? – I thought her lover Faulkland had enured her to it.'[12]

Absolute is frustrated by Lydia's 'dev'lish romantic, and very absurd' notions, and Julia is wearied by Faulkland's self-tormenting impulses. But as Julia criticises Lydia, Absolute censures Faulkland:

FAUKLAND: Now, Jack, as you are my friend, own honestly – don't you think there is something forward – something indelicate in this haste to forgive? …

ABSOLUTE: I have not patience to listen to you: – thou'rt incorrigible! … a captious sceptic in love, – a slave to fretfulness and whim – who has no difficulties but of *his own* creating – is a subject more fit for ridicule than compassion.[13]

The first critics of *The Rivals* do not seem to have shared Absolute's exasperation with his friend, but on the contrary took Faulkland as a model of delicacy and refined sensibility.[14] Furthermore they felt that Lydia's romantic notions would be best suited to Faulkland's neurotic musings, although this would reduce the comedy arising from the contrasts between the lovers and their counterparts.[15]

The Rivals employs a series of commonsense, sceptical figures who provide an ironic contrast with the sentimental characters, and who directly challenge their pretensions. Sheridan levels his critique at sentimentalism by contrasting sensible and rational figures with their opposites, who not only stand in direct contrast to their more foolish counterparts but openly avow their disapproval of them. This principle of pairings defines his comic effect. By doubling up the romantic leads, Sheridan fully exploits the contrasts between the two female friends and the two males, as well as those between the pairs of lovers.

The Rivals was an important influence on Jane Austen's exploration of sensibility in her first published novel. Critics who have sought literary antecedents in Austen's use of 'sense' and 'sensibility' characters as foils to one another have neglected the influence of stage models.[16] *The Rivals* was the most celebrated example of the 'sense' and 'sensibility' opposition in comic stage heroines, though other playwrights had explored the comic potential of antithetical characters. This tradition of contrasting foils is prevalent in the dramatic tradition. In *The Funeral: or Grief à-la-Mode* (1701), Richard Steele dramatised two sisters of contrasting characters, Harriot and Sharlot. The coquettish and giddy Harriot is contrasted with the graver Sharlot. In Cibber's *The Careless Husband* (1704), the coquettish Lady Betty Modish is contrasted with her virtuous friend Lady Easy. And in Hugh Kelly's *False Delicacy* (1768), another play satirising excessive sensibility, the sentimental heroine Lady Betty is contrasted with the commonsensical Mrs Harley. When Lady Betty's personal happiness with Lord Winworth is compromised by her belief in the 'laws of delicacy' (one element being that 'a woman of real delicacy shou'd never admit a second impression on her heart'), she is roundly scolded by her friend Mrs Harley:

> What a work there is with you sentimental folks ... thank heaven my sentiments are not sufficiently refin'd to make me unhappy ... the devil take this delicacy; I don't know any thing it does besides making people miserable.[17]

Kelly's comedy, like *Sense and Sensibility*, shows that sustained mockery of sensibility may coexist with a strong sympathy for it.[18] Although there is no direct evidence that Austen knew the play, she certainly knew *The Rivals*, which, like Kelly's play, dramatises a giddy and a wise female duo.

Austen's principle of pairings is the structural base of *Sense and Sensibility*, and is developed in the contrasting and comparable characters of the two heroines. An antithetical position of representing one sister with sense, Elinor, and the other sister with sensibility, Marianne, is set up, only to be subsequently undermined. So much so that by the end of the novel it is the sensible sister who makes a romantic marriage, and the romantic sister who makes a sensible marriage. Like *False Delicacy*, Austen's satire of sensibility is less straightforward than it appears. The book is consciously structured around a series of ironic oppositions, which work to deflate fixed notions. Having two heroines allows the author's sympathy to be balanced between them as they are played off against one another.

The rationalism of Julia and Jack in *The Rivals*, which actively condemns sensibility, is reworked in *Sense and Sensibility*, where Elinor's dry responses to Marianne's impassioned outbursts often, though not always, prick the bubble of her excessive sensibility. In *The Rivals*, Julia Melville is amused and exasperated by her friend's distorted notions of romance, and provides a dramatic foil to Lydia's romantic notions. In *Sense and Sensibility*, Austen also uses contrasts and parallels between two seemingly different heroines to attack excessive sensibility. One of Marianne's most impassioned outbursts about falling autumnal leaves is dryly condemned by Elinor, 'It is not everyone who has your passion for dead leaves' (SS, p. 88). Julia Melville's genuine pain is keenly dramatised, whereas Lydia's pain is satirised because it is chiefly of her own making. Similarly, we feel limited sympathy for Faulkland's self-destructive impulses. In Sense and Sensibility, Elinor's internal suffering is keenly dramatised, while Marianne's is often satirised, largely because it is of her own creation: 'Marianne would have thought herself very inexcusable had she been able to sleep at all the first night after parting from Willoughby ... Her sensibility was potent enough' (SS, p. 83).

In The Rivals, Sheridan's principle of pairings allows him to exploit the comic possibilities that arise from the conflicts between reason and feeling, sense and sensibility. But we are meant to distinguish between Faulkland's problems of temperament and Lydia's quixotic errors. The quixotic figure is clearly to be considered differently to the melancholic figure, deriving from one of the most influential of all sentimental novels, Goethe's The Sorrows of Young Werther.

Though Faulkland's expectation of female decorum in courtship is derived from his distorted sentimental notions, the implication seems to be that they are imbibed not necessarily from romantic fiction, but from the effects of a melancholic, neurotic nature. After expecting that he is to be rejected by Julia, he is only more distressed to find that he has been forgiven; forgiveness does not accord with his preconceived notion that a lover must be made to suffer. 'Don't you think there is something forward – something indelicate in this haste to forgive? Women should never sue for reconciliation.'[19]

It is therefore striking that Faulkland puts Lydia's flaw down to 'the errors of an ill-directed imagination', while his own he describes as a problem of temperament and the effects of 'an unhappy temper'.[20] This perhaps makes Faulkland a closer model for Marianne Dashwood in Sense and Sensibility, and Benwick in Persuasion, whose melancholic temperaments are partly instrumental in their own misery. In Northanger Abbey, the quixotic Catherine Morland is famously reproached by Henry Tilney for the liberty of her imagination (NA, p. 199), but her danger to herself is not life-threatening.

Marianne Dashwood's romantic ideas, like those of Lydia Languish, are derived from the books that she reads. Jane Austen gains much comic mileage from her young heroine's faith in her own originality, although, ironically, her conduct places her as a rather conventional comic type. Both Lydia and Marianne are slavishly following the dictates of romantic novels where economic realities are disregarded. Lydia insists on marrying a penniless ensign and Marianne wonders 'What have wealth or grandeur to do with happiness?' (*SS*, p. 91). Her romantic sentiments are contrasted with her sister's more practical considerations, yet as Elinor paradoxically suggests, 'we may come to the same point. *Your* competence and *my* wealth are very much alike'. Ironically, Marianne's 'competence' of two thousand a year is greater than Elinor's 'wealth' of one thousand. This is an example of how the same thing or idea (wealth or competence) can be seen or be represented from two diametrically opposed and yet similar angles. This surprising doubleness becomes a main feature of the novel's dynamic.

In this conversation Austen is still drawing out the contrasts between her two heroines. Initially, she appears to be making broad antithetical judgements between the sisters. *Sense and Sensibility* is a deliberately undemanding title (each sister implicitly representing the antithetical position), suggesting a fairly primitive schematisation. But the novel subsequently proceeds to undermine this expectation. Both sisters have sense and sensibility, though in different proportions.

In the main plot a very similar situation of courtship is set up between the two sisters, and between the men that they are in love with, in order to invite parallels, contrasts and ironic reversals. Towards the end of volume one, Austen draws a structural parallel where both Willoughby and Edward have left Barton with no adequate explanation, nor any promise of return. In contrast to the conduct of her sister, Elinor 'does not adopt the method so judiciously employed by Marianne, on a similar occasion, to augment and fix her sorrow, by seeking silence, solitude and idleness' (*SS*, p. 104). Elinor's cheery selflessness spares her mother and sisters 'much solicitude on her account'. Nevertheless, she suffers quite considerably throughout much of the novel, especially as she is forced to endure Lucy Steele's spiteful taunting. Marianne's 'method' of coping with a broken heart is, of course, selfish and indulgent, and she sees nothing to be recommended in Elinor's self-control. For Marianne, bouts of hysterics, tears and melancholy are the legitimate response to thwarted love, and she equates Elinor's silent grief with an absence of 'strong affections'.

Jane Austen satirises the bullying egotism that is implicit in Marianne's excessive sensibility: 'She expected from other people the same opinions and feelings as her own, and she judged of their motives by the immediate effect of their actions on herself' (SS, p. 202). Didactic expectations are, however, confounded by the similarities between the sisters. Marianne's romantic notions are frequently punctured by Austen, who uses Elinor to expose her sister's contradictory views and lack of self-knowledge, just as Sheridan uses Julia Melville to counterbalance Lydia. But the irony is also pitted against Elinor, who is frequently mistaken and misguided in her notions. The irony is directed at both heroines and both types of conduct: 'Their means were as different as their objects, and equally suited to the advancement of each' (SS, p. 104).

At the end of volume two, in another structural parallel, both heroines prepare to leave London for home, having been jilted by their lovers, who are now engaged to other women. Marianne herself shows her awareness of the similarities of their positions when she shrewdly remarks that they are both behaving in a curiously similar and yet diametrically opposed way: 'We have neither of us anything to tell; you, because you communicate, and I, because I conceal nothing' (SS, p. 170).

Austen begins by satirising Marianne's sensibility but later moves to an imaginative imposition that is clearly on her side. Though Marianne is initially presented as a quixotic heroine, her genuine sensibility is never in doubt. Marianne is a far more vulnerable figure than Lydia Languish, whose conduct often borders on the absurd. Lydia's lack of intellectual curiosity is not to be compared with Marianne's inquiring mind. We cannot imagine Lydia reading Thomson's The Seasons, one of Marianne's favourites. Austen early on hints that Marianne's sensibility is a problem of temperament when Elinor perceptively comments that, though her sister is 'earnest' and 'very eager', she is 'not often really merry' (SS, p. 93).

Marianne's melancholy and intensity of feeling, like Faulkland's, add to her own misery. Even after her 'rupture' with Willoughby, Marianne blames herself, and seems bent on a similar course of excessive and obsessive self-destruction when she plans to spend her life in solitary study. Like Faulkland's, Marianne's sensibility can be seen as absurd and self-destructive, but its authenticity is not doubted. If there is any doubt of this, Austen contrasts Marianne's genuine sensibility with the false sensibility of the Steele sisters.

Austen's principle of pairings, as the structural base of *Sense and Sensibility*, allows her to mirror complex comparisons and contrasts between character and behaviour. Her principle of pairings makes the issue more complicated than one person being right and the other wrong. Not only does Austen draw upon comparisons and contrasts between the two Dashwood sisters, but by bringing in two other pairs of sisters who reflect upon our view of Marianne and Elinor, she further complicates the picture. Her principle of pairings is not confined to two heroines as in *The Rivals*, but is developed in two other pairs of sisters, the Jennings sisters (now Lady Middleton and Mrs Palmer) and the Steele sisters.

The discussion about the picturesque with Edward Ferrars allows Austen to draw further parallels between the sisters. Moreover, the arrival of Mr Palmer and the two Jennings sisters offers yet another perspective upon Edward and the Dashwood sisters. Austen juxtaposes the scenes one after another for comic effect, but also to suggest more serious alternative readings of Elinor and Marianne. Lady Middleton's elegance and coldness are contrasted unfavourably to her sister's 'prepossessing manners', her warmth and friendliness and lack of ceremony, which again encourage us to draw contrasts between Elinor and Marianne as sisters and as individuals. The controlled and coldly elegant Lady Middleton could be viewed as a more extreme version of Elinor, and Mrs Palmer, with her prettiness and warmth, as a crude version of Marianne. Mrs Palmer's claims to have almost married Brandon confirm this parallel.

Anne and Lucy Steele are introduced to provide yet another perspective on Elinor and Marianne. As with the Dashwoods, the Steeles are without financial means and are in need of the social patronage of the Middletons. The chief differences are initially summed up in the Dashwoods' refusal to ingratiate themselves into the Middletons' society;

it is always Sir John who presses the girls to accept his invitations. While the Dashwoods refuse to engage in sycophantic behaviour towards the Middletons, the Steeles have the 'good sense to make themselves agreeable' to the lady of the house through courting her odious, and very spoilt, children. This kind of 'sense' is shown in an unfavourable light by the Dashwood sisters, who refuse to pay any attention to the children. This is not lost on the shrewd Lucy Steele, who remarks on their indifference:

'I have a notion', said Lucy, 'you think the little Middletons rather too much indulged ... I love to see children full of life and spirits; I cannot bear them if they are tame and quiet'.

'I confess', replied Elinor, 'that while I am at Barton Park, I never think of tame and quiet children with any abhorrence.' (SS, pp. 122–23)

Elinor deflates yet another convention of sensibility: the idealisation of childhood innocence. One of the plays chosen by the Austen women for the family theatricals in 1805 was the popular farce *The Spoilt Child*, which dramatised the cunning and naughty conduct of a small child.[21]

Austen's principle of pairings is also developed in the contrasting characters of Brandon and Willoughby. They are even summed up like characters in a drama by the costumes they wear. Willoughby is first seen in his hunting clothes, which, to the smitten Marianne, is a mark of his manliness: 'of all manly dresses a shooting jacket was the most becoming' (SS, p. 26). In contrast, Brandon wears a flannel waistcoat which has drearily unromantic associations of 'aches, cramps, rheumatisms, and every species of ailment that can afflict the old and the feeble' (SS, p. 25). In the eighteenth-century farce *My Grandmother*, to which Austen directly alludes in *Mansfield Park*, one of the characters is ridiculed for wearing a flannel waistcoat. Austen's use of the flannel-waistcoat motif from a well-known farce is perhaps a deliberate gesture to suggest the crude contrasts of stage-heroes, whose costumes represent character.

Austen makes less crude comparisons and contrasts between Edward and Willoughby, though she uses a familiar stage device to reveal the differences between them. Both are dependent upon an older woman's authority, which means that they are unable to marry freely the women they love. But in Austen's hands, as in Sheridan's before her, the tradi-tional comic motif of the antagonism between the old order and the new is reversed.

Parental tyranny exercised in the choice of spouse for a son, daughter or ward had long been traditional in comedy, and is paradoxically reworked in *The Rivals*.[22] Sheridan's inversion of this convention is to portray Mrs Malaprop and Sir Anthony Absolute, who, far from dividing the young lovers, only wish to encourage the union. That the marriage is delayed by Jack and Lydia's own perversity, rather than parental interven-tion, is the main comic thrust:

> ABSOLUTE: Sure, Sir, this is not very reasonable, to summon my
> affections for a lady I know nothing of!
> SIR ANTHONY: I am sure, Sir, 'tis more unreasonable in you to *object*
> to a lady you know nothing of.[23]

Sir Anthony's implacable demands of obedience from his son in matters matrimonial become a double-edged comic device in Sheridan's handling of the trope. As soon as Jack discovers that the girl intended for him *is* Lydia Languish, he is all too eager to submit to his father, in what becomes a brilliant inversion of a traditional motif of antagonism between the old and the young:

> ABSOLUTE: 'Tis just as Fag told me, indeed. – Whimsical enough,
> faith! My Father wants to *force* me to marry the very girl I am
> plotting to run away with! … However, I'll read my recantation
> instantly. – My conversion is something sudden, indeed – but I can
> assure him it is very *sincere* …
> SIR ANTHONY: Fellow, get out of my way.
> ABSOLUTE: Sir, you see a penitent before you.
> SIR ANTHONY: I see an impudent scoundrel before me.
> ABSOLUTE: A sincere penitent. – I am come, Sir, to acknowledge my
> error, and to submit entirely to your will … the result of my
> reflections is – a resolution to sacrifice every inclination of my own
> to your satisfaction.[24]

Austen's parody of secret engagements and parental interference makes use of a brilliant device clearly borrowed from *The Rivals*. The pivot of Sheridan's comic plot is his exploitation of the trope of filial disobedience. As discussed already, Austen had used this model in *Love and Freindship* in a reversal of the comic convention where an authority figure prevents the lovers' union. But in *Sense and Sensibility* Austen uses this motif in a far more complex and ambiguous way.

Both Elinor and Marianne wrongly attribute their lovers' inconsistent conduct to parental interference. Mrs Dashwood also falls into the sentimental trap set up by Austen, as she concocts a sentimentalised fantasy of Willoughby's conflict with his patron Mrs Smith: 'I am persuaded that Mrs Smith suspects his regard for Marianne, disapproves of it (perhaps because she has other views for him,) and on that account is eager to send him away' (*SS*, p. 78). Mrs Dashwood's account is highly ironic, as we later discover that Mrs Smith is no ogre, but wishes her nephew to act correctly by the woman he has seduced.

Similarly, Mrs Dashwood attributes Edward's low spirits to Mrs Ferrars's interference: 'attributing it to some want of liberality in his mother, [she] sat down to table indignant against all selfish parents' (*SS*, p. 90). The irony is intensified, as once more we have the same situation, and the same explanation as Mrs Dashwood had excused in the case of Willoughby. Elinor, as well as Marianne, is shown to be capable of error when she attributes Edward's inconsistent behaviour to his mother's influence. She mistakenly attributes Edward's 'want of spirits, of openness, and of consistency' to the interference of Mrs Ferrars, and Austen ironically notes, 'it was happy for her that he had a mother whose character was so imperfectly known to her, as to be the general excuse for every thing strange on the part of her son' (*SS*, p. 101).

The irony is clear: Elinor expresses doubt about Marianne's excuse of parental tyranny dividing her from Willoughby, yet Elinor is willing to use the same excuse when it comes to herself: 'she was very well disposed on the whole to regard his actions with all the candid allowances and generous qualifications, which had been rather more painfully exhorted from her, for Willoughby's service, by her mother' (*SS*, p. 101). Elinor is happy to blame Mrs Ferrars for her interference in her son's affairs: 'The old, well established grievance of duty against will, parent against child, was the cause of all' (*SS*, p. 102). Elinor could not be more wrong.

As in *The Rivals*, parental interference is a red herring. It is the lovers' own conduct and their own irresponsibility that causes them anguish. Although Mrs Ferrars conforms to the stereotype of parental power and authority, she is finally powerless to prevent both sons from marrying whom they want. Conversely, Mrs Smith is not the dictatorial authority figure of stage comedy, nor a Mrs Malaprop, hastening to marry her nephew off to a rich woman. To his horror Willoughby discovers that marrying the heiress Miss Grey has paradoxically alienated him from his benefactor. Miss Smith's desire that he should marry Eliza is a complex reversal of his expectations. So too is his discovery that 'had he behaved with honour towards Marianne, he might at once have been happy and rich' (*SS*, p. 379). It is Willoughby's own conduct that is responsible for his own fate: 'That his repentance of his misconduct, which thus brought its own punishment, was sincere, need not be doubted' (*SS*, p. 379).

Austen draws a final ironic parallel between Elinor and Marianne. On hearing the news of the public revelation of Lucy and Edward's secret engagement, Elinor is made even more painfully aware of this 'resemblance in their situations' (*SS*, p. 261). And Marianne confirms this by seeing Edward as a 'second Willoughby' (*SS*, p. 261).

Early on, when Elinor had been informed of the secret engagement between Edward and Lucy, she had considered the opposition of Mrs Ferrars to this match and perceived that 'melancholy was the state of the person, by whom the expectation of family opposition and unkindness, could be felt as a relief' (*SS*, p. 140). 'Relief' in this context seems to point towards Edward being relieved of his engagement to Lucy through parental opposition, but Elinor is confounded once again by Edward's defiance of his mother.

Edward's situation is now paralleled with Willoughby's – with one important difference, Edward's acceptance of his contract with Lucy Steele. Paradoxically, Edward's defiance of his mother, Mrs Ferrars, adds to his own misery, just as Willoughby's defiance of Mrs Smith brings its own punishment. This is yet another ironic reversal where defiance of parental authority works against the characters' best interests. Edward is made to conform to the picture of the romantic hero, who courageously defies parental authority for the sake of the woman he is engaged to. But this is satirically undermined by the fact that Edward is *not* in love with the young woman: 'Elinor's heart wrung for the feelings of Edward, while braving his mother's threats, for a woman who could not reward him' (*SS*, p. 268).

This is the sort of comic paradox that Sheridan explores to great effect in *The Rivals*. But Austen's ironic reversal of filial disobedience is more complex. Edward's 'honourable' refusal to extricate himself from a hastily formed and unwanted engagement is now compared favourably with Willoughby's refusal to honour either his implicit engagement with Marianne, or his more explicit contract with Eliza. While Mrs Jennings praises Edward's conduct in comparison with Willoughby's 'only Elinor and Marianne understood its true merit. *They* only knew how little he had had to tempt him to be disobedient' (*SS*, p. 270).

Edward's only respite is time: 'everything depended … on his getting that preferment, of which, at present, there seemed not the smallest chance' (*SS*, p. 276). Not even Elinor predicts the final cruel twist, when Brandon, misunderstanding the true state of affairs between Edward and Elinor, provides the means for Edward to marry Lucy.

This is yet another reversal of a sentimental trope. One of the stalwarts of sentimental stage comedy is the last-minute benefactor who unites the young lovers against all odds. Perhaps the most famous eighteenth-century example was Stockwell in Cumberland's *The West Indian*. Brandon's benevolence is partly inspired by his (misplaced) admiration for Edward's chivalric conduct in opposing his mother for the sake of love: 'The cruelty … of dividing, or attempting to divide, two young people long attached to each other, is terrible – Mrs Ferrars does not know what she may be doing – what she may drive her son to' (*SS*, p. 282). Brandon, of course, labours under a mistaken understanding of the situation, and the ironies increase as he makes Elinor his confidante. Brandon's generous interference unites the lovers (who are no longer in love), and seals Elinor's fate.

Austen's satirical inversion of this sentimental convention is in the spirit and manner of *The Rivals*, where the young lovers' union is threatened only by their own behaviour and not by parental interference. In *Sense and Sensibility*, the young men are financially dependent on older authority figures, but they are also free to make their own choices. Edward Ferrars's defiance of his mother for the sake of a woman he no longer loves is dangerously close to the absurd conduct of Edward Lindsay in *Love and Freindship*, who defies his father by his refusal to marry the woman he loves.

Austen's principle of pairings is the structural base of *Sense and Sensibility*. The pairing of Elinor and Lucy is developed through their parallel situation (both women are in love with the same man) in the final chapters leading up to the end of volume one and the closer paralleling of their behaviour in volume two. The revelation of Lucy's secret engagement at the end of volume one echoes the ambiguity surrounding the 'truth' of the secret engagement between Marianne and Willoughby and shows how contrasts, parallels and discordant similarities of action and exchange constantly resonate against each other. Austen thus ends the first volume with a theatrical flourish. And in volume two she deploys a further quasi-theatrical device, the 'set-piece' of a confrontation between two female rivals.

Jane Austen's set-piece between her 'two fair rivals' deliberately appeals to stage comic models. Scenes such as this, which contain pointed exchanges of dialogue and repartee, can be traced back to wit-comedies. The classic example of this kind of dramatic exchange, the 'polite quarrel' between two female characters, is the exchange between Célimène and Arsinoë in Molière's *Le misanthrope*. Henry Fielding used this model in his plays, and then more effectively in his novels.[25] But Austen's dramatic rendering of the polite quarrel in *Sense and Sensibility* achieves a realistic quality that transcends the burlesque absurdities of similar comically stylised exchanges in Fielding's plays and novels.

The scene is set in the Middletons' drawing room, and takes place in the stuffy, dimly-lit environment of the ladies' dining party. The controlling presence of the author is felt in the narrative preliminaries which sketch the unpleasant social atmosphere in which the dialogue takes place. On stage this would be achieved by the actors and the producer. The scene between Elinor and Lucy is introduced by Lady Middleton's proposal of a card game. Jane Austen invites the reader to consider the relationship between game-playing and social conduct.

The dialogue is preceded by a quasi-dramatic monologue in which Elinor's internal thoughts about Lucy's revelation are processed by a circuitous route of disbelief, indignation and, finally, acceptance. Austen thus sets the scene in the context of her heroine's disappointment and pain. Through this internalising of her heroine's thoughts, we discover the reason for Lucy's confidence in Elinor. Elinor discovers that, like Marianne, she has been jilted, but also that her rival is insistent on asserting her prior claim:

> What other reason for the disclosure of the affair could there be, but that Elinor might be informed by it of Lucy's superior claims on Edward, and be taught to avoid him in future? She had little difficulty in understanding thus much of her rival's intentions … (*SS*, p. 142).

Elinor's desire to renew the topic with Lucy in order to ascertain further details is an ironic variant on the confidante role. Just as Austen satirises the stage-convention of filial defiance, she now parodies a favourite sentimental twist: a secret engagement due to the opposition of a cruel parent, and told to a best friend in confidence.

Elinor's decision to accept the role of Lucy's confidante threatens to compromise her integrity. The confidante or 'tame duenna', as Mary Crawford reminds us in *Mansfield Park*, is a conventional trope of stage comedy that had been successfully assimilated into the sentimental novel. In *The Rivals*, Julia acts as Lydia's confidante, although she expands the usual role by virtue of her criticism of her friend. Susanna Centlivre's comedy *The Wonder: A Woman Keeps a Secret* centres its plot on the role of the confidante. The title alone suggests that it is highly unusual for a woman to be trustworthy, even though Centlivre's heroine keeps her friend's secret at great personal cost. Austen's heroine also keeps a secret at great personal cost to her self-respect and dignity. Lucy and Elinor provide a cruel parody of the duenna trope, particularly as we know the reasons why Lucy is confiding in Elinor.

The theatrical tableau set up by Jane Austen is reminiscent of the opening of Congreve's *The Way of the World*. Two gamesters are at cards in a chocolate-house and, as the dialogue begins, the card-game dissolves to become a metaphor for the dramatic action. Mirabell and Fainall each seek to elicit information from the other without revealing his own hand. In Austen's tableau, Elinor and Lucy are working together on a filigree basket; this is extremely delicate ornamental work, which involves twisting, plaiting and weaving together the strands of the basket. While the 'remaining five draw their cards' (SS, p. 145), Lucy and Elinor engage in their more serious game: 'the two fair rivals were thus seated side by side at the same table, and with the utmost harmony in forwarding the same work' (SS, p. 145). Lucy's 'work' is to ensure that she is safe from the interference of Elinor, but she sadistically uses the opportunity to taunt her rival. Elinor's 'work' is to elicit information about the engagement.

The confrontation scene between Elinor and Lucy consists of a whole chapter written mainly in dialogue form. The dramatic element is reinforced by the relative absence of connectives ('he said', 'she said'). The scene is mostly unmediated in terms of authorial voice, although there appears to a conscious sense of a controlling presence from the opening line of the chapter:

In a firm, though cautious tone, Elinor thus began.

'I should be undeserving of the confidence you have honoured me with, if I felt no desire for its continuance, or no farther curiosity on its subject. I will not apologize therefore for bringing it forward again.'

'Thank you,' cried Lucy warmly, 'for breaking the ice; you have set my heart at ease by it; for I was somehow or other afraid I had offended you by what I told you that Monday.'

'Offended me! How could you suppose so? ...'

'And yet I do assure you,' replied Lucy, her little sharp eyes full of meaning, 'there seemed to me to be a coldness and displeasure in your manner, that made me quite uncomfortable.' (SS, p. 146)

The opening sentence seems to be the objective voice of the narrator, but a closer look reveals that this is Elinor's perspective shaping the narrative. The effect of Austen's free indirect speech in this instance is that Elinor's apprehension is conveyed in her desire to appear in control; the implication being that she is not.

Though the confrontation begins politely, the underlying tone of the exchange is established with added interjections, such as 'her little sharp eyes full of meaning'. Again, there is an ambiguity at play. The interjections are very much in the style of Richardson's 'conversations', but the point of view is deliberately muddied. If this is Elinor noting Lucy's aggressive body language, rather than an objective description by the author, the emotional content of the confrontation is intensified. Austen's free indirect speech gives her the means of being simultaneously inside and outside her character.

In the opening dialogue Austen creates a subtle instability of tone. The hints, evasions and insinuations convey the impression of much being withheld, and yet paradoxically revealed. The ritual of social nastiness and feminine swordsmanship truly gets underway with Elinor's sarcastic and uncharacteristic baiting: 'Could you have a motive for the trust, that was not honourable and flattering to me?' (*SS*, p. 146). Thus begins an intricate 'I know that you know that I know' dialogue in the tradition of the multi-layered exchanges to be found in Congreve.

In the opening dialogue of *The Way of the World*, the cause of tension between the two men is Mrs Marwood. Mrs Marwood has frustrated Mirabell's plan to gain Lady Wishfort's approval of his match with Millamant. Mirabell suspects Fainall of being Mrs Marwood's lover and privy to her design. In turn, Fainall suspects Mrs Marwood of being in love with Mirabell and seeks to establish whether Mirabell returns the sentiment or not. Furthermore, part of Mirabell's preoccupation is also to gauge Fainall's relationship with his wife, who happens to be Mirabell's lover. The exchange is thus fraught with innuendo, double meaning and insinuation, as the men play a complex double-game.

In *Sense and Sensibility*, Austen establishes a similar kind of narrative subtlety. Elinor wants to establish certain truths and details, and wishes to convince her rival of her indifference, while Lucy wants to taunt Elinor and keep her away from Edward. But, as the dialogue gets under way, the surface politeness and restraint become increasingly strained and the mutual dislike and jealousy of the two rivals are apparent:

[Lucy] 'If you knew what a consolation it was to me to relieve my heart by speaking to you of what I am always thinking of every moment of my life, your compassion would make you overlook everything else I am sure.'

[Elinor] 'Indeed I can easily believe that it was a very great relief to you, to acknowledge your situation to me, and be assured that you shall never have cause to repent it.' (*SS*, p. 146)

The point-scoring repartee reaches a natural climax in Elinor's (untruthful) plea of indifference:

'... the power of dividing two people so tenderly attached is too much for an indifferent person.'

''Tis because you are an indifferent person,' said Lucy, with some pique, and laying a particular stress on those words, 'that your judgement might justly have such weight with me. If you could be supposed to be biassed in any respect by your own feelings, your opinion would not be worth having.' (*SS*, p. 150)

Lucy implies that Edward has given himself away by talking too much of Elinor, and that she knows the full state of affairs between them, and with her malicious innuendo on 'indifference', incites Elinor's tactical withdrawal: 'Elinor thought it wisest to make no answer to this, lest they might provoke each other to an unsuitable increase of ease and unreserve' (*SS*, p. 150).

In a similar scene, earlier in the novel, Lucy reveals her secret engagement to Elinor. Austen punctuates the dialogue with dramatic interjections: 'eyeing Elinor attentively as she spoke'; 'amiably bashful, with only one side glance at her companion to observe its effect on her'; '"not to Mr Robert Ferrars – I never saw him in my life; but," fixing her eyes upon Elinor, "to his elder brother"' (*SS*, pp. 128–29). The dialogue is reinforced by Lucy's use of props, the reference to the ring and the 'taking a letter from her pocket', asides in the manner of stage directions.

As well as using quasi-theatrical interjections to suggest the emotional force of the confrontation, Jane Austen also shows how seemingly careless actions, such as the rolling of the papers, convey powerful emotional conflict beneath the calm surface. Towards the end of the novel, the unspoken but powerful emotion of Edward's revelation of his release from Lucy is given added force by his action of inadvertently cutting the

sheath into pieces with the scissors. Mindless actions that suggest powerful emotional conflict are in the tradition of the drama.

Jane Austen's set-pieces often have a semi-autonomous quality,
making them resemble individual scenes in a play. But though they may
be presented as self-contained and carefully patterned scenes, which rely
mainly on character-revealing dialogue, they nevertheless establish a
controlling, though often extremely delicate, authorial presence. In this
instance, there is a disquieting sense that the moral order of the novel's
world is threatening to collapse: the danger is that Elinor's aptitude for
dissimulation and disingenuousness is alarmingly akin to Lucy's.

Elinor's complicity in the 'game' of confidences that is duplicitously set
up by Lucy is undermined by the cruel truth that the Dashwood sisters
do not confide in each other. Elinor now seems to be an extension of
Lucy Steele:

> 'If the strength of your reciprocal attachment had failed, as between
> many people and under many circumstances it naturally would during
> a four years' engagement, your situation would have been pitiable
> indeed.'
>
> Lucy here looked up; but Elinor was careful in guarding her counte-
> nance from every expression that could give her words a suspicious
> tendency. (*SS*, p. 147)

The danger that is implied in the adoption and exploitation of Lucy's
methods is swiftly curtailed. Elinor attempts this participation in what is
really an unpleasant social game only once: 'From this time forth the
subject was never revived by Elinor … it was treated by the former with
calmness and caution, and dismissed as soon as civility would allow; for
she felt such conversations to be an indulgence which Lucy did not
deserve, and which *were dangerous to herself*' (*SS*, p. 151, my italics).

A further aspect of Austen's principle of pairings between Elinor and
Lucy is the implication for Marianne. If Elinor's extreme is Lucy at one
end and Lady Middleton at the other, Marianne's extreme must be the
garrulous, empty-headed Anne Steele, who at thirty is clearly beyond
marriage prospects, and the rattling Mrs Palmer. Austen is perhaps inviting us to consider that Anne is a version of a character that Marianne

might have become at the end of the novel, after having renounced sensibility, had she not been rescued by Colonel Brandon. As Lucy constantly smoothes over her sister's glaring *faux pas*, so Elinor 'screens' Marianne's deliberate rudeness. Anne Steele at one point is severely rebuked by Lucy for yet another social impropriety. The sharpness of Lucy's reprimand 'though it did not give much sweetness to the manners of one sister, was of advantage in governing those of the other' (*SS*, p. 219). This comment has significance for both pairs of sisters – although Elinor's gentler methods of 'governing' her sister's social conduct are more praiseworthy than Lucy's.

The paralleling of Anne and Marianne's social indiscretions also serves as a method of highlighting Marianne's virtues by contrasting them with an idiot version, much in the way that Mr Darcy is contrasted with Mr Collins. It is striking just how similar Collins's and Darcy's proposal speeches are. By the comparison between the two sets of sisters, Austen implies that Elinor's danger lies in becoming too adept at the social game, becoming dangerously close to Lucy. Through Austen's favourable comparison with Anne Steele, and the contrast between Marianne's genuine sensibility and the false sensibility of the Steeles, Austen is moving towards an imposition which is now on Marianne's side.

Austen's pairing of Lucy and Elinor enables her to make comparisons in ways that reflect favourably on Marianne. Thus when Elinor tries similar Lucy-like behaviour on her sister, Austen censures her duplicity and the authorial sympathy shifts to Marianne:

> Marianne looked at her steadily, and said, 'You know, Elinor, that this is a kind of talking which I cannot bear. If you only hope to have your assertion contradicted, as I must suppose to be the case, you ought to recollect that I am the last person in the world to do it. I cannot descend to be tricked out of assurances, that are not really wanted.' (*SS*, p. 244)

Marianne's outright refusal to participate in this form of social hypocrisy is revealed in an admirable light. The authorial sympathy, at this point, returns to Marianne. Nevertheless, aside from these temporary lapses, Elinor's social conduct perfectly illustrates her doctrine of the important disparity between independence of mind and outward behaviour. When Marianne takes her sister to task for her social conformity, she heartily disputes the accusation: 'No, Marianne, never. My doctrine has never aimed at the subjection of the understanding. All I have ever attempted to influence has been the behaviour. You must not confound my meaning' (SS, p. 94).

It was from the drama that Jane Austen received invaluable training for a novelist interested in scenes and dialogue. Scenes or set-pieces are units of action built around exits and entrances. How do you begin and end a scene except through entrances and exits? They are the markers of beginnings and endings, and of moments of surprise and suspense – of drama. But exits and entrances are not merely the units that mark beginnings and ends in a play; they can also come in the middle of a scene as an element of surprise. Throughout *Sense and Sensibility*, Austen provides us with a running motif of characters who are mistaken for others, as well as unexpectedly appearing and disappearing through doors, as in a farce.

This is particularly the case with her male characters. As one male character enters, the other exits. A morning walk in the country becomes an occasion of thwarted expectation for Marianne when she sees a man on horseback in the distance and immediately presumes that it is Willoughby, 'It is he; it is indeed; – I know it is!' (SS, p. 86), whereas the more sceptical Elinor is sure that it is not. Close up it in fact turns out to be Edward – Elinor is right. But later in the novel this scene is inverted when Elinor sees a gentleman on horseback and assumes it to be Colonel Brandon, only to discover that it is Edward (SS, p. 358). Austen's principle of pairings makes the issue more complex than one character being right and the other wrong. Both sisters misperceive. This exposes an important theme for the novel: the dangers of conjecture and subjective interpretation.

Austen's plot device of having people appear and disappear through doors is a means of exploring the discrepancy between illusion and reality. This is particularly the case with those male characters who disappear for unexplained reasons and reappear again unannounced. Edward absents himself indefinitely from Elinor, Brandon leaves for London unexpectedly, and Willoughby's abrupt departure from Barton cottage is equally mysterious and unexplained.

When the action of the novel shifts to London, a knock on the door is assumed by both sisters to herald Willoughby's long-awaited arrival in Berkeley Street:

> Elinor felt secure of its announcing Willoughby's approach, and Marianne starting up moved towards the door. Everything was silent; this could not be borne many seconds, she opened the door, advanced a few steps towards the stairs, and after listening half a minute, returned into the room in all the agitation which a conviction of having heard him would naturally produce; in the extasy of her feelings at the instant she could not help exclaiming, 'Oh! Elinor, it is Willoughby, indeed it is!' and seemed almost ready to throw herself into his arms, when Colonel Brandon appeared. (SS, p. 161)

The situation of a young girl throwing herself into the arms of the wrong lover is markedly theatrical. But Austen does not employ it here for comic effect. Marianne's disappointment is severe. Furthermore, this quasi-farcical moment points ahead to the union between Marianne and Brandon, in a way that not even Elinor anticipates. This is a scene of dramatic surprise, where the reader is kept in suspense as to who is behind the door.

The comic inversion of this incident is rendered in the great set-piece of Edward Ferrars's unpropitious arrival at Berkeley Street, only to find himself compromisingly positioned between the woman he wishes to marry and the woman he is engaged to marry:

> Elinor was prevented from making any reply to this civil triumph, by the door's being thrown open, the servant's announcing Mr Ferrars, and Edward's immediately walking in.
>
> It was a very awkward moment; and the countenance of each showed that it was so. They all looked exceedingly foolish; and Edward seemed to have as great an inclination to walk out of the room again, as to advance further into it.' (SS, pp. 240–41)

But this scene is one of dramatic irony. When Edward walks through the door to see Elinor, he has no idea that Lucy Steele is in the room. His innate social awkwardness is now ironically transformed to the acute embarrassment of being caught unaware, but being unable to explain himself to either of them. Caught thus between Lucy and Elinor, all he can do is look embarrassed: 'his embarrassment still exceeded that of the ladies in a proportion, which the case rendered reasonable, though his sex might make it rare; for his heart had not the indifference of Lucy's, nor could his conscience have quite the ease of Elinor's' (SS, p. 241).

If this is not sufficient discomfort for him, Austen compounds the comic impact with Marianne's arrival. Her customary directness is agonisingly misplaced as she heavily alludes to Edward's love for her sister in front of Lucy Steele: 'don't think of *my* health. Elinor is well, you see. That must be enough for us both' (SS, p. 242). The dramatic irony is intensified by Marianne's faith in Edward's honour, following her own disappointment in Willoughby, which leads her to magnify Edward's qualities. She is, of course, wildly off beam and misinterprets Edward's evident agitation 'to whatever cause best pleased herself'. Austen, meanwhile, invites us to enjoy his discomfort: 'Poor Edward muttered something, but what it was, nobody knew, not even himself' (SS, p. 243).

In *The Rivals* there are numerous examples of comic embarrassment built around untimely entrances and exits. In one memorable scene, Jack Absolute in the disguise of Ensign Beverley pretends to disguise himself as his own rival, Jack Absolute, in order to simultaneously deceive Mrs Malaprop and Lydia – who both know him as different characters. Just when he thinks that he has got away with deceiving the women, he is caught out by his father, who demands, along with them, that his son confess his true identity. Jack is placed in an impossible position when he is forced to admit his deception and confess his true identity to both Lydia and Mrs Malaprop; caught between offending one or the other and incurring the displeasure of both. In *Sense and Sensibility* we see how Jane Austen adopts similar theatrical devices to Sheridan. She builds her structure through 'scenes' woven around entrances and exits, and uses this as a device of comic embarrassment in the exact manner of eighteenth-century comedy.

If Edward's visit to Elinor is the comic apotheosis of unexpected entrances, Willoughby's equally unexpected arrival at Marianne's sickbed is surely the tragic. As with the mistaken identities of the men on horseback, Austen almost identically parallels Marianne's misconceptions with Elinor's. This time it is Elinor who almost rushes into the wrong man's arms. Upon hearing the sound of an approaching carriage, Elinor assumes that it heralds the imminent arrival of her mother and Brandon at Cleveland. Even though her common sense confounds the probability of this (she knows that it is far too early for their arrival), she vehemently wishes to believe in the truth of the 'almost impossibility of their being already come'.

Austen builds Elinor's anticipation of being reunited with her mother and Brandon in a way that echoes the earlier scene of Marianne's expectation of her imminent reunion with Willoughby: 'the night was cold and stormy ... the clock struck eight'. And, in a structural parallel typical of the novel's dynamic, Austen thwarts Elinor's expectations: 'Never in her life had Elinor found it so difficult to be calm, as at that moment ... The bustle in the vestibule, as she passed along an inner lobby, assured her that they were already in the house. She rushed forwards towards the drawing-room, – she entered it, – and saw only Willoughby' (SS, p. 316).

At various points in the novel Edward is mistaken for Willoughby, Edward is mistaken for Brandon, Brandon is mistaken for Willoughby, and Willoughby is mistaken for Brandon. In a novel that has pointedly alerted its characters to the discrepancies between illusion and reality, and the perplexities of interpretation and misconception, it is finally befitting that Willoughby should present his point of view. Indeed he refers explicitly to the dangers of subjective interpretation: '"Remember", cried Willoughby, "from whom you received the account. Could it be an impartial one?"' (SS, p. 322).

The confusion between the identities of the male characters, though quasi-farcical, poses a more sobering social reality for Austen's female characters. Behind such farcical or burlesque-like absurdities lies a cynical reminder that poverty is one of the best inducements for marriage, reminding us of Jane Austen's advice to her niece, Fanny, on the social and economic realities for dependent women: 'Single Women have a dreadful propensity for being poor – which is one very strong argument in favour of matrimony' (*Letters*, p. 332).

The casualness of husband-hunting is suggested quite early in the novel when Charlotte Palmer claims that she might have married Brandon, 'if Mama had not objected to it', even though he had only seen her twice and had not owned an affection to her: 'he would have been very glad to have had me, if he could. Sir John and Lady Middleton wished it very much. But Mama did not think the match good enough for me, otherwise Sir John would have mentioned it to the Colonel, and we should have been married immediately' (*SS*, p. 117). Mrs Jennings's observation that she has 'the whip hand' of Mr Palmer because 'you have taken Charlotte off my hands, and cannot give her back again' (*SS*, p. 112) also emphasises how women were perceived as burdens on their family.

Austen had earlier observed that having married off her own daughters, Mrs Jennings had now 'nothing to do but to marry all the rest of the world' (*SS*, p. 36). Mrs Jennings shows no compunction in transferring her matchmaking plans from one lover to another. She has no trouble in switching Edward Ferrars's allegiance from Elinor to Lucy Steele, and again in transferring Brandon's from Marianne to Elinor. What is more, Elinor is also suspected by John Dashwood of making a conquest of Brandon: 'A very little trouble on your side secures him' (*SS*, p. 223).

It is not only stage routines, such as entrances and exits, that Austen uses to illustrate the harsh reality of the marriage market. Other artifices from the drama, such as comic misunderstandings and conversations heard at cross-purposes, are also employed to signal this theme. Austen taps into a long theatrical tradition of such overhearings that have either comic effects, as in *Much Ado About Nothing*, or tragic consequences, as in *Othello*. Mrs Jennings misconceives that she has 'overheard' a proposal of marriage between Brandon and Elinor when in fact Brandon has offered to save Edward and Lucy. Mrs Jennings's congratulations to Elinor are taken by Elinor to mean quite the opposite – the impending marriage of Edward and Lucy. The mistake persists, even though Mrs Jennings is amused and surprised by the coolness of the lovers: 'I have not heard of anything to please me so well since Charlotte was brought abed' (*SS*, p. 287). As Brandon apologises for the 'badness of his house', meaning the Delaford parsonage, Mrs Jennings takes it to mean his own estate: 'This set the matter beyond a doubt' (*SS*, p. 281). She is as eager to congratulate Elinor on her good luck, even though previously insistent that Brandon was in love with Marianne. Like John Dashwood, Mrs Jennings expresses indifference as to the identity of the future Mrs Brandon.

The misunderstanding is finally resolved by Mrs Jennings's direct reference to Elinor's marriage to Brandon: 'The deception could not continue after this; and an explanation immediately took place, by which both gained considerable amusement for the moment, without any material loss of happiness to either, for Mrs Jennings only exchanged one form of delight for another, and still without forfeiting her expectation of the first' (*SS*, p. 292). Comic misunderstandings persist to the very end with Mrs Jennings's letter to Elinor, which relates Edward's heartache at having been jilted by Lucy and reveals Brandon's delusions about Edward.

Austen's pointed use of artifices from the drama thus becomes a means of exposing her views on love and marriage. The confusion between the lovers and their arbitrary switching of partners, and the varying levels of deceit and mercenary considerations, provide a satirical exposé of the marriage market. As the various lovers pass in and out of doors, and are mistaken for each other right up to the very end, where Elinor believes that Edward is Brandon, we are encouraged to believe that the plot could go any way. Love becomes a chance encounter; whoever comes through the door could be the man you marry.

Therefore, contrary to critical consensus, no one should be surprised by Lucy's sudden marriage to Robert Ferrars (especially since he is now the new heir), nor by Marianne's union with Brandon, nor Elinor's with Edward. When John Dashwood informs Elinor that his family expect Robert to marry Miss Morton, his sister deftly sums up the situation: 'The lady, I suppose, has no choice in the affair ... it must be the same to Miss Morton whether she marry Edward or Robert' (*SS*, p. 296). John Dashwood's brutal reply reflects the cynicism of the age when he answers, 'Certainly, there can be no difference' (*SS*, p. 297).

* * *

In *Sense and Sensibility*, Jane Austen exploits specific sentimental conventions from stage comedy, devices that had been assimilated into the sentimental novel: filial defiance, romantic heroes, giddy heroines, kindly benefactors. She satirises them in the way that Sheridan had done in *The Rivals*. Furthermore, Austen derives her principle of pairings from the example set by stage models in *The Rivals* and *False Delicacy*. In a kaleidoscopic fashion, her principle of pairings creates a diversion and shifting of sympathies, particularly between the two heroines. Like Sheridan and Hugh Kelly before her, Austen uses her principle of pairings to show that sustained mockery of sensibility may coexist with a strong sympathy for it.

Thus in the filigree basket scene between Elinor and Lucy, Elinor's 'sense' is shown to be as dangerous as Marianne's 'sensibility'. When Elinor feels in danger of entering into a form of social hypocrisy she quickly draws back, but not before the similarities between her and Lucy have been drawn. Austen's principle of pairings is the means to enable her to shift authorial sympathy from one heroine to the other, without a failure in the moral organisation of her fictional world.

In *The Rivals*, the doubling of the female leads enables the satire to be directed against the sentimental Lydia Languish, but Jane Austen's use of this device is far more elaborate than Sheridan's. In her hands, the pairing motif is further complicated. Individual sisters are compared not only with each other, but also with other pairs of sisters. As with Lucy and Anne, we are encouraged not only to draw comparisons between their conduct and that of Elinor and Marianne, but also to draw comparisons between Anne and Marianne, and Lucy and Elinor. Having extreme versions of the foils means that they are not just foils to each other. The Steele sisters and the Jennings sisters provide almost caricature-like versions of the heroines, which encourages us to view Elinor and Marianne and 'sense' and 'sensibility' in different lights. Austen's use of the principle of pairings is far more complex and nuanced than Sheridan's for it enables her to ironise both heroines. Elinor's capacity to be as mistaken as Marianne allows for a shift in our perceptions and the displacement of our expectations, which is an important part of Austen's ironic method. Ironically, Elinor's and Marianne's similarities become more acute than their differences.

Towards the close of *Sense and Sensibility*, Austen upholds an ironic detachment from her characters. The authorial voice accords perfectly with the moral ambivalence achieved by the principle of pairings. Marianne, 'instead of falling a sacrifice to an irresistible passion', falls for a man 'she had considered too old to be married, – and who still sought the constitutional safeguard of a flannel waistcoat' (*SS*, p. 378). Elinor, after succumbing to a fit of sensibility in which she 'bursts into tears of joy', marries the disinherited Edward. The winner is the unscrupulous Lucy Steele:

> The whole of Lucy's behaviour in the affair, and the prosperity which
> crowned it, therefore, may be held forth as a most encouraging instance
> of what an earnest, an unceasing attention to self-interest, however its
> progress may be apparently obstructed, will do in securing every advan-
> tage of fortune. (*SS*, p. 376)

The authorial voice, at the end of *Sense and Sensibility*, is less ostentatious than the absurd Fieldingesque voice at the end of 'Jack and Alice',[26] and the satirical voice at the end of *Lady Susan*.[27]

Jane Austen's principle of pairings, derived from specific stage models, was the means of enabling her to achieve an ironic detachment from her characters which she was to perfect in her later novels by her increasing use of free indirect speech. The technique allows a shift in authorial sympathy and an ambiguity of moral tone. Her use of parallelism and contrast, which, for example, enables her to show a variety of different responses to the same situation, encourages us constantly to call into question the things we take for granted.

7

Pride and Prejudice

Of all Jane Austen's characters, with the possible (and intriguing) exception of Mary Crawford in *Mansfield Park*, Elizabeth Bennet most resembles the lively, witty, independent heroine of Shakespearean and Restoration comedy. And of all the novels, *Pride and Prejudice* most naturally lends itself to dramatic representation, mainly because of its reliance on dramatic speech. Perhaps Richard Brinsley Sheridan (always on the look-out for promising young writers) appreciated its quasi-dramatic qualities when he declared the novel 'one of the cleverest things he had ever read'.[1]

Austen's first critics, sensitive to the close affinity between stage and page in the late Georgian era, admired Elizabeth as a Shakespearean heroine. The *Critical Review* described her as the 'the Beatrice of the tale; [who] falls in love on much the same principles of contrariety'. The same reviewer also noted an allegiance to eighteenth-century, as well as Shakespearean, comedy: 'The character of Wickham is very well pourtrayed; we fancy, that our authoress had Joseph Surface before her eyes when she sketched it; as well as the lively Beatrice, when she drew the portrait of Elizabeth'.[2]

The so-called 'lively lady' and her more serious foil (Beatrice/Hero, Rosalind/Celia) were established character types in Restoration and eighteenth-century comedy. As has been shown, they were duly assimilated into the novel, but in the more sentimentalised comedy of the later eighteenth century there were changes and developments in the pairings. The secondary relationship between the duller and more serious couple was often given more emphasis and interest – consider the pairings of Julia and Faulkland in *The Rivals*, and Jane and Mr Bingley in *Pride and Prejudice*. The secondary love-plot was, furthermore, often

interwoven with that of the witty courtship. Another important development was that the lively heroine was often given a sensible husband
rather than a witty rake for a partner. The coquettish elements of the
heroine were played down and, though clever and independent, she
often proves to be mistaken in the matters of her own heart. In both
Pride and Prejudice and *Emma*, Austen conforms to this new pattern of
romantic comedy. She tempts the heroine with a witty rake (Wickham
and Frank Churchill), but ultimately the heroine chooses a serious and
steady lover, one who is characterised by his inability or refusal to speak
florid protestations of love. When Elizabeth chides Darcy for his reluctance to demonstrate his love by talking to her at dinner, he replies, 'A
man who felt less, might' (*PP*, p. 381). Mr Knightley similarly declares
to Emma, 'If I loved you less, I might be able to talk about it more more'
(*E*, p. 430).

Hannah Cowley's comedy *Which is the Man?* typifies the new kind of
courtship model, where the lively heroine chooses a sensible lover
(Beauchamp) rather than a reformed rake (Lord Sparkle). Lord Sparkle's
cynicism and dissipation are revealed in his attempted seduction of an
innocent country girl unaccustomed to 'the language of the day' which
equates flattery with hard-nosed economics: 'Compliments are the ready
coin of conversation. And 'tis every one's business to understand their
value.'

In the contest for Lady Bell's heart, the superficially glamorous Lord
Sparkle is rejected in favour of his less dazzling but more reliable rival:
'As caprice is absolutely necessary to the character of a fine lady, you will
not be surpris'd if I give an instance of it now; and, spite of your elegance,
your fashion, and your wit, present my hand to this poor soldier – who
boasts only worth, spirit, honour, and love.'[3]

Lady Bell Bloomer is one of the most successful examples of the stock
character of the witty, linguistically sophisticated and fearlessly outspoken lady, who arose from the drama and was developed by Richardson
in the character of Lady G. in *Sir Charles Grandison*.[4] Lady Bell and Lady
G. were two of Jane Austen's best-loved literary heroines. Strikingly, both
hold a more powerful social position than, for example, Elizabeth
Bennet. They are thus able to vent some of their intellectual frustration
upon the men around them. Though Elizabeth is without 'family,

connections and fortune', Austen ensured that her next spirited heroine Emma was not lacking in social status, wealth and power. Like Emma Woodhouse, the witty and popular Lady Bell only realises her love for Beauchamp when she mistakenly believes that he is in love with her friend and confidante, Julia. Lady Bell's jealousy of her friend inspires her moment of epiphany and the revelation that she does not know her own heart: 'the pangs of jealousy prov'd to me, in one moment, that *all* its sense is love'.[5]

Although Lady Bell promises to reform, she nevertheless continues to display her playful spirit with a quip that belies her intent. In response to Fitzherbert's vow to make Beauchamp his heir, Lady Bell protests against this measure to raise her husband's fortune from his modest pension as a soldier: 'Oh, I protest against that! – Our union would then appear a prudent, *sober* business, and I should lose the credit of having done a mad thing for the sake of the man my heart prefers.'[6]

Importantly, as with Elizabeth Bennet and Emma Woodhouse, the self-discovery of Lady Bell's folly and her ensuing marriage with a worthy man do not threaten to stifle her penchant for merriment. As Richardson's Lady G. protests her independence even as she walks up the aisle at her wedding ceremony, so Lady Bell's impending marriage promises not to suppress her spirit. In *Pride and Prejudice*, Darcy has to learn to be laughed at by his future wife, and, after they are married, she shocks his sister by continuing to talk to him 'in a lively, sportive manner' (*PP*, pp. 387–88). Critics have condemned Emma Woodhouse's failure to reform fully, or even to capitulate to her future spouse, but this is to misunderstand the workings of the lively heroine.[7]

Hannah Cowley's comedies also reveal the fascination in the drama of the period with conflict between social classes. In *Who's the Dupe?* (1779), the nimble-witted aristocrat Granger is shown making a fool of the *nouveau riche* merchant Doiley. Though his daughter Elizabeth is in love with Granger, Doiley is determined that she should marry the 'larned' scholar and pedant, Gradus. The witty and outspoken Elizabeth dislikes solemnity and gravity; she loves 'delightful nonsense'. She employs the help of her cousin and friend, Charlotte, to be rid of Gradus, leaving her free to marry Granger. Meanwhile, to Elizabeth's astonishment, Charlotte accepts a proposal of marriage from her rejected suitor.

In *Pride and Prejudice*, Austen echoes this plot-line, and even keeps the names of Elizabeth and Charlotte.

Austen's *Pride and Prejudice* may also have been alluding to another Cowley comedy, *The Belle's Stratagem* (1780), which begins with an account of five sisters from the country who come to town in the hope of finding rich husbands. This play was well known to Austen. She quoted a phrase in a letter to Cassandra in 1801: 'Mr Doricourt has travelled, he knows best.'[8] The vivacious heroine Letitia Hardy made this play Cowley's most popular and lasting comedy.

The plot of *The Belle's Stratagem* pivots upon the unpropitious first impressions of the fashionable Doricourt, when he meets Letitia for the first time. Determined to turn his indifference into love, she affects the manners of an ignorant country bumpkin to put him off, while enchanting him with her gaiety and wit (while in disguise) at a masked ball. When the lovers are finally united, Doricourt rejoices in her independence and liveliness, and confesses that he was deceived by his first impressions: 'You shall be nothing but yourself – nothing can be captivating that you are not. I will not wrong your penetration, by pretending that you won my heart at the first interview, but you have now my whole soul.'[9]

Unfavourable first impressions also provided the plot for *Pride and Prejudice*. Even if Austen was not consciously alluding to Cowley's play, she certainly used a similar comic motif of contrasting different social groups to express her views on morals and manners. The tension between town and country values had long been the staple of Restoration and eighteenth-century stage comedy, and in *Pride and Prejudice* Austen uses this motif for her thoroughgoing exploration of class and social prejudices.

Jane Austen's representation of social class requires an understanding of the indisputable fact – both celebrated and mocked in the drama of the period – of the fluidity and mobility of the middle classes in the late eighteenth and early nineteenth centuries.[10] The later novels, *Emma*, *Persuasion* and *Sanditon*, all register social and economic change, and enact social mobility.[11] But even in *Pride and Prejudice*, Austen celebrates her most upwardly mobile heroine in Elizabeth Bennet, and mocks the almost anachronistic social pride of the well-born Mr Darcy. She shows herself to be sympathetic to the claims of the rising middle classes, and gains much comic mileage from contrasts and comparisons between 'high' and 'low' characters. In this she was influenced by the dramatic tradition.

I have suggested in an earlier chapter that the drama's obsessive interest in the concept of social mobility, the rise of the middling classes, and the comic interplay between high life and low was fuelled by the widely divergent theatre-going public of the late eighteenth century. The usual convention in comic theatre for exploiting social difference was to depict the dramatic and comic situations that arise when a person crosses the boundary from low life to high. In the novel tradition, too, the social metamorphosis of a character such as Richardson's Pamela inspired other writers to explore the morals and manners of socially divergent groups. In *Evelina*, Fanny Burney provided satirical and sharply observed commentary on fashionable London society seen through the eyes of her intelligent ingénue.

The constant theme of Restoration and eighteenth-century comic drama is the contrast between genteel and mercantile values. In the novel tradition, Richardson's *Sir Charles Grandison* advocated the virtues of trade and commerce compared to mere gentility; Fanny Burney's novels and (unpublished and unproduced) stage comedies also suggest sympathy with the respectable merchant classes. Austen followed Burney in her unwillingness to ascribe bad behaviour to one particular class of society – most comedies satirised one social class at the expense of the other – and in her belief that morals and manners are inextricably linked.

The usual way to explore social difference in comedy was to bring the country girl to the town. In *Pride and Prejudice*, Austen brings the town to the country. This was a less conventional move, though Oliver Goldsmith in *She Stoops to Conquer* and Hannah Cowley in *The Runaway* had successfully used a country house setting for their comedies. In *She Stoops to Conquer*, Goldsmith opens his brilliantly conceived plot with two young men of fashion entering the country, one of whom (Marlow) arouses universal contempt for his haughty, supercilious manners, and subsequently falls in love with someone he believes to be a social inferior. The comedy, with its mix of genteel and low characters, is deeply concerned with the concept of social class. Kate Hardcastle, like Letitia Hardy in *The Belle's Stratagem*, deliberately reverses her social station to teach her lover a lesson and win his affections. However, her father's involuntary social metamorphosis – that is, Marlow's mistaken belief that he is an innkeeper – is dependent on the fact that Hardcastle cannot be recognised intrinsically as a gentleman. His lament, 'And yet he might have seen something in me above a common innkeeper',[12] reveals that rank and good breeding are not always concomitant.

In *Pride and Prejudice*, Elizabeth's most damning condemnation of Darcy is that he hasn't behaved as a gentleman.[13] Her stout refusal to equate high social status with intrinsic gentility sweeps away rigid class boundaries, and her marriage with Darcy heralds a more inclusive society. The final words of the novel reveal the realisation of Lady Catherine's fear that old money will mingle with new, that gentility will mingle with trade: 'she condescended to wait on them at Pemberley, in spite of that pollution which its woods had received, not merely from the presence of such a mistress, but the visits of her uncle and aunt from the city' (*PP*, p. 388).

The Gardiners are not the only family in the novel with trade connections. Mr Bingley's fortune has been acquired by trade, and the plot is initiated by his desire to purchase an estate. His sisters are 'fine ladies' who play down their associations with trade: 'They were of a respectable family in the north of England; a circumstance more deeply impressed on their memories than that their brother's fortune and their own had been acquired by trade' (*PP*, p. 15). Bingley's sisters are described as 'supercilious', unlike for example, Sir William Lucas, who has also acquired his fortune in trade, and has 'risen to the honour of knighthood', but 'though elated by his rank, it did not render him supercilious' (*PP*, p. 18).

The battle between town and country is invoked to play off different social groups. Darcy's first appearance at the Meryton Assembly, his slighting of Elizabeth, and his contempt for the 'collection of people in whom there was little beauty and no fashion' (*PP*, p. 16), perfectly express his indifference to the country. Even his swift change of heart towards Elizabeth asserts his town prejudice: 'in spite of his asserting that her manners were not those of the fashionable world, he was caught by their easy playfulness' (*PP*, p. 23). Caroline Bingley echoes this town prejudice with her disapproval of Elizabeth's 'country town indifference to decorum' (*PP*, p. 36). Her attempts to discredit Elizabeth in Darcy's eyes target her lowly origins, and her trade connections:

> 'I think I have heard you say, that their uncle is an attorney in Meryton.'
>
> 'Yes; and they have another, who lives somewhere near Cheapside.'
>
> 'That is capital,' added her sister, and they both laughed heartily.
>
> 'If they had uncles enough to fill *all* Cheapside,' cried Bingley, 'it would not make them one jot less agreeable.'
>
> 'But it must very materially lessen their chance of marrying men of any consideration in the world,' replied Darcy.
>
> To this speech Bingley made no answer; but his sisters gave it their hearty assent, and indulged their mirth for some time at the expense of their dear friend's vulgar relations. (*PP*, p. 37)

Since the Restoration, dramatists and novelists had mocked the 'Cits', the new-moneyed, vulgar-mannered social class that lived in the City of London as opposed to the fashionable West End of London. Austen shows her awareness of London's strict social geography in a discussion between Mrs Gardiner and Elizabeth, where they debate the probability of an encounter between Jane and Bingley: 'Mr Darcy may perhaps have *heard* of such a place as Gracechurch Street, but he would hardly think a month's ablution enough to cleanse him from its impurities, were he once to enter it' (*PP*, p. 141). Elizabeth in particular comprehends the huge social distance between Gracechurch Street (home to the Gardiners) and Grosvenor Street (home to the Bingleys). The residence of the Gardiners in Gracechurch Street is dependent upon practical considerations rather than fashionable ones: 'The Netherfield ladies would have had difficulty in believing that a man who lived by trade, and within view of his own warehouses, could have been so well-bred and agreeable' (*PP*, p. 139).

As has been seen, one of the most important changes in the theatre of the late eighteenth century was the development of increasingly middle-class attitudes and values.[14] The frequent appearance of the newly-rich merchant classes in the drama of the period, sometimes treated sympathetically, sometimes not,[15] suggests the emergence of a new social group. In the novel tradition too, Fanny Burney's *Evelina* drew upon the eighteenth-century stage tradition of playing off different social classes. Burney's hilarious portrayal in *Evelina* of the Branghtons, an archetypal *nouveau riche* family, charmed everyone from Dr Johnson in London to Jane Austen in Steventon – she read the comic parts of the novel aloud to her nieces. Inspired by her success with the Branghtons, and encouraged by the playwright/manager Sheridan, Burney set about writing a comic play which would contrast different social classes. Burney's comedies never reached the stage, so Austen could not have known them when writing *Pride and Prejudice*, but one of her best plays, *A Busy Day*, is striking for the insights into the social structures and manners of the late eighteenth century that it shares with Austen's work.

Burney's *Evelina* and *A Busy Day* exploit the motif of embarrassing relations whose ignorance and selfishness threaten the heroine's happiness. In *A Busy Day*, the heroine Eliza Watts is led to believe that her well-born lover (Cleveland) is repelled by her vulgar relations and low connections. In particular, Cleveland's aristocratic Aunt (Lady Wilhemina) is determined to oppose the match, which she believes to be an injury to her station and rank. Unlike many of the comedies which exploit one social group at the expense of the other, Burney is keen to suggest that ignorance, ill-breeding and selfishness are not the province of one particular social class, but can be seen in all sections of society. Eliza's *nouveau riche* family are vulgar, selfish and money-grubbing, but Cleveland's aristocratic family (the Tylneys) are very much the same. Sir Marmaduke orders his nephew Cleveland to marry a rich heiress to pay off his mortgages, and Lady Wilhemina is the quintessential social snob who worships the aristocracy and despises the lower orders. Burney ends her play with the claim that 'Merit is limited to no spot, and confined to no Class'.

Like her admired Burney, Austen is keen to suggest that bad behaviour is not confined to caste but can be seen in all sections of society, and to emphasise that there are no class boundaries in moral obtuseness, selfishness, vulgarity and rudeness. Caroline Bingley's jealous taunting of Darcy targets his social pride through jibes at Elizabeth's 'vulgar relations': 'Do let the portraits of your uncle and aunt Philips be placed in the gallery at Pemberley. Put them next to your great uncle the judge. They are in the same profession, you know; only in different lines' (*PP*, pp. 52–53). Elizabeth's laughter is the usual corrective to such blatant snobbishness, but she is also made uneasy by the indisputable fact of her mother's vulgarity. The ambiguity of her position is caught in an early exchange between the two circles (town and country – Bingleys and Bennets), where Darcy is indulging a stereotypical notion of country-life:

> 'In a country neighbourhood you move in a very confined and unvarying society.'
>
> 'But people themselves alter so much, that there is something new to be observed in them for ever.'
>
> 'Yes, indeed,' cried Mrs Bennet, offended by his manner of mentioning a country neighbourhood. 'I assure you there is quite as much of *that* going on in the country as in town.'
>
> Everybody was surprised; and Darcy, after looking at her for a moment, turned silently away. (*PP*, pp. 42–43)

Elizabeth's blushes for her mother's social indiscretions reveal not simply a refined sensibility on the model of Burney's heroines but a deeper, more complex sense of the requirements of social conduct. Caroline Bingley's forced politeness fools Mrs Bennet, but not Elizabeth, who notes that 'she performed her part indeed without much graciousness' (*PP*, p. 45). However, Elizabeth also 'trembles ... lest her mother should be exposing herself again'.

Ghastly relatives are a conventional trope in many of the comedies of the period. In Cowley's *Which is the Man?*, the low-born Sophy Pendragon, who is unexpectedly transported to London's high life, remarks, 'What d'ye think one has relations given one for? – To be asham'd of 'em'.[16] Comedies of the late eighteenth century, such as Burney's *A Busy Day* and Colman's *The Heir at Law*, also contain 'low' relations who specifically threaten the social pretensions and aspirations of the newly rich. The best scenes in these plays are the ones where the different sections of society meet in one room. Burney's final act of *A Busy Day* brings all the social classes together in order to play them off against each other. In *Pride and Prejudice*, the Netherfield Ball displays the Bennet family in the worst possible light, filtered through the eyes of the mortified heroine, and shows Austen drawing upon and yet departing from the comic conventions of the drama.

Social embarrassment is one of Austen's great themes in the novel, and at the Netherfield Ball she derives much of her comedy from this. Elizabeth's first mortification is her opening dance with Mr Collins; her 'shame and misery' due to the wrong-footedness and clumsiness of her partner set the tone for her exposure to the more severe embarrassments that are in store for her. Similarly, when asked to dance by Darcy, her unease is intensified by the knowledge that her every move is being closely observed. Strikingly, during the dance Elizabeth and Darcy both use the word 'performance' as a noun for drawing a person's character: 'I could wish, Miss Bennet, that you were not to sketch my character at the present moment, as there is reason to fear that the performance would reflect no credit on either' (*PP*, p. 94). Darcy is, of course, referring to Elizabeth's misreading of his own and Wickham's character, and though she claims that she 'must not decide on my own performance', she has already drawn Darcy's character. In this context, the word carries a resonance of the public perception of the case against Darcy: after all, a 'performance' requires an audience, and Elizabeth's prejudice has been enhanced by the opinions of others.

Ignoring Darcy's warning, Elizabeth blithely takes the bait when Caroline Bingley (rightly) defends Darcy against Wickham. Elizabeth's acute sense of social injustice is aroused by Caroline's attack on Wickham's socially dubious origins: 'he was the son of old Wickham, the late Mr Darcy's steward ... really considering his descent, one could not expect much better' (*PP*, pp. 94–95). Elizabeth's angry retort is typically sound: 'His guilt and his descent appear by your account to be the same ... for I have heard you accuse him of nothing worse than of being the son of Mr Darcy's steward' (*PP*, p. 95). However misguided she may be, her defence of Wickham's lowly origins reveals the heroine in a sympathetic light, in marked contrast to Mr Collins, who incurs contempt for ingratiating himself with those in a higher social position. Though Elizabeth speaks her mind freely when the occasion demands, she nevertheless has a highly developed sense of social protocol, which means that she is horrified when Mr Collins insists on paying his respects to Mr Darcy without a formal introduction. It is Elizabeth, not Mr Collins, who perceives Darcy's contempt, and her discomfort intensifies as her mother repeatedly breaches social etiquette by her indiscreet remarks about Jane and Bingley.

One of the supreme ironies of the novel is that Mrs Bennet is as bad as Darcy thinks she is, and, like Mrs Hardcastle in *She Stoops to Conquer*, has very little to redeem her. The scene is filtered mainly through the eyes of Elizabeth, whose discomfort is intensified by the fact that Darcy is also observing her mother's various improprieties: 'Elizabeth blushed and blushed again with shame and vexation' (*PP*, p. 100). Similarly, Mary's 'exhibition' is equally painful to her because she sees it through the contemptuous eyes of the Bingley sisters and Darcy:

> To Elizabeth it appeared, that had her family made an agreement to expose themselves as much as they could during the evening, it would have been impossible for them to play their parts with more spirit, or finer success … she could not determine whether the silent contempt of the gentleman, or the insolent smiles of the ladies, were more intolerable. (*PP*, pp. 101–2)

The final mortification for Elizabeth is Mrs Bennet's deliberate ploy to delay their departure at the end of the evening, especially as the Bingley sisters fully understand the ruse. Both sisters are patently rude, and the delay provides ample opportunity for the Bennet family to humiliate themselves further. The only other person to be sensible of the awkwardness of the party is her father: 'Mr Bennet, in equal silence, was enjoying the scene' (*PP*, p. 103).

Unlike Mr Bennet, Elizabeth takes no pleasure from the spectacle. Austen's narrative technique ensures that she is not merely a witness to the scene of social embarrassment, but a mortified player. She is forced to endure not only the humiliation of her family's impropriety, but to witness the contempt of others observing her family's humiliation. Austen's doubling of perspectives, Elizabeth watching Darcy watching Mrs Bennet, is a means of intensifying and exacerbating the heroine's shame and embarrassment. This, of course, is more difficult to achieve in the drama. In *A Busy Day*, for example, Burney relies upon the less subtle devices of caricature and verbal exclamation to achieve a similar effect. In other words, the vulgar characters (both high and low) are exaggerated in order for Eliza to express both her distaste of and her distance from them. Furthermore, she often openly expresses her shame and embarrassment at the vulgarity of her family: 'O Cleveland! with elegance like yours, founded on birth, education and intellectual endowments, can I wonder if your mind should involuntarily recoil from an alliance in which shame must continually struggle against kindness, and Pride against Happiness.'[17]

Like Eliza Watts, Elizabeth is forced to endure the spectacle of her vulgar relations at their worst in front of the man she will eventually marry. As in Burney's play, however, Austen replays the motif later in the novel at Darcy's expense. Lady Catherine is Mrs Bennet's comic counterpart, and Austen pricks her pomposity with as much relish as she displays Mrs Bennet's vulgarity. Elizabeth's presentation at Rosings is a scene of high comedy, with its semi-parodic overtones of a presentation at court. Sir William Lucas (himself only recently risen to 'the honour of a knighthood') takes it upon himself to be the expert on the 'manners of the great': 'About the Court, such instances of elegant breeding are not uncommon' (*PP*, p. 160). His daughter Maria 'looked forward to her introduction at Rosings, with as much apprehension, as her father had done to his presentation at St James's' (*PP*, p. 161). Mr Collins's instruction to the ladies not to dress too finely, for Lady Catherine 'likes to have the distinction of rank preserved', makes Maria tremble further. Elizabeth alone remains composed: 'She had heard nothing of Lady Catherine that spoke her awful from any extraordinary talents or miraculous virtue, and the mere stateliness of money and rank, she thought she could witness without trepidation' (*PP*, p. 161).

The group is ceremoniously led into the entrance hall, and through an ante-chamber to where Lady Catherine awaits. Then Jane Austen's comic description of the different responses to the courtly presentation endorses her heroine's equanimity:

In spite of having been at St James's, Sir William was so completely awed, by the grandeur surrounding him, that he had but just courage enough to make a very low bow, and take his seat without saying a word; and his daughter, frightened almost out of her senses, sat on the edge of her chair, not knowing which way to look. Elizabeth found herself quite equal to the scene, and could observe the three ladies before her composedly. – Lady Catherine was a tall, large woman, with strongly-marked features, which might once have been handsome. Her air was not conciliating, nor was her manner of receiving them, such as to make her visitors forget their inferior rank. (*PP*, p. 162)

Lady Catherine is in the comic tradition of redoubtable aristocratic ladies, beloved by Fanny Burney (Lady Smatter, Mrs Delvile, Lady Wilhemina), monsters of egotism, selfishness and pride. She has the same contempt for the lower orders as these other fine ladies, and a misplaced love of her own dignity. Though she is obsessed with the minutiae of social decorum, she is also rude and unfeeling. The comic effect is enhanced by the pairing of the well-built, talkative and domineering mother with her thin, pale and silent daughter. But, on a more sinister note, Lady Catherine's social power is not confined to her own small circle, for, as Elizabeth discovers, she has an effective spy in Mr Collins:

She was a most active magistrate in her own parish, the minutest concerns of which were carried to her by Mr Collins; and whenever any of the cottagers were disposed to be quarrelsome, discontented or too poor, she sallied forth into the village to settle their differences, silence their complaints, and scold them into harmony and plenty. (*PP*, p. 169)

Elizabeth assesses her as self-important and opinionated, reflecting that 'nothing was beneath this great Lady's attention, which could furnish her with an occasion of dictating to others' (*PP*, p. 163). However, she resolutely refuses to be bullied:

'Upon my word', said her Ladyship, 'you give your opinion very decid-
edly for so young a person. – Pray, what is your age?'

'With three younger sisters grown up', replied Elizabeth smiling,
'Your Ladyship can hardly expect me to own it'. Lady Catherine seemed
quite astonished at not receiving a direct answer; and Elizabeth
suspected herself to be the first creature who had ever dared to trifle
with so much dignified impertinence. (*PP*, p. 166)

It is now Darcy's turn to blush for his relations, especially when his aunt
offers Elizabeth the use of her pianoforte, in a part of the house that
nobody uses: 'Mr Darcy looked a little ashamed of his aunt's ill breeding,
and made no answer' (*PP*, p. 173).

Elizabeth is wrong in her estimation that Darcy is culpable of the
'worst kind of pride'. In her view, this is social pride, which distinguishes
and elevates rank before any other considerations, what she describes as
'want of importance in his friend's connections, than from their want of
sense' (*PP*, p. 187). Darcy's self-exculpatory letter, however, makes it
abundantly clear that the real objection to Elizabeth's family is not their
rank, but their behaviour: 'The situation of your mother's family, though
objectionable, was nothing in comparison of that total want of propriety
so frequently, so almost uniformly betrayed by herself, by your three
younger sisters, and even occasionally by your father' (*PP*, p. 198). Most
painful of all for Elizabeth is that 'Jane's disappointment had in fact been
the work of her nearest relations' (*PP*, p. 209). She is made aware from
this point on that breaches of social etiquette hold potentially damaging
consequences.

Nevertheless, even though Elizabeth is finally brought to acknowledge
the truth of Darcy's appraisal of her family, he too must learn to abandon
the social pride that is manifested in his superciliousness towards trade.
When Darcy asks Elizabeth to introduce him to the Gardiners, whom he
mistakes for 'people of fashion', she obliges with the expectation of 'his
decamping as fast as he could from such disgraceful companions' (*PP*, p.
255). His reformation forces a re-evaluation of his social prejudices:
'When she saw him thus seeking the acquaintance, and courting the good
opinion of people, with whom any intercourse a few months ago would
have been a disgrace; when she saw him thus civil, not only to herself, but

to the very relations whom he had openly disdained ... the difference, the change was so great' (*PP*, p. 263). He later confesses that she alone has effected the change, 'By you I was properly humbled' (*PP*, p. 369).

Conversely, Lady Catherine's deeply rooted class prejudices show no such capacity for change. The set-piece of Lady Catherine's memorable encounter with Elizabeth relies upon traditional comic and quasi-theatrical techniques. One of the more classical conventions that Austen draws upon in this scene is the triumph of the new order over the old. Elizabeth's moral defeat of the older woman reveals the shallowness and ignorance of the social distinctions to which Lady Catherine is desperate to cling. Her speech about the importance of continuing the noble line by the union of Darcy and his cousin, and her insistence that Elizabeth – 'a young woman without family, connections, or fortune' – should not 'quit the sphere, in which [she] has been brought up' (*PP*, p. 356), wholly discredit the speaker. By now, it is impossible for the reader to imagine the possibility of a marriage between Darcy and the sickly Anne, especially given the extraordinary vigour of Elizabeth in this scene, and, as a result, Lady Catherine's anachronistic class distinctions lose all credibility and seem merely absurd. Her insistence that the union would 'ruin him in the opinion of all his friends and make him the contempt of the world' (a similar objection that Richardson's Mr B. makes to Pamela) is crushed by Elizabeth's fitting and final words: 'With regard to the resentment of his family, or the indignation of the world, if the former *were* excited by his marrying me, it would not give me one moment's concern – and the world in general would have too much sense to join in the scorn' (*PP*, p. 358).

During the confrontation, Lady Catherine accuses Elizabeth of being 'lost to every feeling of propriety and delicacy', a charge that she equates with her refusal to accept the distinctions of social class. But, as Elizabeth demonstrates, true propriety and delicacy are indicative of manners rather than rank. Furthermore, although Elizabeth refuses to be bullied by authority and exhibits courage and frankness in her private encounter with Lady Catherine, she also has a heightened awareness of the importance of observing social forms in public.

When Elizabeth taxes Darcy on his rudeness and incivility at their first public meeting, this opens up an important discourse on the art of social role-playing. Darcy professes that he lacks the necessary 'talent' for social intercourse, but Elizabeth reminds him that it is more a matter of practice and personal endeavour: 'My fingers do not move over this instrument in the masterly manner which I have seen so many women's do ... but then I have always supposed it to be my own fault – because I would not take the trouble of practising' (*PP*, p. 175). Elizabeth's remonstrance is gently phrased, and her analogy between practising the piano and practising social intercourse also resonates with Lady Catherine's earlier rudeness concerning the use of her piano. Darcy's response, 'we neither of us perform to strangers', is ambiguous; for although she is without affectation or false pretensions, Elizabeth is mindful of the necessity of social performance.

Jane Austen's heightened sense of the complexity of social performance means that even a matter such as a simple leave-taking presents potential conflicts. Elizabeth's farewell to Mr Collins, which 'tried to unite civility and truth in a few short sentences', epitomises the perennial problem of right social conduct. Even Elizabeth, despite her gift for social intercourse, struggles with this. She only succeeds by dint of her highly dexterous verbal skills which, for example, allow her to say with impunity to Mr Collins that 'she firmly believed and rejoiced in his domestic comforts' (*PP*, p. 216).

Elizabeth's social discretion is contrasted with Lydia's reckless want of delicacy. When the Bennet girls are waiting for their carriage at the roadside inn, Lydia is highly amused that Jane and Elizabeth send the waiter away before relating her gossip: 'Aye, that is just like your formality and discretion. You thought the waiter must not hear, as if he cared! I dare say he often hears worse things said than I am going to say. But he is an ugly fellow! I am glad he is gone. I never saw such a long chin in my life' (*PP*, p. 220).

As in *Sense and Sensibility*, Austen is comparing and contrasting different forms of social conduct. Lydia shows no compunction in expressing her feelings about Wickham and the heiress Mary King: 'I will answer for it he never cared three straws about her. Who *could* about such a nasty little freckled thing' (*PP*, p. 220). Elizabeth is shocked by her sister's candour, in part because she feels the same way: 'Elizabeth was shocked to think that, however incapable of such coarseness of *expression* herself, the coarseness of the *sentiment* was little other than her own breast had formerly harboured and fancied liberal!' (*PP*, p. 220). Once again, Austen illustrates the disparity between inward feeling and outward conduct that is so beautifully expressed by Elinor Dashwood in *Sense and Sensibility*: 'My doctrine has never aimed at the subjection of the understanding. All I have ever attempted to influence has been the behaviour' (*SS*, p. 94).

One of Elizabeth's rare lapses of decorum is brought on by the news of the match between Charlotte and Mr Collins. Her shock when she learns of the engagement is 'so great as to overcome at first the bounds of decorum ... "Engaged to Mr Collins! My dear Charlotte, – impossible!"' (*PP*, p. 124). It is Charlotte who is dismayed and confused by 'so direct a reproach' and Elizabeth ensures that her blunder is smoothed over and appropriate congratulations offered. In private, she laments the match and makes one of her most damning judgements when she refutes Jane's defence of Charlotte: 'You shall not, for the sake of one individual, change the meaning of principle and integrity, nor endeavour to persuade yourself or me, that selfishness is prudence, and insensibility of danger, security for happiness' (*PP*, pp. 135–36).

Elizabeth's own refusal of Mr Collins comically reveals the complexities of social conduct for young women on the subject of marriage. Mr Collins assumes her rejection of him is a ruse to increase his ardour, 'according to the usual practice of elegant females', but she insists 'I would rather be paid the compliment of being believed sincere ... Do not consider me now as an elegant female intending to plague you, but as a rational' creature speaking the truth from her heart' (*PP*, pp. 108–9).

Elizabeth is mortified that her refusal is taken as the 'affectation and coquetry of an elegant female'. And although this is the sort of paradox in social conduct that Austen exploits for comic effect, there are moral implications too. Both Jane and Elizabeth discuss the impossibility of right female conduct within courtship. Jane defends Bingley's flirtation – 'Women fancy admiration means more than it does' – but her sister retaliates sharply: 'And men take care that they should.' Elizabeth, furthermore, assesses the moral implications of ambiguous social conduct, whereby harm can be done without design: 'but without scheming to do wrong, or to make others unhappy, there may be error, and there may be misery. Thoughtlessness, want of attention to other people's feelings, and want of resolution, will do the business' (*PP*, p. 136).

Elizabeth's belief in 'attention to other people's feelings' is reflected in her private conduct as well as public. She shows propriety and delicacy in her attitude towards Jane, in her refusal to speculate upon Mr Bingley's return to Netherfield, though 'no such delicacy restrained her mother' (*PP*, p. 129). Similarly, she shows her capacity to 'unite civility with truth' in her rapprochement with Wickham, and her tacit championing of Darcy: 'In essentials, I believe, he is very much what he was' (*PP*, p. 234). Her stout refusal to be once again drawn in by Wickham ensures that 'they parted at last with mutual civility, and possibly a mutual desire of never meeting again' (*PP*, p. 235).

It is striking that no such decorum is necessary for the union between Elizabeth and Darcy. Indeed, their relationship is defined by their mutual candour, and their unwillingness to dissemble, which is perhaps what Darcy implies in his remark that 'neither of us performs to strangers'. Their earliest exchanges convey a refreshing irreverence that belies their strong mutual attraction, as when Elizabeth's challenge, '*your* defect is a propensity to hate everybody', is countered with Darcy's swift return, 'And yours is wilfully to misunderstand them'. In a later erotically charged exchange, he shows that he is more than equal to her spirit of independ-ence: 'I have had the pleasure of your acquaintance long enough to know, that you find great enjoyment in occasionally professing opinions which in fact are not your own' (*PP*, p. 174).

The quality of the wit-combats was what inspired Austen's first critics to see shades of Shakespeare's Beatrice in Elizabeth. They are independ-ent-minded young women each of whom 'falls in love on the same prin-ciples of contrariety'. Certainly, as Darcy confesses, the effect of Lady Catherine's interference 'had been exactly contrariwise' and 'taught him to hope'. For, as Darcy well knows, 'had you been absolutely, irrevocably decided against me, you would have acknowledged it to Lady Catherine, frankly and openly'. Elizabeth's witty response accepts the veracity of his charge: 'Yes, you know enough of my *frankness* to believe me capable of *that*. After abusing you so abominably to your face, I could have no scru-ple in abusing you to all your relations' (*PP*, p. 367). Here, as so often, the development of the courtship proceeds through razor-sharp dialogue in the exact manner of that tradition of witty stage comedy which runs from *Much Ado About Nothing* through the Restoration to Hannah Cowley.

Elizabeth shows her grasp of the particular dynamic of their relationship when she assesses the qualities with which Darcy fell in love:

> 'My beauty you had early withstood, and as for my manners – my behaviour to *you* was at least always bordering on the uncivil … Now be sincere; did you admire me for my impertinence?'
>
> 'For the liveliness of your mind, I did.'
>
> 'You may as well call it impertinence at once. It was very little less. The fact is, that you were sick of civility, of deference, of officious attention. You were disgusted with the women who were always speaking and looking, and thinking for *your* approbation alone. I roused, and interested you, because I was so unlike *them.*' (*PP*, p. 380)

It is precisely Elizabeth's irreverence and frankness that make possible a private language between them that transcends a society dependent upon conformity to social mores.

In her next two novels, *Mansfield Park* and *Emma*, Jane Austen returned to many of the themes of *Pride and Prejudice*. Her interest in the concept of social class and the quest to discover a language truthful to emotional experience were explored with even greater depth and insight. As this chapter has demonstrated, one of the great lessons that Austen took from the drama was the idea that social life always requires a strong element of role-playing. *Mansfield Park* and *Emma* are, respectively, her most complex and her wittiest explorations of this idea. In different ways, each novel owes much of its profundity to a highly fruitful engagement with the dramatic tradition.

8

Lovers' Vows

Mansfield Park is considered to be Jane Austen's problem novel, contrasting sharply with the comic brilliance of its predecessor, *Pride and Prejudice*.[1] Its depiction of an awkward, shy and socially displaced heroine – the diametric opposite of the lively, unrestrained Elizabeth Bennet – has aroused considerable hostility.[2] Yet Austen was an author who constantly experimented with narrative style and technique: it is characteristic that she should have transposed the role of the witty stage-heroine to the anti-heroine, Mary Crawford, and depicted the heroine, Fanny Price, as a reliable but dull understudy waiting in the wings.[3]

The theatrical metaphor is apt, as the novel ambitiously undertakes to depict the consciousness of not one, but a whole cast of characters. Jane Austen focuses her plot more broadly than usual, exploring the development of not one or two but four young women. With most of the action taking place in a large country house, the dynamics of the plot are rendered through the grouping and regrouping of her large cast of characters. As in the other novels, relationships are developed in the setting of the formal or semi-formal occasion: balls, outings, dinner parties, family visits.

Austen expressed dissatisfaction with the 'playfulness and epigrammatism' of *Pride and Prejudice*, and in *Mansfield Park* returns to the morally ambiguous and uncertain territory of *Sense and Sensibility*. In deliberate contrast to *Pride and Prejudice*, she sets a more sober tone from the outset. Nevertheless, comedy permeates the novel, especially in the events surrounding the amateur theatricals. Of all Austen's mature works, *Mansfield Park* is the one that most systematically engages with the drama. This is primarily because the novel's plot is interwoven with the plot of a controversial eighteenth-century play, *Lovers' Vows*.

* * *

The critical debate that continues to surround Jane Austen's use of *Lovers' Vows* is, in part, due to the ideological concerns raised by the play's authorship. The play rehearsed for the Mansfield theatricals is Elizabeth Inchbald's expurgated version of August Kotzebue's *Das Kind der Liebe*. Inchbald softens the original title, a literal translation of which would be *The Love-Child*. According to Mrs Inchbald's first biographer, James Boaden, a translation of Kotzebue's popular melodrama was brought to her in 1798 by the manager of Covent Garden, who 'desired her to fit it to the English stage'.[4] Under the title of *Lovers' Vows*, Mrs Inchbald's play was performed at Covent Garden in 1798. Its continuing popularity throughout the 1798–99 Covent Garden season (forty-two performances) was assured by favourable reviews and high receipts.[5] In the next few years the play was staged at Drury Lane, the Haymarket and the Theatre Royal, Bath. It was publicly performed in Bath at least seventeen times when the Austens lived there between 1801 and 1806.[6]

Much has been made in recent years of the political implications of the play-within-the-novel. For some critics, what is particularly attractive about Austen's choice of play is the opportunity it has given them to construe *Mansfield Park* as an attack upon the drama, and Kotzebue in particular.[7] One of the problems with this argument is that Austen enjoyed going to see Kotzebue plays. As has been shown, she saw various Kotzebue adaptations at the professional theatre, including *The Birth-Day*, *Of Age Tomorrow* and *The Bee-Hive*. She attended a performance of the last of these as late as 1813. Two of the most frequently performed roles of her admired Elliston were those of the heroes of immensely popular Kotzebue adaptations: *The Stranger* and *Pizarro*. She clearly also knew *Lovers' Vows* extremely well.

Jane Austen may even have attended an amateur version of *Lovers' Vows* in a private theatre. Three letters written to Cassandra in 1814 repeatedly refer to General Chowne, a family friend, as 'Frederick'.[8] In the same letters, there are comments about *Mansfield Park*. Austen remarks, 'I shall be ready to laugh at the sight of Frederick again' (*Letters*, p. 256), and finds Chowne much changed when she sits next to him at the theatre: 'he has not much remains of Frederick' (*Letters*, p. 258). Her final reference to Chowne connects him once again with 'Frederick': 'We met only Gen. Chowne today, who has not much to say for himself. – I was ready to laugh at the remembrance of Frederick, and such a different Frederick as we chose to fancy him to the real Christopher!' (*Letters*, p. 262). The most plausible explanation of this play on the name is that Chowne acted the part of Frederick in an amateur production of *Lovers' Vows*, and that this is what was being remembered with amusement by Jane and Cassandra.[9]

Speculative as this supposition may be, it cannot be disputed that Jane Austen attended rather than boycotted Kotzebue plays at the public theatre. She even took her impressionable young nieces along with her. As we have seen, she joked about her role as the young girls' chaperone. Equally, at the time she was reading the moralistic and anti-theatrical Thomas Gisborne, she was performing private theatricals with her nieces.

This is not to suggest that Austen was unaware of the controversial aspects of *Lovers' Vows*.[10] Indeed, she draws some of her most effective irony from her different characters' reaction to the chosen play. Edmund's sarcastic suggestion that the theatrical party put on a 'German play' shows him taking a rather conventional stance of high-minded prejudice against German drama. The Earl of Carlisle, writing his *Thoughts upon the Present Conditions of the Stage* in 1808, lamented a decline in standards due to 'those vicious productions of the German writers': 'This accounts for what appears to be a most vitiated taste of the public in the endurance of those childish pantomimes, Blue Beard, etc. on the very boards where Shakespeare and Otway once stormed the human heart.'[11]

When Edmund's ironic suggestion is turned against him and the group settles on *Lovers' Vows*, his shocked reaction to the female parts also conforms to a very stereotypical prejudice against the character of the fallen woman. Austen makes it clear that it is the fallen Agatha rather than the coquettish Amelia who is the cause for concern. When Edmund pointedly asks Maria 'what do you do for women?', she is unable even to speak the name of Agatha: 'I take the part which Lady Ravenshaw was to have done' (*MP*, p. 139).

The rendering of the plight of fallen women was not uncommon on the eighteenth-century stage. Nicholas Rowe's tragedy *Jane Shore*, which Austen satirised in her juvenilia, was a vehicle for stars like Siddons, and later O'Neill, to arouse pity and feeling for the abject figure of the fallen woman. Hastings's attempted rape of Jane Shore and the humiliating treatment she suffers at his hands are partly punishment for her lapse from virtue, but she is portrayed, ultimately, as a dignified and repentant figure. Though she attains her husband's forgiveness in her final moments, one of her most famous speeches is a reminder of the harsh, but inescapable, truth of the inequality of women:

> Why should I think that man will do for me
> What yet he never did for wretches like me?
> Mark by what partial justice we are judged:
> Such is the fate unhappy women find,
> And such the curse intail'd upon our kind,
> That man, the lawless libertine, may rove,
> Free and unquestion'd through the wilds of love;
> While woman, sense and nature's easy fool,
> If poor weak woman swerve from virtue's rule,
> If, strongly charm'd, she leave the thorny way,
> And in the softer paths of pleasure stray;
> Ruin ensues, reproach and endless shame,
> And one false step entirely damns her fame.
> In vain with tears the loss she may deplore,
> In vain look back to what she was before,
> She sets, like stars that fall, to rise no more.[12]

Charles Inigo Jones, in his memoir of Eliza O'Neill, was keen to stress her ability to impart purity to Kotzebue's fallen women. He isolated Jane Shore's speech as the linchpin of English morality: 'These sentiments of Rowe may be considered as the standard English opinion on the subject of female frailty, contrasted with the modern school of Kotzebue, as inferred by his portrait of Mrs Haller in *The Stranger*.'[13]

Kotzebue's fallen women, such as Elvira in *Pizarro* and Mrs Haller in *The Stranger*, are certainly more defiant figures than their English counterparts, and it was therefore vital that actors such as Siddons and O'Neill displayed the requisite purity and dignity: 'The sterling good sense of this country is not easily led astray by the sophistry of the new philosophy ... A Mrs Haller and a Mary Wolstancroft [*sic*] are the same; and if their morality is to be the guide and standard of female excellence, virtue will be but an empty name, and guilt lose all its turpitude.'[14]

William Dunlap in his memoir of G. F. Cooke took a rather more liberal view of Kotzebue's fallen women than the conventional one put by Austen into the mouth of Edmund Bertram: 'What torrents of abuse have been turned upon Kotzebue for uniting *Agatha Fribourg* in wedlock to her seducer, after twenty years of exemplary conduct and exemplary suffering.'[15] Dunlap complained that while George Colman the Younger's *Peregrine* was seen as a lesson in high morality – 'Its great object is to excite a just detestation of the character of a seducer, and to inculcate mercy and forgiveness to the seduced' – Kotzebue was damned for the same lesson: 'The reprehension of the crime, and the exhibition of the consequences are stronger in Kotzebue than in Colman. But German literature had become at one period too brilliant, too fashionable, and usurped too much attention – it became the interest of certain English writers to put it down.'[16]

Edmund thus adopts a conventional stance of trashing German drama and condemning the figure of Agatha Friburg, although his moral indignation does not prohibit him from taking part in *Lovers' Vows*. Dunlap's memoir of Cooke was first published in 1814, which suggest that the controversy about Kotzebue and Agatha Friburg was still topical when *Mansfield Park* was published (Dunlap had that same year also adapted *Lovers' Vows* in America).[17]

Kotzebue is only part of the story. Austen and her readers would also have been aware of the fact that *Lovers' Vows* was translated and adapted by Elizabeth Inchbald.[18] Inchbald's reputation as a writer was well-established and she was highly respected in literary London. She had at one time been in close association with Jacobin circles, yet in her preface to *Lovers' Vows* she indicates that she was no extremist.[19]

In her preface Inchbald also showed her sensitivity to the issue of female propriety. She accordingly altered Amelia's 'indelicately blunt' proposal of love to suit the sensibilities of her English audience by replacing 'coarse abruptness' with 'whimsical insinuations'.[20] Furthermore she removed sensitive political references such as Count Cassel's description of the attack on him in Paris at the start of the Revolution.[21] She also increased the comedy by building up the part of Verdun the butler.

Austen's deliberate omission of Kotzebue's name from the text of *Mansfield Park* only draws further attention to Mrs Inchbald.

The connection is particularly striking when viewed in the light of the fact that Inchbald had already invented a love affair between a priest and a coquette in her novel *A Simple Story*. *Lovers' Vows* ideally suited Austen's intentions of interweaving a dramatic counter-text with the plot of her novel. The particular rendering of a relationship between a coquette and a clergyman in this play, for example, has no other precedent in the drama. And the character of Agatha Friburg, perhaps one of the most notorious portrayals of a fallen woman, resonates with Austen's own depiction of a fallen woman.

Elizabeth Inchbald's play raises considerations about the right of women to choose their own husbands, about a father's responsibilities to his children, and, perhaps most radically, about the validity of innate merit rather than social position. In *Mansfield Park* Jane Austen is deeply engaged with all of these issues. In order for her to develop further her interest in the relationship between role-playing and social behaviour, she needed a play that could be interlinked with the characters in her novel. The sub-plot of *Lovers' Vows* parallels the main plot in *Mansfield Park*: the prohibited love between a heroine and the clergyman/mentor who is responsible for forming her mind and her values. Additionally, the counter-text allows Austen to explore the 'dangerous intimacies' between the pairings of Edmund/Mary and Henry/Maria, with Fanny weaving between the two couples. There was simply no other play that could have done this as well as *Lovers' Vows*.

Austen describes the seemingly careless gesture of Tom Bertram flicking through the pages of the eclectic volumes of plays that line the table, only to chance upon the script of *Lovers' Vows* – but of course the choice has been carefully and consciously made, long before the heir of Mansfield Park triumphantly alights upon it. As Yates insists, 'After all our debatings and difficulties, we find there is nothing that will suit us altogether so well, nothing so unexceptionable, as Lovers' Vows' (*MP*, p. 131).

Jane Austen's intricate interweaving of novel and play depends upon an assurance of her readers' familiarity with *Lovers' Vows*. Notably, Fanny is the only principal character in the novel who has not read or seen the play. Tom Bertram defends the educational benefit of play-*reading*, and insists on its efficacy for improving public speaking. Tom's conviction of his father's tacit approval of the amateur theatricals is rather loosely based upon Sir Thomas's encouragement of youthful recitations – an essential part of male education. Even the relatively humble Robert Martin in *Emma* 'would read something aloud out of *Elegant Extracts*' (*E*, p. 29).

Tom, Edmund, Henry and Rushworth all refer to their visits to the public theatre, whereas among the female characters only Lady Bertram does so. This suggests that Maria and Julia have derived their prior knowledge of *Lovers' Vows* from reading rather than viewing. (The sale of the family's town house to settle Tom's debts could have made theatre-going more difficult for the young ladies.) When Edmund urges Maria to give the play up, he makes the assumption that she hasn't *read* it carefully enough, but Maria quickly confirms that she is 'perfectly acquainted' with *Lovers' Vows*. Play-reading is a prerequisite for a would-be heroine. Ironically, Maria, unlike Catherine Morland in *Northanger Abbey*, fails to learn the lessons from the printed text.[22]

Fanny Price has no qualms about 'reading' *Lovers' Vows*. Play-reading is her only source of dramatic entertainment until she is awakened, by Henry Crawford, to the pleasures of 'good hardened real acting' (*MP*, p. 124). In *Mansfield Park* Jane Austen not only directly shows her own heroine in the act of reading plays, she also indirectly encourages play-reading in her own readers by assuming prior knowledge of Mrs Inchbald's play – even today, readers who enjoy the novel are tempted to go on to the play. Much of the first volume of *Mansfield Park* is only partially intelligible without knowledge of *Lovers' Vows*. If Austen really did make the assumption that her readers had direct access to the play, this makes clear her reason for directly quoting only one speech from it. She simply believed that her readers, like herself, held the text in their memories or had it in their libraries. With this is mind I would like to argue for a closer reading of *Lovers' Vows* than has previously been attempted.[23]

*   *   *

In *Lovers' Vows*, Baron Wildenhaim has seduced and then abandoned a chambermaid, Agatha Friburg, in his youth. When the play opens Agatha is in a state of poverty, where she is found by her illegitimate son Frederick, now a soldier. When he learns the true story of his birth, he goes out to beg in order to help his mother. He happens to meet his father and tries to rob him. When he is arrested he reveals the identity of himself, the Baron and his mother. With the aid of the pastor, Anhalt, he persuades the Baron to marry Agatha. The Baron also consents to the marriage of his daughter, Amelia, to Anhalt, instead of forcing her to marry Count Cassel, a rich but brainless fop he had in mind for her.[24]

The casting eventually agreed at Mansfield is as follows:

MEN
Baron Wildenhaim – Mr Yates
Count Cassel – Mr Rushworth
Anhalt – Edmund Bertram
Frederick – Henry Crawford
Verdun the Butler – Tom Bertram
Landlord – Tom Bertram
Cottager – Tom Bertram

WOMEN
Agatha Friburg – Maria Bertram
Amelia Wildenhaim – Mary Crawford
Cottager's Wife – Fanny Price

Austen's introduction of *Lovers' Vows* into the action of *Mansfield Park* is a much more serious and far-reaching matter than the arbitrary choice of a play for an entertaining diversion during the absence of the father of the house. The choice of play signals Austen's engagement with the subject of prohibited relationships and with a long-standing debate about women's autonomy in courtship.

In *Northanger Abbey*, Austen had mocked Samuel Richardson's claim that no woman should fall in love with a man before he had made his proposal.[25] In her first published novel, *Sense and Sensibility* (1811), she had depicted two heroines who love without promise, and explored the implications of this condition for young, penniless women. In her later novels, *Mansfield Park* and *Persuasion*, she dramatises the effect of constrained love upon her displaced heroines. Throughout *Mansfield Park*, Fanny Price is portrayed in the uncompromising position of loving without invitation, and, much worse, loving without hope.

In *Mansfield Park* Austen explores female consciousness in four young women, and focuses upon the comparisons and contrasts of female conduct in the courtship process. The prototype for this type of narrative was her admired *Sir Charles Grandison*. Richardson's novel was among the first of its kind to describe female consciousness in detail, and its depiction of Harriet Byron's entrance into the world was a theme taken up most successfully by female authors such as Fanny Burney in *Evelina* (1771) and Maria Edgeworth in *Belinda* (1801).

The first three volumes of Richardson's lengthy novel depict his heroine's difficulty in deciding whether she should conceal or admit her love for Sir Charles before he has addressed her with a formal declaration. The character of Amelia Wildenhaim in *Lovers' Vows* is the stage prototype of a woman who unequivocally defends her right to love before her love is returned. From Richardson's portrayal of his heroine's dilemma in courtship to Inchbald's depiction of a brazen coquette initiating her own right to choose there is a huge leap in notions of female propriety. Inchbald, via Kotzebue, takes up the cause of a woman's right to court.

Lovers' Vows and *Mansfield Park* are both explorations of the *Grandison* theme: the difficulties of a prohibited relationship, from a woman's perspective.[26] The most obvious parallel between *Mansfield Park* and *Lovers' Vows* is that each work gives prominence to a relationship between a coquette and a clergyman. Inchbald was drawn to this kind of relationship partly for personal reasons – she was in love with John Kemble, who had abandoned his clerical vocation in order to become an actor – but the motif also arose from the eighteenth-century resurrection of the medieval love story of Eloise and Abelard.[27] Inchbald's first novel, *A Simple Story* (1791), depicts a prohibited love affair between a pious Catholic priest and his lively and outspoken ward, Miss Milner. Her interest in this kind of prohibited relationship perhaps contributed to her decision to adapt *Lovers' Vows*. In *Mansfield Park* Austen orchestrates parallels with and deviations from the coquette/clergyman theme brought to her by Inchbald.

Mansfield Park has its own triangle of lovers: a coquette, a prude and a clergyman. In seeking a model for Mary Crawford's attempt to divert Edmund from his calling, Austen would have had to look no further than Inchbald's *Lovers' Vows*. In seeking a model for Fanny Price's concealed passion, she would also find one in the play. It may even be that *Lovers' Vows* actually gave Austen the impulse to broach this set of relationships in her novel.

On a superficial level, when the amateur theatricals take place at Mansfield Park, the characters seem to be cast into roles that are appropriate for them. But on more detailed examination we see that this is not always the case. Jane Austen uses the play as a point of reference for the novel's principal relationship, that between Fanny and Edmund; but, rather than the heroine being characterised as a charming coquette, Fanny is divested of superficial sexual charisma and behaves as a model of modesty and prudence. In *Mansfield Park* the plot is complicated by the presence of a third force, and the character of the winning coquette is displaced onto the anti-heroine, Mary Crawford, whose role is that of the seductress who poses a threat to the heroine's happiness. Mary acts as a dramatic foil to the shy, prudish heroine, and Fanny's jealousy of her dazzling rival prompts much of the novel's dynamic.

In character and situation both Mary and Fanny present a variation on the *Lovers' Vows* theme. Amelia Wildenhaim, a beautiful coquette, is secretly in love with the clergyman who has been responsible for her education. In *Mansfield Park* Mary Crawford exhibits similar qualities of wit and vivacity that tempt the prudish Edmund to waver from his duty. But Fanny Price is also offered as a modification of the *Lovers' Vows* theme; she loves a man destined for the clergy who is prohibited to her, and refuses a more lucrative offer of marriage from an unworthy suitor.

As Fanny is willing to defy Sir Thomas in refusing a man she doesn't love, so Amelia disregards wealth and status in favour of love. Amelia's disregard of the binding rules of courtship decorum obscures neither her ability to recognise and value Anhalt's understated qualities, nor her readiness to put personal happiness before material considerations. Mary Crawford recognises Edmund's worth and is attracted by his steadiness and integrity, but cynically insists that there is no glamour in being 'honest and poor' – 'I have a much greater respect for those that are honest and rich' (*MP*, p. 213). Mary will not lower herself to marry a clergyman, in particular a clergyman with a serious vocation: 'It was plain that he could have no serious views, no true attachment, by fixing himself in a situation which he must know she would never stoop to' (*MP*, p. 228). Amelia, like Miss Hastings in Goldsmith's play, will 'stoop to conquer'. Mary will not.

Mary Crawford's faults are primarily attributed to a lack of the right sort of education: she has had an education in fashionable accomplishments rather than in good principles and morals. Her verbal indiscretions are the indelible marks of her educational deficiencies. They alert both Fanny and Edmund to her casual disregard of propriety. In the Sotherton chapel, Mary's indecorous quip about the 'former belles of the house of Rushworth' making eyes at the chaplain confirms the Abelard and Eloise theme of *Lovers' Vows* and *Mansfield Park*: 'The young Mrs Eleanors and Mrs Bridgets – starched up into seeming piety, but with heads full of something very different – especially if the poor chaplain were not worth looking at' (*MP*, p. 87).

Mary's irreverent remark also reveals an irony at her own expense, for it coincides with her discovery that Edmund is to be a clergyman. Mary's remark, pointedly made in a disused family chapel, is a covert hint at her contempt for Edmund's chosen profession, which she subsequently and quite openly attempts to undermine. Edmund Bertram is undoubtedly modelled upon the lover/clergyman hero of Pope and Rousseau, modified by Inchbald and Kotzebue, and brought to Austen's *Mansfield Park* directly and indirectly through Edmund's role as Anhalt in *Lovers' Vows*. Edmund closely resembles Anhalt in character and in situation. They have chosen the same profession: the church. They are both responsible for nurturing a young woman who responds by falling in love with them, and they are both captivated by a fashionably accomplished woman who happens to be attractive, witty and verbally imprudent. The incident in the chapel heralds the long conflict ahead for Mary and Edmund that ends with his discovery of her 'corrupted, vitiated mind' (*MP*, p. 456).

Mary's fondest memory of Edmund is recalling him in a position of sexual submission:

The scene we were rehearsing was so very remarkable! The subject of it so very – very – what shall I say? He was to be describing and recommending matrimony to me. I think I see him now, trying to be as demure and composed as Anhalt ought, through the two long speeches … If I had the power of recalling any one week of my existence, it should be that week, that acting week. Say what you will, Fanny, it should be *that*; for I never knew such exquisite happiness in any other. His sturdy spirit to bend as it did! Oh! it was sweet beyond expression. (*MP*, p. 358)

For Austen it is the friction ensuing from the clash between the sexually confident coquette and the grave, prudish, religious figure that gives the relationship its dynamic.[28] Mary Crawford's persistent attempts to dissuade Edmund from his decision to be ordained not only reflect her desire to continue in the lifestyle to which she has become accustomed: they also increasingly become a struggle for the control of Edmund's spirit, something she clearly finds thrilling. Although some critics have puzzled over Mary's admiration of the rather stolid Edmund, this is to misunderstand the workings of the coquette/clergyman relationship. Mary's rival is the church. Mary's conflict with Edmund's religious vocation is no less than a fight for his soul, and this is why Fanny is so dead set against Mary and why Edmund is portrayed as a character divided against himself.

Mary's attempts to dissuade Edmund range from gentle persuasion – 'You really are fit for something better. Come, do change your mind. It is not too late. Go into the law' – to cruel attempts to emasculate him: 'Men love to distinguish themselves, and in either of the other lines, distinction may be gained, but not in the church. A clergyman is nothing' (*MP*, pp. 92–93). Eventually, when she is no longer convinced of her powers of persuasion, she pointedly insists that she 'never has danced with a clergyman … and never *will*' (*MP*, p. 268). Later, she ridicules his profession to his face (*MP*, p. 279). Having succeeded once in getting him to change his mind over playing Anhalt, Mary is angered to discover, during the card game Speculation, that she is deceived about her dreams of Edmund as an unordained 'gentleman of independent fortune.'[29]

Austen makes the comparison between Edmund and Anhalt abundantly clear from the outset of the theatrical episode in her telling description of Edmund caught 'between his theatrical and his real part' (*MP*, p. 163). Mary's comment about Edmund's performance of Anhalt's spiritual struggle, '*his* sturdy spirit to bend as it did', is thus deliberately ambiguous.

Edmund's long-drawn-out temptation is a source of provocation and anguish to his 'confessor', Fanny, who condemns him for his weakness and urges him to make up his mind: 'Finish it at once. Let there be an end of this suspense. Fix, commit, condemn yourself' (*MP*, p. 424). One of the cruelties of Fanny's position as confessor is that she is forced to listen to Edmund expressing both his admiration for, and his doubts about, Mary:

'I have been pained by her manner this morning, and cannot get the better of it. I know her disposition to be as sweet and faultless as your own, but the influence of her former companions makes her seem, gives to her conversation, to her professed opinions, sometimes a tinge of wrong. She does not *think* evil, but she speaks it – speaks it in playfulness – and though I know it to be playfulness, it grieves me to the soul'. 'The effect of education,' said Fanny gently. (*MP*, pp. 268–69)

Mary's verbal indiscretions frequently have a sexual content. Her remarks range from the mildly inappropriate – she jokes about the amorous servants lying in bed on a Sunday instead of going to chapel – to the more risqué joke about *Rears* and *Vices*. Her verbal improprieties, which reveal worldliness and knowingness, clearly hold a fascination for Edmund, which both attracts and repels. Yet although he is aware of her educational limitations, Austen reminds us that 'had he been able to talk another five minutes, there is no saying that he might not have talked away all Miss Crawford's faults and his own despondence' (*MP*, p. 270).

In *Lovers' Vows* Amelia promises to reimburse Anhalt's teaching by payment in kind. She will turn tutoress and so teach him how to love: 'none but a woman can teach the science of herself: and though I own I am very young, a young woman may be as agreeable for a tutoress as an old one'.[30] In contrast to the frivolously accomplished Bertram sisters and Mary Crawford, Fanny Price has had the 'proper' sort of education, nurtured by her cousin Edmund: she responds by loving him.

In both *Mansfield Park* and *Lovers' Vows* the young heroine falls in love with the man she holds responsible for her education. Paradoxically, then, it is Fanny, not Mary Crawford, who correlates with Amelia Wildenhaim in refusing a brilliant match with a rich but unworthy lover because her heart is pre-engaged to the man who has nurtured and educated her.

Alexander Pope in his poem *Eloise to Abelard* (1717) wrote of love:

Of all affliction taught a lover yet,
'Tis sure the hardest science to forget.[31]

The idea of love as a 'taught science' appears in all of the eighteenth-century resurrected versions of Eloise and Abelard. In *Lovers' Vows* the pious young clergyman, Anhalt, like Rousseau's St Preux in *La nouvelle Héloïse*, has been responsible for the tutoring of the Baron's family. Amelia unequivocally states, 'My father has more than once told me that he who forms my mind I should always consider as my greatest benefactor. And my heart tells me the same' (act 3, scene 2). Amelia inverts social convention when she candidly offers to teach Anhalt 'the science of herself', to repay him for the 'education' he has given her. This very closely parallels Rousseau, where Julie (the Eloise figure) explains to her father that her education is due to the exertions of her tutor: 'but all this could not be mine without a master: I told him mine, enumerating at the same time all the sciences he proposed to teach me, except one.'[32]

More radically, Amelia makes, in Fanny's words, 'very little short of a declaration of love' to her tutor: a shocking concept to Fanny, who is embarrassed by the similarity of her own situation to Amelia's. However, the idea of declaring that love, let alone making a proposal of marriage, is inconceivable to Fanny. Behind Fanny's discomfort of witnessing the 'dreaded scene' from *Lovers' Vows* is the cruel irony of her own similarity to Amelia. Edmund's searching out of Fanny to read Amelia's part against his Anhalt is potentially even more distressing than her being forced to watch Edmund and Mary rehearse the scene.

One of the ironies of Fanny's situation is that she is unable to express her true feelings directly to the one person who would listen, and a further cruel irony is that she is forced to accept the role of confidante to that same person. Fanny is aware of the cruelties of her position, yet is powerless to stem the force of her feelings:

> To think of him as Miss Crawford might be justified in thinking, would in her be insanity. To her, he could be nothing under any circumstances – nothing dearer than a friend. Why did such an idea occur to her even enough to be reprobated and forbidden? It ought not to have touched on the confines of her imagination. (*MP*, pp. 264–65)

Like Amelia in *Lovers' Vows*, Fanny is unmoved by the temptations of wealth, status and sexual conquest.[33] When she is given the rare opportunity to express her feelings, she does not hold back, as is shown in her gentle, but spirited, defence of her right to her 'negative':

> 'I *should* have thought … that every woman must have felt the possibility of a man's not being approved, not being loved by some one of her sex, at least, let him be ever so generally agreeable. Let him have all the perfections in the world, I think it ought not to be set down as certain, that a man must be acceptable to every woman he may happen to like himself … In my situation, it would have been the extreme of vanity to be forming expectation on Mr Crawford … How then was I to be – to be in love with him the moment he said he was with me? How was I to have an attachment at his service, as soon as it was asked for?' (*MP*, p. 353)

This speech is remarkable for its encapsulation of the paradoxes of courtship conduct for women, particularly those of a low status.

Fanny's 'settled dislike' of Crawford is not enough for Sir Thomas, or indeed Edmund, because Crawford is perceived as a socially acceptable 'catch'; yet, paradoxically, it is precisely Fanny's lowly social status which precludes her from forming any expectations of Henry in the first place. Furthermore, when she is condescended to be noticed by a man of means, a man whom she has no right to consider in the first place, she is immediately expected to switch on her feelings, 'as soon as it was asked for'. The further layer of irony exposed by this double standard is Fanny's concealed love for Edmund, to whom she is making this speech. Fanny's own impropriety in imagining Edmund as a sexual partner has been reproved by her own conscience, for daring 'to have touched on the confines of her imagination'. But, paradoxically, the knowledge that Edmund 'could be nothing [to her] under any circumstances' does not stop the idea occurring to her 'even enough to be reprobated and forbidden' (*MP*, pp. 264–65). This is precisely because feelings cannot be switched off and on at random.

Fanny, of course, is not in Amelia's position of choosing her own husband, but she nevertheless exercises her right to refusal, as do most of Jane Austen's heroines. In *Sir Charles Grandison* Harriet Byron complains to her confidante about the unfairness of courtship decorum: 'What can a woman do who is addressed by a man of talents inferior to her own? She cannot pick and choose, as men can. She has only her negative.'[34] Austen has Henry Tilney advocating women's 'power of refusal' in *Northanger Abbey*,[35] but in *Pride and Prejudice* she conveys the limitations of a woman's 'no' in Mr Collins's and Darcy's refusal to accept Elizabeth's refusal.

In Henry Mackenzie's Rousseauistic novel *Julia de Roubigné* the heroine is frustrated by the Count's persistent pursuit of her hand, and complains of the injustice for women in courtship: 'Is this fair dealing … that his feelings are to be an apology for his suit, while mine are not allowed to be a reason for refusal.'[36] In *Mansfield Park*, Henry's reluctance to accept Fanny's refusal is proof of his gross selfishness. Even when she is softened by his conduct at Portsmouth, she still hopes to be released from his attentions: 'might not it be fairly supposed, that he would not much longer persevere in a suit so distressing to her?' (*MP*, p. 414).

Now it is Fanny who parallels Amelia in refusing an unwanted offer of marriage. While no one could claim that she shares Amelia's vivacity, she does share, to use Sir Thomas's term, an 'independence of spirit' (*MP*, p. 318). Neither Fanny nor Amelia will marry from a sense of duty. Amelia openly flirts with the reticent clergyman, but her intentions are deadly serious. She genuinely loves him and defiantly claims 'If you then love me as you say, I will marry; and will be happy – but only with you' (*LV*, act 3, scene 2). Paradoxically, it is Maria Bertram who, in refusing to be released from her engagement to Rushworth, does not exercise her right to refusal.

* * *

Many critics have noted the analogy between the two 'fallen woman', Agatha Friburg and Maria Bertram. The casting of Maria as Agatha is apt because, like her stage counterpart, she eventually becomes a social outcast through sexual misconduct. But Maria's character and situation are markedly different from those of her stage counterpart, just as Mary Crawford's and Amelia's situations are not as close as has usually been assumed. It is essential to the complex, ironic relationship between *Mansfield Park* and *Lovers' Vows* that not all the characters in the novel are, as superficially seems to be the case, cast in the parts that are appropriate for them – as we have seen from the greater resemblance of Amelia to Fanny Price than Mary Crawford.

Paradoxically, though Maria's situation as a fallen woman is different from Agatha's (she is the eldest daughter of a great family, not a seduced chambermaid), it does correspond with the role of the second female lead, Amelia. Both young women have an offer of marriage from men they despise, both are secretly in love with another man, both are under the jurisdiction of their fathers. Maria shares with her cousin, Fanny, the situation of being in love with an inaccessible man. Similarly, Sir Thomas's interviews with Maria and Fanny on the subject of the marriage transaction mirror each other.

One of the most striking parallels between *Lovers' Vows* and *Mansfield Park*, which is wholly lost on a reader unfamiliar with the play, is that between Sir Thomas Bertram and Baron Wildenhaim. As will be seen in the next chapter, Austen particularly relishes the great comic stage confrontation between Sir Thomas and Yates in the role of the Baron. In *Lovers' Vows* the loving and affectionate relationship between father and daughter is a striking reversal of the convention of the tyrannical Gothic father-figure so popular in late eighteenth-century fiction.

In *Mansfield Park* Wildenhaim's parental concern is echoed by that of Sir Thomas when he learns that his daughter's betrothed, James Rushworth, is empty and foolish. Rushworth's foppishness is likewise indicated by an 'unmanly' obsession with his 'finery'. His incessant references to his dressing-up clothes, in particular his pink satin costume, are a constant source of amusement to the other actors. That Rushworth is chosen to play the part of the despised suitor, Count Cassel, confirms the parallel between Sir Thomas and Wildenhaim.

Both Sir Thomas and the Baron hope for an improvement in their future sons-in-law: 'Mr Rushworth was young enough to improve; – Mr Rushworth must and would improve in good society' (*MP*, p. 201). Similarly Wildenhaim entreats the religious and spiritual guidance of Anhalt to improve Cassel, 'Take him under your care, while he is here, and make him something like yourself ... Form the Count after your own manner' (*LV*, act 2, scene 2). Both fathers act responsibly in their attempts to gauge their daughters' happiness, both profess an unwilling-ness to 'sacrifice' that happiness to financial gain, and both wish to become better acquainted with their future sons-in-law before express-ing their consent to marriage. Sir Thomas determines to spend more time with Rushworth in the hope of discovering the truth of Mrs Norris's promise that 'the more you know of him, the better you will like him' (*MP*, p. 190). Wildenhaim, likewise, is prepared to give his daughter time:

No, I shall not be in a hurry: I love my daughter too well. We must be better acquainted before I give her to him. I shall not sacrifice my Amelia to the will of others, as I myself was sacrificed. The poor girl might, in thoughtlessness, say yes, and afterwards be miserable. (*LV*, act 2, scene 2)

The Baron's concern for his daughter's marital felicity places him as a considerate and responsible parent. Similarly Sir Thomas decides to 'observe' Maria and Rushworth to ascertain the strength of her feelings:

He had expected a very different son-in-law; and beginning to feel grave on Maria's account, tried to understand *her* feelings. Little observation there was necessary to tell him that indifference was the most favourable state they could be in. Her behaviour to Mr Rushworth was careless and cold. She could not, did not like him ... Advantageous as would be the alliance, and long standing and public as was the engagement, her happiness must not be sacrificed to it. (*MP*, p. 200)

Wildenhaim's soliloquy is strikingly echoed in Sir Thomas's internal monologue. Both fathers condemn the idea of 'sacrifice' by an unhappy liaison, regardless of material advantage. Both fathers use the same strategy to ascertain the truth by resolving to speak seriously to their daughters in a private interview. Both fathers seem to be a reversal of the Gothic patriarch of stage and page.

Austen takes from *Lovers' Vows* the scene of a confrontation between father and daughter on the subject of marriage, and extends and modifies it on two separate occasions. As in the play, the novel has a meeting between the Baron(et) and his daughter in which he (feebly) attempts to discover her true feelings for her suitor. Austen invites us to consider the similarities and differences between the two fathers.

In *Lovers' Vows* the interview between father and daughter is light-hearted and comic. Baron Wildenhaim begins his paternal speech by urging openness: 'Amelia, you know you have a father who loves you … tell me candidly how you like Count Cassel? … to see you happy is my wish' (*LV*, act 2, scene 2). The exchange is punctuated by Wildenhaim's insistence on candour: 'but be sure to answer me honestly – Speak truth,' and 'Nor ever *conceal* the truth from me' (*MP*, p. 495). The comic irony springs from the knowledge that Amelia is barely attempting to conceal her secret love for her tutor, but Wildenhaim is too blind to notice her hints:

BARON: Psha! I want to know if you can love the Count. You saw him
  at the last ball when we were in France: when he capered around
  you; when he danced minuets; when he –. But I cannot say what his
  conversation was.

AMELIA: Nor I either [*sic*] – I do not remember a syllable of it.

BARON: No? Then I do not think you like him.

AMELIA: I believe not.

BARON: Do not you wish to take his part when his companions laugh
  at him?

AMELIA: No: I love to laugh at him myself. (*LV*, act 2, scene 2)

The potential seriousness of the father/daughter scene is undercut by Amelia's casual indifference to the whole transaction. Her most serious stated reservation about marriage with Cassel is that he steps on her toes at balls. Although Cassel's status and wealth are vigorously stressed by the Baron, Amelia defends her view that 'birth and fortune are inconsiderable things, and cannot give happiness'. The convention that is being satirised in this scene is the confrontation with the tyrannical father. Far from being ill at ease and powerless, as is the expectation of a dependent daughter refusing a wealthy and approved suitor, Amelia upturns the convention by coolly and openly acknowledging her contempt for her betrothed, and it is Wildenhaim who is embarrassed and flustered by his own clumsy attempts to do his fatherly duty. In *Mansfield Park*, compared with the friendly banter between Amelia and the Baron, there is a chilling lack of feeling between Maria and her father, as he attempts to follow up the observations that have stared everyone else in the face since her hasty engagement.

The interview between father and daughter is deliberately brief. Austen sets out the position in reported speech: 'With solemn kindness Sir Thomas addressed her; told her his fears, inquired into her wishes, entreated her to be open and sincere, and assured her that every inconvenience should be braved, and the connection entirely given up, if she felt herself unhappy in the prospect of it. He would act for her and release her' (*MP*, p. 200). The lack of dramatic impetus in the rendering of Sir Thomas's 'paternal kindness' is a deliberate and conscious device of distancing. Maria's dismissal of his fears is dutiful and equally polite, but it strikes a false note, which conveys her proud intransigence in the face of her father's probings:

> She thanked [Sir Thomas] for his great attention, his paternal kindness, but he was quite mistaken in supposing she had the smallest desire of breaking through her engagement, or was sensible of any change of opinion or inclination since her forming it. She had the highest esteem for Mr Rushworth's character and disposition, and could not have a doubt of her happiness with him. (*MP*, p. 200)

Any young woman on the verge of marriage might express fears or doubts if asked, but Maria's exaggerated claims of conviction produce little sympathy. Her stubborn bravado is expressed through her choice of words, and the rhythms of her speech: '*quite* mistaken', 'the *smallest* desire', 'the *highest esteem*', '*not a doubt of* her happiness with him'.

As in *Lovers' Vows*, there is dramatic irony at work in the daughter's concealment of knowledge from her father, in Maria's case that of her attachment to Henry Crawford and his rejection of her. In *Lovers' Vows* the irony is unambiguously directed against the father, who misinterprets his daughter's secrecy (the result of her love for Anhalt) as virgin modesty, while the audience enjoys her handling of the joke at his expense.[37] In *Mansfield Park*, on the other hand, the irony encompasses both Sir Thomas and Maria.

In the aftermath of the conference, both are left to reflect on their parts. His happiness in escaping 'the embarrassing evils of a rupture' assuages his doubts: 'Sir Thomas was satisfied; too glad to be satisfied perhaps to urge the matter quite so far as his judgement might have dictated to others' (*MP*, p. 201). Maria's response is to strengthen her resolve to 'behave more cautiously to Mr Rushworth in future, that her father might not be again suspecting her' (*MP*, p. 201). Austen reminds us that they have both got what they wanted: Maria has 'pledged herself anew to Sotherton' and prevented 'Crawford [from] destroying her prospects', and Sir Thomas has secured 'a marriage which would bring him such an addition of respectability and influence'. Austen spares neither father nor daughter: 'To her the conference closed as satisfactorily as to him.'

The Baron, like Sir Thomas, holds 'birth and fortune' high in the marital stakes, but Sir Thomas strikingly deviates from Wildenhaim in condoning a marriage without love, a reflection perhaps on his own mistake in marriage: 'A well-disposed young woman, who did not marry for love, was in general but the more attached to her own family' (*MP*, p. 201). A further irony is that Sir Thomas's timing is out: he is 'three or four days' too late, after Maria's wounded feelings have been tranquillised and replaced by 'pride and self-revenge' (*MP*, p. 202). Matrimony becomes her means of escape. She enters into marriage with a man she despises in order to get away from a father she resents:

Independence was more needful than ever; the want of it at Mansfield more sensibly felt. She was less and less able to endure the restraint which her father imposed. The liberty which his absence had given was now become absolutely necessary. She must escape from him and Mansfield as soon as possible, and find consolation in fortune and consequence, bustle and the world, for a wounded spirit. (*MP*, p. 202)

It is clear that Sir Thomas's intervention helps to push Maria over the edge. Ironically his 'solemn kindness', far from releasing her fears, precipitates her decision to marry Rushworth and leave Mansfield. In *Lovers' Vows*, Wildenhaim is more alert to the dangers of the kind of parental interference that is common in Gothic drama and fiction. He vows to remain impartial: 'I shall not command, neither persuade her to the marriage. I know too well the fatal influence of parents on such a subject' (*LV*, act 2, scene 2). Again the Gothic element is overturned in *Lovers' Vows*, but in *Mansfield Park* Sir Thomas's control and restraint are merely presented as a more subtle form of imprisonment.

So much for Maria and her father. Sir Thomas is pleased with the outcome of the conference. Once Maria and Julia have left for London, he is 'observing' once more, and this time it is an advantageous match for Fanny that interests him:

and though infinitely above scheming or contriving for any the most advantageous matrimonial establishment that could be among the apparent possibilities of any one most dear to him, and disdaining even as a littleness the being quick-sighted on such points, he could not avoid perceiving in a grand and careless way that Mr Crawford was somewhat distinguishing his niece – nor perhaps refrain (though unconsciously) from giving a more willing assent to invitations on that account. (*MP*, p. 238)

This passage is loaded with authorial irony. The mock-lofty tone of the first sentence deliberately undercuts the baronet's dignified intent; we already know that he has sanctioned an advantageous liaison for one 'most dear to him' in the full knowledge that it is marriage without affection or love, so we are clearly required to mistrust the authorial voice, and to accept this statement ironically. Nor are we meant to be fooled by Sir Thomas's casual admission of his observation of Henry's attention to Fanny, and his concession to the 'littleness' of such an observation. This is especially intriguing because the self-knowledge that is implied by such an admission is in fact more an assumption that Sir Thomas is making about himself, rather than a representation of his conscious thoughts. The inherent untrustworthiness of Sir Thomas's admission is subtly conveyed through free indirect speech, which simultaneously manages to excuse and condemn, to conceal yet reveal. The voice that seems to approve of the delicacy of Sir Thomas's motives is in fact exposing its distrust of his motives. Furthermore, the latter half of the sentence flatly contradicts the first. Sir Thomas's active encouragement of the Crawfords' company reveals that he is as scheming as Mrs Norris when it comes to contriving a lucrative marriage.

The irony, continuing in the same mocking vein, undermines Sir Thomas's screening of his own 'unconscious' scheming: 'for it was in the course of that very visit, that he first began to think, that any one in the habit of such idle observation *would have thought* that Mr Crawford was the admirer of Fanny Price' (*MP*, p. 238). Sir Thomas objectifies his observations to conceal his true motives from himself. This conscious concealment of his less honourable intentions is reinforced later in the novel, at the ball that he has so carefully stage-managed for the purpose of promoting Henry and Fanny's attachment. Austen deliberately employs an ambiguous language for Sir Thomas in which we can read his true motives beneath his words, even as he deludes himself in the process: 'He remained steadily inclined to gratify so amiable a feeling – to gratify *any body else* who might wish to see Fanny dance' (*MP*, p. 252, my italics). The 'any body else' is of course Henry Crawford, and this is confirmed by Sir Thomas's approval when Fanny is engaged for the first two dances by Henry, and his invitation to Henry at the end of the ball:

> and the readiness with which his invitation was accepted, convinced him that the suspicions whence, *he must confess to himself*, this very ball had in great measure sprung, were well founded, Mr Crawford was in love with Fanny. (*MP*, p. 280, my italics)

Most interesting in this passage is Sir Thomas's need to confess to himself fully. At last it is openly stated. Austen delivers her strongest indictment of Sir Thomas's control of Fanny: 'Sir Thomas was again interfering in her inclination by advising her to go immediately to bed. "Advise" was his word, but it was the advice of absolute power' (*MP*, p. 280). By the end of the ball, there is no ambiguity in Austen's presentation of Sir Thomas: 'In thus sending her away, Sir Thomas perhaps might not be thinking merely of her health. It might occur to him that Mr Crawford had been sitting by her long enough, or he might mean to recommend her as a wife by shewing her persuadableness' (*MP*, p. 281). This ironically anticipates Fanny's withstanding of Sir Thomas in her own conference scene, which forms a contrast to his scene with Maria. The complexity of Austen's use of narrative control to expose the workings of Sir Thomas's mind takes her far beyond *Lovers' Vows*.

The similarity of Fanny's position to that of her cousin Julia is made strikingly clear throughout the theatrical saga: neither of them wants to take part in the play because their rival is cast opposite the man they desire themselves. Less obviously, Fanny's correspondence with Maria is apparent from the similar situation in which they find themselves when in conference with Sir Thomas. Both girls are secretly in love, and unable to express that love to Sir Thomas, but are pressured into matrimony with a rich, unsuitable man. Fanny, in refusing Crawford, differs from her cousin, but shares the dilemma of being forced to conceal and dissemble.

Inchbald had parodied the theme of patriarchal power in *Lovers' Vows* by means of Amelia's control over her father. Austen has presented us early on in *Mansfield Park* with a kindly, if misguided father, who offers to release his daughter from her unhappy engagement. This time it is Fanny who is urged by a father-figure to accept a lucrative but unwanted marriage proposal, while she is forced to conceal the truth of a secret attachment. The contrast of this scene to Sir Thomas's early triumph with Maria is in its boldly theatricalised presentation of patriarchal power.

The scene with Sir Thomas in the East Room is preceded by Henry's passionate proposal to Fanny. This encounter between Fanny and Henry is almost comically presented, as her horror at his passionate words only increases his ardour. The comic irony springs from *her* disbelief of his intentions – 'it was like himself and entirely of a piece with what she had seen before' – and *his* misapprehension of her evident reluctance: 'to part with her at a moment when modesty alone seemed to his sanguine and pre-assured mind to stand in the way of the happiness he sought'. The quasi-farcical encounter is ended when Fanny 'bursts away from him' upon hearing Sir Thomas and 'rushed out at an opposite door from the one her uncle was approaching' (*MP*, p. 302).

The final volume of *Mansfield Park* opens with the heroine hiding in her room to avoid Henry. The sounds of her uncle's footsteps outside the door set her trembling like a Gothic heroine awaiting her terrible fate:

> Suddenly the sound of a step in regular approach was heard – a heavy step, an unusual step in that part of the house; it was her uncle's; she knew it as well as his voice; she had trembled at it as often, and began to tremble again, at the idea of his coming up to speak to her, whatever might be the subject. (*MP*, p. 312)

Sir Thomas comes his closest yet to making an apology to Fanny on his discovery that there is no fire in her room: 'you will feel that *they* were not least your friends who were educating and preparing you for that mediocrity of condition which *seemed* to be your lot' (*MP*, p. 313). Now that Henry's offer of marriage has raised the stakes, Sir Thomas entreats Fanny not to 'harbour resentment' over past grievances. His opening speech begins on the subject of 'birth and fortune'. In *Lovers' Vows* the Baron, when asked what can interest him in favour of a man 'whose head and heart are good for nothing', replies 'birth and fortune': as in *Mansfield Park*, the question of social status is raised as an important part of the marriage contract.

Just as in the interview with Maria, Sir Thomas is in control. He does not expect any problem at all from the shrinking girl he has fostered, and again the irony springs from the reversal of expectations. Sir Thomas expects problems from his daughter's 'disposition' but does not anticipate any struggle from Fanny's gentle nature. But it soon becomes clear that he is less concerned with romantic notions of marital felicity than with encouraging an advantageous alliance of means. He is stunned by Fanny's refusal to ally herself to a gentleman of such favourable prospects.

The scene is characterised by a fundamental clash of values. Sir Thomas's initial mistake is to assume that Fanny will behave as a dutiful daughter and accept the man of his choice. Given that Crawford is a man of sense, as well as fortune, he is even more confounded by Fanny's uncompromising refusal to accept him. Moreover, because she is without position and means, she has less reason to refuse him than the Bertram daughters would have:

> 'Am I to understand', said Sir Thomas, after a few moments' silence, 'that you mean to *refuse* Mr Crawford?'
> 'Yes, Sir'.
> 'Refuse him?'
> 'Yes, Sir'.
> 'Refuse Mr Crawford! Upon what plea? For what reason?'
> 'I – I cannot like him, Sir, well enough to marry him.' (*MP*, p. 315)

The fear that Fanny expresses to her uncle contrasts not only with Amelia's teasing but loving relationship with her father, but also with Maria's polite indifference to Sir Thomas. The tone of the interview shifts from friendly paternal consideration to outright emotional blackmail when Sir Thomas realises that she indeed means to defy him and refuse Crawford.

The scene gains suppleness from the quasi-theatrical device of dramatic irony whereby, like Maria and Amelia, Fanny is concealing vital information. Both Fanny and Sir Thomas are at cross-purposes. In *Lovers' Vows* the cross-purposes between father and daughter work effectively on a comic level. While it is obvious to the audience that Amelia is in love with Anhalt, when she drops hints to enlighten her father he blindly misinterprets her romantic allusions to the chaplain:

> BARON: Have you not dreamt at all tonight?
> AMELIA: Oh yes – I have dreamt of our chaplain, Mr Anhalt.
> BARON: Ah ha! As if he stood before you and the Count to ask for the ring.
> AMELIA: No: not that. (*LV*, act 2, scene 2)

Sir Thomas, too, is blind to the full state of affairs because Fanny withholds information. But his lack of comprehension, and her dissembling, do not work for comic effect. Her motives can only be cleared by implicating those of her female cousins:

> her heart sunk under the appalling prospect of discussion, explanation and probably non-conviction. Her ill opinion of him was founded chiefly on observations, which, for her cousins' sake, she could scarcely dare mention to their father. Maria and Julia – and especially Maria, were so closely implicated in Mr Crawford's misconduct, that she could not give his character, such as she believed it, without betraying them. (*MP*, pp. 317–18)

Ironically the suitor is Henry Crawford, Maria's secret lover, and Fanny's secret lover is Edmund. The conference scene between Fanny and Sir Thomas is one of the most powerful in the novel. Fanny's motives are misunderstood and misrepresented by Sir Thomas, who is more and more bewildered by her refusal. His final admonishing speech is intended to hurt and humiliate. Sir Thomas accuses his niece of ingratitude, selfishness and wilfulness. The kindly baronet has turned into a stage monster, rather as General Tilney, in *Northanger Abbey*, causes distress to the heroine which is more real to her than that inflicted by any Gothic tyrant she has read about.

The greatest blow to Fanny is her discovery that the uncle that she admires so much is inflexible in refusing to accept her rejection of Henry: 'She had hoped that to a man like her uncle, so discerning, so honourable, so good, the simple acknowledgement of settled *dislike* on her side, would have been sufficient. To her infinite grief she found it was not' (*MP*, p. 318). In *Lovers' Vows*, we find a similar turn of phrase to express Wildenhaim's sense of the limit of parental pressure: 'Yet, if I thought my daughter absolutely disliked him.' For Amelia's father, 'settled dislike' *is* sufficient.

In *Mansfield Park*, the scene is not without comic irony. Sir Thomas's melodramatic accusation that Fanny is acting 'in a wild fit of folly' is utterly inappropriate for her gentle, hesitant repudiation of Henry: 'His attentions were always – what I did not like' (*MP*, p. 319). Similarly, Sir

Thomas's abrupt change of heart in keeping Fanny apart from Crawford is portrayed as a calculating move: 'When he looked at his niece, and saw the state of feature and complexion which her crying had brought her into, he thought there might be as much lost as gained by an immediate interview' (*MP*, p. 320). He still believes that he will win.

The most significant irony of this scene is Sir Thomas's refusal to perceive Fanny's true motives in refusing Crawford. In the scene with Maria, the thought that his daughter might have formed another attachment does not even enter his head. But with Fanny he permits the thought to enter his consciousness: 'Young as you are, and having scarcely seen anyone, it is hardly possible that your affections –' (*MP*, p. 316). At this juncture the close verbal parallels with *Lovers' Vows* resume significance. The Baron confides his fears for his daughter's impending marriage to the man that she is secretly in love with. The secret that Anhalt is the true recipient of Amelia's love is withheld from the unsuspecting father, just as Fanny's love for Edmund is concealed from Sir Thomas. The dramatic irony continues with Baron Wildenhaim's claim – addressed to Anhalt – that, although birth and fortune are important, love and affection must come first:

> Yet if I thought my daughter absolutely disliked him, or that she loved another, I would not thwart a first affection; no, for the world I would not. [*Sighing.*] But that her affections are already bestowed is not probable. (*LV*, act 2, scene 2)

The thought is allowed to flit across Wildenhaim's consciousness before he dismisses it as 'improbable', while the embarrassed chaplain squirms under his gaze. The same happens with Fanny, who, like Anhalt, is in love with her social superior. Sir Thomas momentarily permits the possibility of Fanny's affections being engaged, but, just as readily as he allows himself to be led out of his deep fears for Maria and Rushworth, he dismisses the idea of Fanny having a pre-engaged heart:

> He paused and eyed her fixedly. He saw her lips formed into a *no*, though the sound was inarticulate, but her face was like scarlet. That, however, in so modest a girl might be very compatible with innocence;

and chusing at least to appear satisfied, he quickly added, 'No, no, I know *that* is quite out of the question – quite impossible.' (*MP*, p. 316)

Amelia's lips would never have formed into a 'no' in this way. She is the least devious of the three young women. Her witty attempts to drop hints to her father are, at least, honest. Conversely, Fanny is forced to act a part: she would 'rather die than own the truth' (*MP*, p. 317).

In *Mansfield Park* Austen uses her two interview scenes to explore socially acceptable and unacceptable marriages. But the authorial voice probes critically at both Fanny and Sir Thomas, and Maria and Sir Thomas, in a way that is not possible in drama. On each occasion Sir Thomas chooses 'to appear satisfied' by his 'daughter's' attempts to deceive him. Yet on each occasion his conduct is reprehensible. He has no qualms at all about marrying the two young women to men they cordially loathe, as long as, in the eyes of the world, it looks like an advantageous match.

Sir Thomas and Baron Wildenhaim have different values. Both respect the dual claims of 'birth and fortune' in matrimony, but Sir Thomas is prepared to overlook the claims of love and affection. Austen ironises his propensity for righteous self-justification. Sir Thomas condones Maria's loveless marriage: 'without the prejudice, the blindness of love ... and if she could dispense with seeing her husband a leading, shining character, there would certainly be everything in her favour' (*MP*, p. 201). Conversely, he scorns Fanny for harbouring romantic notions: 'because you do not feel for Mr Crawford exactly what a young, heated fancy imagines to be necessary for happiness, you resolve to refuse him' (*MP*, p. 318).

In his defence, Sir Thomas is only partially aware of the truth. Fanny later comforts herself with this knowledge: 'and when she considered how much of the truth was unknown to him, she believed she had no right to wonder at the line of conduct he pursued' (*MP*, p. 331). But the irony begins again with a suggestion that, even if Sir Thomas had known 'the truth', it would not have made much difference. That he can describe Maria as 'nobly married' is proof enough of his insensibility (*MP*, p. 319). Fanny's harshest condemnation of her beloved uncle confirms this: 'He who had married a daughter to Mr Rushworth. Romantic delicacy was certainly not to be expected of him' (*MP*, p. 331).

Jane Austen reworks the interview scene from *Lovers' Vows* twice over, first with Maria, and then, more profoundly, with Fanny, to show the inadequacies of their relationship with Sir Thomas. She also shows that a woman who cannot admit her love has no choice but to conceal and deceive. Neither woman is in a position to reveal their secret passions, especially to a father-figure so insensitive to their feelings. Amelia and Baron Wildenhaim are revealed in a more favourable light by force of contrast.

As we have seen, the analogies between the play and novel are not solely to do with the casting parallels. The most important are the similarities and differences between Sir Thomas and Baron Wildenhaim in their relationship to their daughters, and the parallels and contrasts between Amelia and the three young women in *Mansfield Park*, Fanny, Mary and Maria. Both fathers urge candour and honesty, but both are patently blind to the fact that there may be a prior attachment. The fathers do not ask, and the daughters do not tell. But where Maria crucially deviates from Amelia is in lying about Rushworth. Maria's dissimulation is thus made clear.

The Baron's objections to the Count are not only his arrant stupidity: 'But when you find a man's head without brains, and his bosom without a heart, these are important articles to supply' (*LV*, act 2, scene 2). The man whose head is without brains is of course fitting for Rushworth, of whom even the tolerant Edmund cannot refrain from speaking ironically: 'If this man had not twelve thousand a year, he would be a very stupid fellow' (*MP*, p. 40). But the man whose 'bosom is without a heart' is, ironically, not the man Maria is engaged to, the Count Cassel figure, but the one who has secretly claimed her heart and who coolly endeavours to make a 'hole in Miss Price's heart': Henry Crawford.

Count Cassel in *Lovers' Vows* thus provides a character type for each of Maria's suitors. Cassel, although a rich fool, is a well-travelled, sophisticated man, 'an epitome of the world' (*LV*, act 2, scene 2). Part of his worldly education includes making and breaking lovers' vows: 'for me to keep my word to a woman would be deceit: 'tis not expected of me. It is in my character to break oaths in love.' Amelia's dislike of the Count is connected to his seduction techniques, which she describes as 'barbarous deeds', and his false promises of love: he has 'Made vows of love to so many women, that, on his marriage with me, a hundred female hearts will at least be broken' (*LV*, act 4, scene 2).

In *Mansfield Park*, Henry Crawford is the worldly, sophisticated seducer of women. When, like Cassel, he finally is conquered by one woman, Fanny Price, hundreds of woman are expected to be broken-hearted: 'Oh! the envyings and heart-burnings of dozens and dozens' (*MP*, p. 360). Mary Crawford entreats Fanny to bask in the conquest she has made over so many women, 'the glory of fixing one who has been shot at by so many'. But Fanny, like Amelia, 'cannot think well of a man who sports with any woman's feelings' (*MP*, p. 363).

Fanny and Amelia have no joy in such 'sportful' behaviour, unlike Mary Crawford and her friends. Amelia is unimpressed that marrying the Count means scoring off hundreds of heart-broken women, and instead she feels compassion for the waiting-girl who has been seduced. Fanny also shows female solidarity in both keeping Maria's secret from Sir Thomas and refusing to think well of a man who sports with any woman's feelings. I have already noted how Fanny is placed in an analogous situation with Amelia, in that both heroines are secretly in love with a clergyman/tutor. But their refusal to equate a good marriage with wealth and status, and their respect for other women, draws them even closer together. The surprising kinship between the superficially very different heroines of novel and play reveals the depth of Austen's engagement with *Lovers' Vows*.

A detailed analysis of the complex relationship between the two works suggests that, although Sir Thomas Bertram condemns the theatricals, Jane Austen does not. The opposite is more true, thanks to the contrast between the two fathers: it is the theatricals that condemn Sir Thomas.

9

Mansfield Park

I now want to set aside the play that is chosen at Mansfield Park and instead consider some other dimensions of the novel's interest in the drama, including the play that is not chosen. By doing so, I hope to demonstrate that, in both the range of its allusiveness and the variety of its quasi-dramatic techniques, *Mansfield Park* is much more deeply involved with the theatre than has hitherto been assumed.

We have already seen how thoroughly Jane Austen was indebted to the theatrical 'set-piece' or scene, how many of the most memorable moments in her works may be perceived in terms of their dramatic impact. Austen's novels are 'dramatic' in the sense that her scenes were often conceived and conducted in stage terms. The prevalence of character-revealing dialogue is the most far-reaching theatrical debt. It should be considered alongside the collecting of characters in appropriate groups, and the contriving of entrances and exits.

The first group activity in *Mansfield Park*, before the play sequence is introduced, is the outing to Sotherton Court, ostensibly for the purpose of advising its owner on the efficacy of landscape improvement. The family visit to Sotherton and the *Lovers' Vows* sequence are firmly linked in Fanny's consciousness as the two social events in which illicit misconduct goes unwarranted and unchecked.[1]

The outing to Sotherton is used primarily to explore the initial stages of the courtship between Mary and Edmund, and Maria and Henry. It also prefigures later important events: Edmund's ordination and Maria's marriage. Furthermore, the flirtations that get under way in the grounds of Sotherton between the two pairs of lovers (Mary and Edmund, Maria and Henry) are further developed in the rehearsals of *Lovers' Vows*.

There are parallels between the improving party and the theatrical party. Both schemes spring from the desire to alleviate boredom in the country, and both events incorporate the use of theatrical language to mask the unlicensed love-play that takes place between the characters. The events at Sotherton are the first steps in seduction, and, in the style of Restoration and eighteenth-century comedy, pairings of lovers are explored as the characters wander, aimlessly, around the grounds of Sotherton Court. The Sotherton episode could be described as a prelude to the mainpiece of *Lovers' Vows*.

It has been suggested that in the Sotherton episode Austen is alluding to Shakespeare's *As You Like It*. There is a pastoral setting and, more specifically, the mock marriage ceremony in the Jacobean family chapel (proposed by the jealous Julia) has shades of the mock marriage performed by Celia to unite Rosalind and Orlando.[2] *Mansfield Park* certainly shares with Shakespearean comedy an interest in role-play and overhearing. Fanny Price is accused by Mrs Norris of excessive 'lookings on': 'these are fine times for you, but you must not be always walking from one room to the other and doing the lookings on, at your ease, in this way' (*MP*, p. 166).[3]

The connection between the pastoral tradition and a kind of unlimited freedom of behaviour does derive from Shakespearean comedy, but the pastoral location is usually the wood or forest, as in the Italian tradition from which the genre derived. The use of the park or garden of a country estate is the Restoration variation of pastoral that was also the model for eighteenth-century comedy. Austen's use of the garden to dramatise freedom of conduct shows an allegiance less directly to Shakespeare than to recent and contemporaneous stage comedy. I believe that the Sotherton episode both alludes to and adapts one of the most popular comedies of the eighteenth-century stage.

From an early age, Jane Austen was familiar with George Colman and David Garrick's highly successful comedy, *The Clandestine Marriage*. She makes an explicit reference to the play in her early novel, *Love and Freindship*.[4] In 1813, she attended a production of the play at Covent Garden, commenting on the new Lord Ogleby, and complaining that the acting was only 'moderate'.[5] Colman and Garrick's comedy is the first of a number of contemporary plays that Austen deploys in *Mansfield Park*.

It has a heroine called Fanny and uses a garden setting to dramatise illicit love-play.

In *The Clandestine Marriage* the various love intrigues of the play are conducted in the extensive grounds of Sterling's country estate.[6] The conventional comic situation of love-play outdoors, assimilated from Restoration comedy, is given an eighteenth-century slant through an emphasis on the trend for landscape improvements. 'The chief pleasure of a country-house is to make improvements', remarks the master of the house, as he shows his guests around the grounds of his huge estate.[7] Sterling's 'improvements' naturally include the needless destruction of trees: 'We were surrounded with trees. I cut down above fifty to make the lawn before the house, and let in the wind and sun – Smack smooth – as you see.' Sterling's fashionably slavish desire for picturesque 'ruins' is mocked: 'It has just cost me a hundred and fifty pounds to put my ruins in thorough repair.'[8]

Austen provides her own parody of the picturesque in the portrayal of the foolish improver, Rushworth. He has already cut down 'two or three fine old trees ... that grew too near the house' and talks of cutting down the avenue at Sotherton, something that Fanny laments, quoting from Cowper's *The Task* in defence of the fate of the elm (*MP*, pp. 55–56).

The numerous puns on 'improvements' in *The Clandestine Marriage* are specifically given a lascivious *double entendre*. Sterling's fake church spire against a tree 'to terminate the prospect' is commented upon by the lecherous Lord Ogleby: 'Very ingenious, indeed! For my part, I desire no finer prospect than this I see before me. [*Leering at the Women.*] Simple, yet varied; bounded, yet extensive.' Ogleby continues to makes puns on this theme: 'We're in the garden of Eden, you know; in all the region of perpetual spring, youth and beauty [*Leering at the Women*].'[9]

The metaphor of the garden of Eden is extended by Ogleby's reference to a 'serpentine path':

STERLING: How d'ye like these close walks, my lord?

LORD OGLEBY: A most excellent serpentine! It forms a perfect maze, and winds like a true lover's knot.[10]

The lover's knot, which becomes increasingly entangled, is the secret love affair between Fanny and Lovewell. A comic love triangle is created when Fanny unburdens herself to Lord Ogleby, who mistakenly believes that he is the recipient of Fanny's secret affections. The 'lover's knot' is further complicated by the unexpected and genuine conversion of the rake, Sir John Melvil, who also falls in love with Fanny. It is out in the garden that Melvil makes the confession that, although engaged in a treaty of marriage with the elder sister, he is now in love with the younger. As in a Restoration comedy, the garden is the scene of seduction and intrigue. The physical landscape of the garden, its winding paths and sheltered walkways, screens the illicit behaviour of the characters.

Jane Austen adapts the theatrical device of love-play outdoors and uses a serpentine path symbolically to suggest her own 'lover's knot'. Edmund walks the path with Fanny and Mary on each arm. As in *The Clandestine Marriage*, a connection between sexual temptation and the Garden of Eden is suggested by the serpentine path. It is no coincidence that Mary first tries to tempt Edmund from his religious vocation on the serpentine path. Illicit misconduct and sexual temptation are suggested in Austen's language from the moment when the young people come to a door leading out to the garden, 'temptingly open on a flight of steps which led immediately to turf and shrubs, and all the sweets of pleasure-grounds, as by one impulse, one wish for air and liberty, all walked out' (*MP*, p. 90).

A second 'lover's knot' is explored in the secret flirtation between Henry Crawford and Maria Bertram, who is betrothed to John Rushworth. It is Mrs Grant who first makes a pun on the word 'improvements' with her insinuating remark that Maria will be Sotherton's finest 'improvement': 'Sotherton will have *every* improvement in time which his heart can desire', and this is spoken to Mrs Norris with 'a smile' (*MP*, p. 53). Henry Crawford picks up the metaphor when he is flirting with Maria before the iron gate: 'I do not think that *I* shall ever see Sotherton again with so much pleasure as I do now. Another summer will hardly improve it to me' (*MP*, p. 98).

Henry Crawford's surreptitious flirtation with Maria is conducted in quasi-theatrical terms. As Mary Crawford is the witty heroine of eighteenth-century comedy, so her brother is the charming rake of sentimental comedy, whose 'reformation' is at stake. Austen's implementation of a brother-sister duo who infiltrate a different society is a striking reversal of a popular eighteenth-century comic convention. Colman the Younger's *The Heir at Law* and Hannah Cowley's *Which is the Man?* rely upon a conventional comic plot device. Both plays introduce a pair of rustics, a brother and sister, whose entrance into London society gives rise to many incongruities and misunderstandings. In these plays, different styles of language and action are attached to different classes and ironically juxtaposed.

In *Mansfield Park* Austen reverses this convention. The brother-sister duo are sophisticated Londoners who leave town to enter the country. If the prosaic conversations of Fanny and Edmund seem dull by comparison, this is precisely the effect that Austen wants to create. As Edmund warns Mary, there is no fear of him saying 'a bon-mot, for there is not the least wit in my nature' (*MP*, p. 94). In contrast, the Crawfords' sparkling dialogue and witty repartee, with just a lacing of French phrases, reflect their cosmopolitan lifestyles: they are the kind of sophisticated Frenchified types parodied in Garrick's satire against fashionable gallantry, *Bon Ton: or High Life Above Stairs*.

In the chapel at Sotherton, Henry plays the part of the charming rake with characteristic aplomb. The striking tableau that is set up in the family chapel foreshadows and supplants the actual marriage ceremony between Maria and Rushworth, which later takes place 'off-stage'. Julia draws the group's attention to the 'performance': 'Do look at Mr Rushworth and Maria, standing side by side, exactly as if the ceremony were going to be performed' (*MP*, p. 88). As readers, we are encouraged to watch the group audience themselves watching the acting out of the future marriage ceremony between Maria and Rushworth that finally takes place unobserved by the reader. The emphasis on the visual tableau is undercut by Henry's whisper to the bride 'in a voice which she only could hear, "I do not like to see Miss Bertram so near the altar"' (*MP*, p. 88).

Maria's complicity is suggested in her acceptance of Henry's challenge and she continues the intimate banter by asking if he would 'give her away'. His response is equally provocative: '"I am afraid I should do it very awkwardly," was his reply with a look of meaning' (*MP*, p. 88).

Henry's flirtatious 'asides' to Maria set the tone for the repartee that is continued in the grounds in front of the iron gate. Austen contrasts the posed and confined indoor scene of the private chapel with the liberating outdoor scene. The indoor scene centres upon the legitimising of love-play by its public acknowledgement in marriage, while the outdoor scene embraces the idea of unlicensed, clandestine love-play. Thus, the cool chapel, where marital love is sanctioned, is contrasted with the flaming heat of the outdoors.[11]

The substantial stretch of direct speech between Maria and Henry, in front of the iron gate with Fanny as audience, is virtually a ready-made dramatic script, complete with directions for the actors (note the interjected instructions such as 'speaking rather lower' and 'smiling'):

[*Henry*] 'I find [Sotherton] better, grander, more complete in its style, though that style may not be the best. And to tell you the truth,' speaking rather lower, 'I do not think that *I* shall ever see Sotherton again with so much pleasure as I do now. Another summer will hardly improve it to me.'

After a moment's embarrassment the lady replied, 'You are too much of a man of the world not to see with the eyes of the world. If other people think Sotherton improved, I have no doubt that you will.'

'I am afraid that I am not quite so much the man of the world as might be good for me in some points. My feelings are not quite so evanescent, nor my memory of the past under such easy dominion as one finds to be the case with men of the world.'

This was followed by a short silence. Miss Bertram began again.

'You seemed to be enjoying your drive here very much this morning. I was glad to see you so well entertained. You and Julia were laughing the whole way.'

'Were we? Yes, I believe we were; but I have not the least recollection at what. Oh! I believe I was relating to her some ridiculous stories of an old Irish groom of my uncle's. Your sister loves to laugh.'

'You think her more light-hearted than I am.'

'More easily amused', he replied, 'consequently you know,' smiling, 'better company. I could not have hoped to entertain *you* with Irish anecdotes during a ten miles' drive.'

'Naturally, I believe, I am as lively as Julia, but I have more to think of now.'

'You have undoubtedly – and there are situations in which very high spirits would denote insensibility. Your prospects, however, are too fair to justify want of spirits. You have a very smiling scene before you.'

'Do you mean literally or figuratively? Literally, I conclude. Yes, certainly the sun shines and the park looks very cheerful. But, unluckily that iron gate, that ha-ha, give me a feeling of restraint and hardship. I cannot get out, as the starling said.' As she spoke, and it was with expression, she walked to the gate; he followed her. 'Mr Rushworth is so long fetching this key.'

'And for the world you would not get out without the key and without Mr Rushworth's authority and protection, or I think you might with little difficulty pass round the edge of the gate, here, with my assistance; I think it might be done, if you really wished to be more at large, and could allow yourself to think it not prohibited.'

'Prohibited! nonsense! I certainly can get out that way, and I will. Mr Rushworth will be here in a moment you know – we shall not be out of sight.'

'Or if we are, Miss Price will be so good as to tell him, that he will find us near that knoll, the grove of oak on the knoll.'

Fanny, feeling all this to be wrong, could not help making an effort to prevent it. 'You will hurt yourself, Miss Bertram,' she cried, 'you will certainly hurt yourself against those spikes – you will tear your gown – you will be in danger of slipping into the ha-ha. You had better not go.'
(*MP*, pp. 98–100)

This dialogue between Henry and Maria, the rake and the flirt, recalls the verbal fencing and lovers' wit-combat of Restoration and eighteenth-century stage comedy. Henry's challenging pun on 'improvement' is met with Maria's cool response: 'If other people think Sotherton improved, I have no doubt that you will.'

Many of Austen's dialogues consist of a rapid exchange of debating points, as in the confrontation between Lady Catherine and Elizabeth in *Pride and Prejudice*, and that between Elinor and Lucy in *Sense and Sensibility*. The set-piece between the clandestine lovers in *Mansfield*

Park is striking, however, for its use of silence to delineate the characters and attitudes of the speakers. Maria's jealousy and chagrin are expressed, finely, in the pause between her remarks regarding her impending marriage and her accusatory comments about Julia and Henry: 'You seemed to be enjoying your drive here very much this morning.'

The provision of 'stage directions' is a device that Austen uses to reinforce and sometimes contradict the spoken word. In Henry's case, the directions 'smiling' and 'speaking rather lower' reveal the hollowness of the verbal facade. The use of *double entendre* enhances the illicit tone of the banter; and, if we are in any doubt of the sub-text, Maria, with surprising clarity, focuses the reader with her question, 'Do you mean literally or figuratively?' With this breakthrough of consciousness, the authorial sympathy shifts to Maria momentarily with her poignant declaration 'I cannot get out, as the starling said'. Austen's allusion to Sterne's imprisoned starling in *A Sentimental Journey*, singing 'I can't get out, I can't get out', is highly significant. Shortly before he hears the bird's 'song for liberty', Yorick is contemplating confinement in the Bastille, which he describes as 'but another word for a house you can't get out of'. Maria Bertram describes Sotherton as 'dismal old prison' (*MP*, p. 53), and her words also resonate with those of another notorious Maria, Wollstonecraft's trapped heroine of *The Wrongs of Woman*, who declares that 'Marriage had bastilled me for life'.[12]

The remaining dialogue forecasts Maria's adultery, and the point of view moves to Fanny, who is suddenly reintroduced into the narrative with the warning cry: 'You will certainly hurt yourself against those spikes – you will tear your gown – you will be in danger of slipping into the ha-ha.'

This unexpected intrusion, with its overt prediction of sexual misconduct ('spikes', torn clothing, descent into ill-fame), has the effect of distancing Maria as it simultaneously draws the narrative focus back to Fanny. Just as Henry and Maria have forgotten about Fanny's presence, so too has the reader. The relative absence of authorial intervention in the long dialogue between Henry and Maria is emphasised by the sudden reappearance of the heroine, and the reader is jolted into remembering that Fanny has witnessed this highly-charged exchange. Only at this point does the authorial perspective return to Fanny's predictable conclusion: 'Fanny was again left to her solitude, and with no increase of pleasant feelings, for she was sorry for almost all that she had seen and heard, astonished at Miss Bertram and angry with Mr Crawford' (*MP*, p. 100).

The scene before the iron gate continues to be conducted in stage terms, not only in the use of dialogue but also in the contriving of exits and entrances. The single setting is retained throughout, with Fanny seated on the bench. The rest is as follows: initially Mary and Edmund exit from the bench as Rushworth, Maria and Henry enter. Rushworth exits for the key. Maria and Henry exit around the locked gate. Julia enters, and exits, around the locked door. Rushworth enters with the key and exits through the gate. Enter Edmund and Mary. Subordinate dialogues take place, leaving Fanny to contemplate the outcome of events from the central position of the bench. Confusingly, Fanny's ubiquitous presence, rather than focusing the ironies of the scene, offers a disarming lack of perspective. Throughout the quasi-farcical entrances and exits of the various characters, her thoughts are shaped, largely, by her jealous concern for Edmund. But though she seems to be little more than a conduit, it is significant that she should witness Henry in action. Her knowledge of his duplicitous conduct prepares her for her rejection of his advances in the third volume of the novel.

One of the most unexpected twists of *Mansfield Park* is the controversial reformation of the rake, Henry Crawford. The reformed rake had been a favourite stage type ever since the reformation of Loveless in the very first sentimental drama, Colley Cibber's *Love's Last Shift* (1696). In an important conversation that takes place shortly after Maria's marriage to Rushworth, Henry is reminded of Fanny's status as a silent witness to his conduct at Sotherton. Mary Crawford's commendation of her brother's behaviour at Sotherton makes her complicit in his misconduct: 'Only think what grand things were produced there by our all going with him one hot day in August to drive about the grounds and see his genius take fire. There we went, and there we came home again; and what was done there is not to be told!' (*MP*, p. 244). But it is Fanny's reaction to this comment that discomposes Henry:

Fanny's eyes were turned on Crawford for a moment with an expression more than grave, even reproachful; but on catching his were instantly withdrawn. With something of consciousness he shook his head at his sister, and laughingly replied, 'I cannot say there was much done at Sotherton; but it was a hot day, and we were all walking after each other and bewildered'. As soon as a general buz gave him shelter, he added, in a low voice directed solely at Fanny, 'I should be sorry to have my powers of *planning* judged of by the day at Sotherton. I see things very differently now. Do not think of me as I appeared then.' (*MP*, pp. 244–45)

For Henry, part of Fanny's charm is her indifference to him. What begins as a game to make 'a small hole in Fanny Price's heart' becomes a challenge when he discovers that she does, in fact, dislike him: 'Her looks say, "I will not like you, I am determined not to like you," and I say, she shall' (*MP*, p. 230). Henry's unexpectedly genuine conversion to love is of no greater surprise to anyone but himself: 'I am fairly caught. You know with what idle designs I began – but this is the end of them' (*MP*, p. 292).

The most influential example of a reformed rake in the novel tradition was Mr B. in Richardson's *Pamela*, who is tamed by the virtue and religious principles of a lowly maidservant.[13] But in the relationship between Fanny Price and Henry Crawford readers would have recognised allusions to *The Clandestine Marriage*, not least because its heroine Fanny Sterling – whose very name anticipates the solid worth and reliable qualities of Austen's heroine – rejects the proposals of a reformed rake. Sir Thomas comes to prize in Fanny 'the *sterling* good of principle' (*MP*, p. 471, my italics). Fanny Sterling is described as possessing 'delicacy' and a 'quick sensibility'. She is gentle and amiable, though is often misunderstood as being 'sly and deceitful': 'She wants nothing but a crook in her hand, and a lamb under her arm, to be a perfect picture of innocence and simplicity.'[14] Subjected to the jealousy of an elder sister, and in possession of a secret that renders her helpless to resist the unwanted attention of her sister's lover, Fanny is a target for ill-treatment – until the unexpected twist in the plot of *The Clandestine Marriage*, the conversion of the rake, Melvil.

I came into this family without any impressions on my mind – with an unimpassioned indifference, ready to receive one woman as soon as another. I looked upon love, serious, sober love as a chimera, and marriage as a thing of course, as you know most people do. But I, who was lately so great an infidel in love, am now one of its sincerest votaries. – In short, my defection from Miss Sterling [Fanny's elder sister] proceeds from the violence of my attachment to another ... who is she! who can she be, but Fanny – the tender, amiable engaging Fanny?[15]

The rake has become conscious of the superior attractions of the demure Fanny: 'was it possible for me to be indulged in a perpetual intercourse with two such objects as Fanny and her sister, and not find my heart led by insensible attraction towards her?'

Fanny's conduct is persistently misunderstood. Her repulsion of Melvil does not appease her sister, nor are her claims for female solidarity understood: 'If I forebore to exert a proper spirit nay, if I did not even express the quickest resentment at your behaviour, it was only in consideration of that respect I wish to pay you, in honour to my sister: and be assured, sir, that woman as I am, that my vanity could reap no pleasure from a triumph that must result from the blackest treachery to her.'[16]

Despite Fanny's protestations and anger at Melvil's persistence, his ardour is only increased by her resistance: 'And yet, opposition, instead of smothering, increases my inclination. I must have her.' Fanny's final declaration that she can never love Melvil likewise falls on stony ground: 'Hear me, sir, hear my final declaration. Were my father and sister, as insensible as you are pleased to represent them; were my heart forever to remain disengaged to any other, I could not listen to your proposals.' Unable and unwilling to return his affections, Fanny is 'packed off' to town to 'send her out of the way'.[17]

Like her predecessor, Fanny Price is in possession of a secret (her attachment to Edmund), and her attempts to conceal this secret cause her conduct to be consistently misunderstood. Fanny's gentle repulses only increase Henry's ardour, for he does not realise that she has a pre-engaged heart. Furthermore, she takes no pleasure in scoring against the opposite sex, or indeed her own sex, telling Mary that she cannot think highly of a man 'who sports with any woman's feelings' (*MP*, p.

363). Fanny Price's rejection of a reformed rake mirrors Fanny Sterling's rejection of Melvil, and, as a final remedy, she in turn is packed off to Portsmouth to be taught the 'value of a good income' (*MP*, p. 369). In *The Clandestine Marriage*, one of the most popular comedies of the period, there is a whole range of techniques that Austen assimilates into the Sotherton episode: the dramatic setting of the garden of a large country estate, the use of a serpentine path, flirtatious banter between quasi-theatrical types such as 'the flirt' and 'the rake', puns and innuendoes specifically linked to the idea of 'improvements', exits and entrances, and a keen sense of audience and looking on.

Furthermore, Austen borrows the name Fanny for her heroine (who has similar sterling qualities as Garrick and Colman's Fanny), and specifically uses the word 'clandestine' to describe Henry Crawford's conduct at Sotherton in a revealing passage that connects Sotherton with *Lovers' Vows*. Fanny firmly links the two episodes together when she too feels herself in danger of being seduced by Crawford: 'Mr Crawford was no longer the Mr Crawford who, as the clandestine, insidious, treacherous admirer of Maria Bertram, had been her abhorrence ... She might have disdained him in all the dignity of angry virtue, in the grounds of Sotherton, or the theatre at Mansfield Park; but he approached her now with rights that demanded different treatment' (*MP*, pp. 327–28).

The seed for Jane Austen's idea for the inclusion of private theatricals in a novel can be found in a short sketch written in about 1792. In 'The Three Sisters', the greedy, pleasure-seeking Mary Stanhope demands a private theatre as part of her marriage settlement: 'You must do nothing but give Balls & Masquerades. You must build a room on purpose & a Theatre to act Plays in. The first Play we have shall be *Which is the Man?*, and I will do Lady Bell Bloomer' (*MW*, p. 65).

Towards the end of *Love and Freindship*, Austen depicts the problems facing a small company of strolling actors in a manner that surely recalls her own family's difficulties in finding suitable plays for their amateur dramatics:

our Company was indeed rather small, as it consisted only of the Manager his wife & ourselves, but there were fewer to pay and the only inconvenience attending it was the Scarcity of Plays which for want of People to fill the Characters, we could perform –. We did not mind trifles however –. One of our most admired Performances was *Macbeth*, in which we were truly great. The Manager always played *Banquo* himself, his wife my *Lady Macbeth*. I did the *Three Witches* & Philander acted *all the rest*. (*MW*, p. 107–8)

The absurdity of Philander playing the parts of characters who appear on the stage at the same time, such as Macbeth and Macduff, and Gustavus playing all three witches, will especially amuse anyone who has had to work within the limitations of a small theatre company. The Austens sometimes solved their casting problems by inviting neighbouring families to take part in their performances. It is, of course, in order to avoid just such a measure that Edmund Bertram reluctantly agrees to join the theatrical ensemble in *Mansfield Park*.

The interest that was sparked by the Steventon theatricals and flickered through Jane Austen's juvenilia was rekindled in the writing of *Mansfield Park*. Significantly though, she focuses that interest on the pre-production, rehearsals and aftermath of *Lovers' Vows*, rather than the actual performance of the play, which is so memorably pre-empted by Sir Thomas's return. Her satirical treatment of the 'inconveniences' attached to 'scarcity of plays' in *Love and Freindship* is reworked in the Mansfield theatricals, where, ironically, the search for a suitable play is dramatised more fully than the play itself:

'Oh! no, *that* will never do. Let us have no ranting tragedies. Too many characters – Not a tolerable woman's part in the play – Anything but *that*, my dear Tom. It would be impossible to fill it up – One could not expect any body to take such a part – Nothing but buffoonery from beginning to end. *That* might do, perhaps, but for the low parts – If I *must* give my opinion, I have always thought it the most insipid play in the English language – *I* do not wish to make objections, I shall be happy to be of any use, but I think we could not choose worse.' (*MP*, p. 131)

Clearly Austen was no stranger to the exigencies of choosing a suitable play for home representation, and she delights in the sheer egomania of the would-be actors, who find it so hard to make a decision, chiefly because they all want the 'best characters'. Fanny Price, like her author, is 'not unamused' by this picture of 'disguised' selfishness. Fanny seems only too happy to observe the theatrical events: 'For her own gratification she could have wished that something might be acted, for she had never seen half a play, but everything of higher consequence was against it' (*MP*, p. 131).

Fanny forewarns Edmund that the group's theatrical preferences are markedly dissimilar: 'Your brother's taste, and your sisters', seem very different.' Edmund and Fanny even cherish hopes that the theatrical project will never get off the ground because there are too many people to be pleased. Austen ominously details the practical arrangements which begin to escalate in scale and expense – the carpenter has taken measurements and is already at work erecting a stage, the housemaids are making up the curtain – even before a choice of play has been fixed upon. The 'great irreconcileable difference' is over comedy or tragedy, and choosing a suitable play becomes an all-consuming task.

Shakespeare's tragedies, *Hamlet*, *Macbeth*, *Othello*, together with Moore's *The Gamester* and Home's *Douglas* (probably the two most popular 'sentimental' tragedies of the eighteenth century), are rejected as unsuitable. *The Rivals*, *The School for Scandal*, *The Wheel of Fortune* and *The Heir at Law* are eschewed by the tragedians 'with yet warmer objections' (*MP*, p. 131). While the majority view holds out for tragedy, Tom Bertram's preference is clearly for comedy; and, although he is tacitly seconded by Mary Crawford, 'his determinateness and his power, seemed to make allies unnecessary' (*MP*, p. 130). Tom insists upon a comedy, or at least a comic part for himself: 'I take any part you choose to give me, so as it be comic. Let it but be comic, I condition for nothing more' (*MP*, p. 131). Tom is 'exactly adapted to the novelty of acting' by dint of his 'lively talents' and 'comic taste'.

Tom Bertram is the character who is most deeply 'infected' by the vogue for amateur theatricals. Few have noticed how central he is to the theatricals.[18] Of all the characters, he appears to be the one with the most detailed and enthusiastic knowledge of the drama. Initially he doesn't want a sentimental play like *Lovers' Vows* – he wants to put on a comedy.

Tom's suggested plays, all well-established comedies of the London stage, represent a cross-section of some of the best works of a number of successful eighteenth-century playwrights, Sheridan, George Colman the Younger and Richard Cumberland. *The Rivals* and *The School for Scandal* were obvious choices for Austen, as both of these plays had been performed by her own family. Cumberland's sentimental comedy, *The Wheel of Fortune*, as the title suggests, presents a profligate, Woodville, who has squandered his fortune at the gaming table, enabling his arch enemy, Penruddock – a role made famous by John Philip Kemble – to exact revenge on him. It hardly hardly needs to be emphasised that Tom Bertram has already squandered part of his father's fortune on gambling losses, and cost Edmund his clerical living at Mansfield. *The Wheel of Fortune* dramatises a failed relationship between father and son. While the son has been off fighting for his country, his father has lost his home and wife through his addiction to gambling.

But it is *The Heir at Law* that Tom earnestly proposes five times. There are two parts that Tom considers for himself; one is the famed comic role of the great opportunist Dr Pangloss, the other is Lord Duberley – the comically displaced heir-at-law.[19] Tom's choice of play and role provide a significant insight into his character, which is wholly lost on a reader today.

George Colman the Younger, playwright and manager of the Haymarket Theatre, produced *The Heir at Law* on 15 July 1797.[20] The play enjoyed over a hundred years of success before disappearing from the boards; a performance was even noted as late as 1906.[21] Colman's play is another striking example of the era's devotion to comedies depicting social transformations. The device of bringing together contrasting 'types' allowed Colman to exploit fully the comic potential of the juxtapositions of 'high' and 'low' life in Georgian England, and to please the upper galleries as well as the pit.

The eponymous heir-at-law, Lord Duberley formerly Daniel Dowlas, is a common tradesman who in the absence of a natural heir has inherited a title and an estate belonging to a distant cousin. Uncomfortable with his role of nobleman, he secretly employs the services of Dr Pangloss for the purpose of 'fashioning his discourse' so that he can assume his 'rightful' place in genteel society. Meanwhile, the true heir, Henry Moreland, supposedly lost at sea, returns to England, only to find a common merchant in his father's place. The play is full of lively, displaced characters, uncomfortable with the roles that either society or fortune has apportioned them.

Colman's play shows that 'the fickle world is full of changes'. The plot revolves around inequalities of birth, where 'chance may remove one man so far from another, in the rank of life', and social mobility, where one's fortune can be made by improving a vulgar family's 'cacology', by becoming a rich man's mistress or by winning the lottery.[22] Colman's socially displaced characters are made miserable by their shifting roles and positions in society. At the play's denouement they are all restored to their original status, with the exception of the rustic, Zekiel Homespun, who confounds all social classifications by his win on the lottery. Daniel Dowlas is only too relieved to relinquish his burdensome rights and responsibilities to the real heir, Moreland, whose return from the 'watery grave' restores the authentic peer to his estate.

Plays depicting incongruous social reversals, such as *The Heir at Law* and Townley's *High Life Below Stairs*, were the particular favourites of the amateur theatricals of the public schools, military academies and spouting clubs. These exclusively male dilettante theatricals favoured comedies where social roles were turned topsy-turvy. Part of the attraction was the opportunity for enacting scenarios of social transformation. Navy theatricals, for instance, enabled officers to indulge themselves in coveted 'low-life' roles.[23] By the same account, Tom Bertram's interest in *The Heir at Law* and his desire to perform the role of Lord Duberley encourage us to reconsider his position of heir to the Mansfield Park estate.

His choice of the role of Lord Duberley is especially revealing, for the character is a fake aristocrat, a pretender. Thus the heir to the Mansfield estate wishes to play the part of the vulgar tradesman playing the part of the aristocratic lord. The desire to play the inauthentic peer instated by a 'freak of fortune' suggests Tom's uneasiness with the role of elder son – a role that he persistently rejects. Lord Duberley's character, decent and genial, but totally unfit for high office, accords well with Tom's cavalier attitude towards the responsibilities of his position and his light regard towards his duties as a future landowner. Mary Crawford quickly realises that the quickest way to Tom's heart is through horse-racing and gambling – his real love – and just as quickly perceives that his first priorities are to himself:

> his lengthened absence from Mansfield, without any thing but pleasure in view, and his own will to consult, made it perfectly clear that he did not care about her; and his indifference was so much more than equalled by her own, that were he now to step forth the owner of Mansfield park, the Sir Thomas complete, which he was to be in time, she did not believe that she could accept him. (*MP*, p. 114)

Mary's piqued reflections highlight the dangers which face the baronet in Antigua; at any moment Tom may be requested to 'step forth' into his father's shoes. The fear for Sir Thomas's safety is constantly emphasised, disproportionately by Mrs Norris who longs to be the bearer of the news of his untimely decease. One of Edmund's many reasons for opposing the theatricals is fear for his father's safety: 'It would show great want of feeling on my father's account, absent as he is, and in some degree of constant danger' (*MP*, p. 125). Although the danger is not specified, the threat is from not only the 'unfavourable circumstances' in Antigua, but more significantly the dangers of the voyage home. In the event of a disaster at sea, Sir Thomas's death would place Tom in the same position as Lord Duberley, who is heir at law by dint of the shipwrecked and supposedly drowned Henry Moreland.

Austen makes it clear that Tom is *in loco parentis* in the absence of his father: 'the inclination to act was awakened, and in no one more strongly than in him who was now master of the house' (*MP*, p. 123). Tom's wish to escape the role of 'the Sir Thomas complete' is undoubtedly reflected in his desire to play the part of Lord Duberley, the comically unsatisfactory heir to the estate. If he had had his way with the Colman play, his best scene as Lord Duberley, one of mistaken identity and misapprehension, would have suggested a particularly significant reading of his relationship to his father and the estate. In this scene, Stedfast, Moreland's friend, confuses Dowlas with the original Lord Duberley. The comic appeal is dependent upon the fragile equation of virtue with rank, which in this instance is shown to be falsifying:

> Ignorance may palliate meanness and buffoonery, and merely meet contempt, but want of feeling excites indignation. You have shocked me, and I leave you. From exalted rank like yours, my lord, men look for exalted virtue; and when these are coupled, they command respect, and grace each other: – but the coronet, which gives and receives splendour, when fixed on the brow of merit, glitters on the worthless head, like a mark of disgrace, to render vice, folly and inhumanity conspicuous.[24]

The joke is compounded by Stedfast's surprise at finding so little physiognomical evidence of the dignity and nobility that he has been encouraged to take for granted in a peer of the realm. Stedfast's high expectations stem from an earlier scene where the reputation of Lord Duberley has been warmly expounded by his son, who excuses his father's social reserve as a mark of his dignity:

> but I confess to those who are unacquainted with them, these qualities are concealed by a coldness in his manner … a long habit too of haranguing in Parliament, gives a man a kind of dignity of deportment, and an elevation of style not to be met with every day you know. But Gentleman is written legibly upon his brow; erudition shines thro' every polished period of his language; and he is the best of men, and of fathers, believe me.[25]

In Colman's play appearances are deceptive. Dowlas neither looks nor speaks like a nobleman, and, although his good nature is undeniable, he is scorned for his natural vulgarity and 'lowness'. Conversely, Moreland's description of his father's noble physiognomy reminds us of another lofty baronet whose countenance is repeatedly described as being marked with solemn dignity, whose coldness is felt by his children, and whose conduct is not always presented as virtuous or gentlemanly: Sir Thomas Bertram. One of the most shocking moments for Fanny is when she realises that her uncle's motives and conduct towards her are far from disinterested and noble. To her own 'infinite grief', she discovers that she has been deceived by the baronet's outward appearance.

When Sir Thomas inadvertently makes his debut on the stage of his son's theatre, we are surely invited to consider the difference between the old Sir Thomas and the future 'Sir Thomas complete'. Tom Bertram is as uncomfortable with his future role as 'plain Daniel Dowlas of Gosport' is at playing the part of Lord Duberley. In Colman's comedy all comes right in the return of the true heir who restores everyone to their rightful social positions; the fake lord is ejected, and the social order is maintained. Of course, in the conventions of comic theatre, appearances that seem deceptive are revealed in their true light. It is only Daniel Dowlas who is surprised by the discovery that he has been merely *locum tenens* in the absence of Henry Moreland: a 'peer's warming pan'.[26]

In the more complex world of *Mansfield Park*, the social order is not so easily restored. Nor are appearances always a reliable guide to conduct, as Fanny discovers. Tom Bertram appears to be little more than a 'warming pan', as his self-inflicted illness almost threatens to grant Mary Crawford her desire to see the younger brother become 'Sir Edmund' Bertram. But the heir by birth, who is the fake heir by nature, finally does inherit Mansfield, and the heroine, the spiritual heir to the 'great' house, is displaced to the vicarage.

It is unsurprising that the other role to appeal to Tom's theatrical inclinations is that of Dr Pangloss. If he is not to play the part of Lord Duberley, he covets the great comic role of Colman's doctor-on-the-make. When he is denied his preferred choice of play by the opposition of the rest of the cast, he happily assents to *Lovers' Vows*, rejects the paternal role of Baron Wildenhaim and is content to appropriate a suitably humbler part to himself – the comic, rhyming Butler.[27] Even though he has not got his way over *The Heir at Law*, Tom is still able to make his descent down the social scale: the *de facto* master of the house adopts the stage role of a servant.

In the real life amateur theatricals of the period, Lord Barrymore played the roles of rustics and servants in his Wargrave playhouse. This kind of theatrical slumming was a striking reversal of the convention of the public theatre where a low-born actor could successfully portray the role of a gentleman. As we have seen, the actor William 'Gentleman'

Lewis was famous for his rendering of 'high society' roles. At Wargrave, the low-born professional actress Elizabeth Edwin often played the parts of aristocratic ladies to Lord Barrymore's rustics.[28]

When Elizabeth Farren, formerly a child actor in a company of strolling players in the provinces, became famous for her depiction of elegant and well-bred ladies at Drury Lane and Covent Garden, she was courted by the Earl of Derby.[29] Farren's meteoric rise from obscurity to the highest stratum of society, from 'a Barn to a Court', was complete when she became a countess and was presented at Court. She had become the very character that had sustained her in her numerous stage roles. Having grown to be highly respected – her behaviour won the approval of Queen Charlotte – she insisted that her former life should never be mentioned.

Austen's interest in social mobility is inextricably bound up with her knowledge of eighteenth-century theatre, both public and private, where reversals of rank and station were commonplace. Lord Barrymore's well-publicised theatricals were made even more notorious by the presence and 'princely patronage' of the Prince of Wales.[30] The Prince's connections with low-born actresses, most famously Mary 'Perdita' Robinson, no doubt added to the controversy. Austen's juvenilia shows her poking fun at the Prince's notorious relationships with low-born women.[31]

The first part of this book has demonstrated that Austen particularly relished cross-over farces such as *The Devil to Pay* and *High Life Below Stairs*, where reversals of rank and station were employed to reflect upon social conduct, and where low life was used to criticise high life. In *Mansfield Park*, her preoccupation with the blurring of the boundaries between the ranks is suggested from the opening pages where Sir Thomas and Mrs Norris are keen that Fanny should know her place and not be considered '*a Miss Bertram*' (*MP*, p. 10). Sir Thomas is keen to emphasise that the cousins are not 'equals': 'Their rank, fortune, rights, and expectations, will always be different' (*MP*, p. 11). However, by the end of the novel, he is compelled to reassess his thinking about the differences between the 'low' Price children and his own highly-bred children. Sir Thomas duly acknowledges, 'In [Susan's] usefulness, in Fanny's excellence, in William's continued good conduct, and rising fame, and in the general well-doing and success of the other members of the family, all assisting to advance each other ... the advantages of early hardship and discipline, and the consciousness of being born to struggle and endure' (*MP*, p. 473).

Jane Austen's unashamed delight in Elizabeth and Jane Bennet's social mobility in *Pride and Prejudice* is somewhat tempered in her depiction of the ascent of Fanny and Susan Price, where endurance and hard work are emphasised. With William Price – and Captain Wentworth in *Persuasion* – Austen uses the naval profession to emphasise the claims of innate merit and talent over social position and inherited wealth. In eighteenth-century comedies, such as *The Heir at Law* and *She Stoops to Conquer*, the stock character of the profligate son and heir to the estate who refuses to commit to his appropriate social role is used to reflect favourably upon lesser-ranking characters.

Tom's preoccupation with *The Heir at Law* suggests, even more forcibly, that Jane Austen was well attuned to the nuances of eighteenth-century social class and identity, as explored in the drama. Tom's uneasiness with his identity as heir to Mansfield Park is connected to his sense of the quasi-theatrical artifice of social behaviour. His amusing account of his social blunder over the mysteries of female protocol, of the Miss Anderson who was 'not out', and the Miss Sneyd who was 'out' (*MP*, p. 50), is in the style of eighteenth-century comedy's playful confusion of rank and manners – to which, we must assume, he has been attuned by his theatre-going.

Miss Anderson's ambiguous social conduct is a source of embarrassment to Tom. Her behaviour when she is 'not out' is not so much excessive modesty as downright rudeness: 'I could hardly get a word or a look from the young lady – nothing like a civil answer – she screwed up her mouth, and turned from me with such an air!' (*MP*, p. 50). But when he meets her again when she is 'out', she displays a pushy, flirtatious manner in public: 'She came up to me, claimed me as an acquaintance, stared me out of countenance, and talked and laughed till I did not know which way to look. I felt that I must be the jest of the room at the time – and Miss Crawford, it is plain, has heard the story' (*MP*, p. 50). His sense of the absurd is tickled by the artificiality of the girl's social conduct, which verges from one extreme to another.

Likewise, Tom's 'dreadful scrape' at Ramsgate with the younger Miss Sneyd who is 'not out' is caused by misleading female dress codes that fail to denote behaviour. Mary Crawford's distinction between the protocol of the 'out' and the 'not out' girl is 'a close bonnet' (*MP*, p. 49), but Tom's blunder is occasioned by Miss Sneyd's failure to appear in an appropriately coded costume: 'The close bonnet and demure air ... tell one what is expected; but I got into a dreadful scrape last year from the want of them' (*MP*, p. 51).

In Goldsmith's *She Stoops to Conquer* (1771), a comedy premised on the ambiguities of social class and the discrepancies between rank and manners, the plot is based upon a similar social blunder by a young gentleman. Marlow mistakes a gentleman for an innkeeper partly because 'manners and appearance' are 'so totally different' (*MP*, p. 49). Furthermore, Kate Hardcastle's disguise as a barmaid is a voluntary undertaking of the reversal of the class roles in order to 'conquer' the socially awkward Marlow, who is reduced to inarticulacy by genteel women.[32] But it is Kate's father's insistence on her wearing a plain dress which first confuses Marlow, and the success of her plot is dependent upon the bonnet she wears in their first meeting which enables her to carry out her disguise.

Tom Bertram's impatience with the mores of civilised society is shown by his languid observations on dancing (an important and necessary part of the social environment), and his focusing of the scene into a fantasy of sexual intrigue:

> 'I only wonder how the good people can keep it up so long. – They had need be *all* in love, to find any amusement in such folly – and so they are, I fancy. If you look at them, you may see they are so many couple of lovers – all but Yates and Mrs Grant – and, between ourselves, she, poor woman! must want a lover as much as any one of them. A desperate dull life her's must be with the doctor.' (*MP*, pp. 118–19)

His observation on the Grants' ill-suited marriage comes straight out of stage comedy. Dr Grant's pretty wife is 'fifteen years his junior' and suffers at the hands of her gourmandising husband. Their type of union, the sexually deficient older man who risks being cuckolded by his beautiful young wife, had been a staple of comedy ever since its origins in ancient Greece. Eighteenth-century comedy is full of plot lines where young wives, like Sheridan's Lady Teazle, are tempted by rakes, repent of their flightiness, and are reconciled to their old spouses. Tom's speculation about Mrs Grant's sexually unfulfilled marriage suggests Yates as a candidate for the lover she needs to assuage her 'desperate dull life'.

Tom's aside reveals a comic propensity for viewing life through the spectacles of theatre, a propensity which should not be underestimated in a novel which uses theatricality and role-playing to comment upon social behaviour. It is in yet another of his seemingly careless asides that he first draws an explicit parallel between real life and theatricality. Yates's endless preoccupation with the termination of the private theatricals at Ecclesford, due to the death of a dowager grandmother, provokes another theatrical joke from Tom: 'An after-piece instead of a comedy … Lovers' Vows were at an end, and Lord and Lady Ravenshaw left to act My Grandmother by themselves' (*MP*, pp. 122–23).

Ostensibly, Tom's comment reveals how he has such a vast repertoire of eighteenth-century plays in his head that he can produce a theatrical witticism for any occasion. *My Grandmother*, a popular farce by Prince Hoare, was indeed performed as an 'afterpiece' to the main play, as were most eighteenth-century farces.[33] After the death of the dowager and the departure of the young people, Lord and Lady Ravenshaw are left to perform that ultimate after-piece, a funeral. But Tom's remark shows a more complex investment in theatricality than merely a knowledge of contemporary plays.

His pun is dependent upon us perceiving a literal interpretation of the plays' titles to convey the 'real' situation (the death of a grandmother, or love-play between young people), and it also confirms a literal understanding of the nature of the relationship between title and plot. This makes it startlingly clear that 'Lovers' Vows' is to be regarded as *double entendre* for young lovers engaging in love-play, making and breaking promises.[34] Tom is thus the first character to make the fertile connection between real life and theatricality, which is then further explored not only by the way in which the stage-lovers act out their real feelings by way of *Lovers' Vows*, but also by the broader correspondence between social conduct and artful play.

* * *

Once Edmund Bertram has finally been persuaded to participate in the theatricals, he soon begins to confuse 'his theatrical and his real part' (*MP*, p. 163). Although he initially expresses doubt about his closeness to the role of Anhalt – 'the man who chooses the profession itself, is, perhaps, one of the last who would wish to represent it on the stage' (*MP*, p. 145) – he is unable to resist the allure of Mary's bold request, 'What gentleman among you am I to have the pleasure of making love to?' (*MP*, p. 143). In 'making love' to Mary in their rehearsal scene, Edmund finds himself expressing his own real feelings as well as those of his character.

So too with Henry and Maria as Frederick and Agatha: acting gives the lovers freedom to express their real feelings. Fanny notes that 'Maria … acted well – too well' (*MP*, p. 165). And Mary Crawford quips that 'those indefatigable rehearsers, Agatha and Frederick' should excel at their parts, for they are so often embracing: 'If *they* are not perfect, I *shall* be surprised' (*MP*, p. 169). Mary's reference to Henry and Maria by their stage names is a reminder of their emotional identification with the roles of Agatha and Frederick.

The stage directions of the first act of *Lovers' Vows* reveal the 'dangerous intimacy' of Tom's theatre (*MP*, p. 462): '[*Rising and Embracing him*]', '[*Leans her head against his breast*]', '[*He embraces her*]', '[*Agatha presses him to her breast*]', '[*Frederick with his eyes cast down, takes her hand, and puts it to his heart*].' This final direction is at the point where Henry and Maria are later interrupted by Sir Thomas's arrival. This shows how closely Austen followed Mrs Inchbald's stage directions. Ironically, Agatha's words preceding this direction are, 'His flattery made me vain, and his repeated vows –' (*LV*, act 1, scene 1). Henry's act of retaining Maria's hand after Julia's melodramatic announcement of Sir Thomas's arrival gives Maria the false impression that the gesture denotes an implicit lover's vow, and she fully expects that this will be followed by a formal declaration for her hand.[35] After days of anxious waiting, 'the agony of her mind was severe' when she discovers that no declaration is to be made: 'The hand which had so pressed her's to his heart! – The hand and the heart were alike motionless and passive now!' (*MP*, p. 193).

As well as watching Henry and Maria engaging in love-play, Fanny is compelled to be the 'judge and critic' of the rehearsal between Mary and

Edmund. She reflects afterwards on the unhappy experience: 'she was inclined to believe their performance would, indeed, have such nature and feeling in it, as must ensure their credit, and make it a very suffering exhibition to herself' (*MP*, p. 170). Fanny's observation is, of course, heavily ironic: she is referring, not to the acting abilities of Edmund and Mary, but to the display of their real feelings. The combination of the words 'nature and feeling' in the context of acting would, however, have had deep resonance for Austen's early readers, especially since at the time of the novel's publication Edmund Kean had recently made his electrifying debut on the London stage. Kean's 'natural' style fuelled a long-standing debate, going back to Charles Macklin and David Garrick, about traditional styles of acting in tragedy versus the new naturalism.

The declamatory, rhetorical approach, with its 'rants' and 'starts', represented by the Cibber school of acting was slowly reformed by a shift in emphasis from exaggeration to 'naturalism', from tradition to originality.[36] The formal, rhetorical tradition represented by James Quin was challenged by Macklin and Garrick, whose new 'naturalist' approach accepted the actor's right to freedom of interpretation. The birth of the new naturalist approach is memorialised in the story of Garrick's appearance at Goodman's Fields in *Richard III* and Quin's shocked exclamation, 'That if the young fellow was right, he, and the rest of the players, had been all wrong'.[37] Richard Cumberland, who saw Garrick and Quin acting the principal male leads in *The Fair Penitent*, was astonished by Garrick's performance: 'it seemed as if a whole century had been stepped over in the transition of a single scene'.[38] Even before Garrick, however, Macklin had challenged the rhetorical and formal tradition to acting. For example, his unconventional approach to Hamlet's first meeting with the ghost was played with an understated simplicity and respect rather than the expected exaggerated and bombastic 'starts' and 'rants'.[39]

The 'rant', which was the conventional mode of delivery for tragedy, became 'the most unvarying subject of attack by theatrical critics'.[40] Both Arthur Murphy and Thomas Davies in their biographies of Garrick describe him as having banished 'ranting'.[41] Jane Austen shows her own awareness of the practice of ranting in *Mansfield Park* when she depicts her dilettante actor John Yates as one who 'rants' and 'starts' in the style of the old school: 'Mr Yates was in general thought to rant dreadfully' (*MP*, p. 164). At Ecclesford, Yates had 'grudged every rant of Lord Ravenshaw's and been forced to re-rant it all in his own room' (*MP*, p. 132).

On the other hand, Henry Crawford is regarded by the theatrical party as an accomplished actor: 'he had more confidence than Edmund, more judgment than Tom, more talent and taste than Mr Yates' (*MP*, p. 165). It is little surprise that the only character, apart from Rushworth, to dislike Henry's acting style is Yates, who exclaims against 'his tameness and insipidity' (*MP*, p. 165). The histrionic, ranting Yates would, of course, find Henry's naturalism too tame. Fanny, on the other hand, finds Henry's style 'truly dramatic': 'His acting had first taught Fanny what pleasure a play might give' (*MP*, p. 337).

In Austen's era, actors such as Cooke and Siddons followed Garrick in their belief that it was not enough to copy nature. They believed that good acting also required emotional identification with the part. Leigh Hunt observes that Siddons 'has the air of never being the actress; she seems unconscious that there is a motley crowd called a pit waiting to applaud her, or that there are a dozen fiddlers waiting for her exit'.[42] But not every actor worked on the principle of emotional identification. Samuel Johnson enquired of Siddons's brother Kemble, 'Are you, sir, one of those enthusiasts who believe yourself transformed into the very character you represent?' Boswell records, 'Upon Mr Kemble's answering that he never felt so strong a persuasion himself; "to be sure not, Sir (said Johnson) the thing is impossible. And if Garrick really believed himself to be that monster, Richard III, he deserved to be hanged every time he performed it."'[43]

In *Tom Jones*, Henry Fielding's comic depiction of the debate is mediated through the less sophisticated viewpoint of Partridge. Tom Jones is eager for a criticism of Garrick 'unadulterated by art' and informed by 'the simple dictates of nature'. He therefore appeals to the foolish schoolmaster, only to discover to his amusement that Partridge dislikes Garrick's Hamlet because it is too true to life: 'why I could act as well as he myself. I am sure if I had seen a ghost, I should have looked in the very same manner, and done just what he did.'[44] Partridge prefers the exaggerated histrionic acting of the old-school player of Claudius because he 'speaks all his words distinctly, half as loud again as the other. – Any body may see he is an actor.'[45]

Fielding's fictionalising of Garrick's naturalistic performance seen through the eyes of the naive Partridge is a reminder of the way in which the actor's art became the subject of analysis and discussion in the Georgian era.[46] In *Mansfield Park*, Austen uses private theatricals rather than the public theatre to explore her own interest in the debate. Her allusions to the 'nature and feeling' of her four principals, and her comparison of the ranting Yates with the naturalism of Henry Crawford, would not have been lost on her first readers, especially as the novel was published soon after the debut of Edmund Kean, who was regarded as the first actor for a generation to raise stage feeling to the heights of Garrick.[47]

Although Kean made his debut shortly after Jane Austen finished *Mansfield Park*, it is nevertheless intriguing that she writes about him in the context of her novel. In the midst of her enthusiasm about her new novel, her train of thought slides from Henry Austen's reading of it to Henry Crawford to Kean:

Henry has this moment said that he likes my M. P. better & better; – he is in the 3d. vol. – I beleive [sic] now he has changed his mind as to foreseeing the end; – he said yesterday at least, that he defied anybody to say whether H. C. would be reformed, or would forget Fanny in a fortnight. – I shall like to see Kean again excessively, & to see him with You too; – it appeared to me that there was no fault in him anywhere. (*Letters*, p. 258)

Critics have perceived a source for Henry Crawford in the theatre-loving, soldier-turned-banker-turned-clergyman Henry Austen. But what is striking about this letter is the enthusiasm for Kean and the theatre in the context of 'H. C.' It is highly appropriate that Henry Crawford wishes to 'undertake any character that ever was written, from Shylock or Richard III' (*MP*, p. 123), for those were the two parts with which Kean made his name.

Having just completed the novel that dealt most extensively with her interest in the relationship between art and life, Austen was disposed to be pleased with the style of acting heralded by Kean. Unlike Dr Johnson, she did not express any moral concern for the actor's emotional and intellectual identification with the role, but saw, on the contrary, that it created 'exquisite acting'. Even the sincere and demure Fanny takes pleasure in acting: she masters not only Rushworth's part, but every other role in the play in her unofficial capacity as prompter. So it is that she is eventually persuaded to play the role of Cottager's Wife.

Far from proposing that acting encourages a kind of insincere role-playing in life, Austen suggests in her depiction of polite society that an ability to perform socially is often a necessity.[48] Buoyed by her interest in the arts of the theatre, she explores how social mores require characters to adopt particular roles. In *Sense and Sensibility*, Mrs Dashwood anxiously demands if Willoughby has 'been acting a part' throughout his courtship of Marianne. In the morally ambiguous world of *Mansfield Park*, Austen consistently puns on the words 'act' and 'acting' to blur the distinctions between role-playing and social conduct. So, for instance, when Henry Crawford informs Fanny of his reformation from the role of absentee landlord to that of responsible master, Austen alerts us to the possibility of doubt: 'This was aimed, and well aimed, at Fanny. It was pleasing to hear him speak so properly; here, he had been acting as he ought to do' (*MP*, p. 404).

In contrast to the Crawfords, who have mastered the art of social role-playing, Tom Bertram is rendered uneasy by the rules of civilised society, for, as he has discovered with Miss Sneyd and Miss Anderson, they often breed deception and confusion. More than any other character in the novel, Tom is alert to the discrepancy between manners and appearance, and the theatricality of social conduct, and thus it is through his eyes that we witness the grand climax of the *Lovers' Vows* sequence: Sir Thomas Bertram's stage debut.

Austen distinguishes the fashionably elite theatricals of the aristocracy from those of the squirearchy in her portrayal of Tom's aristocratic 'friend', the Honourable Mr Yates, who brings the 'itch' for acting from the Ecclesford theatricals. The name Yates had a venerable theatrical pedigree. Richard Yates (1706–96) was the popular comedian who was the first Oliver Surface in Drury Lane's *The School for Scandal*. He was part of a famous acting couple, with his wife Mary Anne Yates (1728–87), one of Garrick's leading ladies, a famous tragedian often compared to Siddons.[49]

Mrs Yates was also often compared with another leading actress of the eighteenth-century stage, the tragedienne Mrs Ann Crawford (1734–1801).[50] Crawford was known as the 'lover of the stage'.[51] She was also part of a famous acting couple with the notoriously 'handsome, volatile, and noisy' Thomas (Billy) Crawford (1750–94).[52] Campbell wrote in his biography of Sarah Siddons: 'Next to Mrs Pritchard in point of time, our two greatest actresses were Mrs Yates and Mrs Crawford. They were contemporaries and great rivals; the former bearing the palm for dignity and sculpturesque beauty, while the latter, though less pleasing in looks, had more passion and versatility.'[53] The names Yates and Crawford were thus linked in the theatre world, not only because they were famous tragediennes in their own right, but because they were both married to famous actors.

Austen's use of the names Yates and Crawford in the context of her private theatre may well have been noted with amusement by readers familiar with the famous eighteenth-century theatrical dynasties. The romantic pairings of the real-life Yateses and Crawfords add an extra dimension to *Mansfield Park*. Ironically, the two characters who are excluded from the theatrical party, Fanny Price and Julia Bertram, come closer to the Georgian theatrical world when they (potentially, in Fanny's case) become Mrs Crawford and Mrs Yates.

The events at Ecclesford are curiously proleptic of the events at Mansfield Park. *Lovers' Vows* is provokingly interrupted on both occasions. The Ecclesford group are banished upon grounds of strict propriety: 'Lord Ravenshaw, who I suppose is one of the most correct men in England, would not hear of it' (*MP*, p. 122). Similarly, the impropriety of putting on a play when Sir Thomas is 'in some degree of constant danger' is one of Edmund's objections. Death has broken up the Ecclesford theatre. Even the public theatres closed for the day when a royal death occurred. The point is clear: that if news came back of Sir Thomas's death, the play would be interrupted in the same way as at Ecclesford, and *Lovers' Vows* would again be broken up, this time leaving Lady Bertram alone to act the after-piece of 'The Widow' or *The Distressed*

Mother. Lady Bertram certainly 'acts' the part of a grieving mother when she hears the news of Tom's decline: 'It was a sort of playing at being frightened' (*MP*, p. 427).

Lord Ravenshaw's theatrical party, which includes a scattering of the aristocracy (Lord and Lady Ravenshaw are joined by the Honourable John Yates, a Sir Henry, and even a Duke), is conducted on suitably lavish terms. Tom's desire to 'raise a little theatre at Mansfield' (*MP*, p. 123) evinces an ambition for something more extravagant than the makeshift theatres of the gentry. His longing for the 'Ecclesford theatre and scenery to try something with' is contrasted with Maria's entreaty to 'make the *performance*, not the *theatre*, our object' (*MP*, p. 124). Even Henry's suggestion that there is more to a theatre than the buildings and scenery fails to satisfy Tom: 'and for a theatre, what signifies a theatre? We shall only be amusing ourselves. Any room in this house might suffice.' Tom concedes to a makeshift theatre on the proviso that there are at least some theatrical accoutrements, a 'green curtain and a little carpenter's work' (*MP*, p. 127). Only then can he begin to envisage a prospective theatrical venue ensuing from the conversion of two rooms by 'merely moving the book-case in my father's room' (*MP*, p. 125).

Tom concentrates his theatrical energies behind the scenes. He is a committed manager, obsessed with the minutiae of stagecraft: he consults with the carpenters; he sets up a committee to pore over the text, to cut and lop where necessary; he suggests ideas for Fanny's costume and stage make-up; he is even prepared to ride across the country to find one more actor for his company (*MP*, p. 148). His efforts to professionalise the theatre are compounded by an adoption of theatrical language: he speaks of his 'company' and of Sir Thomas's study as the 'green room', while the billiard room is now '*the Theatre*'. Rather than respecting the 'privacy of the representation' he gives 'an invitation to every family who came in his way' (*MP*, p. 164). Having learned his part, 'all his parts', he is impatient to act.

Tom's attempts at *bon ton* theatricals are reminiscent of Lord Barrymore's theatrical excesses at Wargrave. Soon after his death, Barrymore was condemned for engaging in 'the most ridiculous, expensive, profuse and prodigal scheme, that ever signalized a predeliction for *private theatricals*'. Tickets were 'distributed to all the families of fashion and eminence in the surrounding neighbourhood', and 'sums exceeding all rational comprehension, all *common* credulity (to the amount of forty or fifty thousand) have been most degradingly lavished in every scene of riot, debauchery and extravagance'. Barrymore's 'infatuation' with his theatre was condemned: 'he became so severely infected with the deceptive *glee*, the affected *mirth*, the superficial *wit*, the interested *politesse*, the *political attachment*, the general *levity*, the characteristic *indigence*, and attracting tout ensemble of a green room'. Only after his death were the house and village rescued from 'the appearance of a *metropolis* in *miniature*' and restored to a 'truly remote and rusticated village'.[54]

Tom's desire to ape Lord Ravenshaw, not only by choosing *Lovers' Vows* but by longing for 'the Ecclesford theatre and the scenery', resonates with the fashionably elite theatricals of the aristocracy. His rendering of the 'low roles', the Butler and Cottager, also repeats Barrymore's performance of rustics and servants at Wargrave. Tom's responsibility for the theatricals is made clear: 'the inclination to act was awakened, and in no one more strongly than in him who was now master of the house' (*MP*, p. 123).

The disruptive consequences of Tom's theatricalising are most powerfully realised at the end of the first volume of *Mansfield Park* by the unexpected return of Sir Thomas. The first full dress rehearsal of *Lovers' Vows* has just begun when Sir Thomas makes his own melodramatic entrance from the West Indies. Sir Thomas interrupts a moment of high drama on stage, leading to a moment of high drama off stage.

The whole sequence of Sir Thomas's return and the termination of the *Lovers' Vows* is deliciously comic. The opening scene of the play is interrupted at the precise moment when Agatha is explaining the circumstances of her seduction and ruination to her son Frederick. At this point in Inchbald's play the stage directions reveal that Frederick 'takes the hand of Agatha and puts it to his heart'. Austen's specificity reveals her close knowledge of the play: 'Frederick was listening with looks of devotion to Agatha's narrative, and pressing her hand to her heart' (*MP*, p. 175). This moment occurs about ten minutes into the opening scene, at the end of Agatha's speech:[55]

he talked of love and promised me marriage ... His flattery made me vain, and his repeated vows – Don't look at me, dear Frederick! – I can say no more. [*Frederick with his eyes cast down, takes her hand, and puts it to his heart.*] Oh! Oh! my son! I was intoxicated by the fervent caresses of a young, inexperienced, capricious man, and did not recover from the delirium till it was too late. (*LV*, act 1, scene 1)

The tableau on stage is framed, specifically, within the structure of the novel. In the chapel at Sotherton, Julia had directed the rest of the group to the visual tableau of the marriage between Rushworth and Maria. Now Austen repeats the motif, except that, even more spectacularly, she uses the moment to end the first volume of the novel. Furthermore, this time the tableau is itself a theatrical one – quite literally it forms the first scene of the first act of *Lovers' Vows*. Instead of Maria and Rushworth at the altar, a legitimate and formalised version of love, we now see Maria and Henry in a physical embrace. It is Julia who once again, as in the chapel, directs our gaze to the tableau, but this time there is a double focus: the reader watches a character in the novel watching a character on stage. Furthermore, the scene is not filtered through the eyes of Fanny, for she is also on the stage, about to take her part. It is Julia's re-entrance and horrified cry that ends the first volume: 'My father is come! He is in the hall at this moment' (*MP*, p. 172).

At the beginning of the second volume Austen raises the curtain to reveal the frozen tableau of the cast on stage, motionless and fearful in the 'terrible pause' which precedes 'the corroborating sounds of opening doors and footsteps' (*MP*, p. 175). Once again, silence is used to characterise the attitudes of the group. In *Mansfield Park*, Frederick's pointed gesture of retaining Agatha's hand close to his heart does not go unnoticed by Julia, who literally exits the stage in protest with a suitably frosty closing line, '*I* need not be afraid of appearing before him' (*MP*, p. 175). Austen's reference to Henry and Maria by their stage names signifies that we are watching the lovers on a stage, rehearsing their opening scene, the sentimental reunion of a mother and her son. But offstage we are also about to witness another reunion scene, that between Sir Thomas and his family.

The tone of the narrative lightens with the piqued exit of Julia breaking the on-stage tableau. The Bertram brothers also exit hastily, 'feeling the necessity of doing something'. While the Bertrams hurriedly leave the stage to face their father in the drawing room, Austen completes the scene with the rake, Henry, wickedly encouraging the fop, Rushworth, to 'pay his respects to Sir Thomas without delay' and sending him through the door after the others 'with delighted haste' (*MP*, p. 176). The Crawfords, naturally, make their own perfectly timed exit and Fanny exits hesitatingly, leaving Yates centre stage.

Sir Thomas's family reunion in the drawing room is one of intense dramatic irony, for we know, along with Fanny, that at any minute 'unsuspected vexation was probably ready to burst on him' (*MP*, p. 178). His entrance into the drawing room is comically marked by Mrs Norris's 'instinctive caution with which she had whisked away Mr Rushworth's pink satin cloak as her brother-in-law entered' (*MP*, pp. 179–80).

Jane Austen invites us to enjoy the discomfort of a pregnant and highly awkward social situation. Furthermore, rather than the Gothic father-figure that Fanny has come to expect, Austen delights in surprising her with a much-changed Sir Thomas. He has altered both physically and in character: 'His manner seemed changed; his voice was quick from the agitation of joy, and all that had been awful in his dignity seemed lost in tenderness' (*MP*, p. 178). Furthermore, 'the delights of his sensations in being again in his own house, in the centre of his family, after such a separation, made him communicative and chatty in a very unusual degree' (*MP*, p. 178).

But it is not only the master of the house who seems predisposed to chat. In the 'elation of her spirits Lady Bertram became talkative'. And it is her unusual garrulousness that so comically lets the cat out of the bag: 'How do you think the young people have been amusing themselves lately, Sir Thomas? They have been acting. We have been all alive with acting' (*MP*, p. 181). Austen adds, mischievously, 'and what were the sensations of her children upon hearing her'.

The culmination of the theatrical saga comes in the uproariously comic moment of Sir Thomas's own stage debut. Wishing to take a look at his 'own dear room' the master of the house enters his study to discover general confusion and upheaval, notably the removal of the bookcase from the adjoining door, which we know leads directly to 'the theatre'. Hearing a strange 'hallooing' in the next room Sir Thomas passes through the door and finds himself face to face with the ranting Yates 'who appeared likely to knock him down backwards' (*MP*, p. 182). This moment of quasi-farcical humour is compounded by the sardonic description of Yates 'giving perhaps the very best start he had ever given in the whole course of his rehearsals' as he almost knocks the august Sir Thomas off balance.

The moment of Sir Thomas's great comic entrance onto the stage at Mansfield crystallises Austen's interplay between life and theatre, novel and play. What is most striking about this scene is that it is witnessed by Tom Bertram from the back of what has become the auditorium. The ironies of the scene are focused through the eyes of Tom, who can barely contain himself with laughter at the sight of his father's embarrassment. Crucially, it is only Tom who witnesses this piece of real-life theatre.

Tom's amusement runs deeper than an impartial appreciation of the farcical potential of the scene: 'His father's looks of solemnity and amaze-ment on this his first appearance on any stage, and the gradual metamor-phosis of the impassioned Baron Wildenhaim into the well-bred and easy Mr Yates, making his bow and apology to Sir Thomas Bertram was such an exhibition, such *a piece of true acting*, as he would not have lost upon any account' (*MP*, p. 182, my italics). The fluidity of the sentence, itself metamorphosing through four personae from 'His father – to Baron Wildenhaim – to Mr Yates – to Sir Thomas Bertram', is richly suggestive of the blurring of distinctions between theatricality and real-ity. Yates and Sir Thomas are first startled, then recover themselves to perform their social roles, which create the exhibition of 'true acting'. 'His father', unintentionally, becomes an actor in a scene before reverting to his role as 'Sir Thomas Bertram'. Mr Yates is startled from his melodra-matic posture as the ranting Baron Wildenhaim before he recovers to perform the social grace of a visitor presenting his formal compliments to his host.

The ability to adopt a social role is not to be confused with the poly-morphic skills of Henry Crawford, but Yates's metamorphosis from the 'impassioned Baron Wildenhaim' into 'the well-bred and easy Mr Yates' is a complex reversal of the requirements of the acting process. In meta-morphosing back into himself he is abandoning his usual histrionic style and is now acting naturalistically: what for Tom Bertram is 'true acting' is that absence of posturing which for Partridge, watching Garrick, was bad acting. But paradoxically, as Tom understands, Yates's bow and apology to 'Sir Thomas Bertram' is merely another form of social acting.

The ingenuity of describing this encounter through Tom's perspective is that, unlike Fanny, he understands the absurdities of social performance. Tom's desire to play the displaced Lord Duberley in Colman's *The Heir at Law* first identifies his understanding of the interchangeability of social roles, and the unstable relationship between status and conduct – perhaps first initiated by his confusion about Miss Anderson whose 'out' behaviour he found so perplexing. It is this understanding of the art of social role-playing that now shapes one of the most important scenes of the novel, the encounter between Yates and Sir Thomas, a slice of 'real-life' theatre: 'It would be the last – in all probability the last scene on that stage; but he was sure there could not be a finer. The house would close with the greatest eclat' (*MP*, pp. 182–83). Nowhere is Jane Austen's own *éclat* more evident than in this scene, with its dissolution of the distinction between acting on a stage and in social situations.

10

Emma

The *Lovers' Vows* debacle reveals that for Jane Austen acting is not so much an aberration as an inevitability. The great lesson she took from the drama, that social life requires a strong element of role-playing, is also one of the guiding principles of her next novel. In addition, *Emma* returns to the territory of *Pride and Prejudice*: the interplay of different social classes and the quest to discover a language truthful to emotional experience.

The depiction in *Pride and Prejudice* of a fine lady who is also an unregenerate snob is brilliantly reworked in *Emma*. This time, however, rather than the heroine being the victim of the cruelty and injustice of social snobbery, she is its perpetrator. Like Lady Catherine de Bourgh, Emma is concerned with preserving 'the distinctions of rank', and, in spite of the novel's deep engagement with the concept of social mobility, she is initially resistant to social change, unless upon her own terms.

The most traditional method of movement between the classes was through marriage and in *Emma* there are a number of intermarriages. The novel begins with the marriage between a former governess, Miss Taylor, and a highly respected, albeit self-made, gentleman, Mr Weston.[1] This union finds its correlation towards the close of the novel with the marriage between a woman on the brink of becoming a governess and a wealthy gentleman, who is the son of Mr Weston. Furthermore, the novel ends with the promise of future marriages (and matchmaking) between the daughter of the Westons and the offspring of the most genteel characters, the Knightleys.[2]

The assimilation of the social classes through marriage was one of the great themes of the drama, and alliances between 'blood' and 'money', or 'old' money and 'new', were the focuses of many successful comedies of the period.[3] In the novel tradition, Richardson's *Pamela* was the prime exemplar of an unlikely but successful union between a lowly servant girl and her master. In *Emma*, the theme of intermarriage comes full circle when Emma is faced with what she thinks is the probability, not merely the possibility, of a union between illegitimate Harriet and the well-born Mr Knightley: 'Mr Knightley and Harriet Smith! – Such an elevation on her side! Such a debasement on his! ... Could it be? – No; it was impossible. And yet it was far, very far, from impossible' (*E*, p. 413). When Emma finally accepts that Harriet could well be 'the chosen, the first, the dearest, the friend, the wife to whom he looked for all the best blessings of existence', her wretchedness is increased by the reflection that 'it had been all her own work' (*E*, pp. 422–23).

While Harriet Smith is no Pamela or Evelina, resembling more the simple country girl of David Garrick's popular comedy, she does possess the capacity for improvement. Eventually, Mr Knightley is forced to reconsider his opinion of her character, and admit her to be Mr Elton's equal: 'An unpretending, single-minded, artless girl – infinitely to be preferred by any man of sense and taste to such a woman as Mrs Elton' (*E*, p. 331).

Austen's comedy of errors between Emma, Elton and Harriet in the first volume of the novel is, however, dependent on the finely nuanced renderings of rank and station so beloved of eighteenth-century comedy. The comic misunderstandings between the three characters are made possible by their tenuous grasp of social realities. Harriet believes (or is made to believe) that she is worthy of Mr Elton, while he, in turn, believes that he is worthy of Emma. Emma's concurrence in the misunderstandings is in no small part due to the fact that she is unable to conceive that Mr Elton could aspire to her own lofty level.

The misunderstandings within the Emma/Harriet/Elton love triangle are very much in the tradition of stage comedy. In Hannah Cowley's *The Runaway* a similar set of comic misunderstandings (known in the period as equivoques) occur between a father and son. The son (George Hargrave) mistakenly believes that the elderly Lady Dinah is intended for his father, and duly shows his happiness and approval of the match as he unwittingly courts the lady. The situation allows for many opportunities for comic misunderstandings until the son is suitably enlightened and horrified to learn that he, not his father, is the true object of desire. Likewise, Emma woos on behalf of Harriet until the comic epiphany of Mr Elton's proposal. Though aware of his drunken state, Emma foolishly believes that she can restrain his advances by talking of the weather, and is astonished to find her efforts repulsed: 'It really was so. Without scruple – without apology – without much apparent diffidence, Mr Elton, the lover of Harriet, was professing himself *her* lover' (*E*, p. 129).

In *Pride and Prejudice*, Austen had displayed the range of her comic skills in the great proposal scene between Elizabeth Bennet and Mr Collins, and in *Emma* she reworks the idea to depict the discrepancy between male and female behaviour in the courtship process. The high comedy of Elton's proposal is greatly enhanced by Emma's unknowing compliance in the mistake, yet the scene is also charged with the archetypal male arrogance which little expects anything but grateful acceptance from the female:

> 'I have thought only of you. I protest against having paid the smallest attention to any one else. Every thing that I have said or done, for many weeks past, has been with the sole view of marking my adoration of yourself. You cannot really, seriously, doubt it. No! – (in an accent meant to be insinuating) – I am sure you have seen and understood me.' (*E*, p. 131)

As with that other obtuse clergyman, Mr Collins, Elton interprets the lady's stunned silence as consent: 'allow me to interpret this interesting silence. It confesses that you have long understood me' (*E*, p. 131). Emma's incredulity at finding herself the object of Elton's desire is paralleled with his disdain at the discovery that the illegitimate Harriet is intended for himself: '*I* think seriously of Miss Smith! … no doubt, there are men who might not object to – Every body has their level' (*E*, pp. 131–32).

The narrative of *Emma* moves with great speed and skill between external events and the inner consciousness of the heroine. Dramatic dialogue is thus often followed by 'free indirect discourse' in which the third-person narratorial voice follows the unfolding of Emma's thoughts.[4] The carriage scene is mainly rendered in dialogue, but it is immediately followed by Emma's ruminations on Elton. She quickly realises that 'there had been no real affection either in his language or manners', though 'sighs and fine words had been given in abundance' (*E*, p. 135). Furthermore, she understands that he is a social climber who 'only wanted to aggrandize and enrich himself' (*E*, p. 135). The great comic paradox is that Emma is angry with Elton for looking down on Harriet, but is equally furious that he looks up to her level: 'that he should suppose himself her equal in connection or mind! – look down upon her friend, so well understanding the gradations of rank below him, and be so blind to what rose above' (*E*, p. 136). Having shown the worst effects of social snobbery in Elton's dismissal of Harriet, the authorial irony re-establishes its attack on Emma, whose snobbishness has yet to be purged: 'He must know that the Woodhouses had been settled for several generations at Hartfield, the younger branch of a very ancient family – and that the Eltons were nobody' (*E*, p. 136).

Eighteenth-century drama's obsession with the comic interplay of rank and manners depended upon discrepancies between outward appearance and inner reality. Plays such as *She Stoops to Conquer*, *The Heir at Law*, *The Belle's Stratagem* and *The Clandestine Marriage* all exploited the comic possibilities of mistaken identity and social displacement. Emma's lack of judgement is most apparent in her opinions of Mr Elton and Robert Martin. Her conviction that the handsome and gallant Mr Elton is a 'model' of good manners is as wrong-headed as her observation of Robert Martin's 'clownish' manners. Her comments are restricted to Martin's outward lack of polish, his 'unmodulated voice', and she duly condemns him as 'a completely gross, vulgar farmer – inattentive to appearances, and thinking of nothing but profit and loss' (*E*, p. 33). Emma's absurd remark that Robert Martin is 'not Harriet's equal' is angrily quashed by Mr Knightley: 'No, he is not her equal indeed, for he is as much her superior in sense as in situation' (*E*, p. 61).

The intricacies of social class are clearly understood by Robert Martin, who fears that Harriet is now 'considered (especially since *your* making so much of her) as in a line of society above him' (*E*, p. 59). Both Robert Martin and Mr Knightley know that Emma is to blame for her friend's recent social elevation. Yet again, there are distinctions made between different social levels. Emma thinks Robert Martin is unworthy of

Harriet, and Mr Knightley considers Harriet unworthy of Robert Martin: 'my only scruple in advising the match was on his account, as being beneath his deserts, and a bad connexion for him' (*E*, p. 61). Emma, sounding dangerously like Lady Catherine de Bourgh, stoutly refuses to concede: 'The sphere in which she moves is much above his. – It would be a degradation' (*E*, p. 62).

While Emma initially thinks of compatibility in terms of rank and station, Mr Knightley puts equal emphasis on compatibility of mind and disposition: 'A degradation to illegitimacy and ignorance, to be married to a respectable, intelligent gentleman-farmer'. Knightley approves of Robert Martin for being all that is 'open' and 'straightforward': 'Robert Martin's manners have sense, sincerity and good humour to recommend them; and his mind has more true gentility than Harriet Smith could understand' (*E*, p. 65). Mr Knightley perceives that Harriet's obscure origins are the insuperable social barrier to her making a good marriage (and Mr Elton's comments confirm this truth). Nevertheless, Emma is caught up in the romantic idea that the natural child is of noble birth: 'That she is a gentleman's daughter, is indubitable to me' (*E*, p. 62). Such is her faith in Harriet's true gentility that she fires a parting shot that will later rebound upon her: 'Were you, yourself, ever to marry, she is the very woman for you' (*E*, p. 64).

Social mobility achieved either through intermarriage between the classes or by means of trade and commerce provided stage comedy and fiction with the perfect vehicle for comparing and contrasting different social types. Austen's own fascination with social mobility, explored in *Pride and Prejudice*, is given fuller emphasis in *Emma*, where there is a greater depiction of the assimilation of the trading classes into gentility. While Miss Bates and Jane Fairfax are seen to be downwardly mobile, Mr Perry and the Coles are on the rise.[5] The Cole family, who are described as 'of low origin, in trade, and only moderately genteel', have risen to be 'in fortune and style of living, second only to the family at Hartfield', yet they still struggle to rise above the stigma of trade.

Emma initially sets herself against social mobility, for she has the common prejudice against trade and commerce, 'I have no doubt that he *will* thrive and be a very rich man in time – and his being illiterate and coarse need not disturb *us*' (*E*, p. 34). She dislikes visiting the Bateses at their humble home for fear of 'falling in with the second and third rate of Highbury, who were calling on them for ever'. Like Lady Catherine de Bourgh, Emma wishes to preserve the distinctions of rank, and is therefore rendered uncomfortable by events that dissolve social distinctions, such as the Coles's dinner party and the ball at the Crown Inn. Emma needs to be reassured that there will be no difficulty, 'in everybody's returning into their proper place the next morning' (*E*, p. 198).

But to her own astonishment, she discovers how much she enjoys the Coles's party (in contrast to the two more exclusive social gatherings at Donwell and Box Hill), finding the Coles to be 'worthy people', capable of giving 'real attention' (*E*, p. 208). This is in contrast to the vulgar Mrs Elton, who confirms Emma's worst prejudices about trade, with her airs and pretensions. Mrs Elton is a wonderful comic creation – in the mould of Fanny Burney's *nouveau riche* characters – with her incessant boasting of the Sucklings of Maple Grove and her horror of upstarts such as the Tupmans, 'encumbered with many low connections, but giving themselves immense airs' (*E*, p. 310). Her idiosyncratic speech captures her own particular brand of vulgarity: 'A cousin of Mr Suckling, Mrs Bragge, had such an infinity of applications; every body was anxious to be in her family, for she moves in the first circle. Wax-candles in the school-room! You may imagine how desirable!' (*E*, pp. 299–300). As with Burney's comic monsters, however, her moral inferiority is suggested in her treatment of her servants.[6] Whereas Emma and her father talk of James and Hannah with easy familiarity, Mrs Elton barely remembers the names of her servants: 'The man who fetches our letters every morning (one of our men, I forget his name)' (*E*, p. 295).[7]

Mrs Elton also uses her position of 'Lady Patroness' to bully Jane Fairfax and, together with her husband, to humiliate Harriet Smith: 'the enmity which they dared not shew in open disrespect to [Emma], found a broader vent in contemptuous treatment of Harriet' (*E*, p. 282). Mrs Elton takes up Jane Fairfax because timidity is prepossessing in those 'who are at all inferior' (*E*, p. 283). But, in an important speech, Mr Knightley conveys his understanding of the 'littleness' of her character:

Mrs Elton does not talk *to* Miss Fairfax as she speaks *of* her. We all know the difference between the pronouns he or she and thou, the plainest-spoken amongst us; we all feel the influence of a something beyond common civility in our personal intercourse with each other – a something more early implanted. We cannot give any body the disagreeable hints that we may have been very full of the hour before. We feel things differently. (*E*, p. 286)

This elusive 'something' that Knightley speaks of is crucial to an understanding of the relationship between outward behaviour and inner feeling that permeates Austen's moral vision. The 'something beyond common civility' is of course precisely what Emma transgresses on Box Hill, but this must be understood as an uncharacteristic act, otherwise it would have no effect.

Jane Austen's interest in the disparity between what characters think and what they say and do is an essential part of her dramatic inheritance. We have seen how, from the juvenilia onwards, her works were in various ways shaped by the comic drama of the period. But more than this, her very vision of human beings in society is profoundly tied to her thinking about acting and role-playing. Throughout the novels, she resorts to a lexicon of theatre to explore the notion of the performed self. *Mansfield Park* explicitly revealed the theatricality of the self, above all in the great scene between Sir Thomas and Mr Yates; now in *Emma*, Austen explores this idea more implicitly, through social structure and the interplay of character more than in any particular incident.

Emma, though an 'imaginist', possesses a realistic grasp of the importance of social performance. She duly enacts her disappointment on behalf of the Westons when Frank Churchill fails to appear at Randalls: 'She was the first to announce it to Mr Knightley; and exclaimed quite as much as was necessary (or, being acting a part, perhaps rather more) at the conduct of the Churchills, in keeping him away' (*E*, p. 145).

When Frank himself dissembles on the subject of his prolonged absence from Highbury, she accepts his duplicity with equilibrium: 'still if it were a falsehood, it was a pleasant one, and pleasantly handled' (*E*, p. 191). At the same time, she observes him closely to ascertain 'that he had not been acting a part, or making a parade of insincere professions' (*E*, p. 197). Emma comprehends that, while she must act a part, she must also be on her guard to recognise acting in others. When sharing the news of her engagement to Mr Knightley, she is happy that 'Mrs Weston was acting no part, feigning no feelings in all that she said to him in favour of the event' (*E*, p. 467).

While Emma accepts that 'acting a part', playing a social role, is sometimes 'necessary', she draws the line at the sort of affectation and disingenuousness that disclaims the practice. On hearing Frank profess, 'I am the wretchedest being at the world at a civil falsehood', Emma cannot help but retort: 'I do not believe any such thing ... I am persuaded that you can be as insincere as your neighbours, when necessary' (*E*, p. 234).

The disparity between outward conduct and inner feeling is also a source of endless amusement. Emma's impatience at having to observe right social form is sometimes mocked, as, for example, when decorum demands that she ask after Miss Fairfax, even though she doesn't want to:

'Have you heard from Miss Fairfax so lately? I am extremely happy. I hope she is well?'

'Thank you. You are so kind!' replied the happily deceived aunt. (*E*, p. 157)

Miss Bates and even Jane Fairfax demand Emma's polite forbearance, but most trying of all is Mrs Elton. Emma's solitary outbursts are all the more comic, as they contrast so vividly with her repressed politeness:

'Knightley! – I could not have believed it. Knightley! – never seen him in her life before, and call him Knightley! – and discover that he is a gentleman! A little upstart, vulgar being, with her Mr E., and her *caro sposo*, and her resources, and all her airs of pert pretension and under-bred finery. Actually to discover that Mr Knightley is a gentleman! I doubt whether he will return the compliment, and discover her to be a lady.' (*E*, p. 279)

Though Emma heartily dislikes Mrs Elton, and finds that on occasion 'the forbearance of her outward submission' is put to the test, she (crucially) keeps her disgruntled feelings to herself.[8]

Austen's most discerning heroines, such as Elinor Dashwood and Elizabeth Bennet, possess the skill of appearing courteous in public without sacrificing their personal integrity. Emma also well understands the discrepancy between what Elinor describes as the 'behaviour' and the 'understanding'. Thus when Mr Weston claims that Mrs Elton 'is a good-natured woman after all', she finds the appropriate response: 'Emma denied none of it aloud, and agreed to none of it in private' (E, p. 353). Similarly, when Mr Elton's romantic attentions become annoyingly clear, Emma finds refuge in her ability to act a part but remain true to herself: 'she had the comfort of appearing very polite, while feeling very cross' (E, p. 119). Even when her forbearance is most sorely tested, by Harriet's disclosure of her love for Mr Knightley, Emma's response is magnanimous: 'She listened with much inward suffering, but with great outward patience' (E, p. 409). In each case, the phrasing is weighted by the opposites – denied/agreed, appearing/feeling, inward/outward – to express the conflict between social and private expression.

Even when dealing with extremely difficult family members, such as John Knightley and Mr Woodhouse, Emma shows her capacity for 'uniting civility with truth'. Thus, when John Knightley begins a typically antisocial rant concerning a dinner party at Randalls, Emma is unable to give him the 'pleased assent, which no doubt he was in the habit of receiving'. Rather, we are told, 'she could not be complying, she dreaded being quarrelsome; her heroism reached only to silence' (E, p. 114).

Throughout the novel, Austen explores the importance of silence, plain-speaking and non-verbal communication, offset against verbal ambiguities, equivocations, comic misunderstandings, riddles and word-games. In the first half of the novel, techniques such as riddles and verbal ambiguities are used with great effect to exploit the comic misunderstandings between Emma and Mr Elton. The novel's engagement with a more sophisticated exploration of language and communication coincides, however, with the arrival of Frank Churchill, who is the prime exemplar of verbal charm and social manipulation.

Professional versus Private Theatricals: *Blowing up the Pic Nics* by James Gillray. Sheridan, manager of Drury Lane, leads a protest against the amateur aristocratic Pic Nic Society. The amateurs are performing *Tom Thumb*, while the professionals march under the banner of Shakespeare and Kotzebue (author of the German original of *Lovers' Vows*).

Dora Jordan, the greatest comic actress of the age, painted by Hoppner as the Comic Muse (left, with mask of comedy, supported by the grace Euphrosyne, escaping the advances of a satyr).

The Comic Muse unveils herself and
inspires the pen of Hannah Cowley:
Jane Austen had particular admiration
for comic plays written by women.

The Pantheon in Oxford Street where
Austen's brother Henry owned a box.

Early nineteenth-century theatre-going: pit, boxes and stage,
showing the experience that Jane Austen loved.

The 'illegitimate' Astley's, visited by Jane Austen and the location of the rekindling of the love affair between Harriet Smith and Robert Martin in *Emma*.

Jane Austen's favorite comic actor: her 'best Elliston'.

Eliza O'Neill as Juliet: Jane Austen called her 'an elegant creature' who 'hugs Mr Younge [her co-star] delightfully' – but did not live up to the example of the great Mrs Siddons.

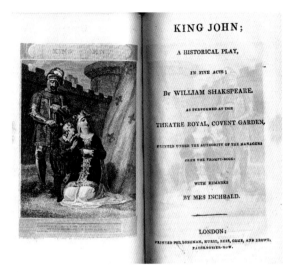

Sarah Siddons as Constance in Shakespeare's *King John*: 'I should particularly have liked seeing her in Constance, and could swear at her for disappointing me,' wrote Austen in 1811.

Frontispiece to the published text of *Lovers' Vows*, revealing its risqué content.

Mrs Inchbald's version of *Lovers' Vows* was immensely popular. Staged at the Theatre Royal, Bath, when Austen lived there, in 1799 it travelled as far as Philadelphia.

Emma Woodhouse, alias Alicia Silverstone as Cher, *Clueless* in Beverly Hills.

Fanny Price and Mary Crawford in Patricia Rozema's controversial *Mansfield Park*.

Mansfield Park made *Metropolitan* in upper-crust Manhattan.

Lady Susan: Whit Stillman's *Love & Friendship* takes Austen back to her comic origins.

From the outset, the Knightley brothers are associated with a lack of gallantry and a love of plain-speaking. For instance, when the brothers meet, they welcome each other in the 'true English style', which though plain and unaffected is not lacking in feeling: "'How dy'e do, George?', and John, how are you?"... burying under a calmness that seemed all but indifference, the real attachment which would have led either of them, if requisite, to do every thing for the good of the other' (E, pp. 99–100). But whereas John Knightley's forthrightness often verges on rudeness, George's rarely does. Furthermore, he is attuned to the fact that the language of gallantry used by other men, such as Frank and Mr Elton, is merely a means to an end. He warns Emma that Mr Elton speaks a different language in 'unreserved moments, when there are only men present'. Mr Elton's more private language reveals that 'he does not mean to throw himself away' (E, p. 66).

George Knightley is similarly intolerant of Frank Churchill's dandyish manners. His own bluntness, which is contrasted with Frank's excessive gallantry, conceals his genuine concern for others. For example, Frank's insinuating praise and his importuning Jane Fairfax to continue singing, in spite of a hoarse voice, is contrasted with Mr Knightley's peremptory and blunt command: 'That will do ... You have sung quite enough for one evening – now, be quiet ... Miss Bates, are you mad, to let your niece sing herself hoarse in this manner? Go, and interfere' (E, p. 229). As Emma observes of Mr Knightley, 'He is not a gallant man, but he is a very humane one' (E, p. 223).

Frank Churchill's gallantry and charm, on the other hand, are manifested by his love and mastery of word-play. This is at its most skilful and scintillating when he is able to play Emma and Jane Fairfax off against each other, such as on the occasion when Emma discovers him mending Mrs Bates's spectacles, and at Box Hill. On both occasions, however, the verbal acrobatics and double-meanings are so brilliantly executed and multi-faceted that they become almost mentally wearying, especially when Emma invariably takes up Frank's challenge. Mr Knightley's habitual brevity of speech, which usually terminates the verbal games, is therefore welcomed. His barely concealed jealousy and disapproval of Frank Churchill, however, puts its own spin on the proceedings.

When Emma interrupts the lovers in the Bateses' sitting room to hear Jane Fairfax perform at her pianoforte, she mistakenly ascribes Jane's evident discomposure to nerves: 'she must reason herself into the power of performance'. However much Jane dislikes having to rouse herself to 'perform' a social lie, Frank relishes the opportunity to flex his verbal muscles by playing a flirtatious double game with the two women. He uses the opportunity to make love to Jane, while simultaneously continuing the Dixon pretence with Emma and using her as a blind. Thus he speaks of the pianoforte as a gift 'thoroughly from the heart. Nothing hastily done; nothing incomplete. True affection only could have prompted it' (*E*, p. 242). Emma, thinking he alludes to Dixon, is quick to reprimand Frank's indiscretion – 'you speak too plain' – but he replies with insouciance, 'I would have her understand me. I am not in the least ashamed of my meaning' (*E*, p. 243).

When Mr Knightley passes the window on horseback, he is drawn into conversation with Miss Bates. Not only does his bluntness amidst so much verbal ambiguity come as a most welcome relief, but the highly comical dialogue between him and the garrulous Miss Bates, which is audible to the small audience in the apartment, makes his feelings about Frank Churchill all too clear:

[Knightley] cut her short with,

'I am going to Kingston. Can I do anything for you?'

'Oh! dear, Kingston – are you? – Mrs Cole was saying the other day she wanted something from Kingston.'

'Mrs Cole has servants to send. Can I do anything for *you*?'

'No, I thank you. But do come in. Who do you think is here? – Miss Woodhouse and Miss Smith … Do put up your horse at the Crown, and come in.'

'Well,' said he in a deliberating manner, 'for five minutes, perhaps.'

'And here is Mrs Weston and Mr Frank Churchill too! – Quite delightful; so many friends!'

'No, not now, I thank you. I could not stay two minutes.' (*E*, p. 244)

It is unsurprising that Mr Knightley, the advocate of forthrightness, dislikes Frank Churchill, although jealousy distorts his judgement. When he and Emma discuss Frank's absence from Highbury, she shows herself to be highly sensitive to the social pressures upon a young man who is almost entirely dependent upon the will of a woman such as Mrs Churchill. As she sharply reminds Knightley, 'You are the worst judge in the world of the difficulties of dependence ... You do not know what it is to have tempers to manage' (*E*, p. 146). No doubt she is alluding to the management of the more awkward members of her own family: 'Nobody, who has not been in the interior of a family, can say what the difficulties of any individual of that family may be' (*E*, p. 146).

Emma understands that forthrightness is a privilege of the powerful, not the disenfranchised. When Knightley suggests to her the simple and resolute speech that Frank should make to the Churchills in order to break free of their claims, she mocks his social naivety:

> Such language for a young man entirely dependent to use! – Nobody but you, Mr Knightley, would imagine it possible. But you have not an idea of what is requisite in situations directly opposite to your own. Mr Frank Churchill to be making such a speech as that to the uncle and aunt, who have brought him up, and are to provide for him! – Standing up in the middle of the room, I suppose, and speaking as loud as he could! How could you imagine such conduct practicable? (*E*, p. 147)

Paradoxically, although Austen is sensitive to the idea that it is not always 'practicable' to be forthright, especially where there is an imbalance of power, she also exploits the tragi-comic possibilities of social decorum that proscribes circumlocution. Emma's final and most painful misunderstanding occurs precisely because of social equivocations, which lead her to believe that Harriet is in love with Frank Churchill rather than Mr Knightley. Emma, resolving to herself that 'Plain dealing was always best' (*E*, p. 341), encourages Harriet to confess her new love, but adds an important codicil: 'Let no name ever pass our lips. We were very wrong before; we will be cautious now' (*E*, p. 342). The misunderstandings persist as the women, with due propriety, agree upon the superior merits of the 'gentleman' in question for rendering Harriet an elusive 'service':

'I am not at all surprised at you, Harriet. The service he rendered you was enough to warm your heart.'

'Service! oh! it was such an inexpressible obligation! – The very recollection of it, and all that I felt at the time – when I saw him coming – his noble look – and my wretchedness before. Such a change! ... From perfect misery to perfect happiness.' (*E*, p. 342)

Emma, of course, refers to Frank's rescue of Harriet from the gypsies, whereas she remembers the far more painful social snub of being 'cut' by Mr Elton at the dance, and saved by Mr Knightley.

The confusion arises partly because social form dictates that the young women cannot be too explicit, that the man cannot be named. This is the sort of comic misunderstanding that is exploited in the drama. For example, in *The Clandestine Marriage* one of the best scenes involves a misunderstanding between the lovely young heroine and the lecherous Lord Ogleby. Fanny's equivocations on the delicate subject of her situation (she is secretly married and pregnant) mislead the debauched aristocrat to believe that she is in love with him. This is a classic example of the problems arising from the exigencies of female propriety. Of course, in *Emma*, the irony is intensified, as Emma is determined not to repeat her earlier misunderstanding with Harriet and Elton, and is therefore especially self-satisfied with her discretion and 'plain-dealing'. When the mistake finally comes to light, it is the catalyst for Emma's double epiphany: the revelation of her own love for Mr Knightley and the realisation of her own wrong-doing.

Jane Austen shows how language and propriety are vulnerable to evasions and misconstructions, but offsets this by demonstrating the unmistakable power of non-verbal communication. The most memorable moments in the novels are often those expressed by wordless actions. Few can forget the emotional impact of Captain Wentworth silently removing the small child from Anne's back in *Persuasion* or Mr Knightley almost kissing Emma's hand. Elinor Dashwood's tears of joy at the news that Edward is released from his engagement express her deep emotion, as do Emma's quiet, uncontrollable tears after Box Hill. Very often, strong feeling is rendered by the frequency with which characters look at each other. Darcy's love for Elizabeth is expressed by the manner in which he fixes his eyes upon her. Mr Knightley rumbles Frank Churchill and Jane Fairfax long before anyone else does because he has noticed the way they look at each other: 'I have lately imagined that I saw symptoms of attachment between them – certain expressive looks, which I did not believe meant to be public' (*E*, p. 350).

In *Emma* Jane Austen explores the impact of a particular kind of telepathy between couples. When Harriet is snubbed by Mr Elton at the Crown Inn ball, it is made clear that Mrs Elton is complicit: 'smiles of high glee passed between him and his wife' (*E*, p. 328). But when Harriet is saved by Mr Knightley, we witness the loving telepathy between him and Emma: 'She was all pleasure and gratitude … and longed to be thanking him; and though too distant for speech, her countenance said much, as soon as she could catch his eye again' (*E*, p. 328). Later, 'her eyes invited him irresistibly to come to her and be thanked' (*E*, p. 330). Similarly, Knightley expresses his own approbation and strength of feeling non-verbally when he discovers that Emma has visited Miss Bates following the Box Hill episode: 'It seemed as if there were an instantaneous impression in her favour, as if his eyes received the truth from her's, and all that had passed of good in her feelings were at once caught and honoured. – He looked at her with a glow of regard' (*E*, p. 385).

Their mutual respect and compatibility are also revealed by the frankness of expression in their conversation. They quarrel and spar in private, showing they are intellectual equals. Emma refuses to be intimidated by Knightley's brusqueness. She dares to contradict him, to accuse him of being manipulative and very fond of 'bending little minds' (*E*, p. 147), and of being full of 'prejudice' against Frank Churchill. She deliberately provokes him by taking views opposite to his. She confesses that even as a young girl she called him George, 'because I thought it would offend you' (*E*, p. 463). In public, their dialogue is distinguished by an economy of expression, which contrasts refreshingly with the tortuous, circuitous way in which, for example, Frank Churchill and Jane Fairfax are forced to communicate in public.[9]

In the dialogue between Emma and Mr Knightley there is an easiness and familiarity, even when they touch upon delicate subjects. When Emma attempts to ascertain his feelings towards Jane Fairfax, with the words 'The extent of your admiration may take you by surprise one day

or other', he blithely responds, 'Oh! are you there? – But you are misera-
bly behindhand. Mr Cole gave me a hint of it six weeks ago' (*E*, p. 287).
Strikingly, their romantic involvement is characterised by an absence of
sentimental language and false courtesy:

> 'Whom are you going to dance with?' asked Mr Knightley.
>
> She hesitated a moment, and then replied, 'With you, if you will ask
> me.'
>
> 'Will you?' said he, offering his hand.
>
> 'Indeed I will. You have shown that you can dance, and you know we
> are not really so much brother and sister as to make it at all improper.'
>
> 'Brother and sister! no, indeed.' (*E*, p. 331)

Even when the lovers discuss their impending marriage, there is a
distinct lack of sentiment: 'The subject followed; it was in plain, unaffected, gentleman-like English, such as Mr Knightley used even to the
woman he was in love with' (*E*, p. 448).

The association of a particular kind of brusqueness and forthrightness
with genuine feeling is used repeatedly in *Emma* to encapsulate the very
essence of Englishness. The true affection that belies the gruff exterior of
the language between the Knightley brothers, which Austen described as
'the true English manner', is now revealed in the union between Emma
and Mr Knightley. It is, furthermore, Frank Churchill's language,
expressed in a 'fine flourishing letter, full of professions and falsehoods',
which enables Mr Knightley to clarify the indefinable 'something' that
had previously eluded him in his early analysis of what constitutes right
moral conduct: 'No, Emma, your amiable young man can be amiable
only in French, not in English ... he can have no English delicacy towards
the feelings of other people' (*E*, p. 149). As in a long tradition within the
drama, English plainness is contrasted with French affectation.

As Austen makes clear, this 'English delicacy' is not confined to rank
or station. Even Emma recognises that Robert Martin and his sisters
possess 'genuine delicacy', and that their exemplary conduct following
Harriet's rejection is 'the result of real feeling' (*E*, p. 179). Yet this delicacy
eludes the Eltons, who in particular show 'injurious courtesy' towards
those who are socially inferior, and in need of protection, such as Jane

Fairfax and Harriet Smith. Momentarily, Emma makes a similar trans-gression to this when she humiliates Miss Bates at Box Hill.[10] Mr Knightley duly emphasises the matter of social inequality when he censures Emma's treatment of Miss Bates: 'Were she your equal in situa-tion – but, Emma, consider how far this is from being the case' (*E*, p. 375). Emma swiftly make reparations with the consciousness of his words guiding her response: 'It should be the beginning, on her side, of a regular, equal, kindly intercourse' (*E*, p. 377).

Austen's happiest alliances are those between equals, not necessarily social equals, but those in whom there is compatibility of mind, and mutual respect and understanding. In the union between Emma and Knightley there is the promise of an equal discourse. Integral to Austen's resolutions is the way that her spirited heroines, in the best tradition of the lively ladies of comic tradition, never relinquish their penchant for merriment. Those critics who insist that Emma's reformation is not genuine cite the impudence of her remark to her future spouse: 'I always expect the best treatment, because I never put up with any other' (*E*, p. 474). To regard this as merely a continuation of Emma's egotism is to misunderstand the workings of the lively lady, such as Austen's favour-ites, Lady G. and Lady Bell Bloomer: comedy proposes that a woman may marry a worthy and upright man without fear that her high spirits will be stifled.

Mr Knightley declares to Emma after Box Hill: 'I will tell you truths while I can.' There is only one final agonising encounter when they fail to communicate fully, a last misunderstanding when each believes the other to be in love with someone else. But this is short-lived, for Emma, having first begged Mr Knightley not to speak of his love, will not ulti-mately sacrifice their friendship: 'I will hear whatever you like. I will tell you exactly what I think' (*E*, p. 429). When the misunderstanding is happily resolved, he shows his characteristic awkwardness with the language of sentiment: 'I cannot make speeches ... If I loved you less, I might be able to talk about it more. But you know what I am. You hear nothing but truth from me' (*E*, p. 430).

Paradoxically, however, Mr Knightley's pursuit of absolute truth is presented as touchingly idealistic: 'Mystery; Finesse – how they pervert the understanding! My Emma, does not every thing serve to prove more and more the beauty of truth and sincerity in all our dealings with each other?' (*E*, p. 446). His noble sentiment is ironically undercut by Emma's 'blush of sensibility on Harriet's account', for she is conscious that she is withholding the full truth of her friend's love for him, and her own part in it. It is only when Harriet is safely married to Robert Martin that 'the disguise, equivocation, mystery, so hateful to her to practise, might soon be over. She could now look forward to giving him that full and perfect confidence which her disposition was most ready to welcome as a duty' (*E*, p. 475). Whether or not Emma finally does reveal the whole truth to Knightley is left open. But this ambiguity should come as no surprise, for the authorial voice has already warned the reader: 'Seldom, very seldom, does complete truth belong to any human disclosure; seldom can it happen that something is not a little disguised, or a little mistaken' (*E*, p. 431). There is no escape from a little disguise, a little mistakenness: such is the lesson of the theatre.

The acknowledgement of the incompleteness of human disclosure strikes at the very heart of Jane Austen's creative vision. The novel, with its omniscient narrator, is in theory a genre that proposes the possibility of complete truth. Austen, however, is more akin to Shakespeare in her perception of the complexity and ambiguity of artistic truth. Her vision of how human beings behave in society is built on disguise and role-play, equivocation and mystery: arts inextricably associated with the dramatic tradition.

Jane Austen's insistence that all our disclosures are 'a little disguised' calls into question the argument of an influential line of critics who believe that she was suspicious of 'acting' because of the supposed insincerity of role-playing.[11] These critics maintain that the growth of the heroine towards authentic self-knowledge is the key to the moral world of the novels. Such critics are themselves more Knightleys than Austens: they are susceptible to an ideal of truth that is surely unattainable. Rather, from Jane Austen's earliest beginnings in the amateur theatricals at Steventon and her experiments with dramatic form in the juvenilia to her systematic engagement with the drama in the mature novels, we find an implicit belief that the social self is always *performed*. The ultimate model for this way of seeing is the theatre.

11

Why She Is a Hit in Hollywood

Hollywood fell in love with Jane Austen in the mid-1990s, when six film and television adaptations of her novels exploded onto the small and big screen, all of them critical and box-office successes. In 1995, the British actors Emma Thompson and Kate Winslet appeared as Elinor and Marianne Dashwood, alongside Hugh Grant and Alan Rickman, in a lushly romantic film of *Sense and Sensibility*, directed by the Taiwanese-born Ang Lee, who had established his reputation with a sequence of films about family conflicts in the context of traditional Chinese values. In *Eat Drink Man Woman*, a master chef in Taipei struggles with his three daughters' distinctly western views of love and marriage. This interest in the tension between the 'modern' notion of romantic passion as the route to marriage and the traditional idea of marrying for the sake of respectability and property inheritance, in accordance with parental wishes, meant that Lee appeared an ideal candidate to direct *Sense and Sensibility*. Manners matter in Chinese culture, as they did in the world of Jane Austen, and in this respect the marriage between director and material proved a good match. The film duly won critical plaudits and seven Academy Award nominations, with Emma Thompson taking the Oscar for Best Adapted Screenplay.

Persuasion was the debut movie of South African-born Roger Michell, who went on to direct *Notting Hill*, one of late twentieth-century British cinema's most commercially successfully romantic comedies. Michell had cut his directorial teeth in the British stage tradition, with work at the Royal Court and the Royal Shakespeare Company. He knew how to get exceptionally nuanced performances out of a host of established classical actors such as Corin Redgrave, Fiona Shaw, Phoebe Nicholls and Simon Russell Beale. Reviewers especially praised *Persuasion*'s gritty realism and Amanda Root's moving and understated performance of Anne Elliot. The film originally aired on 16 April 1995, when it was broadcast on BBC Two television. It won the BAFTA for the year's best single television drama. Sony Pictures Classics released the film in American cinemas on 27 September 1995. Critics hailed its 'unhurried delicacy' and its authenticity to the novel.[1] The *Los Angeles Times* described it as the most faithful to the spirit of Austen of the several Hollywood adaptations.[2]

On the small screen, also in 1995, the BBC's *Pride and Prejudice*, memorably starring Colin Firth as Mr Darcy in a wet shirt, garnered over eleven million viewers in Britain alone.[3] In America, 3.7 million Americans watched the first broadcast on the A&E Network. The series was spread out over six episodes, and adapted by Andrew Davies, a seasoned converter of classic novels for television. He wanted to produce 'a fresh, lively story about real people', and wanted to emphasise the themes of sex and money that underpin the novel.[4] Davies added extra scenes, including the infamous lake scene, and portrayed Austen's men in sporting activities such as billiards and fencing. He also used voiceovers and flashbacks, and revealed character via letters that the actors were seen reading to themselves and to one another. The series was critically acclaimed and award-winning, and it is still perceived by many as the definitive adaptation. The appearance of three such contrasting but equally well-achieved screen dramatisations meant that 'Austen Mania' was truly underway.

The following year Gwyneth Paltrow starred in a lavish, highly decorative, period drama of *Emma*, directed by Douglas McGrath, with Jeremy Northam as Mr Knightley. Despite its outstanding supporting cast (Juliet Stevenson stole the film with her pitch-perfect rendering of the odious snob Mrs Elton), there was a shallow sheen to the adaptation that belied the complexity of the novel. Beautiful to look at, the movie failed to capture the interior life of the more complex characters. Of all Austen's novels, *Emma* is the most technically proficient in the layering of narrative arc and psychological insight. Adapter and director Douglas McGrath could not find any equivalent for the authorial voice upon which the book is so dependent. The main failure of the movie was Paltrow. Austen's intention was to create an unsympathetic heroine: 'I am going to take a heroine whom no one but myself will much like.' But she was too shrewd a novelist not to be aware that her readers still needed to feel sympathy or admiration for the main character. In the novel, Austen gets around this problem of Emma's 'unlikeability' by two means. First, there is her complex use of irony directed against the heroine, multi-layered and beautifully orchestrated from the opening lines. This is facilitated by Austen's increasing command of the key technique of free indirect speech, in which the reader finds herself both inside and outside the heroine as the narrative is written from her point of view but in the third-person, allowing for the ironic exposure of her prejudices. Secondly, there is the censure of Mr Knightley: 'Better be without sense, than misapply it as you do.'[5]

Here is the opening sentence of the novel: 'Emma Woodhouse, handsome, clever, and rich, with a comfortable home and happy disposition, seemed to unite some of the best blessings of existence; and had lived nearly twenty-one years in the world with very little to distress or vex her.' The word 'seemed' is a vital clue to what will unfold in the course of the narrative. By the time we get to Emma's (faulty) judgement of both Harriet Smith and Jane Fairfax, Austen's use of free indirect speech to ironise her heroine, and to deflate her ego, is in full force:

> She was not struck by any thing remarkably clever in Miss Smith's conversation, but she found her altogether very engaging – not inconveniently shy, not unwilling to talk – and yet so far from pushing, shewing so proper and becoming a deference, seeming so pleasantly grateful for being admitted to Hartfield, and so artlessly impressed by the appearance of every thing in so superior a style to what she had been used to, that she must have good sense and deserve encouragement.[6]

And here is Emma on her rival, Jane Fairfax:

> She could never get acquainted with her: she did not know how it was, but there was such coldness and reserve – such apparent indifference whether she pleased or not – and then, her aunt was such an eternal talker! – and she was made such a fuss with by every body! – and it had been always imagined that they were to be so intimate – because their

ages were the same, every body had supposed they must be so fond of each other. These were her reasons – she had no better.[7]

In both these passages, the reader is being directed by Austen to distrust Emma's judgement. We know that we are present in the company of a flawed heroine, who has great, misguided, faith in the powers of her own intelligence. McGrath's essential problem was that he was too in love with Paltrow's beauty. The camera lingered lovingly on her face; she was lit in the most transcendent light, which made her appear angelic. Without the corrective of Austen's lethal irony and with no cinematic equivalent of her free indirect speech, Emma is a two-dimensional, shallow mannequin. Later, I will suggest how Amy Heckerling circumvents the technical problem of ironising the heroine within the genre of film.

Since 1996, there have been over thirty Jane Austen adaptations and spin-offs, including a dog cartoon series based on *Pride and Prejudice* and *Northanger Abbey* called *Wishbone*; Angel Gracia's *From Prada to Nada*, a Latina spin on *Sense and Sensibility* set in East Los Angeles; and *Scents and Sensibility*, where Elinor is a cleaner in a spa and Marianne makes scented products. The novel *Bridget Jones's Diary* reworked the plot of *Pride and Prejudice*. Colin Firth, who played the role of Darcy in the BBC adaptation, played the role of Helen Fielding's modern-day Darcy in the film of the book. Then there was *Lost in Austen*, a fantasy reworking of *Pride and Prejudice* set in modern times, and *The Lizzie Bennet Diaries*, an American web series conveyed in the form of vlogs. We have had a dramatisation of Austen's own purported love life in *Becoming Jane*; Austen goes to Bollywood in *Bride and Prejudice*; Austen meets murder mystery in P. D. James's *Death Comes to Pemberley*; and Austen meets the horror genre in Seth Grahame-Smith's *Pride and Prejudice and Zombies*, which was first a book and then a movie. The list is endless. One wonders whether there will soon be a TV channel entirely devoted to Jane Austen.

Many explanations have been offered for the resurgence of interest in Jane Austen during the two decades between the mid-1990s and the 2016 celebrations of her endurance two hundred years after her death. Typically, the success of the adaptations has been ascribed to a nostalgic desire to escape from the uncertainties of modern life and return to an age of politeness and social order. As we will see, Jane Austen has been popular in times of war. A key aspect of this explanation is what might be described as 'Big House Syndrome'. The televised *Brideshead Revisited* of 1981 filmed at Castle Howard, the 1995 *Pride and Prejudice* using the National Trust property Lyme Park, and, more recently, *Downton Abbey*, which sent thousands of tourists to Highclere, were all of a piece. They idealised the world of 'upstairs, downstairs'. One of the characteristics of the 'heritage' dramatisations of Austen novels was that the houses were all too big. There was an undifferentiated view of the great families and estates of the past: the productions' designers and location scouts failed to see that Austen tends to speak for the values of the lesser gentry and to scorn such idle, vain aristocrats as Lady Catherine de Bourgh (the embodiment of both pride and prejudice) and the Dowager Viscountess Dalrymple (in *Persuasion*).

The power of escapism and romantic fantasy cannot be gainsaid, but the key to the difference between the merely escapist and romantic screen renditions of Jane Austen and those that truly succeed as works of art in their own right is the adaptation's truth not to the letter of her text – and certainly not to correctness of period detail – but to the spirit of her comedy. The spirit, that is, which she herself learned from the comic theatre.

Austen's career in Hollywood began in 1938. *Pride and Prejudice* was a box-office hit in the MGM movie starring Laurence Olivier and Greer Garson. The idea for a movie version came from Harpo Marx, who saw a theatre adaptation of *Pride and Prejudice* in 1935 and thought it would make a good film, and a perfect vehicle for the actress Norma Shearer. However, there is an even more fascinating, though little known, backstory to the history of *Pride and Prejudice* dramatisation.

One of England's most successful playwrights in the 1920s was a man called Alan Milne, who specialised in comedies with a satirical edge. His work was often compared with that of Noël Coward. By 1922, his plays were being performed simultaneously in London, America and Liverpool. He had also turned his hand to screenwriting, though he considered himself first and foremost a playwright. It was only in the late 1920s that he published the stories for his son Christopher Robin that have totally eclipsed his theatrical achievements: *Winnie-the-Pooh* and *The House at Pooh Corner*.

In 1936, shortly after German troops re-entered the demilitarised zone of the Rhineland, A. A. Milne wrote a letter to his friend Charles Turley Smith, deploring the international situation: 'The world is foul. I hate the insular egotism of France, I loathe the German government, I detest Musso, I abominate Communism.' He was taking comfort in an enterprise that he had been working on for some months; to turn his 'favourite book' into a stage play: 'It was nearly a year's job – six months reading and thinking, six months writing.' It was a labour of love: an adaptation of Jane Austen's *Pride and Prejudice*. For him, his 'liaison with Miss Jane Austen' was one of the most 'difficult' and the 'most delightful' things he had ever done.[8]

His 'liaison' went back a long way and had served him well in difficult times.[9] During the First World War, Milne enlisted as an officer in the Warwickshire Regiment. He was sent out to France in July 1916. After serious action on the Somme, his battalion was resting out of the line before going up again. He had travelled to France with a quiet young boy, whose elder brother had been killed a few months earlier. One evening as the soldier was just settling down to take his tea he was hit by a shell and blown to pieces in front of Milne.

In August 1916, the regiment took part in a new attack. In his dug-out, Milne offered to run out a telephone line on the front line, and asked his sergeant to pick two men to accompany him. Losses had been severe, and the colonel told Milne that he could not afford to lose three signalling officers in a month. Milne knew few of the men, but he had bonded with a young man, Lance Corporal Grainger, over a shared passion for Jane Austen. Like the men in Rudyard Kipling's great story 'The Janeites', they would talk about the novels in the trenches. Alan had loved Austen since he had been a boy at Westminster, as had his schoolmate Lytton Strachey. *Pride and Prejudice* was his favourite novel, along with *The Wind in the Willows*.

Milne's sergeant volunteered himself with a cheery 'I'll come for one, sir'. Grainger was nowhere to be seen. And off they went over the top and into the front line. One of the signal stations had been blown to smithereens and was a pancake of earth. Bodies all around him, Milne expertly joined up the telephone. Pressing the buzzer, he made contact with the colonel, glad to be alive. Milne recounted the story in his autobiography:

> Then with a sigh of utter content and thankfulness and the joy of living,
> I turned away from the telephone. And there behind me was Lance
> Corporal Grainger.
> 'What on earth are *you* doing here?' I said.
> He grinned sheepishly …
> 'I thought I'd just like to come along, sir.'
> 'But *why*?' …
> 'Well, sir, I thought I'd just like to be sure *you* were all right.'
> Which is the greatest tribute to Jane Austen that I have ever heard.[10]

Soon after this episode of Jane Austen in the trenches, Milne was invalided out of the Army. As the war came to an end, he began his career as one of the most successful playwrights of the age.

Milne's first intention for the honouring of his passion on stage was to write a play about the life of Jane Austen. But as he began work on the play, he began to see that he was in fact writing about Elizabeth Bennet. In his preface to the published play, Milne wrote about his change of heart:

> I began by telling myself proudly that I was the one dramatist in England
> who had not written a play about the Brontës; who, moreover, had no
> slightest wish to write a play about the Brontës; who, indeed, if ever he
> wrote that sort of play at all, could only want to write about the divine
> and incomparable Austen. Having allowed that thought a moment's
> lodgings in my mind, I was immediately at its mercy. The characters
> began to assemble on the stage: Mr and Mrs Austen, Cassandra, the
> cheery brothers, Uncle Leigh; and at her table in a modest corner, busy,
> over the chatter, at what the family would call 'Jane's writing', Miss
> Austen herself. Soon she will have to say something. What sort of a
> young woman is she? What will she have to say? And as soon as she had
> said it, I knew that it was just Miss Elizabeth Bennet speaking. So the
> play, then, must be about Elizabeth Bennet. It must in fact be a

dramatisation of *Pride and Prejudice*. Quite impossible, I decided at last, but considerable fun to try.[11]

Milne's play is a *tour de force*, as one might expect from the author of one of the funniest children's books ever written adapting the funniest of female authors. In his preface to the published text, Milne drew attention to the golden rules of dramatisation of novels. The dramatist should be guided by 'truth to the characters' (especially in the case of a beloved classic), but always remember that he is writing a play. Though Austen excelled in dramatic dialogue, Milne insists that the dramatist must 'please himself as to how much or how little of the original dialogue he uses'. 'The play must be written throughout as the dramatist would naturally write it, not as Miss Austen would have written it. That is to say, he must never ask himself: "would Jane Austen have made So and So say this?" But "would So and So have said it?"' This is the absolute key to the distinction between adaptations that succeed and those that fail: the test of every line of fresh dialogue is truth to the character, not truth to the original text. And this, of course, is something that Austen herself had learned from reading and seeing plays, whether by Shakespeare, Sheridan or the now forgotten female playwrights of the eighteenth century: be it in the dialogue of a novel, on stage or on screen, the characters must always maintain *consistency of voice*.

Milne added extra scenes where he felt it necessary. He was puzzled, for example, as to why Austen does not permit the reader to witness a conversation between Jane Bennet and Mr Bingley. Their romance takes place 'off stage':

> It is strange that Miss Austen does not give us a single scene between Jane and Bingley. The dramatist cannot afford a similar reticence; for it is Bingley's attraction to Jane which sets the story moving. Bingley was 'lively' – we have Jane's word for it. At a dance, in the company of the girl he loved, a happy carefree Bingley might almost become a 'rattle'. I maintain that I am historically accurate in saying that he did become a rattle. At least there is no evidence to the contrary.

Thus, Milne reveals what Austen denies the reader: a scene between Jane and Mr Bingley, which fleshes out their characters and develops their burgeoning romance:

> BINGLEY: I am the biggest fool at compliments. I think of them just too late.
>
> JANE: But why should you wish to pay me compliments?
>
> BINGLEY: I don't. I wish to talk very seriously to you about Tithes, my Lord Chatham and the Rotation of Crops. I want you to think to yourself: 'This is the most intelligent man I have ever spoken to in my life, he knows all about the rotation of tithes at Chatham, and one day he will stand for Parliament, and people will cry "Vote for Bingley!"' And all the time I want to talk to you like this I find myself thinking 'Her eyes, her hair, her expression, her smile' – and I am dumb. Miss Jane, as a prospective member of Parliament, can I rely upon you to vote for Bingley when the moment comes?
>
> JANE: [*smiling*] I cannot quite see you in Parliament, sir.
>
> BINGLEY: Nor I. And yet there must be bigger fools there, or else they wouldn't be there at all.

Another clever modification was to include the five daughters in the opening scene, which means that he can establish the different characters of the sisters efficiently:

> MR BENNET: Kitty has no discretion in her coughs. She times them ill.
>
> JANE: Do tell us, ma'am.
>
> MARY: Pray tell us, mamma.
>
> MRS BENNET: Well you must know Lady Lucas tells me that Netherfield is really taken at last by a handsome young man of large fortune from the north of England. He came down …
>
> LYDIA: Did she see him? Is he *very* handsome?
>
> MR BENNET: *All* young men with large fortunes are handsome, Lydia.
>
> MRS BENNET: He came down in a chaise and four –
>
> MR BENNET: In a chaise and four they are particularly handsome.

Milne elaborated upon the character of Mr Bennet, and emphasised the strong bond between father and daughter. It is striking that the final scene of the play is a touching one between father and daughter, not a romantic union between Elizabeth and Darcy. Darcy's character is more open than in the novel. After Elizabeth rejects his marriage proposal, he does not write her a letter explaining his actions, as in the novel, but speaks to her directly. Elizabeth, shocked to hear of Wickham's infamy, expresses her disbelief: 'I do not believe it! It is your jealousy which makes you say so … it is your story against his … horrible, horrible! I will *not* believe it.'[12]

Another of Milne's ground rules for adaptation was not to try to improve on Austen's dialogue, but to move seamlessly between the dramatist's voice and Austen's own: 'The two styles should be equal to each other, simply because they are equal to the same thing: namely, the way these actual people would have talked in those days, and in those situations.'[13] His command of the dialogue is so astonishing that there are moments when it's difficult to distinguish Austen from Milne. Here is Lizzy refusing to dance with Mr Darcy, in a speech that anticipates, brilliantly, her later refusal of his marriage proposal: 'No, Mr Darcy, you may not beg it. Let the refusal seem to come from yourself rather than from me, and your pride will be saved.'

Miss Elizabeth Bennet is faithful to the original, but witty and captivating in its own right. Milne's only egregious mistake was the inclusion of Mrs Norris, who is mentioned as an aunt to the sisters. When a friend spotted the error, Milne was mortified: 'Yes, Norris must have come from *Mansfield Park*. God knows how, I have been going hot and cold ever since. I knew I should make some fantastic mistake somewhere, and this is it.'[14]

On the very day that the play was finished, Milne was dismayed to read that a dramatised version of *Pride and Prejudice* was about to be produced on the New York stage:

Apparently it was Jane Austen who was now fashionable. However, there was still England. Should one hurry to get the play on with any cast that was available, or should one wait for the ideal Elizabeth, now unavailable? In the end the risk was taken; arrangements were made for the early autumn; the Elizabeth I had always wanted began to let her hair grow; the management, the theatre, the producer, all were there ... and at that moment the American version landed in London.[15]

An Australian writer called Helen Jerome had got there first: 28 October 1935 was the night that Harpo Marx attended a Philadelphia preview of Jerome's Broadway-bound dramatisation of *Pride and Prejudice*, which was subtitled 'a sentimental comedy in three acts'. The very next day, Harpo sent the following telegram to film producer Irving Thalberg in Hollywood: 'Just saw Pride and Prejudice. Stop. Swell show. Stop. Would be wonderful for Norma. Stop.'[16]

Production was about to begin in October, with Norma Shearer in the role of Elizabeth and Clark Gable in the role of Darcy, when the boy genius Thalberg suddenly died, and the film stalled. Meanwhile, Milne opened his *Miss Elizabeth Bennet* in Liverpool on 3 September 1936. He went to the opening night and made a speech 'in the absence of Miss Austen'.[17] Eighteen months later, the play opened in London but only for a short run at the People's Palace.

In Hollywood, MGM now decided that the role of Mr Darcy should be given to Laurence Olivier, rather than Gable. Olivier had achieved box-office success with *Wuthering Heights* and *Rebecca*. His dark, brooding looks and proud manner, they reasoned, would be perfect for Austen's Darcy. Olivier wanted to appear alongside his lover, Vivien Leigh, in the role of Elizabeth, but the studio, anxious to avoid a scandal, as Olivier was a married man, eventually decided on Greer Garson.[18]

The studio approached the renowned novelist Aldous Huxley, who was living in Hollywood, to co-write the screenplay with writer Jane Murfin. When war broke out, Huxley was reportedly anxious about being paid so handsomely while his 'family and friends were being starved and bombed in England'. He overcame his scruples and the film was a huge success during the early years of war. The advertising campaign announced: 'Bachelors Beware! Five Gorgeous Beauties are on a Madcap Manhunt'. The movie drew the largest weekly August audience in Radio City Music Hall's history.

The 1940 *Pride and Prejudice* set the mould for most of the Hollywood adaptations of the 1990s. The novel's romantic plot between Elizabeth and Darcy was given emphasis, costumes were elaborate (famously 'Hollywoodised' into Victorian frills rather than streamlined Regency clothes), and settings were sumptuous. It won an Academy Award for Art Direction.

The film was a sentimental and idealised vision of nineteenth-century England: it begins 'It happened in Old England ... in the village of Meryton.' Sequences were added, such as the archery scene with Elizabeth and Darcy, and some of the encounters were radically altered, such as the encounter between Lady Catherine and Elizabeth towards the end of the film. Rather than Lady Catherine doing her utmost to separate the lovers, she is seen to actively encourage the union. However, in contrast with A. A. Milne's seamlessly integrated added dialogue, the extra speeches sometimes have a wholly incongruous tone:

> LADY CATHERINE: She's right for you, Darcy. You were a spoiled child, and we don't want to go on spoiling you. What you need is a woman who can stand up to you. I think you've found her.
> ELIZABETH: You're very puzzling, Mr Darcy. At this moment, it's difficult to believe that you're so ... *proud*.
> DARCY: At this moment, it's difficult to believe that you're so ... *prejudiced*. Shall we not call it quits and start again?

The *New York Times* film critic praised the film as 'the most deliciously pert comedy of old manners, the most crisp and crackling satire in costume that we in this corner can remember ever having seen on the screen'. He also praised the two leads: 'Greer Garson as Elizabeth – "dear, beautiful Lizzie" – stepped right out of the book, or rather out of one's fondest imagination: poised, graceful, self-contained, witty, spasmodically stubborn and as lovely as a woman can be. Laurence Olivier is Darcy, that's all there is to it – the arrogant, sardonic Darcy whose pride went before a most felicitous fall.'[19]

For Huxley, it was a hack job. There is none of the astringency of his own novels of social satire such as *Crome Yellow* and *Antic Hay*. Helen Jerome had bequeathed Hollywood a version of Jane Austen as 'sentimental comedy in three acts'. Had the Milne adaptation been used instead, there might have been a better understanding of Austen as social satirist, verbal ironist and daughter of the muse of comedy as opposed to sentiment.

Back in England, Milne lamented his ill-luck, but the publication of his *Miss Elizabeth Bennet* was well received. And, when war broke out, it found a new life as a radio play. In November 1940, the play was broadcast on the Home Service with Celia Johnson in the role of Elizabeth Bennet. Then in March 1944, it was broadcast again as a special play on Forces radio, with Margaret Rutherford in the role of Mrs Bennet.[20]

Jane Austen's novels were clearly perceived as a morale booster, and an escape from the horrors of war. In the light of his experience on the Somme, Milne was duly gratified. A further example of Jane Austen's capacity to boost spirits during wartime was discovered by the American film critic Kenneth Turan, who was granted access to director Robert Z. Leonard's scrapbooks in the Motion Picture Academy library. Turan noticed a letter tucked away in a scrapbook from a fan in England, telling him that the Olivier/Garson *Pride and Prejudice* movie had produced much-needed comic relief and respite from the desperate realities of bombed-out Southampton:

> My husband is a Naval Officer and a few days ago he had one of his rare afternoons in port and a chance to visit the cinema. We went to see your film made from the book we know and love so well and to our delight were carried away for two whole hours of perfect enjoyment. Only once was I reminded of our war – when in a candle-lit room there was an uncurtained window and my husband whispered humorously, 'Look – they're not blacked out.'
>
> You may perhaps know that this city has suffered badly from air raids but we still have some cinemas left, and to see a packed audience enjoying *Pride and Prejudice* so much was most heartening. I do thank you very much as well as all the actors and actresses for your share in what has given so much pleasure to us.[21]

Milne's *Miss Elizabeth Bennet* succeeded as a play both on the stage and on the radio because, as an experienced dramatist, he instinctively understood that he should not be intimidated by the original version.

The best adaptations of Austen are those that, in Milne's words, reveal 'truth to character', without a slavish devotion to the purity of the text. Indeed, it was vital that he ensured his adaptation was intelligible to anyone who had not heard of *Pride and Prejudice*: 'To assume no special knowledge in an audience is the golden rule of play-writing.'[22]

The Austen film adaptations that work best are those that succeed as films in their own right. Patricia Rozema's audacious *Mansfield Park* (1999) eschews the heritage-style whimsy of the conventional period drama. Its deployment of feminist, gender and post-colonial themes nods to academic literary criticism of Austen, and provides a fascinating shadow story to this most complex of novels. Amy Heckerling's *Clueless* (1995) and Whit Stillman's *Love & Friendship* (2016) are two of the most creative and innovative adaptations: again, they eschew whimsy and sentimentalism. They work as films in their own right, they take risks, and yet they remain true to the spirit of the novels and the essence of the characters. They assume no special knowledge. In both films, the writer/ director captures the comic brilliance of the original, the skilfulness of Austen's plotting and characterisation, her verbal dexterity, and the lack of sentimentality that imbues her novels.

Amy Heckerling made her directorial debut in 1982 with *Fast Times at Ridgemont High*, one of the best coming-of-age teen comedies of the modern era, with a script by Cameron Crowe and outstanding performances from a group of young, not yet famous actors including Sean Penn, Nicolas Cage, Jennifer Jason Leigh, Phoebe Cates, Eric Stoltz and Forest Whitaker. Dissatisfied with the quality of the scripts she was subsequently sent, Heckerling began writing her own. Her first 'written and directed by' credit came in 1989 with *Look Who's Talking*, featuring John Travolta, Kirstie Alley and a baby voiced by Bruce Willis. The voice-over from the baby's point of view revealed to Heckerling that it was possible to achieve a narrative equivalent of the novelist's ironising device of free indirect speech. Her next move was to put together this voiceover technique and the material of *Fast Times* – female friendship, coming-of-age, inter-generational conflict (youthful transgressions, uptight teachers), rock soundtrack. The result was *Clueless*. Released in July 1995, it was an immediate box-office hit, the 'sleeper' success of the year, and soon a cult movie spawning a spin-off television series and innumerable imitations. What the credits did not mention and the first wave of appreciative movie critics did not notice was that Heckerling's script was a close adaptation of *Emma* – transposed to the *Fast Times* setting of a Californian high school.

The plot and most of the characters are faithfully preserved, but Highbury is reinvented as modern-day Beverly Hills, home to the fabulously rich and famous. It retains the air of an English village riven with petty jealousies, competitive consumer consumption, superiority complexes and gossipy cliques. Heckerling reveals the intricate workings of the contemporary American class system (based on beauty, wealth and celebrity) with all the finesse of Austen's take on the gentry of early nineteenth-century England.

The heroine Cher (Alicia Silverstone, nineteen years old and in only her second film) is good-looking, clever and rich. She is at the top of the pecking order in her rarefied, though confined, world. As suggested earlier, the key to *Emma* is Austen's use of free indirect speech, so that she can ironise her flawed heroine, which is difficult to achieve in the genre of film. *Clueless* circumvents this by the use of a first-person voiceover, with which Heckerling had experimented in *Look Who's Talking*. It is clear from the opening that Cher/Emma is being ironised. Her lack of self-knowledge and her skewed perspective are made evident from the first two minutes of the film.

It begins with a montage of glamorous, gorgeous young people, shopping at Tiffany's, swimming in luxurious outdoor pools and driving expensive cars. Cher's voiceover says: 'OK, so you're probably going, "Is this like a Noxzema commercial or what?" But seriously, I actually have a way normal life for a teenage girl. I get up, brush my teeth and I pick out my school clothes.' Noxzema is a cleansing cream, intended to make the skin look young and fresh, a point reinforced by the Supergrass song that soon follows on the soundtrack, with its refrain 'We are young! We run green! Keep our teeth nice and clean!'

Cher then programs her sartorial choices into a computer, which matches up the perfect outfit from a selection of exquisite designer clothes. We thus know instantly that she has a skewed sense of reality; she assumes that everyone has the same lifestyle and privileges. She does not have 'a way normal life'.

Nevertheless, her perfect Hollywood life is not all it seems: 'seemed', that key word in our introduction to Emma Woodhouse. Bored and frustrated, Cher is consumed by matchmaking and 'makeovers'. She sees her opportunity for the ideal makeover when Tai, a Latina girl from a deprived background, allows herself to be transformed by stylish clothes, cosmetics and hairstyle into a Beverly Hills high school girl, a clone of Cher herself.

Cher's catchphrase for her makeovers is 'project'. It's a word that seems contemporary, but it's actually used by Austen in *Emma* on several occasions: 'Emma's *project* of forgetting Mr Elton for a while'; 'It was the discovery of what she was doing; of this very *project* of hers'; 'Your views for Harriet are best known to yourself; but as you make no secret of your love of matchmaking, it is fair to suppose that views, and plans, and *projects* you have'. In the novel, matchmaking and projects (in Cher's parlance 'makeovers') are inextricably linked, but in *Clueless*, Heckerling breathes new life into the word and reveals her close reading of the original text.

Heckerling is astute in her understanding that Cher must be a sympathetic, indeed lovable, character. Despite her flaws, she is a devoted daughter; she is kind, witty and has a good heart. Above all, *Clueless* shines because of Heckerling's mastery of rapier-quick comic dialogue. She has learned from Austen the art that Austen learned from the comic theatre:

TAI: Cher, you're a virgin?

CHER: You say that like it's a bad thing.

DIONE: Besides, the PC term is 'hymenally challenged.'

CHER: You see how picky I am about my shoes and they only go on my feet.

There is the joke that also makes a point about Tai/Harriet's lack of education:

TAI: Do you think she's pretty?

CHER: No, she's a full-on Monet.

TAI: What's a monet?

CHER: It's like a painting, see? From far away, it's OK, but up close, it's a big old mess.

There is the art of repartee:

AMBER: Ms Stoeger, my plastic surgeon doesn't want me doing any activity where balls fly at my nose.
DIONE: Well, there goes your social life.

And the affectionate put-down of Cher/Emma by the Knightley character:

CHER: I want to do something for humanity.
JOSH: How about sterilisation?

Heckerling's inventive use of teen jargon ('buggin', 'Baldwin', 'Betty', 'cake boy', 'Boinkfest', 'As if!') is combined with satirical pseudo-intellectual academic jargon: when Cher's best friend Dione chastises her teenage boyfriend for addressing her as 'woman', he replies: 'Street slang is an increasingly valid form of expression. Most of the feminine pronouns do have mocking but not necessarily misogynistic undertones.'

Clueless is as much a satire on teen movies as it is an homage to *Emma*. Few people, at the time of the release, realised that the film was indeed an adaptation of a Jane Austen novel. The only clue is that the Mr Elton figure is called Elton. It works brilliantly (as A. A. Milne would say) in its own right. But it perfectly captures Austen's interest in class, hierarchy, social status, social mobility, manners, and, at its heart, the film has a moral imperative. Cher learns that before she can help others (or interfere with their lives, and meddle with their happiness) she needs to transform herself: 'I decided I needed a complete makeover, except this time, I'd *makeover my soul*.'

It is her willingness to accept that she is wrong and to make amends that redeems her. Milnean 'truth to character' is upheld throughout. Here is Cher on American isolationism, showing her essential goodness of heart:

So like, right now for example. The Haitians need to come to America. But some people are all, 'What about the strain on our resources?' Well it's like when I had this garden party for my father's birthday, right? I put R.S.V.P. 'cause it was a sit-down dinner. But some people came that like did not R.S.V.P. I was like totally buggin'. I had to haul ass to the kitchen, redistribute the food, and squish in extra place settings. But by the end of the day it was, like, the more the merrier. And so if the government could just get to the kitchen, rearrange some things, we could certainly party with the Haitians. And in conclusion may I please remind you it does not say R.S.V.P. on the Statue of Liberty.

If ever an Austen adaptation film set out to shock its viewers from their complacency and vapid sentimentality, then Patricia Rozema's 1999 *Mansfield Park* was the one. In perhaps the cleverest of all overt Austen adaptations, Rozema set out her goal firmly from the beginning, saying that *Mansfield Park*, which she wrote and directed, was not a Jane Austen film: 'It's a Patricia Rozema film. My job as an artist is to provide a fresh view.'[23] Which was primarily that this is a novel about the corrupt spoils of slavery, though Rozema throws in some incest and lesbianism for good measure. Harold Pinter – an inspired piece of casting – portrays Sir Thomas Bertram as a sadistic patriarch who takes an unhealthy interest in his female slaves.

The novel is the least loved of the Austen canon due to the dullness of its heroine, Fanny Price, who has always divided readers and critics. That was true even among Austen's own family. Her pious Christian brother, Frank, thought Fanny a 'delightful character', but her niece Anna 'could not bear Fanny'. Her mother 'thought Fanny insipid' and her nephew George 'disliked Fanny (interested by nobody but Mary Crawford)'.[24]

Perhaps the long-held reluctance to film *Mansfield Park* was precisely bound up with the essential problem of depicting a dull heroine set against a sexy, witty anti-heroine. In an interview about her adaptation, Rozema described Fanny Price as 'annoying', 'not fully drawn' and 'too slight and retiring and internal'.[25] Rozema's modification was to conflate the character of Fanny Price with the author herself, drawing upon Jane Austen's juvenilia and letters to add colour and spirit to the unpopular heroine.

Given that the young Fanny Price's respite from loneliness, bullying at the hands of Mrs Norris and homesickness for her Portsmouth family is the conduit of writing letters home, then this seems to be a legitimate modification. Furthermore, Austen's mature Fanny Price becomes an avid reader. Her love of books proves to be the most durable and sustainable of all her relationships. A turning point in Fanny's character is when she introduces her sister Susan to the pleasures of a good book and the delights of a circulating library: a lifesaver for both of them.

Rozema's Fanny Price is no shrinking violet trembling at the sound of her uncle's footsteps in the passage, as she is in Austen's novel. It remains to be seen whether it is possible for there to be a faithful dramatisation of *Mansfield Park*, which dares to portray a diffident, anxious heroine who nevertheless displays an iron will. In this regard, Fanny Price is the most interesting of Austen's heroines and the one whom the conventions of modern cinema and television are least well qualified to serve. It was striking that when ITV jumped on the Austen bandwagon with a series of adaptations in 2007, the *Northanger Abbey* with Felicity Jones perfectly caught the naivety of Catherine Morland (not least by playing her off against Carey Mulligan's glorious selfish Isabella Thorpe), whereas the *Mansfield Park* failed because even as fine an actor as Billie Piper failed to capture the simultaneous strength and weakness of Fanny Price.

The problem with Rozema's depiction of Fanny as a young woman who is as spirited and sexy as Mary Crawford was that it lost something vital that Austen was trying to explore: the quiet, watchful, moral, bookish girl who becomes indispensable. Austen is interested in characters who fall in love slowly, stealthily. She is always suspicious of the conventional, sentimental idea of love at first sight. That is why the truest adaptations of her novels are those that cut against the grain of Hollywood convention. Rozema certainly does that, especially in the Sapphic dimension, which owes more to her own earlier films than to any warrant in the novel – though it does nod to a notorious essay of that key Austen year of 1995, in which the lesbian literary theorist Terry Castle proposed in a review of a new edition of Austen's letters that, in the light of her deep affection for her sister Cassandra, the novelist's closest emotional attachments were female, an interpretation that some shocked commentators translated into 'Jane Austen may have been gay'.[26] But the refiguring of Fanny comes at the expense of Austen's very deliberate intention to create a heroine who was the opposite of Miss Elizabeth Bennet.

Mansfield Park is not a coming-of-age novel in any conventional sense. It is an ensemble piece of a group of young people on the brink of adulthood. Edmund Bertram loves Mary Crawford, who makes a play first for Tom Bertram before transferring her attentions to Edmund, who is beloved by Fanny Price, who is loved by Henry Crawford. Sisters Julia and Maria Bertram both love Henry Crawford but Maria is engaged to Rushworth (whom she doesn't love). Henry and Maria have an adulterous affair, and Fanny and Edmund are finally united. In many respects this is a novel about ennui and boredom. Stuck in the country with nothing much to do except fall in and out of love, the group try various schemes to alleviate the hopelessness that seems to envelope them all. Despite it being written at the beginning of a new century, there is a *fin-de-siècle* nihilism that suffuses the novel. Rozema's interpretation captures some of this darkness.

The critic David Monaghan argues that viewers should approach Rozema's *Mansfield Park* as 'an independent work of art rather than an adaptation of Austen's novel'.[27] However, Monaghan takes issue with Rozema's depiction of Fanny's 'enlightened attitudes towards issues of gender, class and race'. He sees this as anachronistic (viewing the past through 'modern values') and as trendy liberal humanism that seeks to make this awkward heroine more acceptable to a modern audience. This seems puzzling as both Jane Austen and her heroine Fanny Price do indeed share enlightened attitudes towards gender, class and race. *Mansfield Park* celebrates meritocracy above the inherited values and privileges of the landed gentry. It is the hard-working, ill-educated lower-class Price children who are the victors in this story. Fanny Price exercises her right of refusal in the marriage market (limited power it may be, but it's effective) and she will not be coerced into marrying Henry Crawford, no matter how good a match.

Nevertheless, as Monaghan explains, 'In the England depicted by Rozema (and indeed by Austen), a woman was made extremely vulnerable by her sexuality'. Those such as Maria Bertram who choose to act on libidinous impulses are ostracised. That Rozema's Fanny Price catches

Maria and Henry *in flagrante delicto* is a stark reminder of her own vulnerability: 'The sight of Maria, naked and exposed to shame and ridicule, is all the evidence Fanny needs of what could well have been her own fate had she let herself fall prey to Henry's undoubted charms.'[28]

Monaghan points out the repeated presence of caged birds in the background of interior shots involving female characters. One of the most memorable scenes in the adaptation comes with Henry's arrangement of a choreographed flock of doves as part of his seduction of Fanny in Portsmouth.[29] Then at the film's close, a flock of wild starlings swoop upwards above the house into the sky. This cinematic device is a perceptive and brilliant reference to female enslavement and oppression. In the novel, Maria Bertram enters into a lucrative but loveless engagement with the foolish Rushworth. In the extensive grounds of his estate, Sotherton Court, she looks out at an iron gate and quotes a passage from Laurence Sterne's *A Sentimental Journey*: 'I cannot get out, as the Starling said.' This is one of the rare instances when the authorial sympathy shifts to Maria. She wants to get married to escape her home and her oppressive father, but is merely exchanging one form of slavery for another. She feels trapped and oppressed, just like the starling in the cage, longing to get out (Sterne makes a reference to the Bastille prison in the same passage). Maria is enslaved by her choices, and her desire for status and power, but also by a culture that, in the first place, views her as a commodity.

For Rozema, another kind of enslavement underpins her adaptation. She wanted to use the film to expose the brutal horrors of the slave trade that bankrolls the lifestyle of the Bertrams. Fanny herself is not exempt from this. A pivotal scene (again, with no source in the novel) is that in which Fanny finds Tom's portfolio of sketches of his time in Antigua on his father's slave plantation. There are drawings of white men raping black women, slaves being tortured and Sir Thomas whipping a slave. Another sketch depicts Sir Thomas forcing a female slave to perform a sexual act. It's a shocking and disquieting scene, all the more powerful when we know that this was a common occurrence among slave owners.[30]

If the backdrop to the novel of *Mansfield Park* is the dark story of the slave trade, then Rozema's film is a *tour de force*. We are never permitted to escape its all-pervading influence. The character of Sir Thomas, played to extremely sinister effect by Harold Pinter, is given extra lines, making clear his views on the female slaves: 'The mulattos are in general well-shaped and the women especially well-featured. I have one – so easy and graceful in her movements and intelligent as well. But strangely, you know, two mulattos will never have children. They are of the mule-kind in that respect.'

Unlike so many of the more conventional adaptations, such as Ang Lee's *Sense and Sensibility*, Rozema eschews the sentimental. This is not the world of heritage Jane Austen. This Georgian country house is not a haven of beauty and elegance. It is no Pemberley in the guise of Chatsworth, as used for the BBC's *Pride and Prejudice*. It's barren and bare, crumbling under the weight of its uneasy past. It's a house built on the blood of slaves. At the end of the film, Fanny and Edmund depart to the parsonage and not to the house with all its corrupt associations. This is not a film for the Austen purists, but it's a powerful and unsettling depiction of this most dark and complex of novels.

For Rozema, the central problem of adapting *Mansfield Park* for a modern audience was the passivity of its heroine. How does one make Fanny Price interesting when all eyes, like those of Austen's nephew George, are on Mary Crawford? Is it possible for a modern audience to like Fanny Price? Whit Stillman, who may lay claim to have been the first writer and director of what has been called the post-heritage genre of Austen adaptation,[31] explores this idea in his superb coming-of-age drama, *Metropolitan* (1990).

The film, a contemporary refashioning of *Mansfield Park*, set in Manhattan's Upper East Side and the Hamptons, has at its centre a shy, moral heroine (Audrey Rouget), who is obsessed by Jane Austen. As in *Mansfield Park*, the group of intelligent, well-bred and educated young people on the verge of adulthood are mainly left to their own devices, without the guiding influence of their parents. The parents (and step-parents) are perceived as feckless and selfish, giving no moral or ethical guidance. It's a brilliant depiction of the manners and mores of upper-class WASP society.

In *Metropolitan*, the young people, who are all first-year college students, are on winter break during the Manhattan debutante season.

The boys form a group calling themselves the Urban Haute Bourgeoisie (UHBs), while the girls form the Sally Fowler Rat Pack. Sally's is the apartment where the highly articulate young people converge after the dinners and dances to discuss issues such as the uncertainties of the future, and questions of class and morality.

The narrative is developed through the eyes of Tom, a cynical, poor but clever outsider accepted into the elite group. Audrey is the moral compass and she falls in love with Tom, while he is still smitten with Serena Slocum, the beautiful, witty and amoral girl, modelled on Mary Crawford. At one point in the film, Audrey and Tom have a debate about Fanny Price as a virtuous heroine, quoting from Lionel Trilling's influential essay on the novel:

> I think he's very strange. He says that 'nobody' could like the heroine of *Mansfield Park*. I like her. Then he goes on and on about how 'we' modern people, today, with 'our' modern attitudes 'bitterly resent' *Mansfield Park* because its heroine is virtuous. What's wrong with a novel having a virtuous heroine? Finally, it turns out he really likes *Mansfield Park*, so what's the point?[32]

Tom agrees with Lionel Trilling about the absurdity of the notion that there is something morally wrong about the young people putting on a play. When Audrey presses him on the issue, he admits that he hasn't in fact read the novel, only the criticism: 'I don't read novels. I prefer good literary criticism – that way you get both the novelists' ideas and the critics' thinking.'

The young people, bored and restless, decide to play a game of 'Truth or Dare'. Audrey refuses to play and as a result is isolated from the group, the equivalent of the *Lovers' Vows* episode in the novel. Unpleasant truths are revealed and the group is irrevocably fractured. Audrey leaves Manhattan for the Hamptons in the company of rich, handsome womaniser Rick von Sloneker, the Henry Crawford figure. While she is there, Tom realises that Audrey is the girl he really loves and sets out to rescue her. The film ends with them hitchhiking back to New York.

Stillman's debut film received an Oscar nomination for Best Original Screenplay. He claimed that *Metropolitan* sparked Hollywood's interest in Jane Austen, and he was asked to direct Emma Thompson's *Sense and Sensibility*, but declined after he read the script.[33] But he wasn't finished with Austen. In 2016, he wrote and directed *Love & Friendship*, a period drama based on Austen's novella *Lady Susan*. But this being Whit Stillman, it is not a conventional Austen period drama. There is no probing of the human heart in this adaptation. It's all about the money. It's an audacious, witty, fast-paced paean to Austen's great comic powers, which restores her to her burlesque and satirical roots. Viewers wanting the Austen of romance and sentiment will not find her in this film. This is not the safe, cosy Regency spinster restoring us to a comforting world of gentility and manners. This is the 'sick and wicked' Austen of the letters: the 'mad beast' who 'cannot help it'. Austen's juvenilia is full of arch manipulators such as Lady Susan, though few have her 'diabolical genius' and charm.

'Love & Friendship' is not of course the title of *Lady Susan*, which Austen herself left untitled – only when it was published after her death was the manuscript named for its anti-heroine. Stillman has borrowed his title from another of Austen's early comic works, in order, very cleverly, to echo *Pride and Prejudice* and *Sense and Sensibility*.

The story revolves around the machinations of Lady Susan, a *femme fatale* in the Mary Crawford model, except that, unlike Mary Crawford, she is allowed both to play the game and win the game. The game is the marriage market, and Lady Susan (Kate Beckinsale) seeks a rich husband for both herself and her (dull) daughter, Frederica (Morfydd Clark). Stillman's relish for Lady Susan, Austen's most naughty, clever and sexy heroine, is evident. She is better than all the men around her, because she is more intelligent and resourceful. She is self-aware, selfish and not self-deluded. She wreaks havoc on those around her, and is gloriously unrepentant. Her beauty, style and grace serve her as currency in the Georgian marriage market, but if she's a commodity then she will play the game her own way, breaking the rules from the inside, along the way. She is a magnificent monster, who imposes her will on her world, but also a liberated woman in an era and culture where women are usually restricted. She's like the bad girls in Austen's juvenilia who refuse to be good daughters, good sisters, good wives. She defies social convention not only by her pursuit of men, but by her refusal to accept the norms of motherhood. She delights in being a bad mother and is all the more refreshing for it. She is indeed the heroine and not the victim of her own life. *Love & Friendship* feels like a film that celebrates women.

Kate Beckinsale (who twenty years earlier played Emma Woodhouse in Andrew Davies's rather flat 1996 television dramatisation for the BBC) is perfect casting for the role, combining beauty and wit with a calculating, predatory cynicism. She does, of course, have all the best lines. Of her best friend's companion she quips: 'What a mistake you made in marrying that man! Too old to be governable, too young to die.' And, 'Facts are horrid things,' she sighs after deflecting an assault on her reputation. When a young rake solicits her on a street, she threatens him with a whipping.

Part of the problem with Austen's incomplete novella is that Lady Susan dominates the narrative. There are few counterbalancing figures of the sort that create such vital foils in her finished novels. Stillman gets around this problem by fleshing out some of the other characters. He builds up the role of Lady Susan's companion, Alicia Johnson, who in his film is American, an opportunity for some colonial jokes from Lady Susan. She describes her friend as an American 'who has none of the uncouthness but all of the candour' of that young country. The colonists who have recently won their independence are 'American ingrates'. Lady Susan confesses her schemes to Alicia, to put the audience in the picture.

The film is visually stunning, juxtaposing town and country brilliantly. In tribute to the epistolary form of *Lady Susan*, Stillman creates intertitles that introduce his characters, in the manner of a silent movie. The contents of letters are also flashed up on the screen. Like A. A. Milne in *Miss Elizabeth Bennet*, Stillman seamlessly interweaves his own masterful comic dialogue with Jane Austen's. After shooting the film, he penned his own tie-in version of *Lady Susan*, rewriting it from the point of view of a minor character whom we never meet. The narrative voice is that of Rufus Martin-Colonna de Cesari-Rocca, nephew to Sir James Martin, who hopes that his book will rehabilitate the reputation of Lady Susan. Austen is the unkind and unfair 'spinster Authoress' who has impugned Lady Susan. Stillman explained in an interview that the idea for Rufus came from the real-life character of Austen's stuffy and rather dim nephew, Edward Austen-Leigh, who wrote the first life of Austen and saw *Lady Susan* into print in 1871.[34] This is a witty and Austen-like joke.

Stillman uses many of Austen's wonderful phrases: for example, 'the Vernon milkiness' to describe the sappiness of the Vernon family, whom Lady Susan is out to destroy. But he adds plenty of his own: 'Partial truth is Falsehood's fiercest bodyguard.' There is a wonderful exchange between Lady Susan and her young toy-boy lover, where she is trying to persuade him that her meek and dutiful daughter is a selfish rebel: 'I would never represent my daughter as worse than her actions show her to be.' That is a sentence truly worthy of Jane Austen's barbed verbal economy.

Stillman's deft literary interpolations and command of voice and irony actually improve on the original. It's the advice that A. A. Milne gave in his preface to *Miss Elizabeth Bennet*: don't try to improve on a Jane Austen sentence, and if you are adding extra lines, write what you think the character might say, not what you think Jane Austen would say.

Critics described Stillman's film as being like an undiscovered Oscar Wilde, revealing a different aspect to Jane Austen, far more risqué, more dangerous than anything in the line of costume dramas and sentimental romances descended from the old Hollywood *Pride and Prejudice*. Stillman's vision is far more true to Austen's comic powers than many of the other period dramas. There's a comic exuberance and joy that restores Austen to herself.

If Jane Austen were alive today, she'd probably be appalled by the movie adaptations of her books. She would be baffled by the fact that the majority of films emphasise the romantic aspect of her novels, when her intention was to subvert and undermine the romantic. Perhaps she would be vexed that her comic genius, and precise social satire, have been subsumed by Regency frocks, beautiful houses and impeccably landscaped gardens. Though the performances in Ang Lee's *Sense and Sensibility* were outstanding, the film's insistence on a highly idealistic presentation of romantic love ultimately promulgates and vindicates precisely the values that the novel satirises.

The adaptations and spin-offs that succeed best – *Miss Elizabeth Bennet*, *Clueless*, *Metropolitan* and *Love & Friendship* – do so because they stand up as works of art in their own right, without requiring the spectator to have any prior knowledge of the original work. Staying true to the spirit of Austen, A. A. Milne, Amy Heckerling and Whit Stillman show how uproariously comic she is, and draw attention to her careful manipulation of character and plot. They do this almost instinctively because they are themselves such brilliant writers of comic dialogue and exponents of the great tradition of comedy of manners. Their union with Jane Austen is a marriage not of convenience but of perfection.

Exits and entrances, great comic types, the move from high to low, supreme skill in comic dialogue that allows characters to reveal themselves through the words they speak, narrative structure in the form of scenes with climactic theatrical 'set-pieces': all these Austen devices, which this book has explored, were derived from her immersion in the great tradition of English drama from Shakespeare to Sheridan to Hannah Cowley and Elizabeth Inchbald. That is why the novels are natural candidates for 'revisioning' in the modern dramatic medium of film. The television sitcom and Hollywood romantic comedies are our equivalents of the theatrical comedies to which Jane Austen and her original readers flocked in London and Bath. The Comic Muse passed from those glorious playhouses to Austen's playful pen, and from her it has been passed onto the screen by way of such modern classics as *Clueless*.

As for the more conventional adaptations, they are above all excellent gateways to the novels. They can enhance our appreciation of Austen's comic genius, but we should not forget that she chose the genre of the novel, becoming one of its chief apologists and transforming the art of English fiction into something entirely original. Ultimately, the value of the direct dramatisations such as Emma Thompson's *Sense and Sensibility* screenplay and Andrew Davies's *Pride and Prejudice* television script was that they introduced new readers to the novels, and sent those who had already read Austen back to the pleasures and rewards of re-reading her.

Notes

Introduction

1. [Richard Whately], 'Modern Novels: *Northanger Abbey and Persuasion*', *Quarterly Review*, 24 (1821), p. 362.
2. In reviews of 1847 and 1851, George Henry Lewes cited an 1843 essay by Thomas Macaulay for the phrase. Macaulay does not use the precise wording, but does describe Austen as second only to Shakespeare. See *Jane Austen: The Critical Heritage*, ed. B. C. Southam, 2 vols (London: Routledge and Kegan Paul, 1968–87), i, pp. 122–25 and 130.
3. George Lewes, 'The Novels of Jane Austen', *Blackwood's Magazine*, 86 (1859), p. 105.
4. [Thomas Lister], *Edinburgh Review*, 53 (1830), p. 449.
5. Henry Austen, 'Biographical Notice', *NA*, p. 7.
6. Caroline Austen, *My Aunt Jane Austen: A Memoir* (Winchester: Sarsen Press, 1991), p. 10.
7. Lewes, 'Novels of Austen', p. 105.
8. In an especially influential essay, Lionel Trilling made the *Lovers' Vows* debacle the starting-point for an argument that hostility to role-playing was crucial to Austen's vision of the integrity of the individual. Trilling, 'Mansfield Park', in *The Opposing Self* (London: Secker and Warburg, 1955), pp. 206–30. In particular, Trilling singles out 'the fear that the impersonation of a bad or inferior character will have a harmful effect upon the impersonator, that, indeed, the impersonation of any other self will diminish the integrity of the self' (p. 218). In a later study, Trilling also compares Plato's moral objection to acting with Rousseau's, suggesting that it encourages a falsifying of the self and a weakening of the fabric of society. See Lionel Trilling, *Sincerity and Authenticity* (London: Oxford University Press, 1972), pp. 64–79.
9. Its dramatic elements are, however, ably discussed by Claude Rawson in his introduction to the World's Classics edition of the novel (Oxford: Oxford University Press, 1990).
10. The most influential reading along these 'conservative' lines is Marilyn Butler, *Jane Austen and the War of Ideas* (Oxford: Clarendon Press, 1975).
11. See Henry James, *The Art of the Novel*, ed. R. P. Blackmur (New York and London: Scribners, 1947), p. 110.

1: Private Theatricals

1. See Sybil Rosenfeld, *Temples of Thespis: Some Private Theatres and Theatricals in England and Wales, 1700–1820* (London: The Society for Theatre Research, 1978), p. 11.

2. Barrymore had employed Cox, the carpenter to Covent Garden, to erect his theatre, which was described by the *London Chronicle* as a model of Vanbrugh's King's Theatre in the Haymarket. Its seating capacity was more likely 400. See Anthony Pasquin, *The Life of the Late Earl of Barrymore: Including a History of the Wargrave Theatricals* (London, 1793), pp. 15–16; *Temples of Thespis*, pp. 16–33. See also Evelyn Howe, 'Amateur Theatre in Georgian England', *History Today*, 20 (1970), pp. 695–703; and George Holbert Tucker, *Jane Austen: The Woman* (New York: St Martin's Press, 1994), pp. 87–88.

3. See Gillian Russell, *The Theatres of War: Performance, Politics, and Society, 1793–1815* (Oxford: Clarendon Press, 1995), pp. 122–30. Amanda Vickery, *The Gentleman's Daughter: Women's Lives in Georgian England* (New Haven and London: Yale University Press, 1998), pp. 235–36.

4. See *Theatres of War*, pp. 122–28.

5. See Sybil Rosenfeld, 'Jane Austen and Private Theatricals', *Essays and Studies*, 15 (1962), pp. 40–51.

6. In 1770 Fanny Burney had objected to performing in the 'shocking' farce *Miss in her Teens*, but in 1771 she was happy to perform scenes from Colley Cibber's *The Careless Husband* in front of a small audience. See Fanny Burney, *The Early Journals and Letters of Fanny Burney*, ed. Lars E. Troide, 3 vols (Oxford: Clarendon Press, 1988), i, pp. 116, 161–63, 171; ii, pp. 238–48.

7. Family tradition records that the plays were presented either in the dining room or the outside barn. See *Jane Austen: A Family Record*, by William Austen-Leigh and Richard Arthur Austen-Leigh, revised and enlarged by Deirdre Le Faye (London: The British Library, 1989; repr. 1993), p. 43. See also George Holbert Tucker, 'Amateur Theatricals at Steventon', in *The Jane Austen Handbook: With a Dictionary of Jane Austen's Life and Works*, ed. J. David Grey (London: Athlone, 1986), pp. 1–5.

8. The collected verses of James Austen, including his prologues and epilogues, were copied out by James Edward Austen-Leigh, *c.* 1834–40. Two copies exist, with some slight differences in content and wording, in the Austen-Leigh archive at the Hampshire Record Office and at Chawton House.

9. Hampshire Record Office, Austen-Leigh Archive, James Austen's verses, copied by James Edward Austen-Leigh, 23 M93/60/3/2.

10. Strikingly, the phrase 'Love and Friendship' (the title of one of Austen's early burlesques) appears in one of Siward's speeches:

   Alas! it rives my soul
   To see the tender bonds of amity
   Thus torn asunder by the very means
   I fondly thought for ever would unite them;

And the fair structure, which my hopes had raised,
Of love and friendship, in a moment shrunk
From its weak base, and buried all in ruin.

See Elizabeth Inchbald, *The Modern Theatre*, 10 vols (London, 1811), vi, p. 43.

11. Hampshire Record Office, James Austen's verses, 23M93/60/3/2.
12. The prologue begins with James's imploring indulgence from his friends and ends with a similar plea to the 'blooming fair' members of the audience.
13. *A Family Record*, p. 46.
14. Claire Tomalin, *Jane Austen: A Life* (London: Viking, 1997), p. 40.
15. Hampshire Record Office, 23M93/60/3/2.
16. Hampshire Record Office, Austen-Leigh Archive, Eliza de Feuillide's Letters, 1790s to 1830s, 23M93/M1, letter 21, from Eliza de Feuillide to Philadelphia Walter, 17 January 1786, on microfiche. Letters are sequentially numbered and subsequent references will be numbered and dated.
17. *A Family Record*, pp. 63–64.
18. R. A. Austen-Leigh, *Austen Papers, 1704–1856* (London: Spottiswoode, 1942), p. 126.
19. *A Family Record*, p. 57.
20. Ibid., p. 58.
21. Ibid.
22. Hampshire Record Office, letter 26, 16 November 1787.
23. Ibid.
24. Hampshire Record Office, letter 27, 28 November 1787.
25. Ibid.
26. Ibid.
27. Claire Tomalin observes: 'It seems that Eliza finally got her chance to play Miss Titupp, and to say the lines which reflected well on her own unsatisfactory marriage: "We must marry, you know, because other people of fashion marry; but I should think very meanly of myself, if, after I was married, I should feel the least concern about my husband". *Jane Austen: A Life*, p. 56. See also *Bon Ton: or High Life Above Stairs*, in *The Plays of David Garrick*, ed. Gerald M. Berkowitz, 4 vols (New York and London: Garland, 1981), ii, p. 2.
28. *The Wonder: A Woman Keeps a Secret*, in *The Plays of Susanna Centlivre*, ed. Richard C. Frushell, 3 vols (New York and London: Garland, 1982), iii, p. 8.
29. Marilyn Butler describes *The Wonder* as 'the only unequivocally feminist work we know Austen knew', arguing that this was the play that Austen covertly used in *Mansfield Park*, because her choice of *Lovers' Vows* with its plot feature 'the woman's proposal of marriage' mirrored that of *The Wonder*. However, Butler's contention that Austen disapproved of this 'outright challenge to the masculine prerogative' flies in the face of everything that she was exposed to at Steventon. See Jane Austen, *Mansfield Park*, ed. James Kinsley, with a new introduction by Marilyn Butler (Oxford: Oxford University Press, 1990), pp. xxi–xxv.

30. Hampshire Record Office, 23M93/60/3/2.
31. See *The British Theatre: or A Collection of Plays … with Biographical and Critical Remarks by Mrs Inchbald* (London, 1808), vol. vi.
32. See Q. D. Leavis, 'A Critical Theory of Jane Austen's Writing', *Scrutiny*, 10 (1941–42), pp. 114–42.
33. James Edward Austen-Leigh, *A Memoir of Jane Austen*, ed. R. W. Chapman (Oxford: Clarendon Press, 1926), p. 49.
34. See Butler's introduction to the Oxford edition, p. xxiii.
35. Hampshire Record Office, 23M93/60/3/2.
36. See *A Family Record*, p. 63.
37. *The Sultan: or A Peep into the Seraglio*, in *The Plays of Isaac Bickerstaffe*, ed. Peter A. Tasch, 3 vols (New York and London: Garland, 1981), iii, p. 13.
38. Hampshire Record Office, 23M93/60/3/2.
39. The private theatricals staged by the Burneys were *Tom Thumb* and *The Way to Keep Him*. Burney's niece took the part of Tom Thumb: 'The meaning & energy with which this sweet Child spoke, was really wonderful; we had all done our best in giving her instructions, & she had profitted with a facility & good sense that, at her age, I do believe to be unequalled.' See *The Early Journals and Letters of Fanny Burney*, ii, p. 246. In the public theatres the part of Tom Thumb was often played by child actors, 'sometimes girls and sometimes as young as five, who would have spoken the heroic bombast with high-pitched voices': see Peter Lewis, *Fielding's Burlesque Drama: Its Place in the Tradition* (Edinburgh: Edinburgh University Press, 1987), p. 119. Jane Austen would have been thirteen when it was performed at Steventon.
40. In a letter to her nephew, James Edward, Austen asks him to thank his father for a present of pickled cucumbers and quotes Lady Bell Bloomer's phrase, 'tell him what you will'. See *Letters*, p. 323.
41. Hampshire Record Office, 23M93/M1, letter 30, 11 February 1789.
42. There is a discrepancy in the dating of James's epilogue for *The Sultan*, which he dates January 1790, though the evidence points to 1789. The Cooper cousins came to Steventon for the Christmas of 1788–89, and in February 1789 Eliza wrote to Philadelphia Walter with news of the performances of *The Sultan* and *High Life Below Stairs*.
43. See Margaret Anne Doody, 'Jane Austen's Reading', in *The Jane Austen Handbook*, p. 351.
44. In writing about the life of Henry IV, Austen parodies Goldsmith's bowdlerising style: 'his son the Prince of Wales came and took away the crown; whereupon the King made a long speech, for which I must refer the Reader to Shakespear's Plays, & the Prince made a still longer' (*MW*, p. 139).
45. See Chapman's index of allusions in his edition of *NA & P*, pp. 317–29.
46. See David Gilson, *A Bibliography of Jane Austen* (Oxford: Clarendon Press, 1982), pp. 438–39.
47. William Hayley, *Poems and Plays*, 6 vols (London, 1785).
48. Ibid., vi, p. 256.
49. Ibid., vi, p. 254.
50. James Austen, *The Loiterer*, 2 vols (Oxford, 1789–90), no. ix, pp. 4–7.

51. Ibid., pp. 6–7.

52. *The Children's Friend: Translated from the French of Mr Berquin by Lucas Williams*, 6 vols (London, 1793), preface in vol. 1 (subsequent quotations also from this preface).

53. Ibid., v, p. 18.

54. Ibid., v, p. 32.

55. Ibid., v, p. 36.

56. Austen's juvenile stories and plays were written for family amusement, and were handed down to family members as treasured heirlooms. Brian Southam suggests that the transcription of the juvenilia into the three-volume notebooks was probably for the purpose of reading aloud to the rest of the family. See B. C. Southam, *Jane Austen's Literary Manuscripts: A Study of the Novelist's Development through the Surviving Papers* (London: Oxford University Press, 1964), p. 14.

57. Southam dates *The Mystery* and *The Visit* around 1787–90 (*Literary Manuscripts*, p. 16). As mentioned earlier, Deirdre Le Faye has suggested that they were probably performed as comic after-pieces to the main play at the Steventon theatricals.

58. Claire Tomalin has also noted Austen's subversion of Berquin: 'Where he sought to teach and elevate, she plunged into farce, burlesque and self-mockery, and created a world of moral anarchy, bursting with the life and energy Berquin's good intentions managed to squeeze out'. (*Jane Austen: A Life*, p. 45).

59. Austen's biographer David Nokes views 'The Visit' as a comic counterpart to Townley's topsy-turvy world where servants feed on 'claret, burgundy and champagne' and eat French delicacies: 'In her own short play, *The Visit*, Jane imagined the exact opposite, a dinner-party of elegant aristocrats consuming the meanest labourer's food: cowheel, tripe and suet pudding, washed down with home-made elderberry and gooseberry wines. Something about the anarchy of such incongruous social reversals appealed to her sense of fictional adventure'. Nokes, *Jane Austen: A Life* (London: Fourth Estate, 1997), p. 113.

60. *A Family Record*, p. 63.

61. See Southam's notes to *MW*, p. 458.

62. There are no 'whispering scenes' in *The Critic*, although there are ludicrously ambiguous 'asides' spoken to great comic effect by two of the characters.

63. George Villiers, Duke of Buckingham, *The Rehearsal*, ed. Montague Summers (Stratford: Shakespeare Head, 1914), p. 16.

64. The ballad-opera, such as Gay's *The Beggar's Opera* (1728), was popular in the first part of the eighteenth century, but after 1750 the comic opera, the operatic farce, the burletta and the musical interlude took over. For the subtle differences between these miscellaneous forms, see Allardyce Nicoll, *A History of English Drama, 1660–1900*, 6 vols (Cambridge: Cambridge University Press, 1955–59), iii, pp. 191–208.

65. *New Brooms*, in *The Plays of George Colman the Elder*, ed. Kalman A. Burnim, 6 vols (New York and London: Garland, 1983), iv, p. 21.

66. The most successful comic opera of the time was perhaps Sheridan's *The Duenna* (1775); unusually for comic opera, it was particularly commended for the richness of its plot. *The Duenna* ran for seventy-five performances, see Nicoll, *History of English Drama*, iii, p. 205. Reviews in the *Morning Post* and the *London Chronicle* praised its richness of plot, as did Hazlitt in his *Lectures on the English Comic Writers*.

67. Oliver Goldsmith's comedy *She Stoops to Conquer* is set in a house that is mistaken for an inn, and contains comical scenes with Tony Lumpkin in a roadside tavern called 'The Three Pigeons'.

68. The 'Chorus of Ploughboys' is probably a parody of the choruses in Frances Brooke's ballad-opera *Rosina* (1782), which contains a semi-pastoral element, although there is also a chorus of rustic harvesters in Dryden and Purcell's *King Arthur* (1691).

69. See below for the influence of the drama on Austen's early works of fiction.

70. Kent County Archives, Centre for Kentish Studies, Knatchbull Manuscript, Fanny Knight's Journals, U951 F24, vols 1–10, on microfilm.

71. Although there is a play called *Irish Hospitality: or Virtue Rewarded* by Charles Dibdin, the characters listed by Fanny Knight suggest that this play was specifically written for the children. *Virtue Rewarded* was the sub-title of Richardson's *Pamela* (1740).

72. Claire Tomalin claims that Anne Sharp wrote this play for the children to perform to amuse the servants. See *Jane Austen: A Life*, p. 136.

73. Kent County Archives, U951 F24/1.

74. Thomas Gisborne, *An Enquiry into the Duties of the Female Sex* (London, 1797), p. 175.

75. The influential critic Marilyn Butler has led the way unchallenged in her conviction that Austen's supposed disapproval of private theatricals echoed Gisborne's. Butler's contention that the theatrical saga in *Mansfield Park* implicitly embraces Gisborne's moral conservatism sits oddly with Austen's evident disregard for Gisborne's strident criticism of private theatricals. Butler's insistence that Austen read Gisborne with approval in 1805 does not square with the Kent private theatricals. See *Jane Austen and the War of Ideas* (Oxford: Clarendon Press, 1975; repr. 1987), pp. 231–32.

76. Gisborne, excerpted in Jane Austen, *Mansfield Park*, ed. Claudia L. Johnson (New York and London: Norton, 1998), p. 401.

77. Although for many years the play's authorship was attributed to the seven-year-old Anna, B. C. Southam has set the record straight, arguing that the extent of Anna's collaboration was to make a few suggestions and alterations (there are pencil scribblings in a childish hand): *Jane Austen's 'Sir Charles Grandison'*, ed. Brian Southam (Oxford: Clarendon Press, 1980), p. 11. Southam argues for composition at an earlier date, but the evidence of Anna's hand suggests completion or revision at this time.

78. See Deirdre Le Faye, 'The Business of Mothering: Two Austenian Dialogues', *Book Collector* (1983), pp. 296–314.

79. Ibid., p. 302.

80. Ibid., p. 308.

81. See Ellen Jordan, 'Mansfield Park', *Times Literary Supplement*, 23 June 1972, p. 719.

2: The Professional Theatre

1. See William Dunlap, *The Life and Time of George Frederick Cooke*, 2 vols (London, 1815), i, p. 183.

2. *Dramatic Essays by Leigh Hunt*, ed. William Archer and Robert W. Lowe (London, 1894), p. 41.

3. *The Complete Works of William Hazlitt*, ed. P. P. Howe, 21 vols (London: Dent, 1930–34), xviii, p. 274.

4. The testimony of Thomas Bellamy, in his *Miscellanies*, 2 vols (London, 1794), i, p. 23.

5. See *A Biographical Dictionary of Actors, Actresses, Musicians, Dancers, Managers and Other Stage Personnel in London, 1660–1800*, ed. Philip H. Highfill, J. R. Kalman, A. Burnim and Edward A. Langhans, 16 vols (Carbondale: Southern Illinois University Press, 1984), xii, p. 222.

6. *Works of Hazlitt*, xviii, p. 274.

7. See *Biographical Dictionary of Actors*, ix, pp. 219–22.

8. See Thomas Frost, *Circus Life and Circus Celebrities* (London, 1875), p. 22, and Isaac J. Greenwood, *The Circus: Its Origin and Growth Prior to 1835* (New York: Dunlap, 1898), p. 19.

9. See Watson Nicholson, *The Struggle for a Free Stage in London* (London: Constable, 1906), p. 283; and Ernest Watson, *Sheridan to Robertson: A Study of the Nineteenth-Century London Stage* (Cambridge, Massachusetts: Harvard University Press, 1926), p. 71.

10. See Edward Wedlake Brayley, *Historical and Descriptive Accounts of the Theatres of London* (London, 1826), p. 62. In 1798, it was styled Astley's Royal Amphitheatre. In 1808, it was known as Astley's Amphitheatre, specialising in 'equestrian melodrama and spectacle'. See Allardyce Nicoll, *A History of Early Nineteenth-Century Drama, 1800–1850*, 2 vols (London, Cambridge University Press, 1930), i, pp. 224–25.

11. See Frost, *Circus Life*, pp. 45–46.

12. The term 'burletta' was used as an umbrella term for performances at the minor theatres that, for legal purposes, included five or six songs per act. For a full account of the circumvention of the law by the illegitimate theatres, see the following: Nicholson, *The Struggle for a Free Stage in London*; Ernest Watson, *Sheridan to Robertson: A Study of the Nineteenth-Century London Stage*, pp. 20–57; Joseph Donohue, 'Burletta and the Early Nineteenth-Century English Theatre', *Nineteenth-Century Theatre Research*, 1 (1973), pp. 29–51; and Dewey Ganzel, 'Patent Wrongs and Patent Theatres: Drama and the Law in the Early Nineteenth Century', *PMLA*, 76 (1961), pp. 384–96.

13. *Restoration and Georgian England, 1660–1778*, ed. David Thomas, *Theatre in Europe: A Documentary History* (Cambridge: Cambridge University Press, 1989), p. 208. See also Joseph Donohue, *Theatre in the Age of Kean* (Oxford: Blackwell, 1975), pp. 2–3; and John Brewer, *The Pleasures of the*

Imagination: English Culture in the Eighteenth Century (London: HarperCollins, 1997), pp. 385–89.

14. See Thomas and Hare, *Theatre in Europe*, pp. 220–23. See also Allardyce Nicoll, *The Garrick Stage: Theatres and Audience in the Eighteenth Century*, ed. Sybil Rosenfeld (Manchester: Manchester University Press, 1980), pp. 4–5.

15. Donohue, *Theatre in the Age of Kean*, p. 38.

16. Brayley's account includes the Adelphi Theatre, Astley's Royal Ampitheatre, the East London Theatre, the English Opera House, the King's Theatre, the Olympic Theatre, the Pantheon, the Regency, the Royal Coburg and Sadler's Wells. Tomlins lists the Adelphi, Astley's Amphitheatre, the English Opera House, the Garrick, the Haymarket, the Little Theatre in the Strand, the Olympic, the Pavilion, the Queen's Theatre, Sadler's Wells and the St James's. See F. G. Tomlins, *A Brief View of the English Stage* (London, 1832), p. 60. More recently, Raymond Mander and Joe Mitchenson have accounted for twenty-eight 'lost theatres' of nineteenth-century London.

17. See *Emma*, chapters 28 and 29.

18. The amphitheatre was closed from Michaelmas to Passion week, see Greenwood, *The Circus*, p. 30.

19. See Raymond Mander and Joe Mitchenson, *The Lost Theatres of London* (New York: Taplinger, 1968), p. 253.

20. See Frost, *Circus Life*, p. 48.

21. Greenwood, *The Circus*, p. 30.

22. See *The Life and Enterprises of Robert William Elliston* (London, 1857), p. 210. See also Mander and Mitchenson, *The Lost Theatres of London*, pp. 255–56, and Christopher Murray, *Robert William Elliston: Manager* (London: Society for Theatre Research, 1975), p. 48.

23. This conflicts with Brayley's observation, in 1826, that the theatre, when full, housed 1300 people. See Greenwood, *The Circus*, pp. 30–31; and Brayley, *Theatres of London*, p. 88.

24. Tomlins, *Brief View*, pp. 60–61.

25. See Brayley, *Theatres of London*, p. 66.

26. See *Emma*, p. 472.

27. The amphitheatre contained one full tier of thirteen boxes, three private boxes to the side and two boxes above the stage doors. See Brayley, *Theatres of London*, p. 65.

28. Elliston also had to pay an annuity to Astley for twenty pounds, see *Life and Enterprises*, p. 211.

29. Frost, *Circus Life*, p. 27. Jane Moody has argued that, although the minor theatres were 'neither unequivocally genteel nor unequivocally plebeian places', they were considered as 'artisan domains' by reviewers, and therefore discriminated against. Not only were they housed in insalubrious locations, they were unrespectable and vulgar, even linked with immorality and disorder. Moody invokes the hostility of genteel reviewers towards populist adaptations of Shakespeare in the minor theatres to make a broader argument about patrician anxiety for the preservation of social and cultural hierarchies: 'The presence of mixed social groups watching these

performances no doubt seemed all the more incomprehensible in view of the increasing segregation of domestic and cultural spaces by class taking place outside the theatre', Jane Moody, 'Writing for the Metropolis: Illegitimate Performances of Shakespeare in Early Nineteenth-Century London', *Shakespeare Survey*, 47 (1994), pp. 61–69. See further, Moody, *Illegitimate Theatre in London, 1770–1840* (Cambridge: Cambridge University Press, 2000).

30. Prices for admission in Astley's were 4*s*. for boxes, 2*s*. for pit and 1*s*. for gallery; whereas in the patents, they were 7*s*. for boxes, 3*s*. 6*d*. for pit, 2*s*. for middle gallery and 1*s*. for upper gallery. See Brayley, *Theatres of London*, p. 88.

31. Kent County Archives, Centre for Kentish Studies, Fanny Knight's Journals, 1 October 1807, U951 F24/4.

32. Towards the end of the novel Charles Musgrove secures a box at the theatre for the party, see *PP*, pp. 223–24.

33. Joshua Reynolds painted her formal portrait as Miss Prue; it was much copied and engraved. See *Biographical Dictionary of Actors*, i, p. 19.

34. See *Biographical Dictionary of Actors*, iv, p. 386. See also George Holbert Tucker, *Jane Austen the Woman* (New York: St Martin's Press, 1994). Tucker cites the review from the *Bath Herald and Reporter* for 29 June 1799, p. 96.

35. See James Boaden, *Life of Mrs Jordan*, 2 vols (London, 1832), ii, p. 14.

36. Chris Viveash, 'Jane Austen and Kotzebue', *Jane Austen Society Report* (1994), pp. 29–31.

37. Thomas Dibdin, *The Birth-Day*, in *A Collection of Farces and Other Afterpieces, Selected by Mrs Inchbald*, 7 vols (London, 1809), ii, p. 8.

38. Captain Bertram discovers Mrs Moral's treachery when Jack Junk persuades him to hide in the closet so as to overhear them plotting. The Bertram brothers are united and the cousins marry one another.

39. Margaret Kirkham has proposed that *Emma* is a conscious adaptation of Kotzebue's play, sharing a similar heroine and major plot-line. See *Jane Austen: Feminism and Fiction* (London: Athlone, 1997), pp. 121–29.

40. Though there are four surviving letters written during May 1801, there is a gap in Austen's correspondence until one isolated letter of 14 September 1804 (*A Family Record*, p. 119).

41. The theatre flourished in these years. The receipts for benefits averaged nearly £150 a night, compared to the usual fifty and sixty pounds. In 1799 Dimond, the manager, realised £161 (Mrs Siddons was playing) and Elliston £146. In 1800 Dimond's benefit brought him £137, Elliston's £150 and Mrs Edwin's £150. See Belville S. Penley, *The Bath Stage* (London, 1892), p. 81.

42. By 1800 royal patents had been granted to Aberdeen, Bath, Bristol, Cheltenham, Chester, Cork, Dublin, Edinburgh, Hull, Liverpool, Manchester, Margate, Newcastle-upon-Tyne, Norwich, Richmond, Weymouth, Windsor, Yarmouth and York. See Donohue, *Age of Kean*, p. 28, and Brewer, *Pleasures of Imagination*, p. 388.

43. The first patent was given to Edinburgh. Within months, the first provincial English city was petitioning for the same protection. An Enabling Act was

passed for the licensing of a playhouse in Bath and was given the royal
assent on 29 January 1768. See Thomas, *Restoration and Georgian England*,
pp. 222–25. See also Penley, *The Bath Stage*, p. 35.

44. See Allardyce Nicoll, *A History of English Drama, 1660–1900*, 6 vols
(Cambridge: Cambridge University Press, 1955), iv, p. 234.

45. Penley, *The Bath Stage*, pp. 50, 82.

46. Siddons returned to Bath in 1799 and again in April and August 1801. See
*Theatre Royal Bath: A Calendar of Performances at the Orchard Street
Theatre, 1750–1805*, ed. Arnold Hare (Bath: Kingsmead Press, 1977), pp.
178–79, 190–93. See also Penley, *The Bath Stage*, p. 88.

47. Elliston contemplated at different times entering the church. His
biographer records that in 1799 he undertook a series of lectures at Bath
and Bristol on morals and general criticism, 'in which the moralist and the
critic, pleasantly impregnated with the popular actor, drew together very
profitable assemblies at both cities' (*Life and Enterprises*, p. 48). He had
even considered buying Albemarle chapel, 'having serious thoughts of
taking Holy Orders and preaching therein himself' (*Life and Enterprises*,
p. 158).

48. See George Raymond, *Memoirs of Robert William Elliston*, 2 vols (London,
1844).

49. See Genest, *Some Account of the English Stage from 1660–1830*, 10 vols
(Bath, 1832), vii, p. 638.

50. See ibid., vii, p. 640.

51. William Reitzel has noted six performances of *Lovers' Vows* during the time
of the Austens' residence in Bath: 7 November 1801, 22 April 1802, 28
January 1803, 2 June 1803, 17 November 1803 and 17 January 1805. See
William Reitzel, '*Mansfield Park* and *Lovers' Vows*', *RES*, 9 (1933), p. 454.
However, Arnold Hare's calendar of Orchard Street performances,
compiled from newspapers and playbills, records a further eleven
performances, as follows: 25 May 1801, 21 September 1801, 13 February
1802, 13 November 1802, 13 June 1803, 21 October 1803, 19 November
1803 (not 17 November, as Reitzel suggests), 22 June 1804, 23 June 1804, 12
November 1804, 17 January 1805 and 10 July 1805. See Hare, *Theatre Royal
Bath*, pp. 191–218.

52. See Joseph Donohue, *Dramatic Character in the English Romantic Age*
(Princeton: Princeton University Press, 1970), p. 147. For the numerous
performances of Kotzebue adaptations between 1801 and 1805, see Hare,
Theatre Royal Bath, pp. 187–218.

53. See Genest, *Some Account of the English Stage*, vii, p. 562.

54. R. A. Austen-Leigh, *Austen Papers, 1704–1856* (London: Spottiswoode,
1942), p. 238.

55. According to Dunlap, Kean moved Cooke's remains from the Stranger's
Vault of St Paul's church to a more prominent location in the centre of the
churchyard: 'it may hereafter be found that his surgeon possesses his scull,
and his sucessor, Kean, the bones of the forefinger of his right-hand – that
dictatorial finger'. See William Dunlap, *A History of the American Theatre*
(New York, 1832), p. 393. This gave birth to one of the strangest legends in

theatre history. One version of the fate of the finger claims that Kean's wife had it thrown away, upon which point Kean left the stage. The skull had supposedly been used in productions of Hamlet after Cooke's death, and was located in Jefferson Medical College in 1967. See Don B. Milmeth, 'The Posthumous Career of George Frederick Cooke', *Theatre Notebook*, 24 (1969–70), pp. 68–74.

56. Dunlap, *Life of Cooke*, i, p. 50.
57. Cooke acted with Siddons in the provinces before she became a London star. See *Life of Cooke*, i, p. 43.
58. Dunlap, *Life of Cooke*, i. p. 206.
59. Penley, *The Bath Stage*, p. 81.
60. See *DNB*, vii, p. 302, and *Memoirs of Elliston*, i, pp. 215–23.
61. See Hunt, *Dramatic Essays*, pp. 85, 90.
62. See *DNB*, vii, p. 302.
63. 'R. W. Elliston, Esq'., *Gentleman's Magazine*, 101, part 2 (1831), p. 184.
64. *Oxberry's Dramatic Biography and Histrionic Anecdotes: or The Green-Room Spy*, 6 vols (London, 1825–27), iii, p. 88.
65. See Charles Lamb, *The Last Essays of Elia*, ed. Edmund Blunden (London: Oxford University Press, 1929), p. 23.
66. See Deirdre Le Faye, 'Journey, Waterparties and Plays', *Jane Austen Society Report* (1986), pp. 29–35.
67. See A. Temple Patterson, *A History of Southampton, 1700–1914*, 11 vols (Southampton: Southampton University Press, 1966), i, pp. 115–16.
68. See R. A. Austen-Leigh, *Jane Austen and Southampton* (London: Spottiswoode, 1949). pp. 30–31.
69. See John Adolphus, *Memoirs of John Bannister*, 2 vols (London, 1839), and *Biographical Dictionary of Actors*, p. 270.
70. Fanny Knight's Journals, U951 F24/1.
71. Arthur Murphy, *The Way to Keep Him*, in *Bell's British Theatre*, 34 vols (London, 1797), xvii, p. 52.
72. Hunt, *Dramatic Essays*, p. 31. Samuel de Wilde painted Bannister as 'Ben the sailor'. See *Biographical Dictionary of Actors*, p. 273.
73. Hunt, *Dramatic Essays*, p. 32.
74. See Thomas Dibdin, *Reminiscences*, 4 vols (London, 1827), ii, p. 239.
75. Michael Kelly, *Reminiscences*, 2 vols (London, 1826), ii, pp. 150–52.
76. Ibid., ii, p. 152.
77. Charles Dibdin, *Of Age Tomorrow* (London, n. d.), p. 18.
78. Kelly, *Reminiscences*, ii, p. 151.
79. Bannister's other cross-dressed role was as Jenny Diver in *The Beggar's Opera Metamorphosed*, which he played alongside his father's Polly Peachum in his first season at the Haymarket. Bannister was also painted in the role of Polly Peachum, so he probably took over this role from his father. See *Biographical Dictionary of Actors*, pp. 268, 273.
80. Charles Dibdin (1745–1814), not to be confused with his illegitimate older son Charles Dibdin the younger (1768–1833), and his illegitimate younger son Thomas Dibdin (1771–1841).
81. Patterson, *History of Southampton*, p. 104.

82. See Paul Ranger, *The Georgian Playhouses of Hampshire, 1730–1830*, Hampshire Papers, 10 (Winchester: Hampshire County Council, 1996), pp. 17–18.

83. Patterson, *History of Southampton*, p. 114.

84. Austen-Leigh, *Jane Austen and Southampton*, p. 46.

3: Plays and Actors

1. Pope's career on the London stage spanned fifty-two years and, from playing sprightly comic roles, she became in Hazlitt's words, 'the very picture of a duenna, a maiden lady or antiquated dowager'. See *Biographical Dictionary of Actors*, xii, pp. 77–84.

2. See David Nokes, *Jane Austen: A Life* (London: Fourth Estate, 1997), p. 323.

3. See Claire Tomalin, *Jane Austen: A Life* (London: Viking, 1997), p. 204.

4. See Raymond Mander and Joe Mitchenson, *The Lost Theatres of London* (New York: Taplinger, 1968), pp. 322–34.

5. Frances Burney, *Evelina*, ed. Edward A. Bloom (London: Oxford University Press, 1970), p. 104.

6. See Thomas Campbell, *Life of Mrs Siddons* (New York, 1834), p. 87.

7. Ibid., p. 89.

8. The 'rant', representing the formal and highly rhetorical approach to tragedy, was decried by the critics. See further discussion in Chapter 9 below.

9. See Leigh Hunt, *Dramatic Criticism*, ed. L. H. and C. W. Houtchens (New York: Columbia University Press, 1949), p. 39.

10. Campbell, *Life of Siddons*, pp. 86–87.

11. For her final season at Covent Garden she also acted Queen Katherine six times, Mrs Beverley five times, Elvira four times, Isabella twice and Lady Randolph once. See Genest, *Some Account of the English Stage*, viii, p. 239.

12. The Drury Lane Company remained at the Lyceum until 1812.

13. Dowton was a notorious figure for reviving the burlesque play *The Tailors* at the Haymarket in 1805, inciting a riot by aggrieved London tailors. See *Oxberry's Dramatic Biography*, iv, pp. 256–57.

14. Hunt, *Dramatic Criticism*, p. 97.

15. Hunt, *Dramatic Essays*, p. 32.

16. Mathews describes his unprepossessing figure in his memoirs, where he relates that from a child he was 'a long, thin skewer of a child' with distorted comical features. Mathews's son, who resembled his father, became known as 'Twig'. See *The Life and Correspondence of Charles Mathews*, ed. Edmund Yates (London, 1860), pp. 5–6, 130. For his account of Wilkinson, see ibid., p. 72.

17. *Life and Correspondence of Mathews*, pp. 148–49.

18. Bickerstaffe's musical version of the play was adapted from Cibber. The witty heroine of Restoration comedy had been replaced in Georgian drama by a new character assimilated from Richardsonian models, in particular the freely spoken, independent Lady G. (née Charlotte Grandison). See below, Chapter 5.

19. The Edwins were at Bath, Bristol and Southampton from 1797–98 to 1803–4. Edwin acted in the provinces throughout the acting career. See

Biographical Dictionary of Actors, p. 34, and Hare's *Orchard Street Calendar*, pp. 170–212.

20. C. Baron Wilson, *Our Actresses*, 2 vols (London, 1844), i, p. 105.
21. Ibid., p. 119.
22. *Oxberry's Dramatic Biography*, iv, p. 209.
23. See James J. Lynch, *Box, Pit and Gallery: Stage and Society in Johnson's London* (Berkeley: University of California Press, 1953), pp. 5–6.
24. *Lord Byron: The Complete Poetical Works*, ed. Jerome J. McGann, 7 vols (Oxford: Clarendon Press, 1986), v, p. 9. Byron became friends with Grimaldi. He first saw him in 1808, and always took a box ticket for his benefit. See *Memoirs of Joseph Grimaldi*, ed. Boz (London, 1869), p. 196. See also *The Theatre of Don Juan: A Collection of Plays and Views, 1630–1963*, ed. Oscar Mandel (Lincoln: University of Nebraska Press, 1963).
25. See *PP*, pp. 152–54.
26. There were three boxes on each side of the proscenium, three tiers or circles of boxes in the auditory (each containing twenty-six) and above them spacious slip boxes (on a level with the gallery). Brayley, *Theatres of London*, p. 19.
27. See Marc Baer, *Theatre and Disorder in Late Georgian England* (Oxford: Oxford University Press, 1992), pp. 135–65, and Gillian Russell, 'Playing at Revolution: The Politics of the O.P. Riots of 1809', *Theatre Notebook*, 44 (1990), pp. 16–26.
28. See *Letters*, p. 419.
29. See Brayley, *Theatres of London*, p. 19.
30. See Donohue, *Theatre in the Age of Kean*, p. 47.
31. He made his debut as Leon in *Rule a Wife and Have a Wife*. See Genest, *English Stage*, viii.
32. See J. G. Lockhart, *Life of Walter Scott* (New York: Cromwell, 1848), p. 271.
33. See *The Letters of Sir Walter Scott*, ed. H. J. C. Grierson, 12 vols (London: Constable, 1932), iii, p. 32.
34. See Genest, *English Stage*, viii, pp. 400–1.
35. By the close of the first fortnight of the 1813–14 season the receipts were worryingly low, averaging £250 a night, compared to £500 in the 1807–8 season. See Harold Newcombe Hillebrand, *Edmund Kean* (New York: Columbia University Press, 1933), pp. 106–13.
36. See F. W. Hawkins, *The Life of Edmund Kean*, 2 vols (London, 1869), i, p. 131.
37. *Works of Hazlitt*, v, p. 179.
38. Hawkins, *Life of Kean*, i, p. 130.
39. *Works of Hazlitt*, v, p. 179.
40. *The Romantics on Shakespeare*, ed. Jonathan Bate (London: Penguin, 1992), p. 160. Coleridge's patron Sir George Beaumont also observed of Kean that 'there was a fire in his acting that was electric'. See Hillebrand, *Edmund Kean*, pp. 119, 365.
41. *The London Theatre, 1811–1866: Selections from the Diary of Henry Crabb Robinson*, ed. Eluned Brown (London: Society for Theatre Research, 1966), pp. 36, 56.

42. Lamb, 'Ellistonia', p. 25.

43. See *DNB*, vii, p. 302, and Hunt's *Dramatic Criticism*, p. 96.

44. *Works of Hazlitt*, xviii, pp. 219, 343.

45. See Hunt, *Dramatic Essays*, p. 67.

46. The success of *Killing no Murder* was attributed to the ability of Mathews and Liston to play into each other's hands.

47. When he first joined Drury Lane he was paid £40 a week, though he was rumoured to have earned £100 a week when he joined the Olympic.

48. *Works of Hazlitt*, v, p. 252.

49. Hunt, *Dramatic Essays*, p. 49.

50. *The Works of Charles and Mary Lamb*, ed. E. V. Lucas, 2 vols (London: Methuen, 1903), ii, p. 148.

51. *Works of Hazlitt*, xviii, p. 402.

52. Hunt, *Dramatic Essays*, p. 60; *Dramatic Criticism*, p. 100.

53. *Works of Hazlitt*, xviii, p. 279.

54. See Genest, *English Stage*, viii, p. 422.

55. See *Oxberry's Dramatic Biography*, iv, p. 8. Hazlitt also complained that Young's Hamlet was a poor imitation of Kemble's.

56. *Oxberry's Dramatic Biography*, iv, p. 10.

57. Hunt, *Dramatic Criticism*, p. 25; *Works of Hazlitt*, xviii, p. 244.

58. See *Oxberry's Dramatic Biography*, i, p. 95.

59. See *Byron's Life, Letters and Journals*, ed. Thomas Moore (London, 1854), p. 252.

60. See Joseph Donohue, *Dramatic Character in the English Romantic Age*, p. 167.

61. *Oxberry's Dramatic Biography*, i, p. 97.

62. *Works of Hazlitt*, xviii, p. 196.

63. *Oxberry's Dramatic Biography*, i, p. 97.

64. See Charles Inigo Jones, *Memoirs of Miss O'Neill* (London, 1816), pp. 8, 47.

65. *Works of Hazlitt*, v, p. 199.

66. Crabb Robinson, *Selections from the Diary*, p. 299.

67. *Works of Hazlitt*, v, pp. 198–99.

68. Jones, *Memoirs of O'Neill*, pp. 50, 90–91.

69. *Oxberry's Dramatic Biography*, i, p. 98.

70. See Brayley, *Theatres of London*, p. 29.

71. Kelly observed that the new Opera House 'was by far the best for sound I ever sang at', and that Mrs Jordan received a great share of the applause. See Kelly's *Reminiscences*, pp. 186–87.

72. See Brayley, *Theatres of London*, p. 29.

73. Her fellow actor William Macready observed, 'If Mrs Siddons appeared a personification of the tragic muse, certainly all the attributes of Thalia were most joyously combined in Mrs Jordan'. See *Macready's Reminiscences*, ed. Sir Frederick Pollock (New York, 1875), p. 46. See also Boaden, *Life of Mrs Jordan*, 2 vols (London, 1831), i, p. 2.

74. The full title of the painting was *The Comic Muse Supported by Euphrosyne, who Represses the Advances of a Satyr*. See Claire Tomalin, *Mrs Jordan's Profession* (New York: Knopf, 1994), pp. 69–71.

75. Genest claimed that she never had a superior in her line and that she was 'second to none', *English Stage*, viii, p. 429. Sir Joshua Reynolds declared that she 'vastly exceeded every thing that he had ever seen, and really *was* what others only affected to be', Boaden, *Life of Jordan*, p. 220.

76. Coleridge sent her a copy of *Lyrical Ballads*, and praised her verse-speaking to Byron as the best he had ever heard. He also claimed that Jordan intended to sing stanzas of 'The Mad Mother' in *Pizarro*. See Tomalin, *Mrs Jordan's Profession*, pp. 179, 181, 270.

77. See *Works of Hazlitt*, xviii, p. 277.

78. See Leigh Hunt, *Dramatic Essays*, pp. 80–81. See also his 'The Comic Actress', in *Dramatic Criticism*, pp. 87–91.

79. Genest, *English Stage*, viii, p. 431.

80. In 1796, the King had presented William with Bushy, a part of the Hampton Court Palace estates. See Tomalin, *Mrs Jordan's Profession*, pp. 156–57.

81. See Genest, *English Stage*, vii, p. 18, and *The London Stage, 1660–1800*, ed. Emmett L. Avery, Charles Beecher Hogan, Arthur H. Scouten, George Winchester Stone Jr and William Van Lennep, 11 vols (Carbondale: Southern Illinois University Press, 1960–68), v, p. 1332.

82. *The Greek Slave*, Huntington Library, MS Larpent 894.

83. *Life of Mrs Jordan*, i, p. 142.

84. Hunt, *Dramatic Criticism*, pp. 87–88.

85. See 'Petronius Arbiter', *Memoirs of the Present Countess of Derby* (London, 1797).

86. Genest notes that Dora Jordan played Nell on 7 March, *English Stage*, viii, p. 423.

87. Elizabeth Inchbald, *A Collection of Farces and Other Afterpieces: Selected by Mrs Inchbald*, 7 vols (London, 1809), vii, p. 119.

88. Jordan had quit the stage in 1811 on the terms of her separation with the Duke of Clarence, which stated that if she returned to the stage she would lose custody of her daughters. She did return to the stage in 1812 in order to pay the debts of her son-in-law and secured an engagement at Covent Garden, making her debut in February 1813.

89. *Works of Hazlitt*, xviii, pp. 277, 234.

90. The three mentioned here, which Austen knew, represent merely a fraction of farces and comedies with a similar theme, dating from Gay's *The Beggar's Opera*, which first combined genres from 'high' and 'low' culture.

91. Garrick's famous epilogue to Murphy's *All in the Wrong* is often seen as representative of the social and architectural stratification of theatre audiences. After the main play, people were admitted into the theatre for half price. Although the assumption is that the upper and middle classes left after the main play and the lower classes gained a low ticket price for entrance to the farce, this wasn't always the case. Austen often seemed to prefer the after-piece to the main play. Nor can we make the assumption that the social stratification of the box, pit and gallery was as circumscribed as is sometimes assumed. Joseph Donohue has shown that the architectural and social division of the auditorium 'by no means created mutually exclusive seating areas', *Theatre in the Age of Kean*, p. 15.

92. See Donohue, *Theatre in the Age of Kean*, p. 17, and Lynch, *Box, Pit and Gallery*, p. 2. The rise of sentimental drama has been ascribed, in part, to the idealising of the aspiring middling classes, and the depiction of the heroic merchant figure, as in *The London Merchant* and *The West Indian*. See Arthur Sherbo, *English Sentimental Drama* (Ann Arbor: Michigan State University Press, 1957), and Ernest Bernbaum, *The Drama of Sensibility: A Sketch of the History of English Sentimental Comedy and Domestic Tragedy, 1696–1780* (Gloucester, Massachusetts: Peter Smith, 1958).

93. D. G. Greene proposes that the unifying theme of Austen's novels is the clash of the rising middle class with the established aristocracy: 'In *Pride and Prejudice* it is the middle-class Bennets and Gardiners who compel the noble Fitzwilliams and Darcys to take them seriously; in *Persuasion*, it is Wentworths against Elliots; in *Northanger Abbey*, Morlands against Tilneys; in *Sense and Sensibility*, Dashwoods against Ferrarses ... her middle-class protaganists are as good a class as those who treat them superciliously.' See D. G. Greene, 'Jane Austen and the Peerage', *PMLA*, 68 (1953), pp. 1017–31, at p. 1028.

94. Naturally, her letters during this time contain various references to *Mansfield Park*, in particular Henry's comments and criticisms. Though Jane Austen wrote that she hoped to see it published 'before the end of April' (*Letters*, p. 262), it was announced by Egerton the publisher in the *Morning Chronicle* of 23 and 27 May and was no doubt published soon afterwards. See introductory note to Chapman's edition of *MP*.

95. During the first few weeks of the winter season, the two patent houses scheduled performances on three nights of the week, moving to six performances per week as the season progressed. See James J. Lynch, *Box, Pit and Gallery*, pp. 12–13.

96. Theatre historians have shown that interest in the theatre was by no means limited to certain social classes or economic groups. See Lynch, *Box, Pit and Gallery*, p. 199.

97. See Lynch, *Box, Pit and Gallery*, p. 143.

98. John Brewer, *The Pleasures of Imagination: English Culture in the Eighteenth Century* (London: HarperCollins, 1997), p. 340.

99. Donohue, *Theatre in the Age of Kean*, p. 144.

100. *Works of Hazlitt*, v, p. 173.

4: Early Works

1. Samuel Johnson's definition of the adjective is: 'Jocular; tending to raise laughter by unnatural or unsuitable language and images', and he defines the noun as 'ludicrous language or ideas; ridicule'. Samuel Johnson, *A Dictionary of the English Language*, 4 vols (London, 1756; repr. 1805). John Loftis in *Sheridan and the Drama of Georgian England* (Oxford: Blackwell, 1976), p. 144, cites the first definition of the noun by the *Oxford English Dictionary*. 'That species of literary composition, or of dramatic representation, which aims at exciting laughter by caricature of the manner or spirit of serious works, or by ludicrous treatment of their subject'. The

key point is that the comic effect is achieved by exaggeration of the original in order to elucidate its absurdities and limitations.

2. Park Honan argues that this article was written with Eliza de Feuillide in mind. She had visited the Austen brothers at Oxford in 1788. Honan, *Jane Austen: Her Life* (1987; revised edn, London: Phoenix, 1997), p. 56. This argument is supported by the fact that one of the sisters in Henry's burlesque is called Eliza. That Eliza was keen on burlesque is perhaps comfirmed by Jane Austen's dedication of *Love and Freindship* to her cousin.

3. James Austen, *The Loiterer*, 2 vols (Oxford: C. S. Rann, 1789–90), no. 32, pp. 13–14.

4. Ibid., p. 14.

5. See above, Chapter 1, for the playlets 'The Visit' and 'The Mystery'. Many of the non-dramatic sketches in *Volume the First*, written around 1787–90 when Jane Austen was between the ages of twelve and fifteen, incorporate farcical action. *Volume the Second* contains the two most sustained burlesques, 'Love and Freindship' and 'The History of England', dated 'June 13 1790' and 'November 26 1791' respectively (*MW*, p. 109 and p. 149). *Volume the Third* (1792–93) begins to show Austen intermingling burlesque with her first experiments in realistic social comedy.

6. John Loftis argues unequivocally that 'the most profound literary consequence of the Act has been the impulse that it gave to the development of the novel'. See John Loftis, *The Politics of Drama in Augustan England* (Oxford: Clarendon Press, 1963), pp. 128–53.

7. *The Tragedy of Tragedies: or Tom Thumb the Great*, in *The Beggar's Opera and Other Eighteenth-Century Plays*, ed. John Hampden (London: Dent, 1974), pp. 192, 201.

8. The most notorious example being the cruel jibe she makes about miscarriage: 'Mrs Hall of Sherbourn was brought to bed yesterday of a dead child, some weeks before she expected, oweing to a fright. – I suppose she happened unawares to look at her husband' (*Letters*, p. 17).

9. Garrick's farce *Bon Ton: or High Life above Stairs* and Townley's *High Life below Stairs* spring to mind.

10. David Garrick, *Bon Ton: or High Life Above Stairs*, in *The Plays of David Garrick*, ed. Gerald M. Berkowitz, 4 vols (New York and London: Garland, 1981), ii, p. 257. 'Love and Friendship' is a familiar phrase in eighteenth-century literature. Austen would have known it from Richardson's *Sir Charles Grandison* (1754), v, pp. 74–75, and from Henry Austen's article in *The Loiterer*. 'Let every girl who seeks for happiness conquer both her feelings and her passions. Let her avoid love and freindship' (no. 29). There is also a novel of the same name listed in the preface to Colman's after-piece *Polly Honeycombe*, which lists novels from a typical eighteenth-century circulating library.

11. The problem of accurately defining sentimentalism is explored by Arthur Sherbo in *English Sentimental Drama* (Ann Arbor: Michigan State University Press, 1957). See also Ernest Bernbaum's *The Drama of Sensibility: A Sketch of the History of English Sentimental Comedy and Domestic Tragedy*,

1696–1780 (Gloucester, Massachusetts: Peter Smith, 1958) for the standard work on English sentimental drama. John Loftis shows the 'two faces' of Sheridan's sentimentalism in *Sheridan and the Drama of Georgian England* (Oxford: Blackwell, 1976). See also Richard Bevis, *The Laughing Tradition* (Athens: University of Georgia Press, 1980), pp. 45–47, and John Mullan, *Sentiment and Sociability: The Language of Feeling in the Eighteenth Century* (Oxford: Clarendon Press, 1988; repr. 1997).

12. At the end of *Volume the First*, Austen had written a fragment called *A Beautiful Description of the Different Effects of Sensibility on Different Minds*. The excessive swooning fits of the dying heroine excite compassion from the author, indifference from her insensible sister, sighs from her melancholy husband and bad puns from the doctor who visits her on her death bed (*MW*, pp. 72–73).

13. Both texts are burlesqued in *Northanger Abbey*. For further examples of the sentimental novel see J. M. S. Tompkins, *The Popular Novel in England, 1770–1800* (Lincoln: University of Nebraska Press, 1932; repr. 1961).

14. *The Dramatic Works of Richard Brinsley Sheridan*, ed. Cecil Price, 2 vols (Oxford: Clarendon Press, 1973), ii, pp. 539–41. Centred text indicates lines from the play-within-the-play.

15. In *The West Indian*, Belcour is reunited with his father:

> STOCKWELL: I am your father.
> BELCOUR: My father! Do I live? … It is too much.

Richard Cumberland, *The West Indian: A Comedy* (London, 1771), repr. in *The Beggar's Opera and other Eighteenth Century Plays*, p. 405. Austen's scene is also a burlesque of Burney's *Evelina*, where Sir John Belmont discovers numerous unknown relatives: 'I have already a daughter … and it is not three days since, that I had the pleasure of discovering a son; how many more sons and daughters may be brought to me, I am yet to learn, but I am already, perfectly satisfied with the size of my family' (*Evelina*, p. 371).

16. *Dramatic Works of Sheridan*, ii, p. 548. Tilburina's speech is most obviously a parody of Ophelia. *Hamlet* was the mainpiece performed on the opening night of *The Critic*.

17. Loftis thus argues: 'His burlesque of the tyranny of the older generation in the persons of Sir Anthony Absolute and Mrs Malaprop should not conceal the force of the social reality which lay behind that tyranny – the custom among affluent families of arranging marriages with close attention to property settlements. Sheridan wrote in the interval between Richardson's *Clarissa*, and Jane Austen's *Pride and Prejudice*'. Loftis, *Sheridan and the Drama of Georgian England*, p. 46.

18. *Dramatic Works of Sheridan*, i, p. 408.

19. See Fintan O'Toole, *A Traitor's Kiss: The Life of Richard Brinsley Sheridan* (London: Granta, 1998), p. 125.

20. *Dramatic Works of Sheridan*, i, p. 415.

21. *Sanditon* also contains some of Austen's funniest satire on sensibility. The absurd Sir Edward Denham's taste for sentimental fiction is satirised, and

his penchant for modelling himself on Richardson's Lovelace suggests the corrupting effects of the 'exceptionable parts' of Richardson's novels (*MW*, p. 358).

5: From Play to Novel

1. Austen's play is quoted from *Jane Austen's 'Sir Charles Grandison'*, ed. Brian Southam (Oxford: Clarendon Press, 1980). For ease of reference, it is cited as 'Grandison', Richardson's novel as *Sir Charles Grandison*.

2. 'Grandison', ed. Southam, pp. 1–34.

3. See Mark Kinkead-Weekes, *Samuel Richardson: Dramatic Novelist* (London: Methuen, 1973); Margaret Anne Doody, *A Natural Passion: A Study of the Novels of Samuel Richardson* (London: Oxford University Press, 1974); Ira Konigsberg, *Samuel Richardson and the Dramatic Novel* (Lexington: University of Kentucky Press, 1968).

4. See George Sherburn, 'Samuel Richardson's Novels and the Theatre: A Theory Sketched', *Philological Quarterly*, 41 (1962), p. 328.

5. Samuel Richardson, *Clarissa*, ed. Angus Ross (London: Penguin, 1985), p. 764. This example is cited by Sherburn, 'Richardson's Novels', p. 328.

6. Sherburn, 'Samuel Richardson's Novels', p. 327.

7. See Konigsberg, *Dramatic Novel*, pp. 33–47.

8. Richardson, *Clarissa*, p. 626.

9. 'The First Epistle of the Second Book of Horace Imitated', line 172, *The Poems of Alexander Pope*, ed. John Butt (London: Methuen, 1963), p. 641.

10. 'What a delightful play might be form'd out of this piece. I am sure Mr Garrick will have it upon the stage': quoted, Doody, *A Natural Passion*, p. 280.

11. Samuel Richardson, *The History of Sir Charles Grandison*, ed. Jocelyn Harris, 3 vols (London: Oxford University Press, 1972), i, p. 273.

12. See *The Early Journals and Letters of Fanny Burney*, ed. Lars E. Troide and Stewart J. Cooke, 3 vols to date (Oxford: Clarendon Press, 1988–94), i, p. 202.

13. Kate Chisholm has noted this as one of many instances where Burney coined words that are now cited in the *OED*. See *Fanny Burney: Her Life* (London: Chatto and Windus, 1998), p. 83.

14. 'Grandison', p. 46. Austen had previously used the same joke in 'The Visit', where two characters are 'discovered': a theatrical term used in stage-directions to indicate that the characters are already on the stage when the curtain rises.

15. Richardson, *Sir Charles Grandison*, ii, p. 408.

16. 'Grandison', p. 44.

17. It is also noteworthy that there were a number of school-room abridgements of *Sir Charles Grandison*. Austen's burlesque play was a mockery not only of the original novel, but also of these popular bowdlerisations. 'The schoolroom versions were notably reticent in retailing the events at Paddington, where the threat of rape hangs heavy in the air. Jane Austen makes this the high point of her comic melodrama.

Far from closing her eyes to the strain of erotic titillation in Richardson, Jane Austen laughs it off the stage.' Southam, introduction to 'Grandison', p. 22.

18. In *The Funeral*, Steele dramatises two sisters of contrasting characters, Harriot and Sharlot. The coquettish and giddy Harriot is contrasted with the graver Sharlot. Doody suggests that Richardson has given his heroines the same names but reversed the roles, Doody, *A Natural Passion*, p. 287.

19. *Sir Charles Grandison*, ii, p. 99.

20. William Congreve, *The Way of the World*, ed. Brian Gibbons (2nd edn, London: A & C Black, 1994), act 1, scene 3, pp. 140–45.

21. See Frank W. Bradbrook, *Jane Austen and her Predecessors* (Cambridge: Cambridge University Press, 1966), p. 74.

22. *Sir Charles Grandison*, ii, p. 340.

23. 'Grandison', pp. 45, 51.

24. *Clarissa*, pp. 426, 430.

25. Ibid., p. 721.

26. Henry Fielding, *The History of the Adventures of Joseph Andrews and of his Friend Mr Abraham Adams and An Apology for the Life of Mrs Shamela Andrews*, ed. Douglas Brook-Davies (Oxford: Oxford University Press, 1980), p. 330.

27. *The Correspondence of Samuel Richardson*, ed. A. L. Barbauld, 6 vols (London, 1804), i, pp. xxviii.

28. *Selected Letters of Samuel Richardson*, ed. John Carroll (Oxford: Oxford University Press, 1964), p. 286.

29. The devices that come closest to doing so are voiceover and ironic editing. It was these techniques that made *Clueless* the most successful of the 1990s adaptations, despite its being the one that was least faithful to the surface of its original. The film took the plot of *Emma* and translated it to Beverly Hills, jettisoning the dialogue and yet retaining the spirit of a young girl's growth to self-knowledge. At the same time, the heroine was ironised by means of an art of directorial control strikingly akin to Austen's own authorial control. On this, see Nora Nachumi's excellent essay, '"As If!": Translating Austen's Ironic Narrator to Film', in *Jane Austen in Hollywood*, ed. Linda Troost and Sayre Greenfield (Lexington: University of Kentucky Press, 1998), pp. 130–37, and my final chapter.

30. This point is very well made by Claude Rawson, *Satire and Sentiment, 1660–1830* (Cambridge: Cambridge University Press, 1994), p. 281.

31. See Elizabeth Inchbald, *A Simple Story*, ed. Pamela Clemit (Harmondsworth: Penguin, 1996), p. viii.

32. See Elizabeth Inchbald, *A Simple Story* (1791) ed. J. M. S. Tompkins with a new introduction by Jane Spencer (Oxford: Oxford University Press, 1988), p. 15.

33. Ibid., p. 16.

34. Ibid., p. 110.

35. Ibid., p. 67.

36. James Boaden, *Memoirs of Mrs Inchbald*, 2 vols (London, 1833), ii, pp. 152–53.

37. Gary Kelly has suggested that the use of gestures supplanting that which words often fail to express came from Inchbald's experience as an actress on the London stage. See Gary Kelly, *The English Jacobin Novel, 1780–1805* (Oxford: Clarendon Press, 1976), p. 88.

6: Sense and Sensibility

1. *The Dramatic Works of Richard Brinsley Sheridan*, ed. Cecil Price, 2 vols (Oxford: Clarendon Press, 1973), i, p. 84.

2. Colman's hostility towards his female quixotic is suggested by the fact that she loses her lover by the end of the play without being cured of her romantically absurd notions. Furthermore, in the first edition of *Polly Honeycombe* (1760), Colman provides a preface warning of the dangers of novel-reading for young women.

3. *The Plays of Richard Steele*, ed. Shirley Strum Kenny (Oxford: Clarendon Press, 1971), p. 233.

4. See *Polly Honeycombe*, in *The Plays of George Colman the Elder*, ed. Kalman A. Burnim, 6 vols (New York and London: Garland, 1983), p. 41.

5. The lovely Arabella is considered to be out of her senses, and Colman picks up the motif: 'She's downright raving – mad as a March hare – I'll put her into Bedlam'. *Plays of Colman*, p. 41.

6. *Dramatic Works of Sheridan*, i, p. 123.

7. See John Brewer, *The Pleasures of the Imagination: English Culture in the Eighteenth Century* (London: HarperCollins, 1997), pp. 169–97.

8. Paradoxically, what Austen's foolish, deluded, novel-reading heroine ultimately discovers is that reading books can prepare you for life, and teach you to distrust paternal authority. See Claudia L. Johnson, *Jane Austen: Women, Politics and the Novel* (Chicago: University of Chicago Press, 1988), pp. 39–43.

9. Colman's exemplification of the traffic between drama and the novel is apparent not only in *Polly Honeycombe*, but also in *The Jealous Wife*, which openly acknowledges a debt to Fielding's *Tom Jones*. See John Loftis, *Sheridan and the Drama of Georgian England* (Oxford: Blackwell, 1976), p. 28.

10. See *PP*, p. 274. Both girls are attracted to 'a bit of red cloth' and show disrespect for Fordyce's sermons. Lydia Languish tears out pages of Fordyce's sermons for curl papers. See also E. E. Phare, 'Lydia Languish, Lydia Bennet, and Dr Fordyce's Sermons', *Notes and Queries*, 209 (1964), pp. 231–32.

11. *Dramatic Works of Sheridan*, i, p. 135.

12. Ibid., i, pp. 135, 82.

13. Ibid., i, pp. 130–31.

14. Ironically, Faulkland was first admired by the public as a true picture of a sentimental hero. As John Loftis argues, 'Faulkland serves as a reminder that the "age of sensibility" had not passed, and Sheridan shares an affectionate regard for sensibility even while burlesquing it'. See Loftis, *Sheridan and the Drama of Georgian England*, p. 51. Eighteenth-century

audiences had more sympathy for him than we have, judging by the reviews. The *Morning Chronicle* wrote, 'he is a beautiful exotic, and tho' not found in every garden, we cannot deny it may be in some; the exquisite refinement in his disposition, opposed to the noble simplicity, tenderness, and candor of Julia's, gives rise to some of the most affecting sentimental scenes I ever remember to have met with'. See *Dramatic Works of Sheridan*, i, p. 47. However John Bernard, in *Retrospections of the Stage* (1830), acidly commented that 'Faulkland and Julia (which Sheridan had obviously introduced to conciliate the sentimentalists, but which in the present day are considered heavy incumbrances) were the characters most favourably received' (ibid., i, p. 55). Sheridan's critique of sentimentalism is perhaps clouded by his ambiguous attitude towards Faulkland, and the fact that he pragmatically increased some of his sentimental speeches after the first unsuccessful performance of the play.

15. See Loftis, *Sheridan and the Drama*, p. 52.
16. See Kenneth Molar, *Jane Austen's Art of Allusion* (Lincoln: University of Nebraska Press, 1977), and J. M. S. Tomkins, '"Elinor and Marianne": A Note on Jane Austen', *Review of English Studies*, 16 (1940), pp. 33–43.
17. *False Delicacy* in *The Plays of Hugh Kelly*, ed. Larry Carver and Mary J. H. Gross (New York and London: Garland, 1980), pp. 19–20.
18. See Claude Rawson's 'Some Remarks on Eighteenth-Century "Delicacy", with a Note on Hugh Kelly's *False Delicacy* (1768)', *JEGP*, 61 (1962), pp. 1–13, at p. 12. Rawson also provides notes on 'Delicacy' in *Order from Confusion Sprung: Studies in Eighteenth-Century Literature from Swift to Cowper* (London: Allen and Unwin, 1985), pp. 341–54.
19. *Dramatic Works of Sheridan*, i, p. 130.
20. Ibid., i, p. 144.
21. This was one of the plays performed in the Kent private theatricals in 1805, with Fanny Knight.
22. Polly Honeycombe's closing lines to her lover, Scribble, are: 'You may depend upon my constancy and affection. I never read of any lady's giving up her lover, to submit to the absurd election of her parents', *Polly Honeycombe*, p. 41. Lydia Languish is distressed to find that her romantic fantasies are dashed when she discovers that she has her guardian's consent to marriage: 'So, while *I* fondly imagined we were deceiving my relations … my hopes are to be crush'd at once, by my Aunt's consent and approbation!' *Dramatic Works of Sheridan*, ii, p. 26.
23. *Dramatic Works of Sheridan*, i, p. 97.
24. Ibid., i, p. 103.
25. See Rawson, *Order From Confusion Sprung*, pp. 271–84, a study of dialogue and authorial presence in Fielding's novels and plays that also has striking implications for Jane Austen's implementation of theatrical devices.
26. 'It may be proper to return to the hero of this Novel, the brother of Alice, of whom I beleive I have scarcely ever had the occasion to speak' (*MW*, pp. 24–25).

27. 'For myself, I confess that *I* can only pity Miss Manwaring, who coming to Town & putting herself to an expense in Cloathes, which impoverished her for two years, on purpose to secure him, was defrauded of her due by a Woman ten years older than herself' (*MW*, p. 313).

7: Pride and Prejudice

1. See W. and R. A. Austen-Leigh, *Jane Austen: A Family Record*, rev. and enlarged by Deirdre Le Faye (London: British Library, 1989), p. 175. Sheridan, as manager of Drury Lane, was quick to persuade the young Fanny Burney to write a stage comedy after the success of *Evelina*. He was impressed with Burney's handling of different social classes, and felt that her comic juxtapositions of vulgar and aristocratic characters would translate well to the stage. The quasi-dramatic qualities of *Evelina* also appealed to Austen, who read the comic parts aloud to her family, her niece Caroline describing the experience as being like a play.

2. *Jane Austen: The Critical Heritage*, ed. Brian Southam, 2 vols (London: Routledge and Kegan Paul, 1968–87), i, pp. 45–46.

3. *Which is the Man?*, in *The Plays of Hannah Cowley*, ed. Frederick M. Link, 2 vols (New York and London: Garland, 1979), i, pp. 51, 53.

4. Cowley's comedy frequently alludes to *Sir Charles Grandison* – Richardson's endless debates between the sexes were often refashioned in the plays of the period.

5. *Which is the Man?*, p. 47.

6. Ibid., p. 54.

7. See, for example, Marvin Mudrick, *Jane Austen: Irony as Defense and Discovery* (Princeton: Princeton University Press, 1952), p. 205.

8. *Letters*, p. 74, quoting act 5, scene 5 of *The Belle's Stratagem*. See *Plays of Hannah Cowley*, i, p. 79.

9. *Plays of Hannah Cowley*, i, p. 81.

10. As one sensitive critic of *Emma* suggests: 'The social world of the novel is peopled with upwardly and downwardly mobile individuals. It is viewed not from the perspective of frozen class division but from a perspective of living change. It is not France in the 1780s but England at the beginning of the nineteenth century.' Julia Prewitt Brown, *Jane Austen's Novels: Social Change and Literary Form*, chapter on *Emma* reprinted in *Jane Austen's 'Emma', Modern Critical Interpretations*, ed. Harold Bloom (New York: Chelsea House, 1987), p. 57.

11. See Marilyn Butler, 'History, Politics, and Religion', in *The Jane Austen Handbook*, ed. J. David Grey (London: Athlone, 1986), p. 202.

12. Act 5, scene 1, in Oliver Goldsmith, *She Stoops to Conquer*, ed. Tom Davis (London: Ernest Benn, 1979), p. 79.

13. Darcy admits how her words stung him: 'Your reproof, so well applied, I shall never forget: "had you behaved in a more gentleman-like manner. " Those were your words. You know not, you can scarcely conceive, how they have tortured me' (*PP*, p. 367).

14. See discussion above in Chapter 2. Also Joseph Donohue, *Theatre in the Age of Kean* (Oxford: Blackwell, 1975), p. 17.

15. Plays such as John Burgoyne's *Heiress* (1786), George Colman the Elder's *Man of Business* (1774), Arthur Murphy's *The Citizen* (1761), Hannah Cowley's *Who's the Dupe?* and George Colman the Younger's *The Heir at Law* (1797) crudely satirised the merchant classes as ignorant, ill-educated and money-grubbing.

16. *Plays of Hannah Cowley*, i, p. 16.

17. *A Busy Day*, act 3, scene 3, in *The Complete Plays of Frances Burney*, ed. Peter Sabor, 2 vols (Montreal: McGill-Queen's University Press, 1995), i, p. 350.

8: Lover's Vows

1. See Marvin Mudrick's influential *Jane Austen: Irony as Defense and Discovery* (Princeton: Princeton University Press, 1952). '*Mansfield Park* has always been more respected than loved', observes Marilyn Butler: Jane Austen, *Mansfield Park*, ed. James Kinsley with a new introduction by Marilyn Butler (Oxford: Oxford University Press, 1990), p. vii.

2. Notably from Kingsley Amis in his 'What Became of Jane Austen?' *Spectator*, 4 October 1957, p. 339. Tony Tanner has observed that 'nobody has ever fallen in love with Fanny Price'. See Tony Tanner, *Jane Austen* (London: Macmillan, 1986), p. 143. Jane Austen's mother thought her 'insipid' and Reginald Farrer declared that Henry Crawford had a 'near miss', since 'fiction holds no heroine more repulsive in her cast-iron self righteousness and steely rigidity of prejudice' than Fanny. See Reginald Farrer, 'Jane Austen's *Gran Refiuto*', in *Sense and Sensibility, Pride and Prejudice and Mansfield Park: A Casebook*, ed. B. C. Southam (London: Macmillan, 1976), pp. 210–11.

3. Pam Perkins has argued that Mary Crawford and Fanny Price represent (respectively) 'laughing' and 'sentimental' comedy. See 'A Subdued Gaiety: The Comedy of *Mansfield Park*', *Nineteenth-Century Literature*, 48 (1993), pp. 1–25.

4. See James Boaden, *Memoirs of Mrs Inchbald*, 2 vols (London: 1833), ii, p. 20.

5. See *The London Stage, 1660–1800*, ed. Emmett L. Avery et al., 5 parts in 11 vols (Carbondale, Illinois: Southern Illinois University Press, 1960–68), part 5, 1776–800, ed. Charles Beecher Hogan, p. 2116, for receipts and *Times* review (13 October 1798): '*Lovers' Vows* continues to exercise a resistless controul over the feelings of the audience. The fifth act is, without exception, worked up with more art and nature, and is more impressive in its termination, than any denouement which the English stage has hitherto furnished.'

6. See above, Chapter 2.

7. Marilyn Butler, for instance, has argued that Kotzebue's name alone would have alerted readers to the moral and political dangers of *Lovers' Vows* because his works were synonymous with the German drama so despised by anti-Jacobins: 'There could be no doubt in the minds of Jane Austen and most of her readers that the name of Kotzebue was synonymous with everything most sinister in German Literature of the period.' Kotzebue is

said to be synonymous with political subversion and dangerous Jacobin messages about 'freedom in sexual matters and defiance of traditional restraints'. Marilyn Butler, *Jane Austen and the War of Ideas* (Oxford: Clarendon Press, 1975), pp. 233–34. This sort of political reading has condemned Austen to the status of a conservative propagandist. Even though Butler has softened her position since the publication of her influential *Jane Austen and the War of Ideas*, she still insists upon 'Austen's evident detestation of Kotzebue's play' (introduction to 1990 Oxford World's Classics edition of *Mansfield Park*). Butler supports her anti-Kotzebue argument with the false supposition that Austen was influenced by the Evangelical movement in her suspicion of theatre. For a demonstration that Austen was not Evangelical, see Michael Williams, *Jane Austen: Six Novels and their Methods* (London: Macmillan, 1986), pp. 92–97; see also David Monaghan, '*Mansfield Park* and Evangelicalism: A Reassessment', *Nineteenth-Century Fiction*, 33 (1978), pp. 215–30.

Butler's influential reading of *Lovers' Vows*, along with the older but still frequently cited work of Lionel Trilling on the novelist's rejection of 'the histrionic art', has put the seal on the critical orthodoxy that asserts Austen's condemnation of private theatricals. Even though the evidence of Austen's life conflicts strongly with the arguments advocated by Butler and Trilling, and even though a plethora of critical ambiguity surrounds the play-acting sequence in *Mansfield Park*, few have challenged the assumption that Austen was hostile to the drama.

8. Margaret Kirkham, 'The Theatricals in *Mansfield Park* and "Frederick" in *Lovers' Vows*', *Notes and Queries*, 220 (1975), pp. 389–99.

9. *Mansfield Park* has often been misread as a result of the misinterpretation of another Austen letter, in which she asks a question about 'ordination' – she does *not* say, as was once supposed, that ordination would be the 'subject' of her new novel. Margaret Kirkham neatly suggests that we would do better to begin *Mansfield Park* with knowledge of the 'Frederick' letter, rather than the 'ordination' one: 'Almost everyone who reads *Mansfield Park* now reads some kind of brief introduction first, so he is more likely than not to believe before he starts that Jane Austen said its subject was ordination and that in this period of her life she had become sympathetic to the Evangelical outlook. If the reader started instead with the knowledge that Jane Austen had once seen a very funny performance of *Lovers' Vows* and that a good many years later, just after *Mansfield Park* was finished, she was ready to laugh at the remembrance of the chief male character in it, he might perhaps begin reading what he would expect to be a comedy. The benefits that this might eventually bring, even if improperly derived, would be very considerable', Kirkham, 'Theatricals', p. 390. Kirkham raises a most telling point when she observes that the misunderstanding of the notorious ordination letter and the misleading application of remarks about the Evangelicals, made in very select circumstances to Fanny Knight, are interpretations that have influenced critical writings on *Mansfield Park*. It is an irony, she argues, that the laughter associated with *Lovers' Vows* has been twisted into moral disapprobation and censure.

10. William Reitzel cites a theatre review from the *Porcupine* in 1801 condemning the play for its dangerous political sentiments as well as its dramatic inferiority: 'Independent of the morality of this piece, the first act is the heaviest bundle of dramatic lumber ever tolerated on the boards of an English theatre.' William Reitzel, '*Mansfield Park* and *Lovers' Vows*', *Review of English Studies*, 9 (1933), p. 453.

11. Frederick Howard, Earl of Carlisle, *Thoughts upon the Present Conditions of the Stage* (London, 1808), pp. 5, 22.

12. Nicholas Rowe, *Jane Shore: A Tragedy as Performed at the Theatre-Royal in Drury Lane, Regulated from the Prompt-Book, by Permission of the Managers, by Mr Hopkins, Prompter* (London, 1776), p. 18.

13. See Charles Inigo Jones, *Memoirs of Miss O'Neill* (London, 1816), p. 61.

14. Ibid., p. 49.

15. See William Dunlap, *The Life and Time of George Frederick Cooke*, 2 vols (2nd edn, London, 1815), p. 295.

16. Ibid., p. 295.

17. William Dunlap, *A History of the American Theatre* (New York, 1832), p. 95.

18. Gary Kelly considers the authorship of Mrs Inchbald's *Lovers' Vows* in *Mansfield Park* as controversial 'because of the impropriety of its social *mores* rather than the Jacobinism of its political views'. See *The English Jacobin Novel, 1780–1805* (Oxford: Clarendon Press, 1976), p. 65.

19. The question of Inchbald's politics remains ambiguous. Although *Lovers' Vows* was rendered less controversial than Kotzebue's original play, Inchbald's liberal sympathies with radical and bohemian circles had been noted in the reaction to many of her works. Her play *Every One Has His Fault* was particularly controversial, inciting a riot in the Portsmouth Theatre in 1795. But according to evidence from her biographer James Boaden, her royalist sympathies and strict sense of female decorum defy stringent readings of her supposed radicalism.

20. Inchbald's phrase for her revision of Amelia's style of language might fittingly be applied to Mary Crawford, the mistress of 'whimsical insinuations'. See *MP*, p. 478.

21. Sheridan's adaptation of Kotzebue's *Pizarro* was also highly successful. Like Inchbald, he showed prudence and business acumen in excising the controversial aspects of Kotzebue's play. In particular the part of Elvira, played by Sarah Siddons, was heightened from a soldier's whore to a dignified fallen woman.

22. In *Northanger Abbey* Austen plays a double game in her literary satire. Far from discovering that books do not equip one for dealing with the harsh realities of social snobbery, Catherine's reading of Gothic fiction *does* prepare and influence her distrust of General Tilney's character, so that by the end of the novel her initial suspicions are confirmed: 'in suspecting General Tilney of either murdering or shutting up his wife, she had scarcely sinned against his character, or magnified his cruelty' (*NA*, p. 247).

23. The most stimulating of previous comparisons of *Lovers' Vows* and *Mansfield Park* is by Dvora Zelicovici, who interprets the allusive relationship as one of calculated counter-effectiveness: 'Far from exalting

sexual liberty, *Lovers' Vows* exposes the viciousness of immoral conduct and its miserable consequences. It does not condone and reward licence, but requires repentance and restitution (not retribution).' The point is that the characters in *Mansfield Park* fail to learn the moral messages of the play. Zelicovici, 'The Inefficacy of *Lovers' Vows*', *English Literary History*, 50 (1983), pp. 531–40.

24. Tony Tanner, *Jane Austen* (London: Macmillan, 1986), p. 164; plot summary based on *The Oxford Companion to English Literature*.

25. In 1751 Samuel Richardson had written in Johnson's *Rambler* (no. 97) 'That a young lady should be in love, and the love of the young gentleman undeclared, is an heterodoxy which prudence, and even policy, must not allow.' Samuel Johnson, *The Rambler* (London: Dent, 1953), p. 168. Austen wittily responded in *Northanger Abbey*: 'for if it be true, as a celebrated writer has maintained, that no young lady can be justified in falling in love before the gentleman's love is declared, it must be very improper that a young lady should dream of a gentleman before the gentleman is first known to have dreamt of her' (*NA*, pp. 29–30).

26. There are different kinds of prohibition dividing the hero from the heroine, ranging from religion in *Grandison* to social status in *Lovers' Vows*.

27. The notorious lovers re-emerged in Pope's *Eloise to Abelard* (1717), in Rousseau's *La nouvelle Héloïse* (1761) and Mackenzie's *Julia de Roubigné* (1777). On this tradition, see my article 'A Simple Story: From Inchbald to Austen', *Romanticism*, 5 (1999), pp. 161–72.

28. Professed indifference to her charms is precisely what animates Lady Susan's interest in De Courcy: 'There is an exquisite pleasure in subduing an insolent spirit, in making a person predetermined to dislike, acknowledge one's superiority' (*MW*, p. 254).

29. Throughout Speculation, both Edmund and Mary are found surreptitiously continuing the underground debate that has been running between them ever since the visit to Sotherton. Under cover of the card game, they make their intentions known to each other in coded comments ostensibly spoken to others. Edmund's guarded remark to Henry that the humble Thornton Lacey 'must suffice me; and I hope all who care about me' is answered by Mary, as is intended, by her equivocal comment to William Price that 'she will stake her last like a woman of spirit'. Both Mary and Edmund continue this surreptitious debate until Sir Thomas's 'sermon' unceremoniously puts an end to it, and 'all the agreeable of *her* speculation was over for that hour' (*MP*, p. 248).

30. Act 3, scene 2 (*MP*, p. 506). *Lovers' Vows* is quoted from the text in Chapman's Oxford edition of *MP*, but so that references may be traced in other editions, references are given in the form of act and scene number. The most readily accessible text is that in the World's Classics, *Five Romantic Plays*, ed. Paul Baines and Edward Burns (Oxford: Oxford University Press, 2000).

31. *Alexander Pope: Selected Poetry* (London: Penguin, 1985), p. 71.

32. Jean-Jacques Rousseau, *Eloisa: or A Series of Original Letters*, 2 vols (1803; repr. Oxford: Woodstock Books, 1989), i, p. 114.

33. Fanny and Amelia show little respect for libertines who trifle with women. Fanny tells Mary: 'I cannot think well of a man who sports with any woman's feelings' (*MP*, p. 363), and Amelia censures Count Cassel for his ill treatment of young women: 'For our Butler told my waiting-maid of a poor young creature who has been deceived, undone; and she, and her whole family, involved in shame and sorrow by his perfidy' (*MP*, p. 516).

34. Richardson, *Sir Charles Grandison*, ed. Jocelyn Harris, 3 vols (London: Oxford University Press, 1972), ii, p. 230.

35. In *Northanger Abbey*, Henry Tilney compares women's choice in marriage to their limited powers in choosing a dancing partner – an effective image of courtship ritual: 'I consider a country dance as an emblem of marriage … in both, man has the advantage of choice, woman only the power of refusal' (*NA*, pp. 76–77). Women are not initiators of choice in courtship, but they can resist an offer, as Elizabeth Bennet proves by her refusal of Collins and Darcy.

36. Henry Mackenzie, *The Man of Feeling: and Julia de Roubigné* (London, 1832), p. 162.

37. Wildenhaim's misapprehension gives rise to a number of puns and *double entendres*:

> BARON: However, I will send Mr Anhalt to you –
> AMELIA: [*much pleased*] Do, papa.
> BARON: He shall explain to you my sentiments. [*Rings.*] A clergyman can do this better than – [*Enter servant.*] Go directly to Mr Anhalt, tell him that I shall be glad to see him for a quarter of an hour if he is not engaged. [*Exit servant.*]
> AMELIA: [*calls after him*] Wish him a good morning from me. (*LV*, act 2, scene 2; in *MP*, p. 496)

9: Mansfield Park

1. Fanny's low opinion of Henry Crawford is compelled to undergo a change when he shows himself capable of 'ardent, disinterested love', though she connects his previous ill-conduct with Sotherton and the private theatricals (see *MP*, p. 328).

2. See Isobel Armstrong, *Jane Austen: Mansfield Park*, Penguin Critical Studies (Harmondsworth: Penguin, 1988), pp. 62–65.

3. Fanny's presence in the rehearsals of *Lovers' Vows* is essential, of course, as she alone must be privy to Henry Crawford's conduct.

4. 'After having so nobly disentagled themselves from the shackles of parental authority, by a Clandestine Marriage …' (*MW*, p. 87).

5. Austen saw *The Clandestine Marriage* on 15 September 1813, at Covent Garden. Her lukewarm reaction to the new Lord Ogleby suggests that she had seen the play before. See above, Chapter 3. *Mansfield Park* was begun about February 1811 and finished 'soon after June 1813' (see Chapman's introductory note to *MP*, p. xi).

6. The plot of Garrick's and Colman's comedy turns upon a secret – the clandestine marriage between Fanny Sterling and Lovewell – which gives

rise to various incongruous and comic misunderstandings. Fanny is bound by a promise to her husband to keep her marriage to Lovewell a secret, until an appropriate time, but in the meantime is harassed by other would-be suitors, one of whom has switched his affections from her elder sister. Lovewell wishes to delay the news, fearing that Fanny's avaricious father and interfering aunt will disinherit them. The lecherous Lord Ogleby mistakenly believes that Fanny's secret love is for him, when she unburdens herself to tell him that she is devoted to another man, and places herself under his protection in a comic scene of misunderstandings and cross-purposes.

7. Elizabeth Inchbald, *The Clandestine Marriage*, in *The British Theatre: or A Collection of Plays, with Biographical and Critical Remarks by Mrs Inchbald*, 25 vols (London, 1808), xvi, p. 36.

8. *The Clandestine Marriage*, pp. 36, 38.

9. Ibid., pp. 38–39.

10. Ibid., p. 37.

11. Both the corpulent Rushworth and the delicate Fanny are rendered breathless by the heat and emotion of the day. The hot weather contributes to the mishaps and confusions.

12. Mary Wollstonecraft, *Mary and The Wrongs of Woman*, ed. James Kinsley and Gary Kelly (Oxford: Oxford University Press, 1980), p. 155. See also Margaret Kirkham, *Jane Austen: Feminism and Fiction* (London; Athlone, 1997), p. 37.

13. In *Clarissa*, the rake Lovelace doesn't repent, unlike the reformed rake Loveless in *Love's Last Shift*. Richardson's deliberate and ironic allusion to Loveless/Lovelace is yet another telling example of the traffic between the drama and the novel. Richardson's assumption is that the reader will know the dramatic repertoire, so the irony of expectation is intensified when Lovelace does not reform.

14. *The Clandestine Marriage*, p. 56.

15. Ibid., pp. 39–40.

16. Ibid., p. 43.

17. Ibid., pp. 44, 63, 64.

18. Tom's importance for the novel more generally is recognised by Roger Sales in *Jane Austen and Representations of Regency England* (London and New York: Routledge, 1994), pp. 93–106.

19. Duberley is spelt thus by Austen and I will use her spelling, although 'Duberly' is printed in the text of *The Heir at Law*.

20. *The Heir at Law*, in *The Plays of George Colman the Younger*, ed. Peter Tasch, 2 vols (New York and London: Garland, 1981).

21. See introduction to Colman's *Plays*, i, p. xli. The play was performed twenty-eight times during the summer of 1797. Austen stayed in Bath during the latter part of 1797, and may well have attended a performance of the play on 19 November.

22. *Heir at Law*, p. 41. 'Cacology' means 'Bad choice of words; bad pronunciation'. Dowlas mispronounces it as 'cakelology'.

23. See Gillian Russell, *The Theatres of War: Performance, Politics, and Society, 1793–1815* (Oxford: Clarendon Press, 1995), p. 132.

24. *The Heir at Law*, p. 38.
25. Ibid., p. 31.
26. Ibid., p. 64.
27. As A. Walton Litz points out, Tom takes on a triple role in *Lovers' Vows*, playing Butler, Landlord and Cottager. A. Walton Litz, *Jane Austen: A Study of her Artistic Development* (London: Chatto and Windus, 1965), p. 123. Tom later regrets this and wishes that the play could be changed.
28. C. Baron Wilson, *Our Actresses*, 2 vols (London, 1844), i, p. 105.
29. See 'Petronius Arbiter', *Memoirs of the Present Countess of Derby* (London, 1797).
30. See *Truth Opposed to Fiction: or An Impartial Review of the Late Earl of Barrymore by a Personal Observer* (London, 1793).
31. See *MW*, p. 29.
32. In Goldsmith's comedy, it is not only Marlow who is uncomfortable with genteel women and happy in the company of 'females of another class'. Tony Lumpkin and Mr Hardcastle are more relaxed in the company of their servants than of their genteel guests. At the arrival of Marlow and Hastings, Lumpkin asks his yokel friends to leave with the words, 'Gentlemen ... they mayn't be good enough company for you'. See Oliver Goldsmith, *She Stoops to Conquer*, ed. Tom Davies (London: A&C Black, 1979), p. 18.
33. *My Grandmother* was first performed 16 December 1793 at the Haymarket Theatre, but soon became so popular that it was performed as a mainpiece.
34. The significance of the play's deeply ironic title is made doubly clear later on in Mrs Norris's description of the play to Lady Bertram, 'It is about Lovers' Vows' (*MP*, p. 167). I cannot concur with Chapman's proposal (*MP*, p. 544) that Austen is suggesting Mrs Norris's theatrical ignorance in this comment. I would suggest quite the reverse: that, although she earlier claims that she doesn't know the play, she knows enough about it to screen her sister from watching the rehearsal. As Mrs Norris bluntly confirms, the play *is* 'about Lovers' Vows'. On the other hand, Rushworth's comment in the first edition *is* highly suggestive of theatrical ignorance. In the first edition he says 'it is to be called Lovers' Vows', but this was changed in the second edition to 'it is to be Lovers' Vows' (*MP*, p. 138). Chapman writes that Austen 'may have repented of the hit at poor Mr Rushworth (perhaps in consideration of his having seen the play in London)', *MP*, p. 544. This seems a good explanation, although we must lament this loss of Rushworth's blunder, which would have played off nicely against Tom's theatrical sophistication and wit.
35. See *MP*, pp. 176 and 191–94.
36. See Alan S. Downer, 'Nature to Advantage Dressed: Eighteenth-Century Acting', *PMLA*, 58 (1943), pp. 1002–37; Lily B. Campbell, 'The Rise of a Theory of Stage Presentation in England during the Eighteenth Century', *PMLA*, 32 (1917), pp. 163–200.
37. See Thomas Davies, *Memoirs of Garrick*, 2 vols (Boston, 1818), i, p. 46.
38. *Memoirs of Richard Cumberland*, ed. Henry Flanders (1856; repr. New York: Benjamin Blom, 1969), p. 47.

39. Davies records: 'After the short ejaculation of "Angels and ministers of grace, defend us!" he endeavoured to conquer that fear and terror into which he was naturally thrown by the first sight of the vision, and uttered the remainder of the address calmly, but respectfully, and with a firm tone of voice, as from one who had subdued his timidity and apprehension.' Thomas Davies, *Dramatic Miscellanies*, 3 vols (London, 1785), iii, p. 30.

40. See Downer, 'Nature to Advantage Dressed', p. 1021.

41. Murphy describes Garrick's rescue of the drama 'from its lowest ebb: in tragedy, declamation roared in a most unnatural strain; rant was passion; whining was grief; vociferation was terror, and drawling accents were the voice of love'. See Murphy's *Life of David Garrick*, 2 vols (London, 1801), i, p. 17. Davies records: 'Mr Garrick shone forth like a theatrical Newton; he threw new light on elocution and action; he banished ranting, bombast and grimace; and restored nature, ease, simplicity, and genuine humour' (ibid., i, p. 45).

42. See Hunt's *Dramatic Essays*, ed. William Archer and Robert W. Lowe (London, 1894), p. 13.

43. See Boswell's *Life of Johnson*, ed. George Birkbeck Hill, 6 vols (Oxford, 1937), iv, pp. 243–44.

44. Henry Fielding, *The History of Tom Jones*, ed. Fredson Bowers, 2 vols (Oxford: Oxford University Press, 1975), ii, pp. 852–57.

45. Ibid., ii, p. 857.

46. A number of acting handbooks were published during the latter part of the eighteenth century. Macklin even established a training school to advocate his naturalistic approach. See *Restoration and Georgian England*, ed. David Thomas, and Arnold Hare, *Theatre in Europe: A Documentary History* (Cambridge: Cambridge University Press, 1989), pp. 342–48.

47. The words 'nature' and 'feeling' were often applied to Kean. Sir George Beaumont raved that 'no actor since Garrick exhibited so much genuine *feeling of nature*', praising Kean as 'wholly free from the measured and artificial practise of the Kemble school'. See Harold Newcombe Hillebrand, *Edmund Kean* (New York: Columbia University Press, 1933), p. 119. Byron was mesmerised by Kean and recorded his impression in his journal: 'Just returned from seeing Kean in Richard. By Jove, he is a soul! Life – nature – truth – without exaggeration or diminution … Richard is a man; and Kean is Richard.' See *Byron's Life, Letters and Journals*, ed. Thomas Moore (London, 1854), p. 222.

48. Austen is keenly aware of the necessity of certain kinds of social conduct, which may conflict with the beliefs of the individual. In *Sense and Sensibility*, Elinor's prudent social conduct is contrasted with Marianne's often ill-judged insistence upon being true to herself. See above, Chapter 6.

49. See *Biographical Dictionary of Actors*, xvi, pp. 314–19.

50. See William Hawkins, *Miscellanies in Verse and Prose and Theatrical Biography* (London, 1792), p. 63.

51. See John Bernard, *Retrospections of the Stage*, 2 vols (London, 1830), i, pp. 278–80.

52. This was Hannah More's description of Crawford in a letter to Garrick. See *Biographical Dictionary of Actors*, iv, p. 34. When Crawford married Ann, in 1778, she was the leading tragedienne at Covent Garden and was able to get an engagement for her husband. They then went to Drury Lane, but left after a season. She soon left him and tried to recover her previous glory. See Thomas Gilliland, *Dramatic Mirror*, 2 vols (London, 1808).

53. Thomas Campbell, *Life of Mrs Siddons* (New York, 1834), p. 87.

54. *Truth Opposed to Fiction*, pp. 34–45.

55. The play opens with a short scene between Landlord/Tom and Agatha/Maria, then with Frederick/Henry, Agatha/Maria and Landlord/Tom, and then the Landlord exits, leaving Agatha and Frederick centre stage.

10: Emma

1. Mr Weston comes from a 'respectable family, which for the last two or three generations had been rising into gentility and property' (*E*, p. 15). His fortune, acquired by trade, has enabled him to purchase a small estate. See Juliet McMaster, 'Class', in *The Cambridge Companion to Jane Austen*, ed. Edward Copeland and Juliet McMaster (Cambridge: Cambridge University Press, 1997), pp. 115–30.

2. Emma is delighted when Mrs Weston gives birth to a daughter: 'She would not acknowledge that it was with any view of making a match for her, hereafter, with either of Isabella's sons' (*E*, p. 461).

3. *The Clandestine Marriage* and *A New Way to Pay Old Debts* held the stage with notable success throughout Austen's lifetime.

4. This technique has been much discussed by critics. See especially A. Walton Litz, *Jane Austen: A Study of her Artistic Development* (London: Chatto and Windus, 1965), pp. 146–47.

5. Julia Prewitt-Brown has noted that Miss Bates's small apartment joins the older gentry (Woodhouses and Knightleys), the new rich (Coles), and the lower-middle to lower-class townspeople and clerks: 'She represents Highbury's fluidity and mobility'. See Prewitt-Brown, 'Civilizations and the Contentment of *Emma*', in *Modern Critical Interpretations: Jane Austen's Emma*, ed. Harold Bloom (New York and Philadelphia: Bloom's Literary Criticism, 1987), p. 55.

6. In Burney's play *A Busy Day* the heroine is devoted to her servant, Mungo, whereas her newly rich family treat him with contempt.

7. Critics have noted the similarities between Emma and Mrs Elton, but, as Claudia Johnson suggests, Austen contrasts them to distinguish between the proper and improper use of social position. Mrs Elton's leadership, for example, depends upon the insistent publicity of herself as Lady Patroness, and the humiliation of those who are socially inferior to her. See Claudia L. Johnson, *Jane Austen: Women, Politics and the Novel* (Chicago: University of Chicago Press, 1988), pp. 129–30.

8. One exception is when she enters a private discussion with her trusted friends, Mrs Weston and Mr Knightley, concerning Mrs Elton's injurious treatment of Jane Fairfax (*E*, pp. 286–89).

9. They conduct a polite row on Box Hill, unbeknown to the rest of the party: 'How many a man has committed himself on a short acquaintance, and rued it all the rest of his life' (*E*, p. 372). Jane replies: 'I would be understood to mean, that it can be only weak, irresolute characters (whose happiness must be always at the mercy of chance), who will suffer an unfortunate acquaintance to be an inconvenience, an oppression for ever' (*E*, p. 373).

10. 'There is a pattern in the novel of vulnerable single woman, whom it is the social duty of the strong and the rich to protect': Marilyn Butler, *Jane Austen and the War of Ideas* (Oxford: Clarendon Press, 1975; repr; 1987), p. 257.

11. Lionel Trilling remains especially influential in this regard. See, in particular, his *Sincerity and Authenticity* (London: Oxford University Press, 1972), pp. 75–78. My own reading of Austen is closer to that of Joseph Litvak in his *Caught in the Act: Theatricality in the Nineteenth-Century Novel* (Berkeley: University of California Press, 1993). Jane Austen's characters act all the time, so even Fanny Price cannot help but play a part: 'All along in eschewing acting, Fanny has in fact been playing a role, albeit "sincerely"… From Henry's performance she learns not the necessity of acting, but the impossibility of *not* acting.' Litvak, *Caught in the Act*, p. 21.

11: Why She Is a Hit in Hollywood

1. Desson Howe, '"Persuasion": Worth Waiting For', *Washington Post*, 20 October 1995.

2. Kenneth Turan, 'Movie Review: An Austen-tatious Year', *Los Angeles Times*, 13 December 1995.

3. Linda Troost and Sayre Greenfield (eds), *Jane Austen in Hollywood* (Lexington: University of Kentucky Press, 1998), p. 130.

4. Sue Birtwistle and Susie Conklin, *The Making of Pride and Prejudice* (Harmondsworth: Penguin, 1995).

5. *E*, chapter 8, p. 64.

6. Ibid., pp. 23–4.

7. Ibid., pp. 166–7.

8. A. A. Milne, *Miss Elizabeth Bennet, A Play from 'Pride and Prejudice'* (Chatto and Windus, 1936), p. viii.

9. The following paragraphs are based on the account in Ann Thwaite, *A. A. Milne: The Man behind Winnie-the-Pooh* (London: Random House, 1990), pp. 175–7.

10. A. A. Milne, *It's Too Late Now: The Autobiography of a Writer* (London: Methuen, 1939), p. 42.

11. Milne, *Miss Elizabeth Bennet*, p. vii.

12. Ibid., pp. 85–6.

13. Ibid., p. x.

14. Thwaite, *A. A. Milne*, p. 413.

15. Milne, *It's Too Late Now*, p. viii.

16. Kenneth Turan, '*Pride and Prejudice*: An Informal History of the Garson-Olivier Motion Picture', *Persuasions*, 11 (1989), 140–43.

17. Thwaite, *A. A. Milne*, p. 413.
18. Turan, '*Pride and Prejudice*', p. 140.
19. See Bosley Crowther, '"*Pride and Prejudice*", a Delightful Comedy of Manners', *New York Times*, 9 August 1940.
20. *Miss Elizabeth Bennet* was broadcast again in 1960 with Dorothy Tutin as Elizabeth and Arthur Lowe as Mr Bennet, and in 1967 with Derek Jacobi as Mr Darcy.
21. Turan, '*Pride and Prejudice*', p. 143.
22. Milne, *Miss Elizabeth Bennet*, p. x.
23. Barbara Kantorowitz, 'Making an Austen Heroine More Like Austen', *New York Times*, 31 October 1999, pp. 17, 26. Quoted in Kathi Groenendyk, 'Modernizing *Mansfield Park*: Patricia Rozema's Spin on Jane Austen', http://www.jasna.org/persuasions/on-line/vol25no1/toc.html.
24. Jane Austen, 'Opinions of Mansfield Park', *MW*, pp. 431–5.
25. David Monaghan, 'In Defence of Patricia Rozema's *Mansfield Park*', http://www.jasna.org/persuasions/printed/number28/monaghan.pdf.
26. Terry Castle, 'Sister-Sister', *London Review of Books*, 3 August 1995, and her follow-up letter of 24 August 1995: http://www.lrb.co.uk/v17/n15/terry-castle/sister-sister.
27. Monaghan, 'In Defence', p. 60.
28. Ibid., p. 62.
29. Ibid.
30. See Paula Byrne, *Belle: The True Story of Dido Belle* (London: William Collins, 2014).
31. See Suzanne R. Pucci and James Thompson (eds), *Jane Austen and Co* (Albany, State University of New York, 2003). Spin-offs such as *Bridget Jones's Diary* and *Ruby in Paradise* are other examples of this genre.
32. Quoted R. V. Young, 'From Mansfield to Manhattan: The Abandoned Generation of Whit Stillman's *Metropolitan*', *Intercollegiate Review*, Spring 2000, pp. 20–27.
33. http://observer.com/2016/05/whit-stillman-talks-love-friendship-austen-adaptations-and-the-rules-of-comedy/.
34. See Ryan Gilbey, http://www.newstatesman.com/culture/film/2016/06/whit-stillman-love-friendship-his-postmodern-love-letter-jane-austen.

Bibliography

JANE AUSTEN

Austen, Jane, *The Novels*, ed. R. W. Chapman, 5 vols (Oxford: Oxford University Press, 1923, 3rd edition, 1932–34).

—, *Minor Works*, ed. R. W. Chapman, revised by B. C. Southam (Oxford: Oxford University Press, 1975).

—, *Sir Charles Grandison*, transcribed and edited by Brian Southam (Oxford: Clarendon Press, 1980).

—, *Lady Susan: A Facsimile of the Manuscript in the Pierpont Morgan Library and the 1925 Printed Edition*, ed. A Walton Litz (New York: Garland, 1989).

—, *Jane Austen's Letters*, ed. Deirdre Le Faye (3rd edn, Oxford: Oxford University Press, 1995).

Austen, Caroline, *My Aunt Jane Austen: A Memoir* (Winchester: Sarsen Press, 1991).

Austen, Henry, 'Biographical Notice', in *Northanger Abbey and Persuasion* (London: John Murray, 1818).

Austen-Leigh, James Edward, *A Memoir of Jane Austen*, ed. R. W. Chapman (Oxford: Clarendon Press, 1951).

Austen-Leigh, R. A., *Austen Papers, 1704–1865* (London: Spottiswoode, Ballantyre, 1942).

Austen-Leigh, William and Richard Arthur, *Jane Austen: A Family Record*, rev. and enlarged by Deirdre Le Faye (London: The British Library, 1989).

Gilson, David, *A Bibliography of Jane Austen* (Oxford: Clarendon Press, 1982).

MANUSCRIPTS AND ARCHIVAL MATERIAL

Bath Public Library
Theatre Royal Playbills, 1771–1805 and 1806–20.

Hampshire Record Office, Winchester
23M93/60/3/2, James Austen's Verses, copied by James Edward Austen-Leigh.
23M93/M1, Eliza de Feuillide's Letters, 1790–1830, on microfiche.

Huntington Library, San Marino, California, USA
HM 31201, Anna Larpent's Methodised Journal, 1773–87.
Larpent Collection of Plays.

Kent Archives Office, Centre for Kentish Studies, Maidstone
U951f24/1–69, Fanny Knight's Journals, 1804–72.

OTHER PRIMARY MATERIAL

Adolphus, John, *Memoirs of John Bannister*, 2 vols (London, 1839).
Arbiter, Petronius [pseudonym], *Memoirs of the Present Countess of Derby* (London, 1797).
Austen, James, *The Loiterer*, 2 vols (Oxford, 1789–90).
Bell's British Theatre, 34 vols (London, 1797).
Bellamy, Thomas, *Miscellanies*, 2 vols (London, 1794).
Bernard, John, *Retrospections of the Stage*, 2 vols (London, 1830).
Berquin, Arnaud, *L'ami des enfans*, 12 vols (London, 1782–83).
—, *The Children's Friend, Translated from the French of Mr Berquin*, by Lucas Williams, 6 vols (London, 1793).
Bickerstaffe, Isaac, *The Plays*, ed. Peter A. Tasch, 3 vols (New York and London: Garland, 1981).
Biographia Dramatica, ed. Stephen Jones, 3 vols (London, 1812).
Boaden, James, *Life of Mrs Jordan*, 2 vols (London, 1831).
—, *Memoirs of Mrs Inchbald*, 2 vols (London, 1833).
Boswell, James, *Life of Johnson*, ed. Birkbeck Hill, 6 vols (Oxford, 1937).
Brayley, Edward Wedlake, *Historical and Descriptive Accounts of the Theatres of London* (London, 1826).
Burney, Fanny, *A Busy Day*, ed. Tara Ghoshal Wallace (1801; New Brunswick, New Jersey: Rutgers University Press, 1984).
—, *Camilla: or A Picture of Youth*, ed. Edward and Lillian Bloom (1796; Oxford: Oxford University Press, 1983).
—, *Cecilia: or Memoirs of an Heiress*, ed. Anne Raine Ellis, 2 vols (London: George Bell and Sons, 1882).
—, *Cecilia: or Memoirs of an Heiress*, ed. Margaret Anne Doody and Peter Sabor (1782; Oxford: Oxford University Press, 1992).
—, *Evelina*, ed. Margaret Anne Doody (1778; Harmondsworth: Penguin Classics, 1994).
—, *The Early Journals and Letters of Fanny Burney*, ed. Lars E. Troide and Stewart J. Cooke, 3 vols to date (Oxford: Clarendon Press, 1988–94).
—, *The Journals and Letters of Fanny Burney (Madame D'Arblay)*, ed. Joyce Hemlow et al., 12 vols (Oxford: Clarendon Press, 1972–84).
—, *The Wanderer*, ed. Margaret Anne Doody and Peter Sabor (1814; Oxford: Oxford University Press, 1991).
—, *The Witlings* (1781), in *The Meridian Anthology of Restoration and Eighteenth-Century Plays by Women*, ed. Katharine M. Rogers (New York: Meridian, 1994).

Byron, Lord, *The Complete Poetical Works*, ed. Jerome J. McGann, 7 vols (Oxford: Clarendon Press, 1980–93).

Campbell, Thomas, *Life of Mrs Siddons* (New York, 1834).

Centlivre, Susanna, *The Plays*, ed. Richard C. Frushell, 3 vols (New York and London: Garland, 1982).

Coleridge, Samuel Taylor, *Specimens of the Table Talk of the Late Samuel Taylor Coleridge*, ed. H. N. Coleridge, 2 vols (London, 1835).

Colman the Elder, George, *The Plays*, ed. Kalman A. Burnim, 6 vols (New York and London: Garland, 1983).

Colman the Younger, George, *The Plays*, ed. Peter Tasch, 2 vols (New York and London: Garland, 1981).

Congreve, William, *The Way of the World*, ed. Brian Gibbons (2nd edn, London: A&C Black, 1994).

Cowley, Hannah, *The Plays of Hannah Cowley*, ed. Frederick H. Link, 2 vols (New York and London: Garland, 1979).

Davies, Thomas, *Dramatic Miscellanies*, 3 vols (London, 1785).

—, *Memoirs of Garrick*, 2 vols (Boston, 1818).

[Dickens, Charles], *Memoirs of Joseph Grimaldi*, ed. Boz (London, 1869).

Dibdin, Charles, *Of Age Tomorrow* (London, n. d.).

Dibdin, Thomas, *Reminiscences*, 4 vols (London, 1827).

Dunlap, William, *A History of the American Theatre* (New York, 1832).

—, *The Life and Time of George Frederick Cooke*, 2 vols (London, 1815).

Edgeworth, Maria, *Belinda* (1801; repr. London: Pandora, 1986).

—, *Patronage* (1814; repr. London: Pandora, 1986).

Fielding, Henry, *The History of the Adventures of Joseph Andrews and of his Friend Mr Abraham Adams and An Apology for the Life of Mrs Shamela Andrews*, ed. Douglas Brooks-Davies (Oxford: Oxford University Press, 1980).

—, *The History of Tom Jones*, ed. Fredson Bowers, 2 vols (Oxford: Oxford University Press, 1975).

Frost, Thomas, *Circus Life and Circus Celebrities* (London, 1875).

Garrick, David, *The Plays*, ed. Gerald M. Berkowitz, 4 vols (New York and London: Garland, 1981).

Genest, John, *Some Account of the English Stage from 1660–1830*, 10 vols (Bath, 1832).

Gilliland, Thomas, *Dramatic Mirror*, 2 vols (London, 1808).

Gisborne, Thomas, *An Enquiry into the Duties of the Female Sex* (London, 1797).

Goldsmith, Oliver, *She Stoops to Conquer*, ed. Tom Davis (London: A&C Black, 1979).

Greenwood, Isaac J., *The Circus: Its Origin and Growth Prior to 1835* (New York: Dunlap, 1898).

Hawkins, F. W., *The Life of Edmund Kean*, 2 vols (London, 1869).

Hawkins, William, *Miscellanies in Verse and Prose* and *Theatrical Biography* (London, 1792).

Hayley, William, *Plays for a Private Theatre* (London, 1784).

—, *Poems and Plays*, 6 vols (London, 1785).

Hazlitt, William, *The Complete Works*, ed. P. P. Howe, 21 vols (London: Dent, 1930–34).

Home, John, *The Plays*, ed. James S. Malek (New York and London: Garland, 1980).

Howard, Frederick, Earl of Carlisle, *Thought upon the Present Conditions of the Stage* (London, 1808).

Hunt, Leigh, *Dramatic Criticism*, ed. L. H. and C. W. Houtchens (New York, 1949).

—, *Dramatic Essays*, ed. William Archer and Robert W. Lowe (London, 1894).

Inchbald, Elizabeth, *A Collection of Farces and Other Afterpieces: Selected by Mrs Inchbald*, 7 vols (London, 1809).

—, *A Simple Story*, ed. J. M. S. Tompkins (1791; Oxford: Oxford University Press, 1988).

—, *A Simple Story* (1791; repr. Harmondsworth: Penguin, 1996).

—, *Lovers' Vows: A Play in Five Acts, Performing at the Theatre Royal, Covent Garden. From the German of Kotzebue* (London: G. G. Robinson, 1798). For ease of reference all quotations are taken from the text of the fifth edition in Chapman's edition of *Mansfield Park*. Also reprinted in *Five Romantic Plays*, ed. Paul Baines and Edward Burns (Oxford: Oxford University Press, 2000).

—, The British Theatre; or A Collection of Plays … *with Biographical and Critical Remarks by Mrs Inchbald* (London, 1808), vi.

—, *The Modern British Drama*, 5 vols (London, 1811).

—, *The Modern Theatre: A Collection of Successful Modern Plays, as Acted at The Theatre Royal, London*, 10 vols (London, 1811).

Jones, Charles Inigo, *Memoirs of Miss O'Neill* (London, 1816).

Kelly, Hugh, *The Plays*, eds. Larry Carver and Mary J. H. Gross (New York and London: Garland, 1980).

Kelly, Michael, *Reminiscences*, 2 vols (London, 1826).

Lamb, Charles, *The Last Essays of Elia*, ed. Edmund Blunden (London: Oxford University Press, 1929).

—, *The Works of Charles and Mary Lamb*, ed. E. V. Lucas, 2 vols (London: Methuen, 1903).

Lewes, George, 'The Novels of Jane Austen', *Blackwood's Magazine*, 86 (1859), pp. 99–113.

[Lister, Thomas], 'Women as They Are', *Edinburgh Review*, 53 (1830), pp. 444–63.

Lockhart, J. G., *Life of Walter Scott*, 6 vols (New York, 1848).

Macready's Reminiscences, ed. Sir Frederick Pollock (New York, 1875).

Murphy, Arthur, *Life of David Garrick*, 2 vols (London, 1801).

Oxberry's Dramatic Biography and Histrionic Anecdotes: or The Green-Room Spy, 6 vols (London, 1825–27).

Pasquin, Anthony [pseudonym], *The Life of the Late Earl of Barrymore Including a History of the Wargrave Theatricals* (London, 1793).

Peake, Richard Brinsley, *Memoirs of the Colman Family* (London, 1841).

Penley, Belville S., *The Bath Stage* (London, 1892).

Pope, Alexander, *The Poems*, ed. John Butt (London: Methuen, 1963).

Raymond, George, *Memoirs of Robert William Elliston Comedian*, 2 vols (London, 1844).

—, *The Life and Enterprises of Robert William Elliston* (London, 1857).

Richardson, Samuel, *Clarissa: or The History of a Young Lady*, ed. Angus Ross (1747–48; repr. Harmondsworth: Penguin, 1985).

—, *Selected Letters of Samuel Richardson*, ed. John Carroll (Oxford: Oxford University Press, 1964).

—, *The Correspondence of Samuel Richardson*, ed. A. L. Barbauld, 6 vols (London, 1804).

—, *The History of Sir Charles Grandison*, ed. Jocelyn Harris, 3 vols (1753–54; repr. London: Oxford University Press, 1972).

Robinson, Henry Crabb, *The London Theatre, 1811–1866: Selections from the Diary of Henry Crabb Robinson*, ed. Eluned Brown (London: Society for Theatre Research, 1966).

Rowe, Nicholas, *Jane Shore: A Tragedy as Performed at the Theatre-Royal in Drury Lane, Regulated from the Prompt-Book, by Permission of the Managers, by Mr Hopkins, Prompter* (London, 1776).

Scott, Sir Walter, *The Letters of Sir Walter Scott*, ed. H. J. C. Grierson, 12 vols (London: Constable, 1932).

Sheridan, Richard Brinsley, *The Dramatic Works*, ed. Cecil Price, 2 vols (London: Oxford University Press, 1973).

Steele, Sir Richard, *The Plays*, ed. Shirley Strum Kenny (Oxford: Clarendon Press, 1971).

Tomlins, F. G., *A Brief View of the English Stage* (London, 1832).

Wilson, C. Baron, *Our Actresses*, 2 vols (London, 1844).

[Whately, Richard] 'Modern Novels: *Northanger Abbey and Persuasion*, *Quarterly Review*, 24 (1821), pp. 352–76.

Yates, Edmund, ed., *The Life and Correspondence of Charles Mathews* (London, i860).

SECONDARY MATERIAL

Amis, Kingsley, 'What Became of Jane Austen?', *Spectator*, 4 October 1957, p. 339.

Armstrong, Isobel, *Jane Austen: Mansfield Park*, Penguin Critical Studies (Harmondsworth: Penguin, 1988).

Austen-Leigh, R. A., *Jane Austen and Southampton* (London: Spottiswoode, 1949).

Avery, Emmett L. et al., eds, *The London Stage, 1660–1800*, 5 parts in 11 vols (Carbondale: Southern Illinois University Press, 1960–68).

Babb, Howard, *Jane Austen's Novels: The Fabric of Dialogue* (Columbus: Ohio University Press, 1962).

Baer, Marc, *Theatre and Disorder in Late Georgian England* (Oxford: Clarendon Press, 1992).

Barish, Jonas, *The Anti-Theatrical Prejudice* (Berkeley: University of California Press, 1981).

Bate, Jonathan, ed., *The Romantics on Shakespeare* (Harmondsworth: Penguin, 1992).

Bateson, F. W., *English Comic Drama, 1700–1750* (Oxford: Clarendon Press, 1929).

Bernbaum, Ernest, *The Drama of Sensibility: A Sketch of the History of English Sentimental Comedy and Domestic Tragedy, 1696–1780* (Gloucester, Massachusetts: Peter Smith, 1958).

Bevis, Richard, *The Laughing Tradition* (Athens: University of Georgia Press, 1980).

Bradbrook, Frank W., *Jane Austen and her Predecessors* (Cambridge: Cambridge University Press, 1966).

—, 'Style and Judgement in Jane Austen's Novels', *Cambridge Quarterly*, 4 (1951), pp. 515–37.

Brewer, John, *The Pleasures of the Imagination: English Culture in the Eighteenth Century* (London: HarperCollins, 1997).

Butler, E. M., '*Mansfield Park* and Kotzebue's *Lovers' Vows*', *MLR*, 38 (1933), pp. 326–37.

Butler, Marilyn, Introduction to *Mansfield Park*, ed. James Kinsley (Oxford: Oxford University Press, 1990).

—, *Jane Austen and the War of Ideas* (Oxford: Clarendon Press, 1975).

Campbell, Lily, B., 'The Rise of a Theory of Stage Presentation in England during the Eighteenth Century', *PMLA*, 32 (1917), pp. 163–200.

Castle, Terry, Introduction to *Northanger Abbey, Lady Susan, The Watsons, and Sanditon*, ed. John Davie (Oxford: Oxford University Press, 1990).

Chapman, R. W., *Jane Austen: Facts and Problems* (Oxford: Clarendon Press, 1948).

—, 'Jane Austen's Library', *Book-Collector's Quarterly*, 11 (1933), pp. 28–32.

Chisholm, Kate, *Fanny Burney: Her Life* (London: Chatto and Windus, 1998).

Conger, Sydney McMillen, 'Reading *Lovers' Vows*: Jane Austen's Reflections on English Sense and German Sensibility', *Studies in Philology*, 85 (1988), pp. 92–113.

Cope, Zachary, 'Who Was Sophia Sentiment? Was She Jane Austen?', *Book Collector*, 15 (1966), pp. 143–51.

Donkin, Ellen, *Getting into the Act: Women Playwrights in London, 1776–1829* (London and New York: Routledge, 1995).

Donohue, Joseph W., 'Burletta and the Early Nineteenth-Century English Theatre', *Nineteenth-Century Theatre Research*, 1 (1973), pp. 29–51.

—, *Dramatic Character in the English Romantic Age* (Princeton: Princeton University Press, 1970).

—, *Theatre in the Age of Kean* (Oxford: Blackwell, 1975).

Doody, Margaret Anne, *A Natural Passion: A Study of the Novels of Samuel Richardson* (London: Oxford University Press, 1974).

—, *Frances Burney: The Life in the Works* (New Brunswick, New Jersey: Rutgers University Press, 1988).

Downer, Alan, S., 'Nature to Advantage Dressed: Eighteenth-Century Acting', *PMLA*, 58 (1943). pp. 1002–37.

Duckworth, Alistair M., *The Improvement of the Estate: A Study of Jane Austen's Novels* (Baltimore: Johns Hopkins University Press, 1971).

Flanders, Henry, ed., *Memoirs of Richard Cumberland* (1856; repr. New York: Benjamin Blom, 1969).

Fleishman, Avrom, *A Reading of 'Mansfield Park'* (Minneapolis: University of Minnesota Press, 1967).

Ganzel, Dewey, 'Patent Wrongs and Patent Theatres: Drama and the Law in the Early Nineteenth Century', *PMLA*, 76 (1961), pp. 384–96.

Garside, Peter, and Elizabeth McDonald, 'Evangelicalism and *Mansfield Park*', *Trivium*, 10 (1975), pp. 34–49.

Gray, Charles Harold, *Theatrical Criticism in London to 1795* (New York: Columbia University Press, 1931).

Greene, D. G., 'Jane Austen and the Peerage', *PMLA*, 68 (1953), pp. 1017–31.

Grey, J. David, ed., *The Jane Austen Handbook* (London: Athlone Press, 1986).

Hahn, Emily, *A Degree of Prudery: A Biography of Fanny Burney* (New York: Doubleday, 1950).

Hare, Arnold, ed., *Theatre Royal Bath: A Calendar of Performances at the Orchard Street Theatre, 1750–1805* (Bath: Kingsmead Press, 1977).

Harris, Jocelyn, *Jane Austen's Art of Memory* (Cambridge: Cambridge University Press, 1989).

Hemlow, Joyce, *The History of Fanny Burney* (Oxford: Clarendon Press, 1958).

Highfill, Philip H., Jr, Kalman A. Burnim and Edward A. Langhans, eds, *A Biographical Dictionary of Actors, Actresses, Musicians, Dancers, Managers and Other Stage Personnel in London, 1660–1800*, 16 vols (Carbondale: Southern Illinois University Press, 1984).

Hillebrand, Harold Newcombe, *Edmund Kean* (New York: Columbia University Press, 1933).

Holland, Peter, 'The Age of Garrick', in *Shakespeare: An Illustrated Stage History*, ed. Jonathan Bate and Russell Jackson (Oxford: Oxford University Press, 1996), pp. 69–91.

—, *The Ornament of Action: Text and Performance in Restoration Comedy* (Cambridge: Cambridge University Press, 1979).

Honan, Park, *Jane Austen: Her Life* (London: Weidenfeld and Nicolson, 1987).

Howe, Elizabeth, *The First English Actresses: Women and Drama, 1660–1700* (Cambridge: Cambridge University Press, 1992).

Howe, Evelyn, 'Amateur Theatre in Georgian England', *History Today*, 20 (1970), pp. 695–703.

Hubback, J. H., 'Pen Portraits in Jane Austen's Novels', *Cornhill Magazine* (July 1928), pp. 24–33.

Hufstader, Alice Anderson, *Sisters of the Quill* (New York: Mead, 1978).

Husbands, Winifred H., '*Mansfield Park* and *Lovers' Vows*: A Reply', *MLR*, 29 (1934), pp. 176–79.

James, Henry, *The Art of the Novel*, ed. R. P. Blackmur (New York and London: Charles Scribner's Sons, 1947).

Johnson, Claudia L., *Equivocal Beings: Politics, Gender and Sentimentality in the 1790s* (Chicago: University of Chicago Press, 1995).

—, *Jane Austen: Women, Politics and the Novel* (Chicago: University of Chicago Press, 1988).

Jordan, Elaine, 'Pulpit, Stage and Novel: *Mansfield Park* and *Lovers' Vows*', *Novel: A Forum on Fiction*, 20 (1987), pp. 138–48.

Kelly, Gary, 'Reading Aloud in *Mansfield Park*', *Nineteenth-Century Fiction*, 37 (1982), pp. 29–42.

—, *The English Jacobin Novel, 1780–1805* (Oxford: Clarendon Press, 1976).

Kenny, Shirley Strum, *British Theatre and the Other Arts, 1660–1800* (Washington: Associated University Presses, 1984).

Kinkead-Weekes, Mark, *Samuel Richardson: Dramatic Novelist* (London: Methuen, 1973).

Kirkham, Margaret, *Jane Austen: Feminism and Fiction* (London; Athlone Press, 1997).

—, 'The Theatricals in *Mansfield Park* and "Frederick" in *Lovers' Vows*', *Notes and Queries*, 220 (1975), pp. 389–90.

Konigsberg, Ira, *Samuel Richardson and the Dramatic Novel* (Lexington: University of Kentucky Press, 1968).

Lascelles, Mary, *Jane Austen and Her Art* (Oxford: Clarendon Press, 1939).

Leavis, Q. D., 'A Critical Theory of Jane Austen's Writing', *Scrutiny*, 10 (1941), pp. 61–90, 114–42.

Le Faye, Deirdre, 'Jane Austen and William Hayley', *Notes and Queries*, 232 (1987), pp. 25–26.

—, 'Journey, Waterparties and Plays', *Jane Austen Society Report* (1986), pp. 29–35.

—, 'The Business of Mothering: Two Austenian Dialogues', *Book Collector* (1983), pp. 296–314.

Lewis, Peter, *Fielding's Burlesque Drama: Its Place in the Tradition* (Edinburgh: Edinburgh University Press, 1987).

Linklater Thomson, C., *Jane Austen: A Survey* (London: Horace Marshall, 1929).

Littlewood, S. R., *Elizabeth Inchbald and her Circle* (London: Daniel O'Connor, 1921).

Litvak, Joseph, *Caught in the Act: Theatricality in the Nineteenth-Century Novel* (Berkeley: University of California Press, 1993).

Litz, A. Walton, *Jane Austen: A Study of Her Artistic Development* (London: Chatto and Windus, 1965).

Loftis, John, *Sheridan and the Drama of Georgian England* (Oxford: Blackwell, 1976).

—, *The Politics of Drama in Augustan England* (Oxford: Clarendon Press, 1963).

Lynch, James, J., *Box, Pit and Gallery: Stage and Society in Johnson's London* (Berkeley: University of California Press, 1953).

McMillin, Scott, ed., *Restoration and Eighteenth-Century Comedy* (New York and London: Norton, 1973).

Mandel, Oscar, *The Theatre of Don Juan: A Collection of Plays and Views, 1630–1963* (Lincoln: University of Nebraska Press, 1963).

Mander, Raymond, and Joe Mitchenson, *The Lost Theatres of London* (New York: Taplinger, 1968).

Manvell, Roger, *Elizabeth Inchbald: A Biographical Study* (Lanham: University Press of America, 1987).

Milmeth, Don. B., 'The Posthumous Career of George Frederick Cooke', *Theatre Notebook*, 24 (1969–70), pp. 68–74.

Molar, Kenneth, *Jane Austen's Art of Allusion* (Lincoln: University of Nebraska Press, 1977).

Monaghan, David, '*Mansfield Park* and Evangelicalism: A Reassessment', *Nineteenth-Century Fiction*, 33 (1978), pp. 215–30.

Moody, Jane, *Illegitimate Theatre in London, 1770–1840* (Cambridge: Cambridge University Press, 2000).

—, 'Writing for the Metropolis: Illegitimate Performances of Shakespeare in Early Nineteenth-Century London', *Shakespeare Survey*, 47 (1994). pp. 61–69.

Mudrick, Marvin, *Jane Austen: Irony as Defense and Discovery* (Princeton: Princeton University Press, 1952).

Mullan, John, *Sentiment and Sociability: The Language of Feeling in the Eighteenth Century* (Oxford: Clarendon Press, 1997).

Murray, Christopher, *Robert William Elliston: Manager* (London: Society for Theatre Research, 1975).

Nicoll, Allardyce, *A History of Early Nineteenth-Century Drama, 1800–1850*, 2 vols (London: Cambridge University Press, 1930).

—, *A History of English Drama, 1660–1900*, 6 vols (Cambridge: Cambridge University Press, 1955–59).

—, *The Garrick Stage: Theatres and Audience in the Eighteenth Century*, ed. Sybil Rosenfeld (Manchester: Manchester University Press, 1980).

Nicholson, Watson, *The Struggle for a Free Stage in London* (London: Constable, 1906).

Nokes, David, *Jane Austen: A Life* (London: Fourth Estate, 1997).

Page, Norman, *The Language of Jane Austen* (Oxford: Oxford University Press, 1972.).

Patterson, A. Temple, *A History of Southampton, 1700–1914*, 11 vols (Southampton: Southampton University Press, 1966).

Ranger, Paul, *The Georgian Playhouses of Hampshire, 1730–1830*, Hampshire Papers 10 (Winchester: Hampshire County Council, 1996).

Rawson, Claude, Introduction to *Persuasion*, ed. John Davie (Oxford: Oxford University Press, 1990).

—, *Order from Confusion Sprung: Studies in Eighteenth-Century Literature from Swift to Cowper* (London: Allen and Unwin, 1985).

—, *Satire and Sentiment, 1660–1830* (Cambridge: Cambridge University Press, 1994).

—, 'Some Remarks on Eighteenth-Century "Delicacy", with a Note on Hugh Kelly's *False Delicacy* (1768)', *JEGP*, 61 (1962), pp. 1–13.

Reitzel, William, '*Mansfield Park* and *Lovers' Vows*', *Review of English Studies*, 9 (1933), pp. 451–56.

Rosenfeld, Sybil, 'Jane Austen and Private Theatricals', *Essays and Studies*, 15 (1962), pp. 40–51.

—, *Temples of Thespis: Some Private Theatres and Theatricals in England and Wales, 1700–1820* (London: The Society for Theatre Research, 1978).

Russell, Gillian, 'Playing at Revolution: The Politics of the O. P. Riots of 1809', *Theatre Notebook*, 44 (1990), pp. 16–26.

—, *The Theatres of War: Performance, Politics, and Society, 1793–1815* (Oxford, Clarendon Press, 1995).

Sales, Roger, *Jane Austen and Representations of Regency England* (London: Routledge, 1996).

Selwyn, David, *Jane Austen and Leisure* (London: Hambledon Press, 1999).

Sherbo, Arthur, *English Sentimental Drama* (Michigan: Michigan State University Press, 1957).

Sherburn, George, 'Samuel Richardson's Novels and the Theatre: A Theory Sketched', *Philological Quarterly*, 41 (1962), pp. 325–29.

Southam, B. C., *Critical Essays on Jane Austen* (London: Routledge and Kegan Paul, 1968).

—, *Jane Austen: The Critical Heritage*, 2 vols (London: Routledge and Kegan Paul, 1968–87)

—, *Jane Austen's Literary Manuscripts* (London: Oxford University Press, 1964).

—, *Sense and Sensibility, Pride and Prejudice, and Mansfield Park: A Casebook* (London: Macmillan, 1976).

Spring, David, 'Aristocracy, Social Structure, and Religion in the Early Victorian Period', *Victorian Studies*, 6 (1963), pp. 263–80.

Staves, Susan, 'Evelina: or Female Difficulties', *Modern Philology*, 73 (1976), pp. 368–81.

Tanner, Tony, *Jane Austen* (London: Macmillan, 1986).

Tasch, Peter A, *The Dramatic Cobbler: The Life and Works of Isaac Bickerstaff* (Lewisburg: Bucknell University Press, 1971).

Thaler, Alwin, *Shakespeare to Sheridan* (Cambridge: Cambridge University Press, 1922).

Thomas, David and Arnold Hare, eds, *Restoration and Georgian England, Theatre in Europe: A Documentary History* (Cambridge: Cambridge University Press, 1989).

Tinker, Chauncey Brewster, *Dr Johnson and Fanny Burney* (New York: Moffat, Yard, 1911).

Tomalin, Claire, *Jane Austen: A Life* (London: Viking, 1997).

—, *Mrs Jordan's Profession* (New York: Knopf, 1994).

Tompkins, J. M. S., '"Elinor and Marianne": A Note on Jane Austen', *Review of English Studies*, 16 (1940), pp. 33–43.

—, *The Popular Novel in England, 1770–1800* (Lincoln: University of Nebraska Press, 1932; repr. 1961).

Trilling, Lionel, *Sincerity and Authenticity* (London: Oxford University Press, 1972).

—, *The Opposing Self* (London: Secker and Warburg, 1955).

Troost, Linda, and Sayre Greenfield, eds, *Jane Austen in Hollywood* (Lexington: University of Kentucky Press, 1998).

Trusler, Simon, ed., *Burlesque Plays of the Eighteenth Century* (London: Oxford University Press, 1969).

Tucker, George Holbert, *A Goodly Heritage: A History of Jane Austen's Family* (Manchester: Carcanet Press, 1983).

—, *Jane Austen: The Woman* (New York: St Martin's Press, 1994).

Vickery, Amanda, *The Gentleman's Daughter: Women's Lives in Georgian England* (New Haven and London: Yale University Press, 1998).

Viveash, Chris, 'Jane Austen and Kotzebue', *Jane Austen Society Report* (1994), pp. 29–31.

Watson, Ernest, *Sheridan to Robertson: A Study of the Nineteenth-Century London Stage* (Cambridge, Massachusetts: Harvard University Press, 1926).

Watt, Ian, ed., *Jane Austen: A Collection of Critical Essays* (Englewood Cliffs, New Jersey: Prentice-Hall, 1963).

Williams, Michael, *Jane Austen: Six Novels and their Methods* (London: Macmillan, 1986).

Zelicovici, Dvora, 'The Inefficacy of *Lovers' Vows*', *English Literary History*, 50 (1983), pp. 531–40.

Index

Abington, Frances, 43
acting styles, 60, 66–70 passim, 220–4
   passim, 230–1
actors and plays *see* plays and actors
amateur theatricals, 2–3, 4, 13, 51
   in *Mansfield Park*, xi–xii, 2–3, 9, 10, 36,
   37, 166, 173, 175, 177–8, 209–10, 223,
   229–30
'Amelia Webster' (Austen), 110
L'ami de l'adolescence (Berquin), 24
L'ami des enfans (Berquin), 24, 26
Amphitheatre of Arts *see* Astley's Theatre
Amphitheatre Riding House *see* Astley's
   Theatre
Amyot, Thomas, 69
Anderson, the Misses (Mansfield Park),
   217, 224, 231
Anti-Jacobin Review, 47
Arne, Thomas, 64–5
As You Like It (Shakespeare), 198
Astley, Philip, 39
Astley's Theatre, 39, 40–2
Austen (Gibson), Mary (sister-in-law of
   Jane Austen), 35, 47, 49
Austen, Caroline, 2
Austen, Cassandra (sister of Jane Austen),
   11, 12, 66, 70–1, 267
Austen, Edward (brother of Jane Austen),
   11
Austen, Francis (Frank) (brother of Jane
   Austen), 35, 49, 61, 266
Austen, Henry (brother of Jane Austen),
   17, 52, 61, 77, 81–2, 223
   and Eliza de Feuillide, 17
   epilogues and prologues, 11, 12
   on Jane Austen, 20
   and *The Loiterer*, 81–2, 85, 93, 116
   theatre patronage, 54, 59
   visits from Jane Austen, 53–6, 58–65, 77

Austen, James (brother of Jane Austen),
   13, 17, 20, 28, 54, 82
   epilogues and prologues, 11, 12, 15–16,
   17, 18, 20
   and *The Loiterer*, 85, 93
Austen, Jane
   acting experience, xii, 3, 33, 34, 35, 36,
   53
   bicentenary, xii–xiii
   Terry Castle's view of, 267
   education, 12
   favourite actor, 4, 46–7, 48, 63–4
   favourite poet, 22
   Fielding's influence on, 82, 83–4, 86, 97,
   99, 112, 115
   Inchbald's influence on, xii, 99
   Kotzebue influence, 45, 58–9
   letters *see* letters of Jane Austen
   narrative method *see* narrative method
   resurgence of interest in (from
   mid-1990s), xii, 249, 252–3
   Richardson's influence on, 35, 102–3,
   112, 115, 173–4
   Shakespeare's influence on, xii, 21, 31
   Sheridan's influence on, 12, 82, 86–7,
   92–3, 96–7
   visits to friends and relatives, 44, 53–6,
   58–65, 77
Austen, Jane, theatre
   influence of in her novels, xii, 3–4, 78,
   253
   knowledge of, 3, 38, 43, 60–1, 76, 78
   love of, xii, 3, 4, 32, 83
   visits and actors seen, 20, 21, 22–9,
   30–1, 44, 49, 54, 58–70, 73–4, 76–7,
   167
   see also theatre
Austen, Mrs Cassandra (mother of Jane
   Austen), 35, 48, 266